SUNZEN!™

VOLUME 1

BY SUSUGI SAKURAI

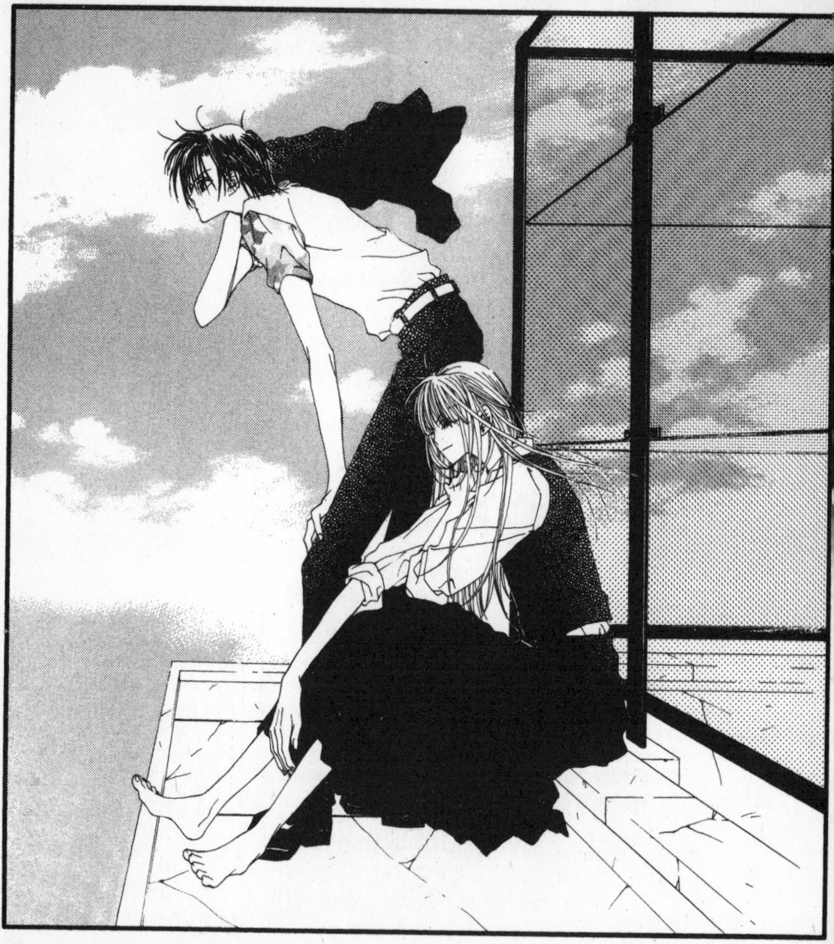

Short Sunzen! Volume 1
Created By Susugi Sakurai

Translation - Kristy Harmon
English Adaptation - Zachary Rau
Retouch and Lettering - Star Print Brokers
Production Artist - Michael Paolilli
Graphic Designer - Jose Macasocol, Jr.

Editor - Hope Donovan and Alexis Kirsch
Digital Imaging Manager - Chris Buford
Pre-Production Supervisor - Erika Terriquez
Production Manager - Elisabeth Brizzi
Managing Editor - Vy Nguyen
Creative Director - Anne Marie Horne
Editor-in-Chief - Rob Tokar
Publisher - Mike Kiley
President and C.O.O. - John Parker
C.E.O. and Chief Creative Officer - Stuart Levy

A **TOKYOPOP** Manga

TOKYOPOP Inc.
5900 Wilshire Blvd. Suite 2000
Los Angeles, CA 90036

E-mail: info@TOKYOPOP.com
Come visit us online at www.TOKYOPOP.com

ISBN: 978-1-59816-937-9

First TOKYOPOP printing: January 2008
10 9 8 7 6 5 4 3 2 1
Printed in the USA

VOLUME 1
BY SUSUGI SAKURAI

HAMBURG // LONDON // LOS ANGELES // TOKYO

CONTENTS

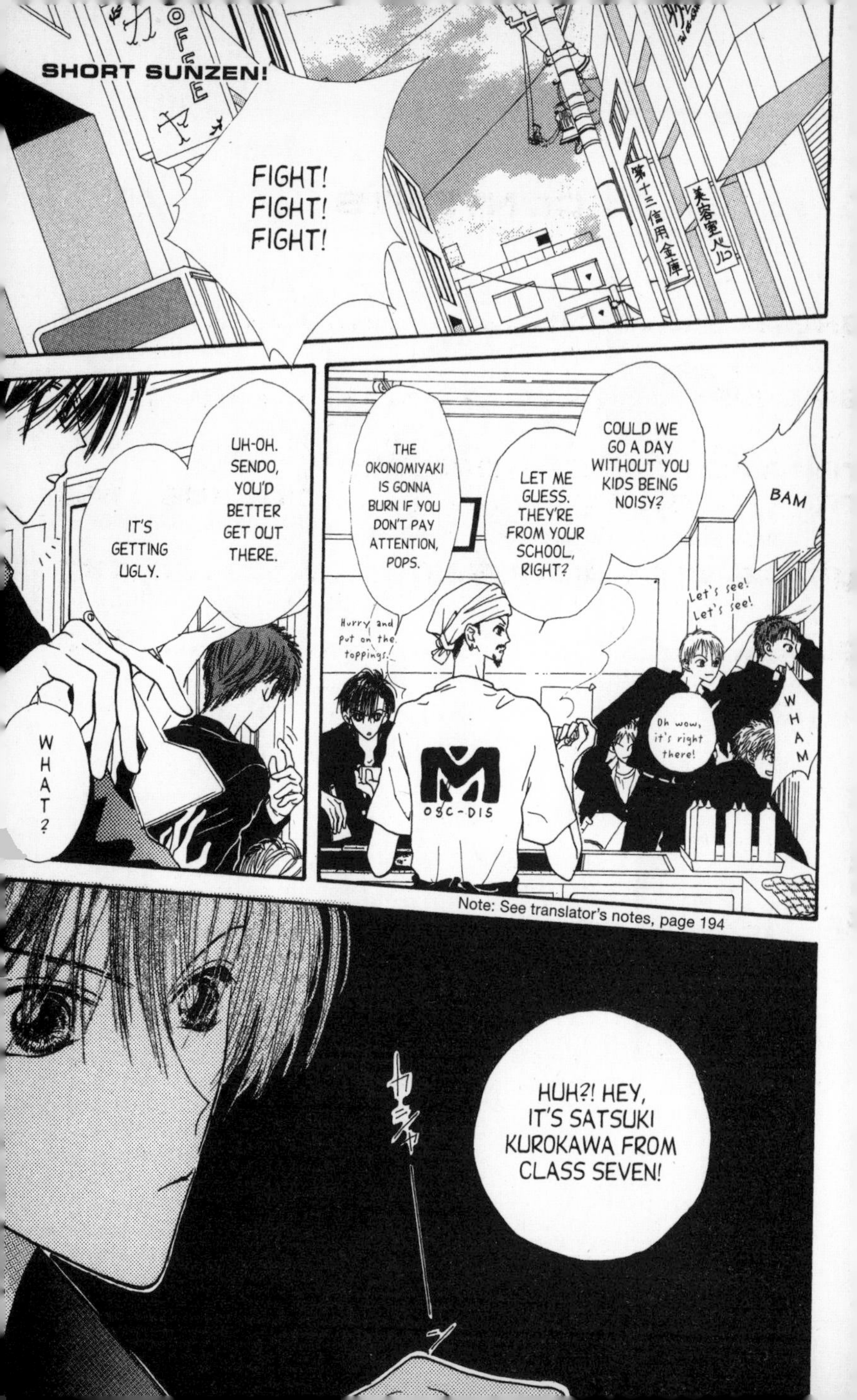
SHORT SUNZEN!
FIGHT! FIGHT! FIGHT!
BAM
COULD WE GO A DAY WITHOUT YOU KIDS BEING NOISY?
LET ME GUESS. THEY'RE FROM YOUR SCHOOL, RIGHT?
THE OKONOMIYAKI IS GONNA BURN IF YOU DON'T PAY ATTENTION, POPS.
Hurry and put on the toppings.
Let's see! Let's see!
Oh wow, it's right there!
WHAM
UH-OH. SENDO, YOU'D BETTER GET OUT THERE.
IT'S GETTING UGLY.
WHAT?
HUH?! HEY, IT'S SATSUKI KUROKAWA FROM CLASS SEVEN!

Note: See translator's notes, page 194

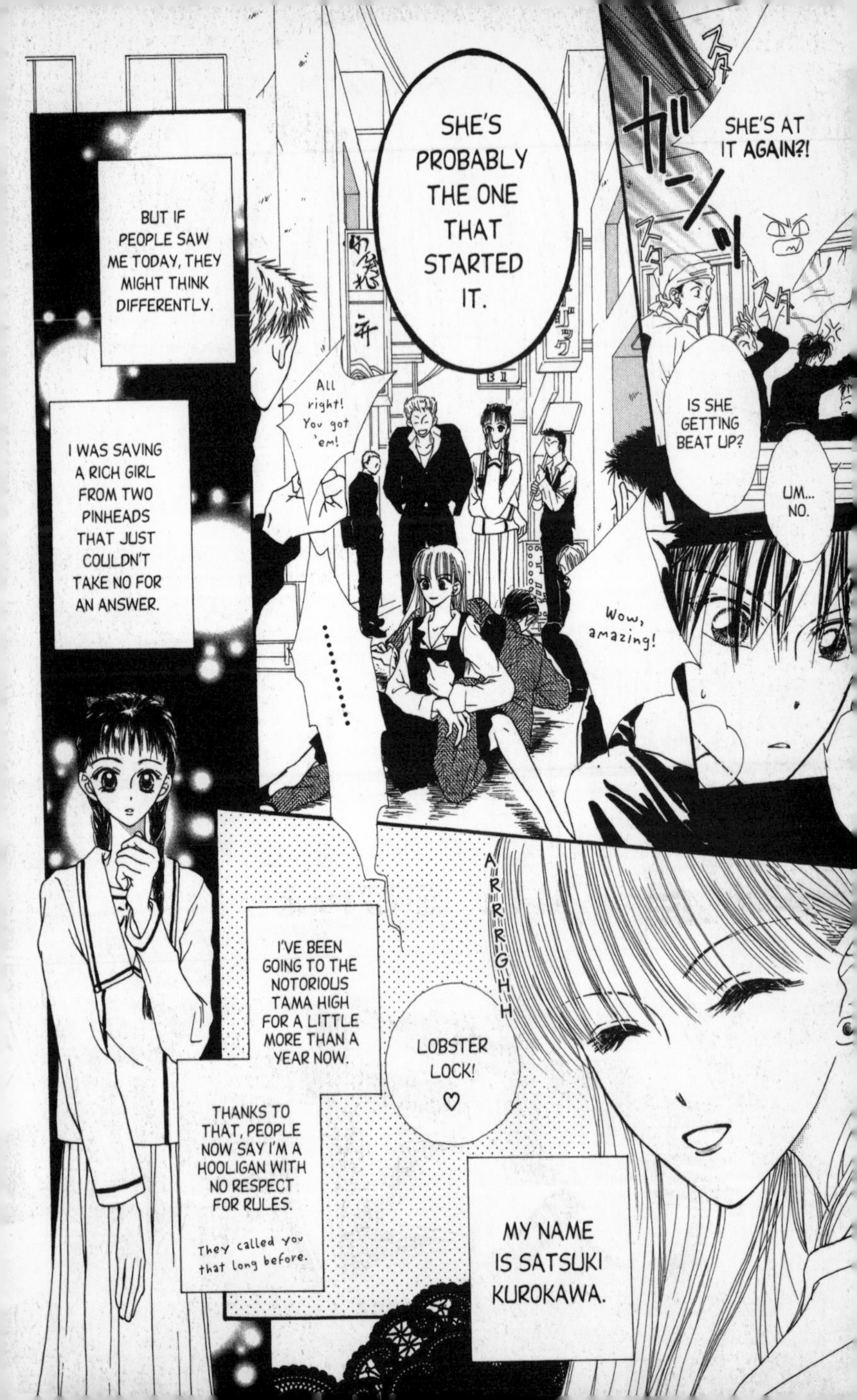
SHE'S AT IT AGAIN?!
IS SHE GETTING BEAT UP?
UM... NO.
Wow, amazing!
SHE'S PROBABLY THE ONE THAT STARTED IT.
All right! You got 'em!
......
BUT IF PEOPLE SAW ME TODAY, THEY MIGHT THINK DIFFERENTLY.
I WAS SAVING A RICH GIRL FROM TWO PINHEADS THAT JUST COULDN'T TAKE NO FOR AN ANSWER.
ARRRGHH
LOBSTER LOCK! ♡
I'VE BEEN GOING TO THE NOTORIOUS TAMA HIGH FOR A LITTLE MORE THAN A YEAR NOW.
MY NAME IS SATSUKI KUROKAWA.
THANKS TO THAT, PEOPLE NOW SAY I'M A HOOLIGAN WITH NO RESPECT FOR RULES.
They called you that long before.

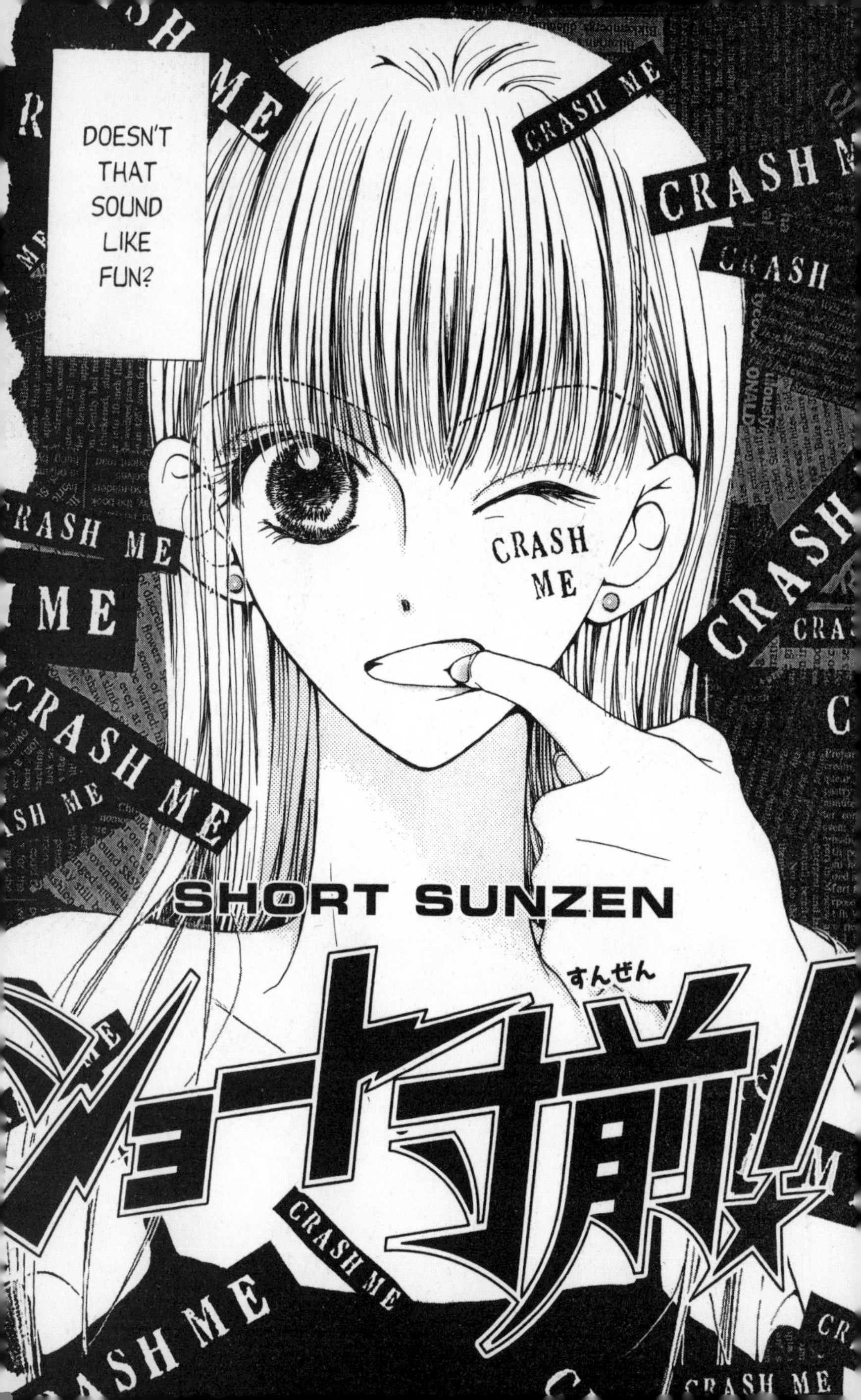
DOESN'T THAT SOUND LIKE FUN?
CRASH ME
SHORT SUNZEN
すんぜん
ショート寸前!

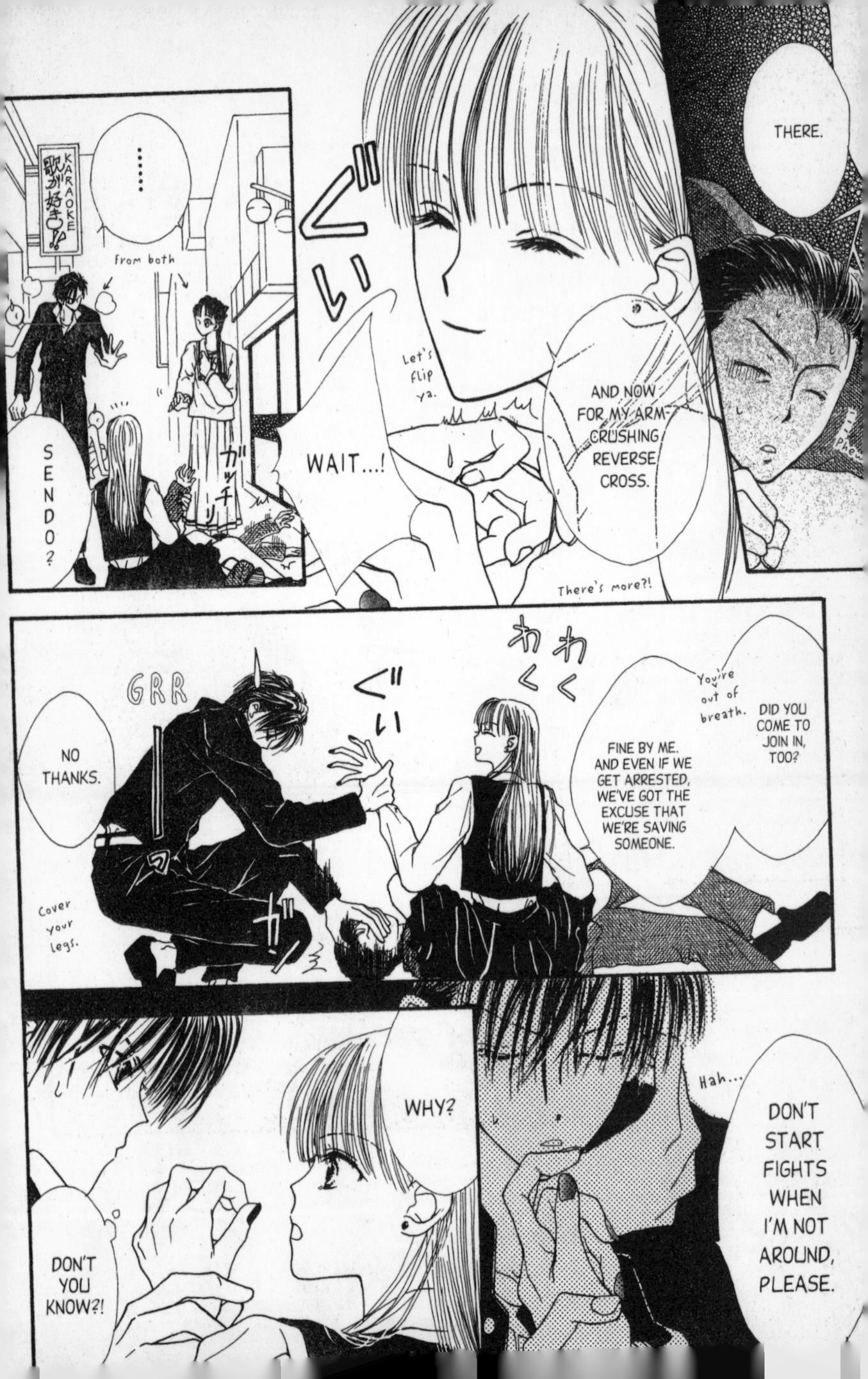

THERE.
Phew
ぐい
Let's flip ya.
AND NOW FOR MY ARM-CRUSHING REVERSE CROSS.
WAIT...!
There's more?!
......
KARAOKE
歌が好き
From both
ガッチリ
SENDO?
You're out of breath.
DID YOU COME TO JOIN IN, TOO?
FINE BY ME. AND EVEN IF WE GET ARRESTED, WE'VE GOT THE EXCUSE THAT WE'RE SAVING SOMEONE.
わくわく
ぐい
GRR
NO THANKS.
Cover your legs.
Hah...
DON'T START FIGHTS WHEN I'M NOT AROUND, PLEASE.
WHY?
DON'T YOU KNOW?!

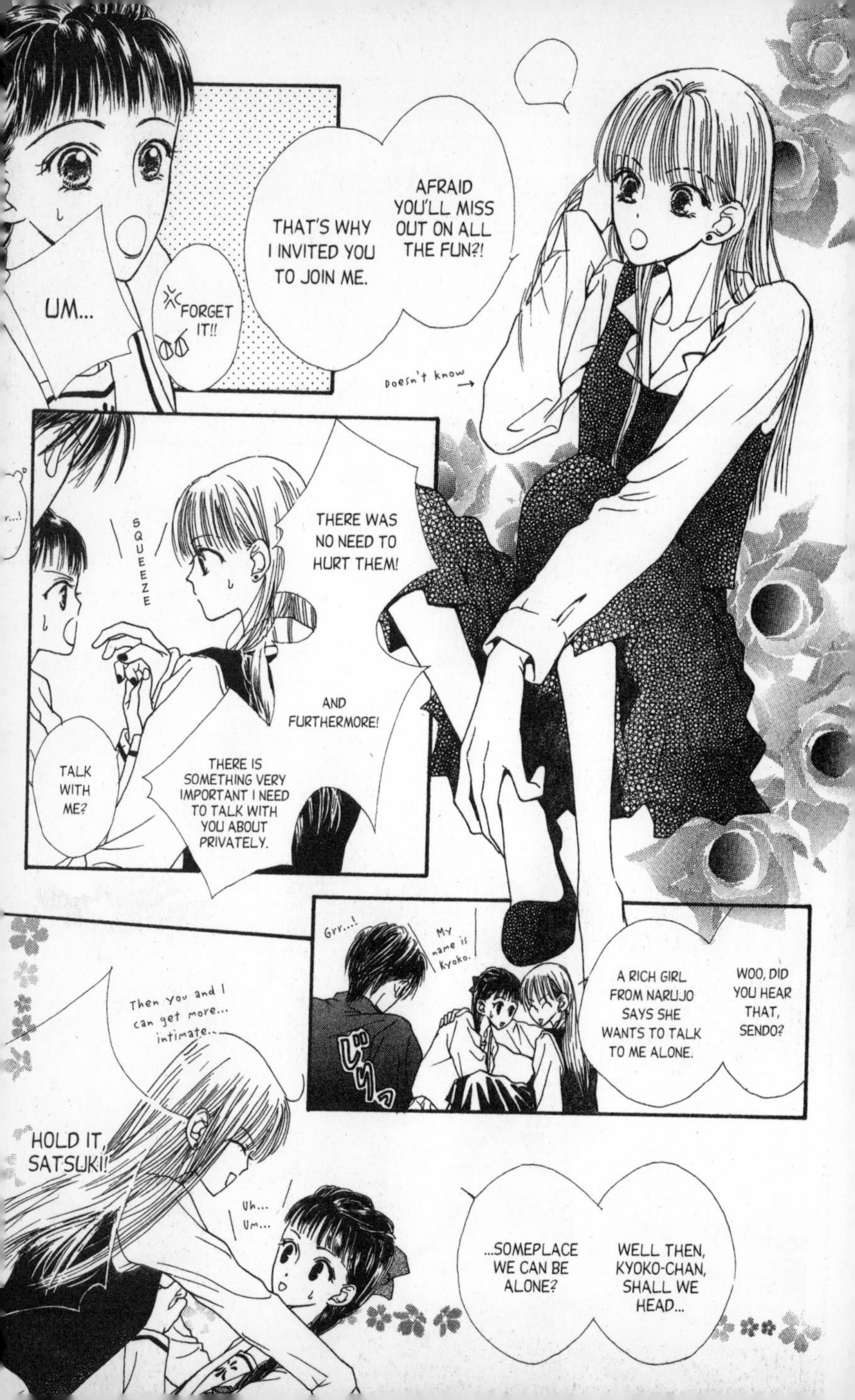
AFRAID YOU'LL MISS OUT ON ALL THE FUN?!
THAT'S WHY I INVITED YOU TO JOIN ME.
FORGET IT!!
UM...
Doesn't know →
THERE WAS NO NEED TO HURT THEM!
SQUEEZE
AND FURTHERMORE!
THERE IS SOMETHING VERY IMPORTANT I NEED TO TALK WITH YOU ABOUT PRIVATELY.
TALK WITH ME?
WOO, DID YOU HEAR THAT, SENDO?
A RICH GIRL FROM NARUJO SAYS SHE WANTS TO TALK TO ME ALONE.
My name is Kyoko.
Grr...!
WELL THEN, KYOKO-CHAN, SHALL WE HEAD...
...SOMEPLACE WE CAN BE ALONE?
Then you and I can get more... intimate...
Uh... Um...
HOLD IT, SATSUKI!

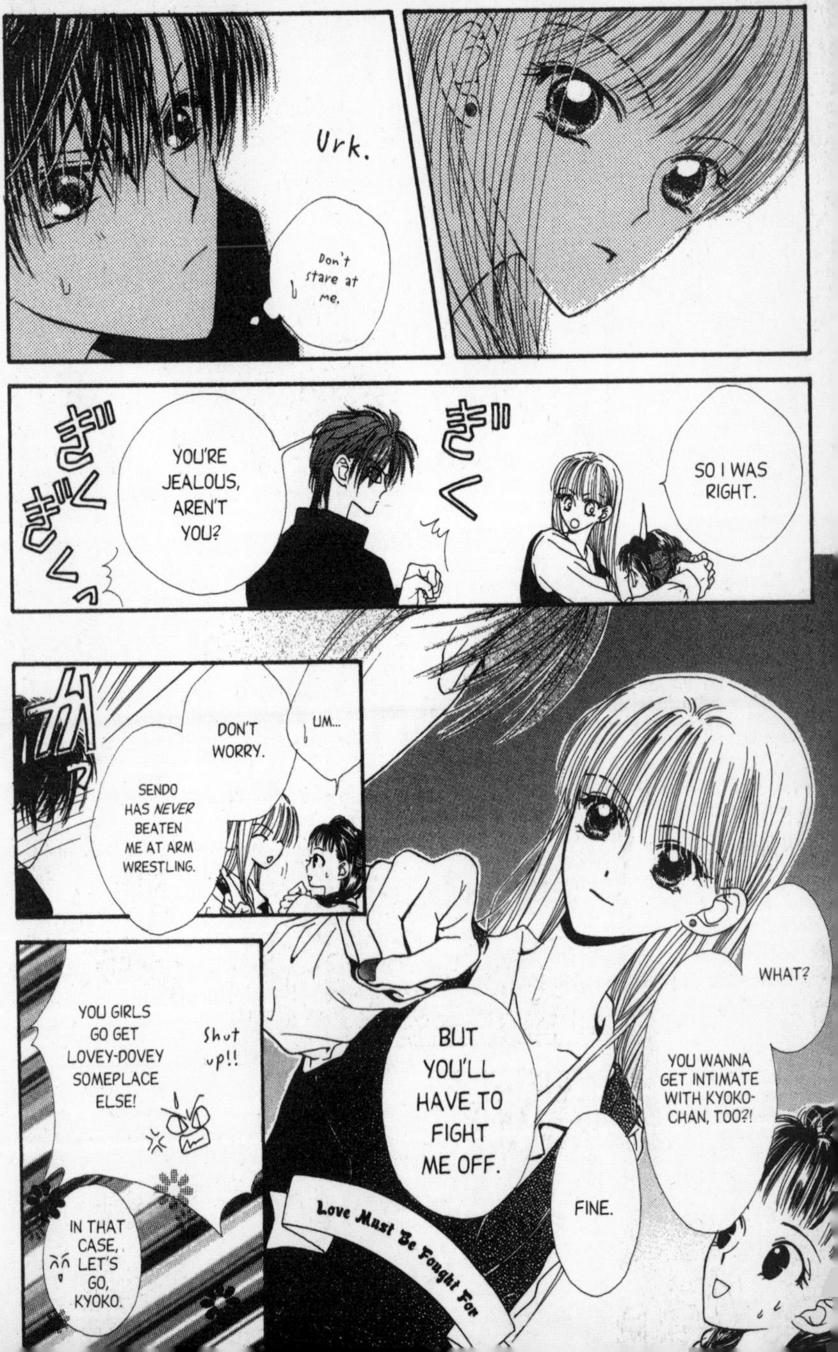
Urk.
Don't stare at me.
SO I WAS RIGHT.
ぎく
YOU'RE JEALOUS, AREN'T YOU?
ぎくぎくっ
WHAT?
YOU WANNA GET INTIMATE WITH KYOKO-CHAN, TOO?!
FINE.
BUT YOU'LL HAVE TO FIGHT ME OFF.
Love Must Be Fought For
UM...
DON'T WORRY.
SENDO HAS *NEVER* BEATEN ME AT ARM WRESTLING.
カァ
YOU GIRLS GO GET LOVEY-DOVEY SOMEPLACE ELSE!
Shut up!!
IN THAT CASE, LET'S GO, KYOKO.

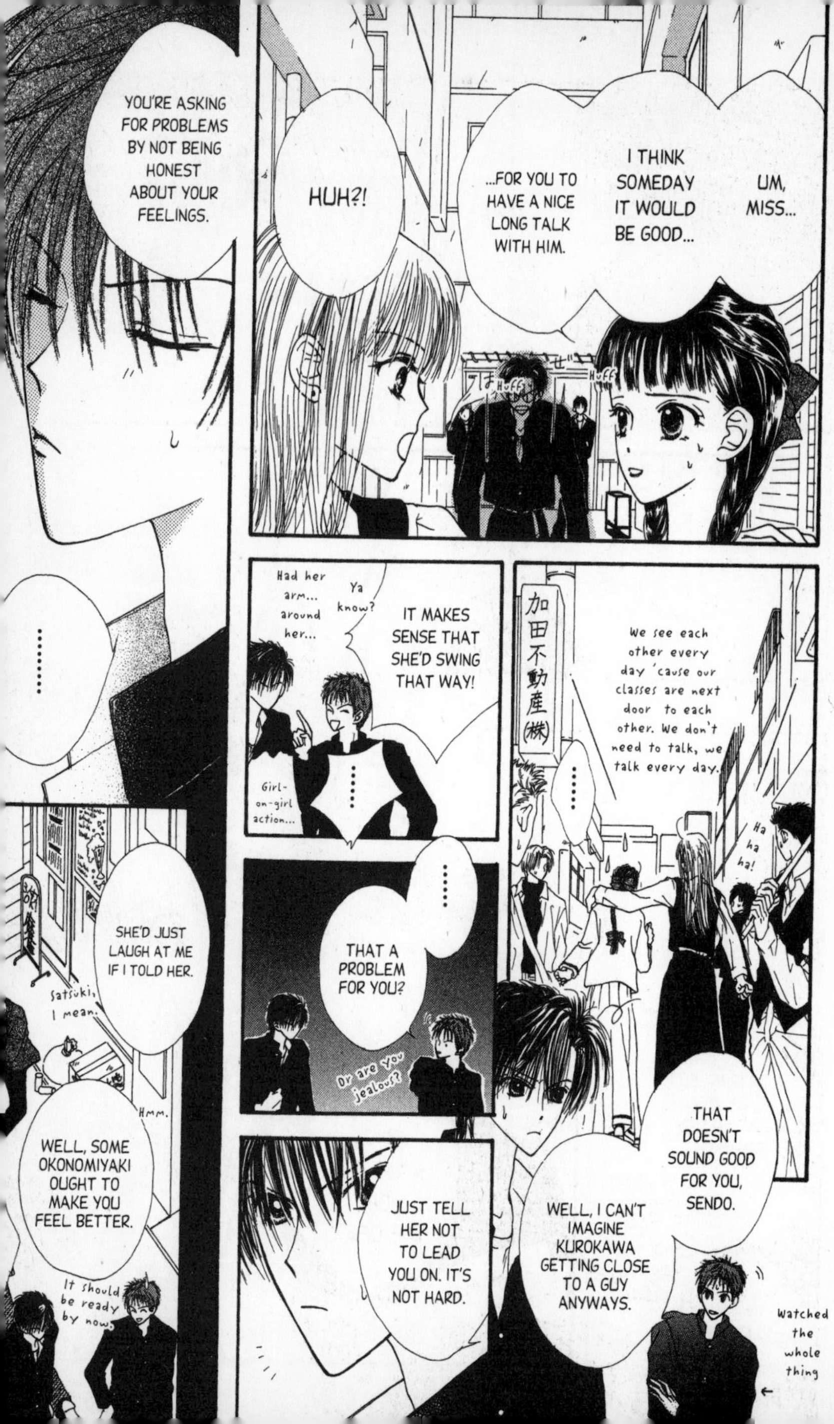
UM, MISS...
I THINK SOMEDAY IT WOULD BE GOOD...
...FOR YOU TO HAVE A NICE LONG TALK WITH HIM.
HUH?!
Huff
Huff
We see each other every day 'cause our classes are next door to each other. We don't need to talk, we talk every day.
......
Ha ha ha!
THAT DOESN'T SOUND GOOD FOR YOU, SENDO.
WELL, I CAN'T IMAGINE KUROKAWA GETTING CLOSE TO A GUY ANYWAYS.
Watched the whole thing
IT MAKES SENSE THAT SHE'D SWING THAT WAY!
Ya know?
Had her arm... around her...
......
Girl-on-girl action...
......
THAT A PROBLEM FOR YOU?
Or are you jealous?
JUST TELL HER NOT TO LEAD YOU ON. IT'S NOT HARD.
YOU'RE ASKING FOR PROBLEMS BY NOT BEING HONEST ABOUT YOUR FEELINGS.
......
SHE'D JUST LAUGH AT ME IF I TOLD HER.
Satsuki, I mean.
Hmm.
WELL, SOME OKONOMIYAKI OUGHT TO MAKE YOU FEEL BETTER.
It should be ready by now.

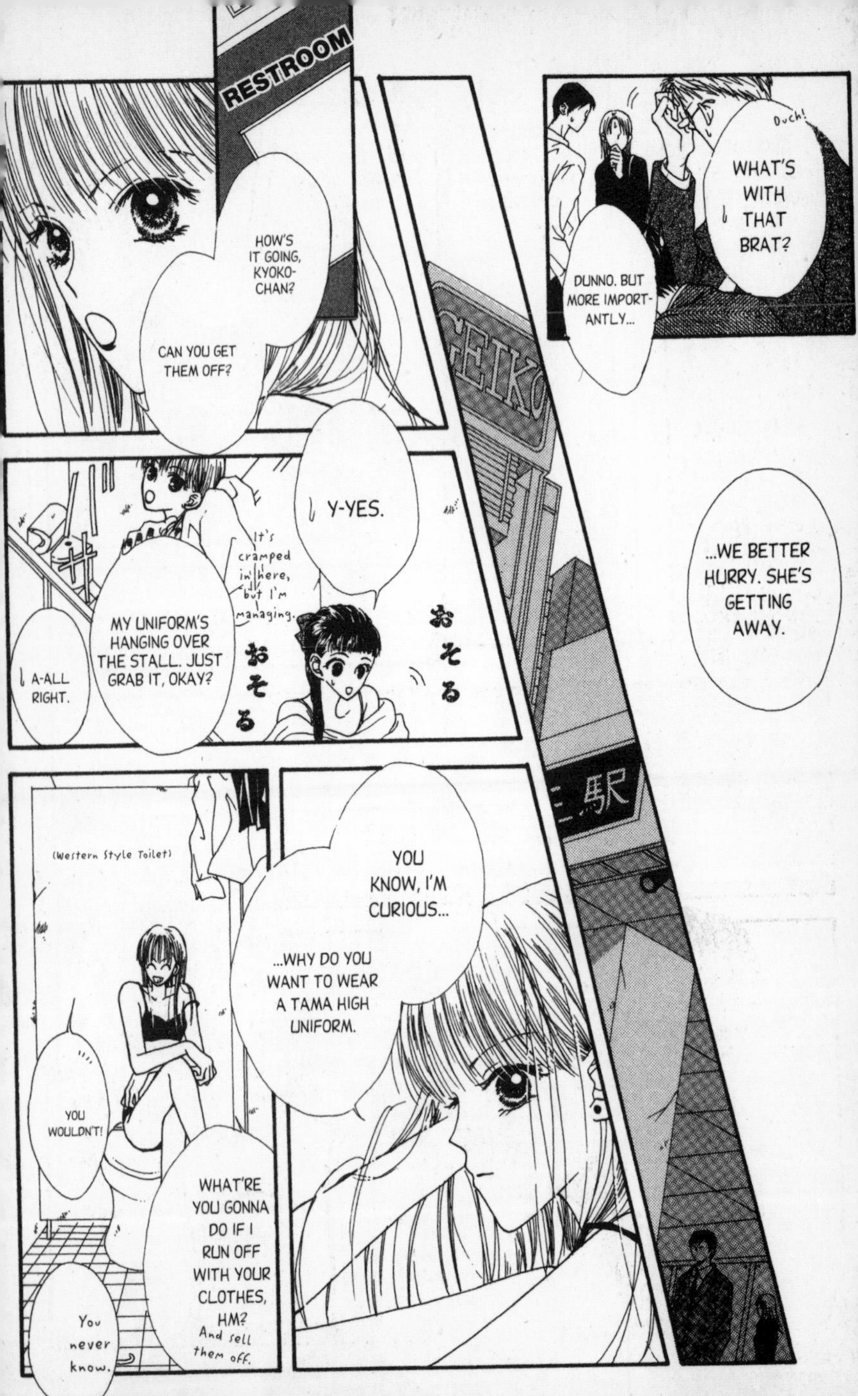
Ouch!
WHAT'S WITH THAT BRAT?
DUNNO. BUT MORE IMPORT-ANTLY...
...WE BETTER HURRY. SHE'S GETTING AWAY.
RESTROOM
HOW'S IT GOING, KYOKO-CHAN?
CAN YOU GET THEM OFF?
Y-YES.
おそるおそる
It's cramped in here, but I'm managing.
MY UNIFORM'S HANGING OVER THE STALL. JUST GRAB IT, OKAY?
A-ALL RIGHT.
YOU KNOW, I'M CURIOUS...
...WHY DO YOU WANT TO WEAR A TAMA HIGH UNIFORM.
WHAT'RE YOU GONNA DO IF I RUN OFF WITH YOUR CLOTHES, HM?
And sell them off.
YOU WOULDN'T!
You never know.
(Western Style Toilet)

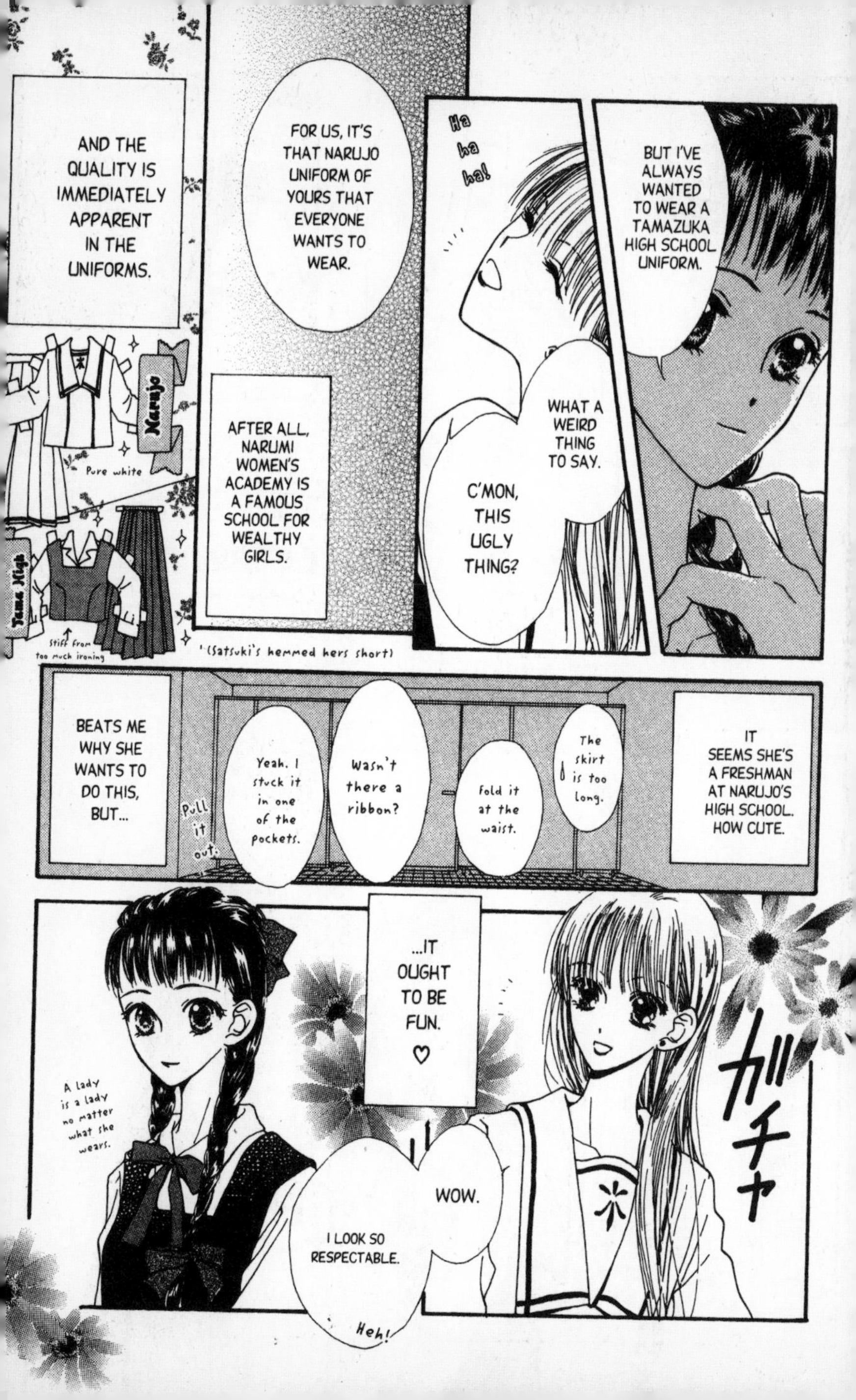
BUT I'VE ALWAYS WANTED TO WEAR A TAMAZUKA HIGH SCHOOL UNIFORM.
Ha ha ha!
WHAT A WEIRD THING TO SAY.
C'MON, THIS UGLY THING?
FOR US, IT'S THAT NARUJO UNIFORM OF YOURS THAT EVERYONE WANTS TO WEAR.
AFTER ALL, NARUMI WOMEN'S ACADEMY IS A FAMOUS SCHOOL FOR WEALTHY GIRLS.
(Satsuki's hemmed hers short)
AND THE QUALITY IS IMMEDIATELY APPARENT IN THE UNIFORMS.
Narujo
Pure white
Tama High
Stiff from too much ironing
IT SEEMS SHE'S A FRESHMAN AT NARUJO'S HIGH SCHOOL. HOW CUTE.
The skirt is too long.
Fold it at the waist.
Wasn't there a ribbon?
Yeah. I stuck it in one of the pockets.
Pull it out.
BEATS ME WHY SHE WANTS TO DO THIS, BUT...
...IT OUGHT TO BE FUN. ♡
ガチャ
WOW.
I LOOK SO RESPECTABLE.
Heh!
A lady is a lady no matter what she wears.

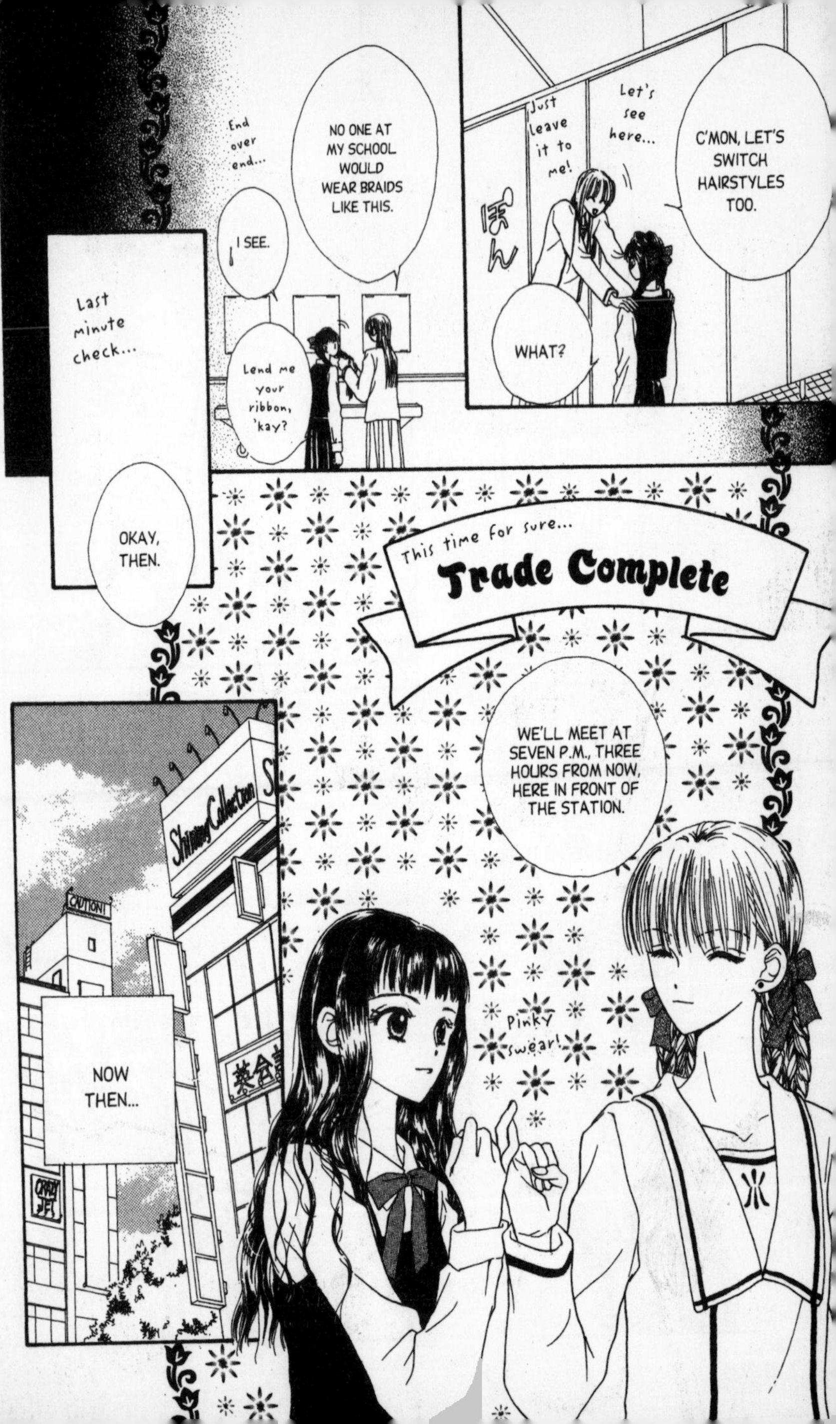
C'MON, LET'S SWITCH HAIRSTYLES TOO.
Let's see here...
Just leave it to me!
ぽん
WHAT?
NO ONE AT MY SCHOOL WOULD WEAR BRAIDS LIKE THIS.
End over end...
I SEE.
Lend me your ribbon, 'kay?
Last minute check...
OKAY, THEN.
This time for sure...
Trade Complete
WE'LL MEET AT SEVEN P.M., THREE HOURS FROM NOW, HERE IN FRONT OF THE STATION.
Pinky swear!
CAUTION!
NOW THEN...

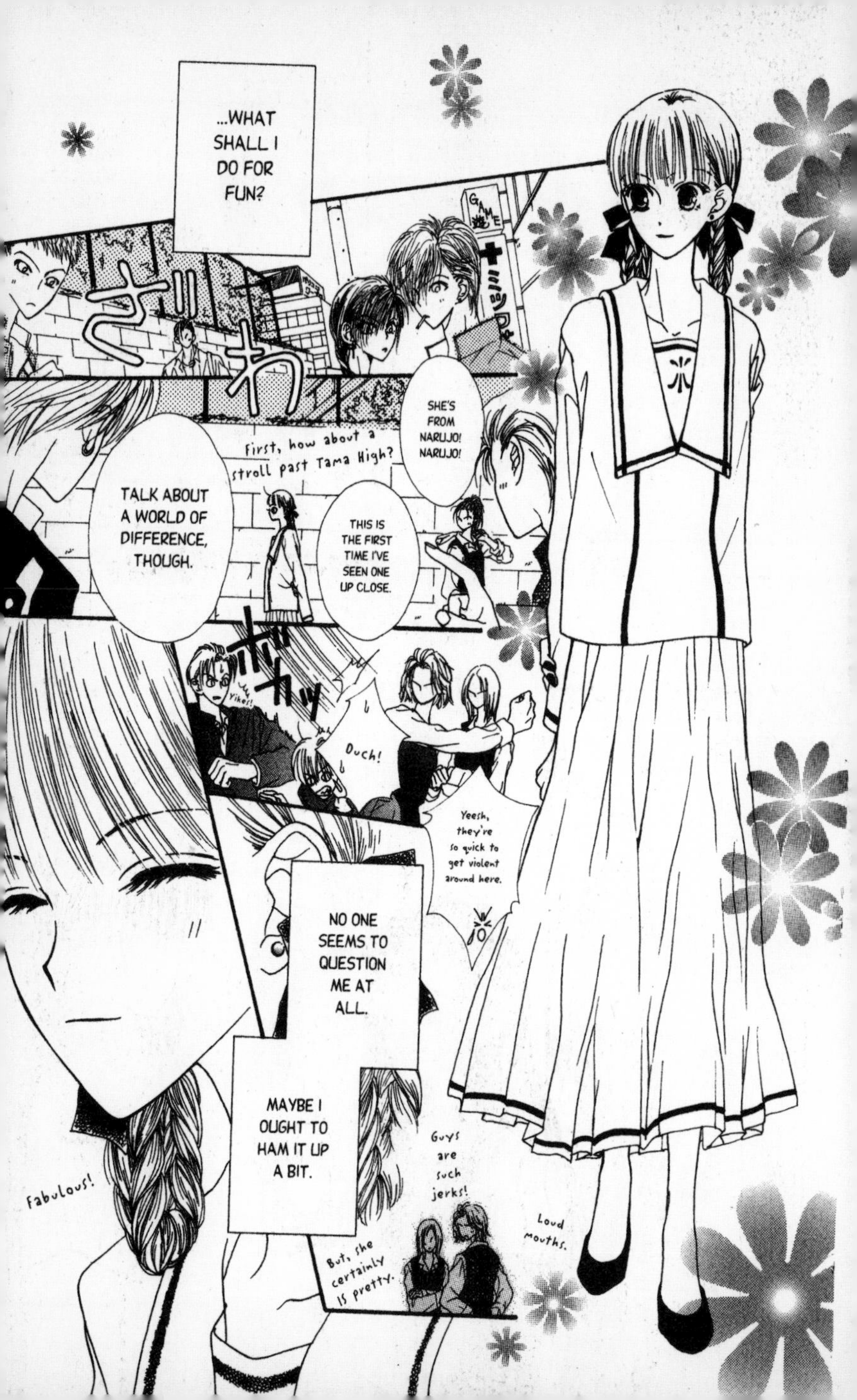
...WHAT SHALL I DO FOR FUN?
SHE'S FROM NARUJO! NARUJO!
First, how about a stroll past Tama High?
THIS IS THE FIRST TIME I'VE SEEN ONE UP CLOSE.
TALK ABOUT A WORLD OF DIFFERENCE, THOUGH.
Yikes!
Ouch!
Yeesh, they're so quick to get violent around here.
NO ONE SEEMS TO QUESTION ME AT ALL.
MAYBE I OUGHT TO HAM IT UP A BIT.
Guys are such jerks!
Loud mouths.
But, she certainly is pretty.
Fabulous!

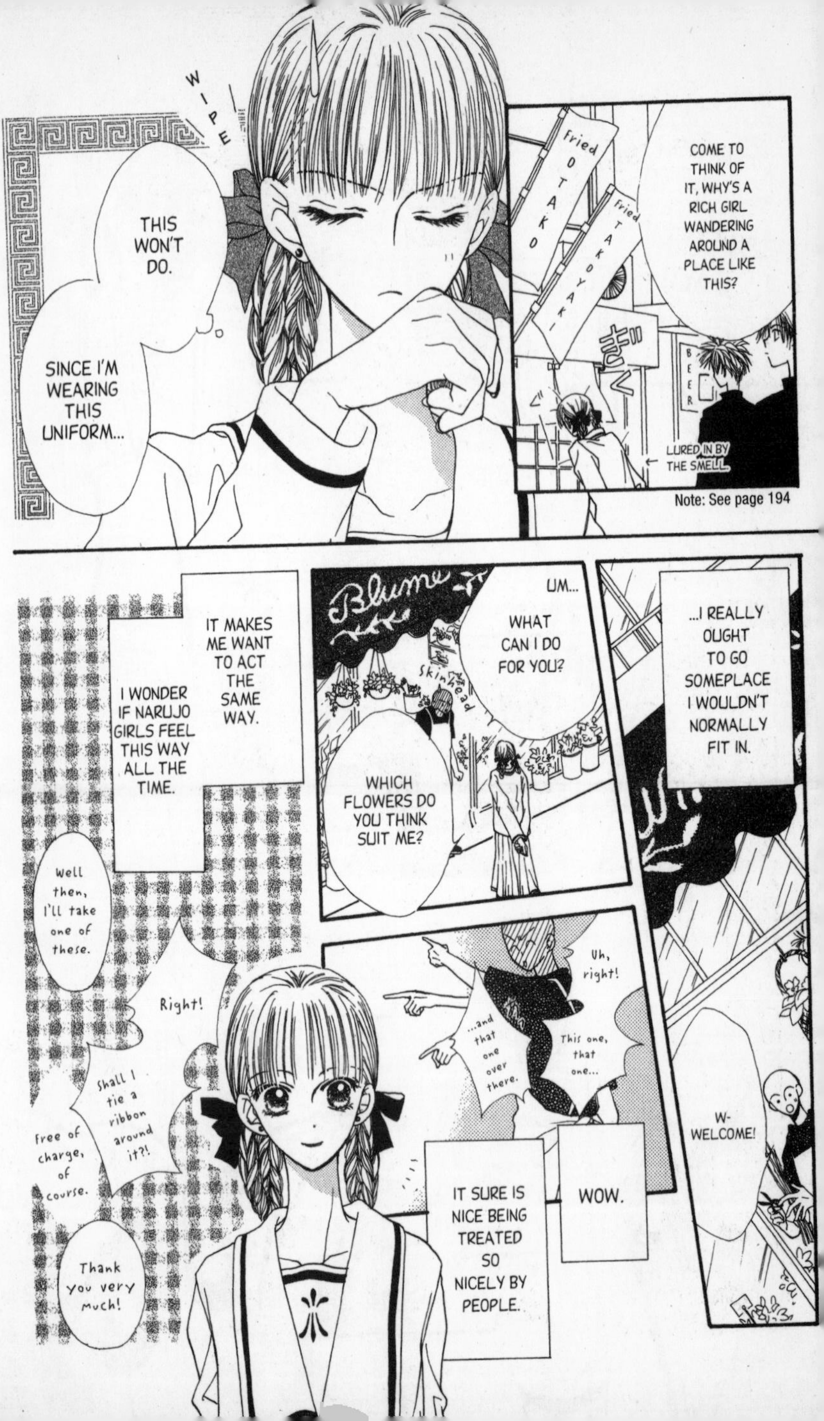
Fried OTAKO
Fried TAKOYAKI
BEER
COME TO THINK OF IT, WHY'S A RICH GIRL WANDERING AROUND A PLACE LIKE THIS?
LURED IN BY THE SMELL.
WIPE
THIS WON'T DO.
SINCE I'M WEARING THIS UNIFORM...
...I REALLY OUGHT TO GO SOMEPLACE I WOULDN'T NORMALLY FIT IN.
W-WELCOME!
Blume
UM...
WHAT CAN I DO FOR YOU?
Skinhead
WHICH FLOWERS DO YOU THINK SUIT ME?
IT MAKES ME WANT TO ACT THE SAME WAY.
I WONDER IF NARUJO GIRLS FEEL THIS WAY ALL THE TIME.
Uh, right!
This one, that one...
...and that one over there.
WOW.
IT SURE IS NICE BEING TREATED SO NICELY BY PEOPLE.
Well then, I'll take one of these.
Right!
Shall I tie a ribbon around it?!
Free of charge, of course.
Thank you very much!
Note: See page 194

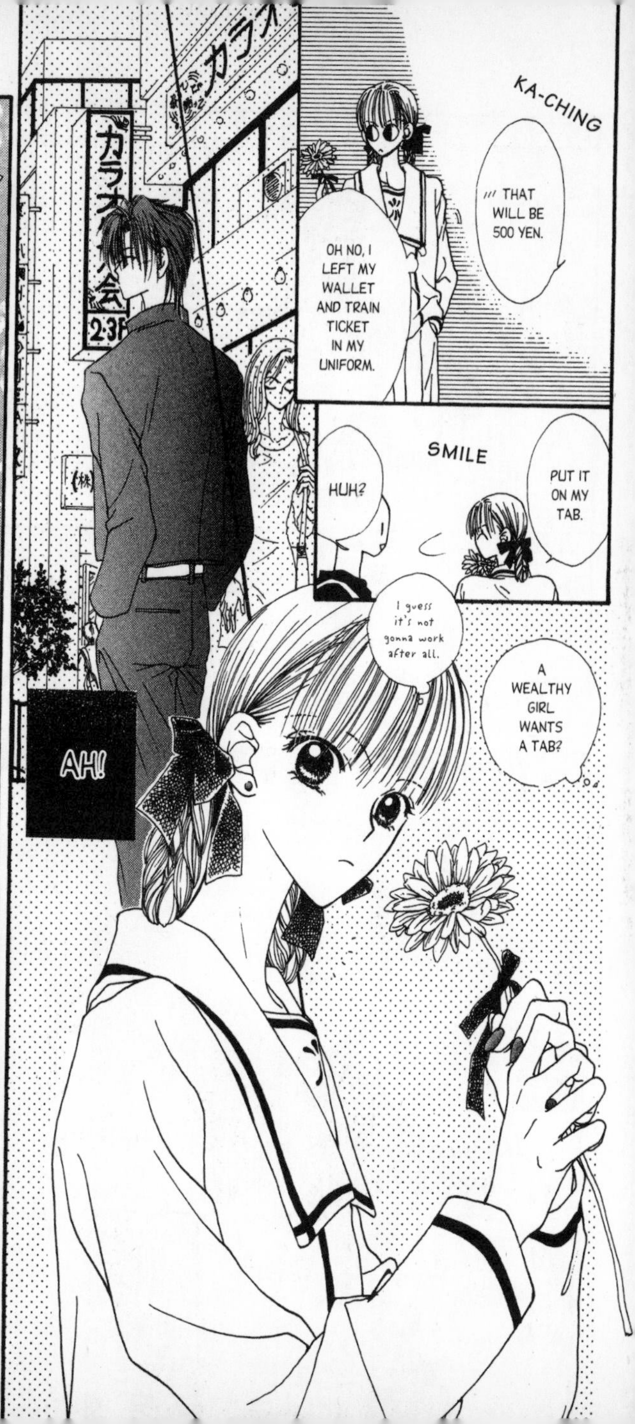
KA-CHING
THAT WILL BE 500 YEN.
OH NO, I LEFT MY WALLET AND TRAIN TICKET IN MY UNIFORM.
PUT IT ON MY TAB.
SMILE
HUH?
A WEALTHY GIRL WANTS A TAB?
I guess it's not gonna work after all.
AH!

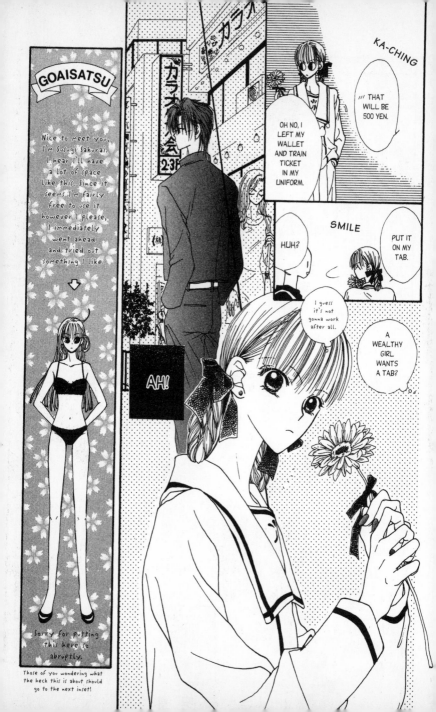

GOAISATSU

Nice to meet you, I'm Susugi Sakurai. I hear I'll have a lot of space like this. Since it seems I'm fairly free to use it however I please, I immediately went ahead and tried out something I like.

↓

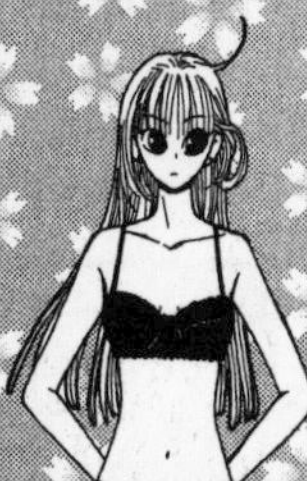

Sorry for putting this here so abruptly.

Those of you wondering what the heck this is about should go to the next inset!

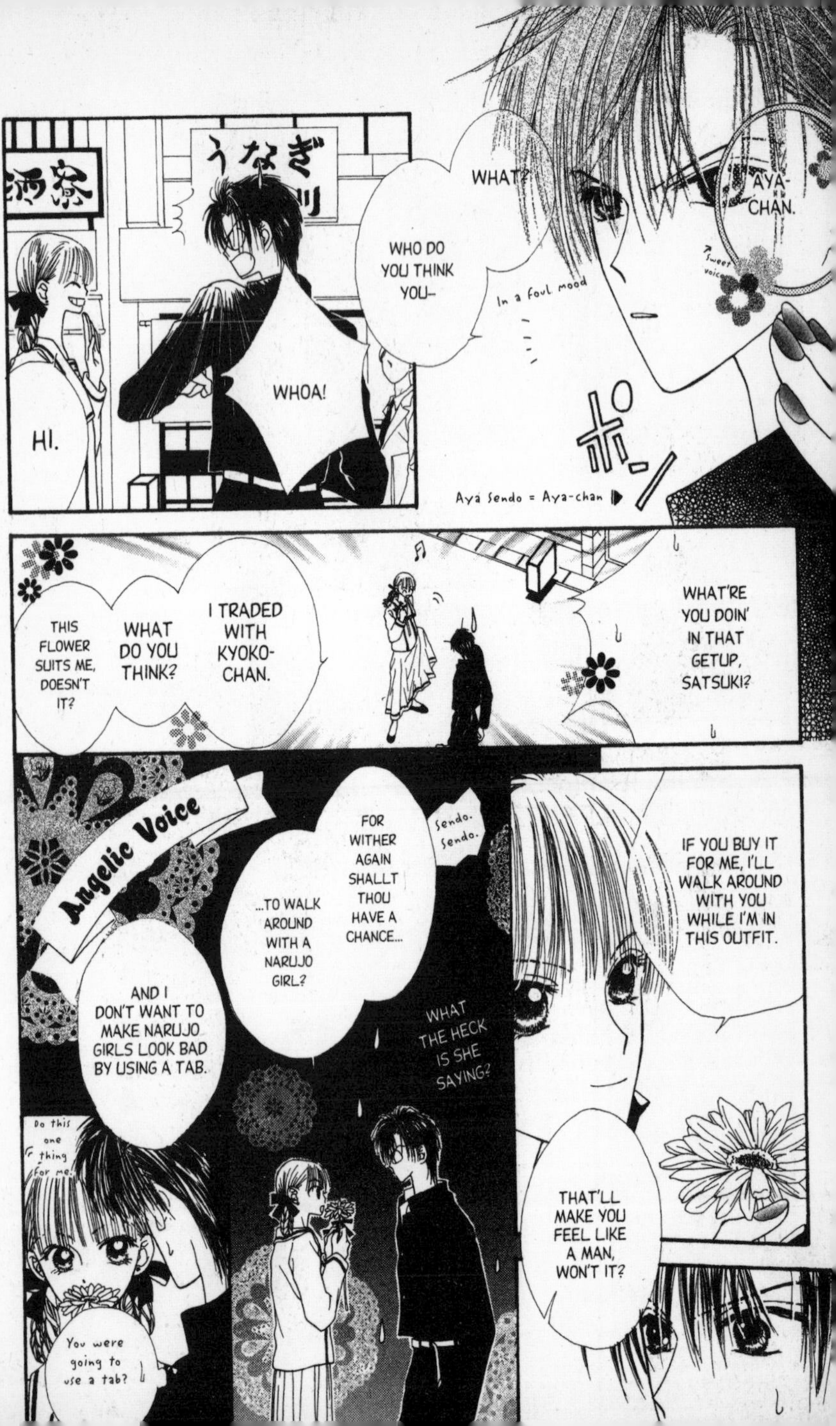
AYA-CHAN.
sweet voice
In a foul mood
WHAT?
ポー
Aya Sendo = Aya-chan
うなぎ
WHO DO YOU THINK YOU–
WHOA!
HI.
WHAT'RE YOU DOIN' IN THAT GETUP, SATSUKI?
I TRADED WITH KYOKO-CHAN.
WHAT DO YOU THINK?
THIS FLOWER SUITS ME, DOESN'T IT?
IF YOU BUY IT FOR ME, I'LL WALK AROUND WITH YOU WHILE I'M IN THIS OUTFIT.
THAT'LL MAKE YOU FEEL LIKE A MAN, WON'T IT?
Sendo. Sendo.
FOR WITHER AGAIN SHALLT THOU HAVE A CHANCE...
...TO WALK AROUND WITH A NARUJO GIRL?
Angelic Voice
WHAT THE HECK IS SHE SAYING?
AND I DON'T WANT TO MAKE NARUJO GIRLS LOOK BAD BY USING A TAB.
Do this one thing for me.
You were going to use a tab?

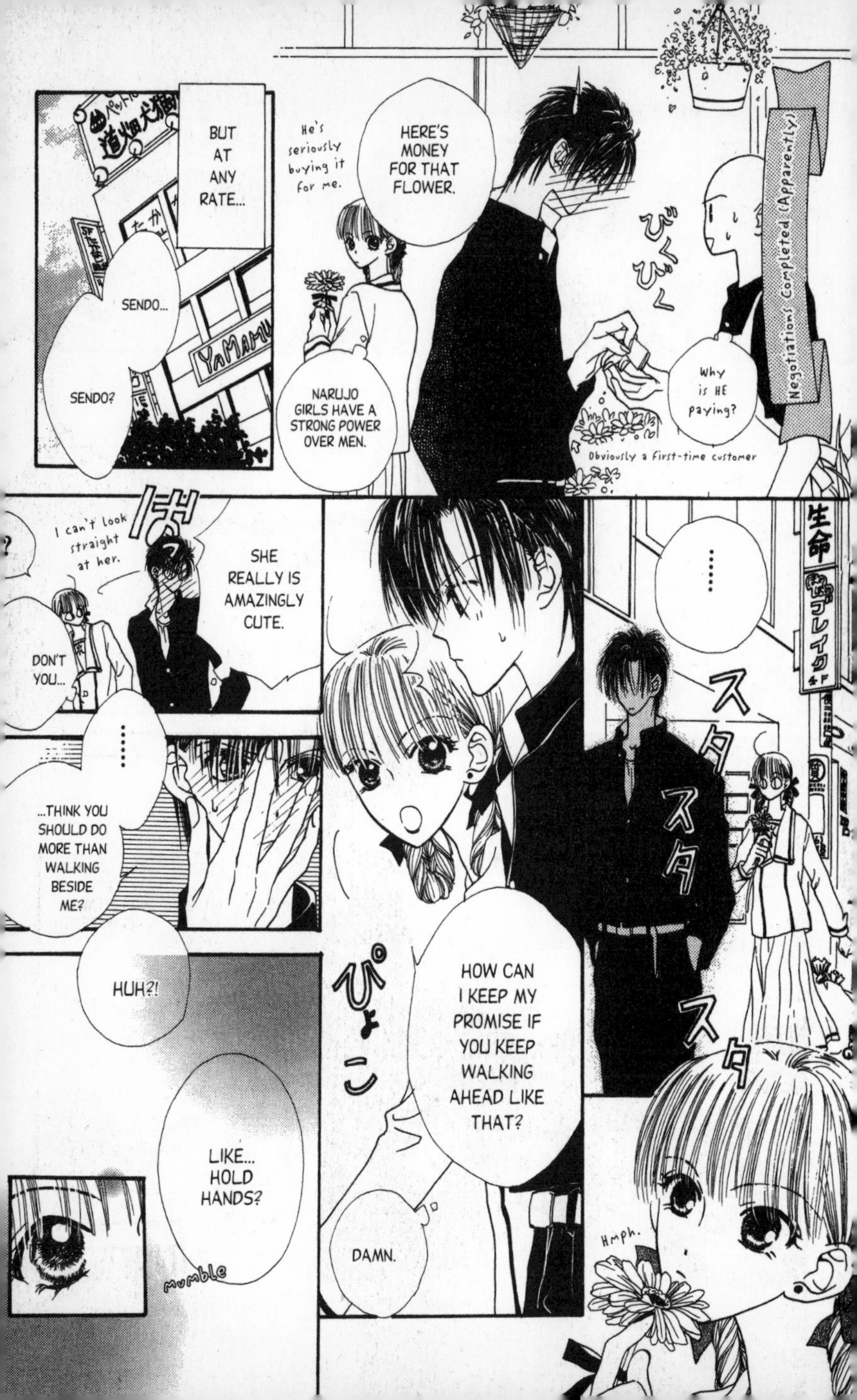
Negotiations Completed (Apparently)
びくびく
Why is HE paying?
Obviously a first-time customer
HERE'S MONEY FOR THAT FLOWER.
He's seriously buying it for me.
NARUJO GIRLS HAVE A STRONG POWER OVER MEN.
BUT AT ANY RATE...
SENDO...
SENDO?
......
スタスタスタ
HOW CAN I KEEP MY PROMISE IF YOU KEEP WALKING AHEAD LIKE THAT?
ぴょこ
Hmph.
DAMN.
ばっ
SHE REALLY IS AMAZINGLY CUTE.
I can't look straight at her.
DON'T YOU...
......
...THINK YOU SHOULD DO MORE THAN WALKING BESIDE ME?
HUH?!
LIKE... HOLD HANDS?
mumble

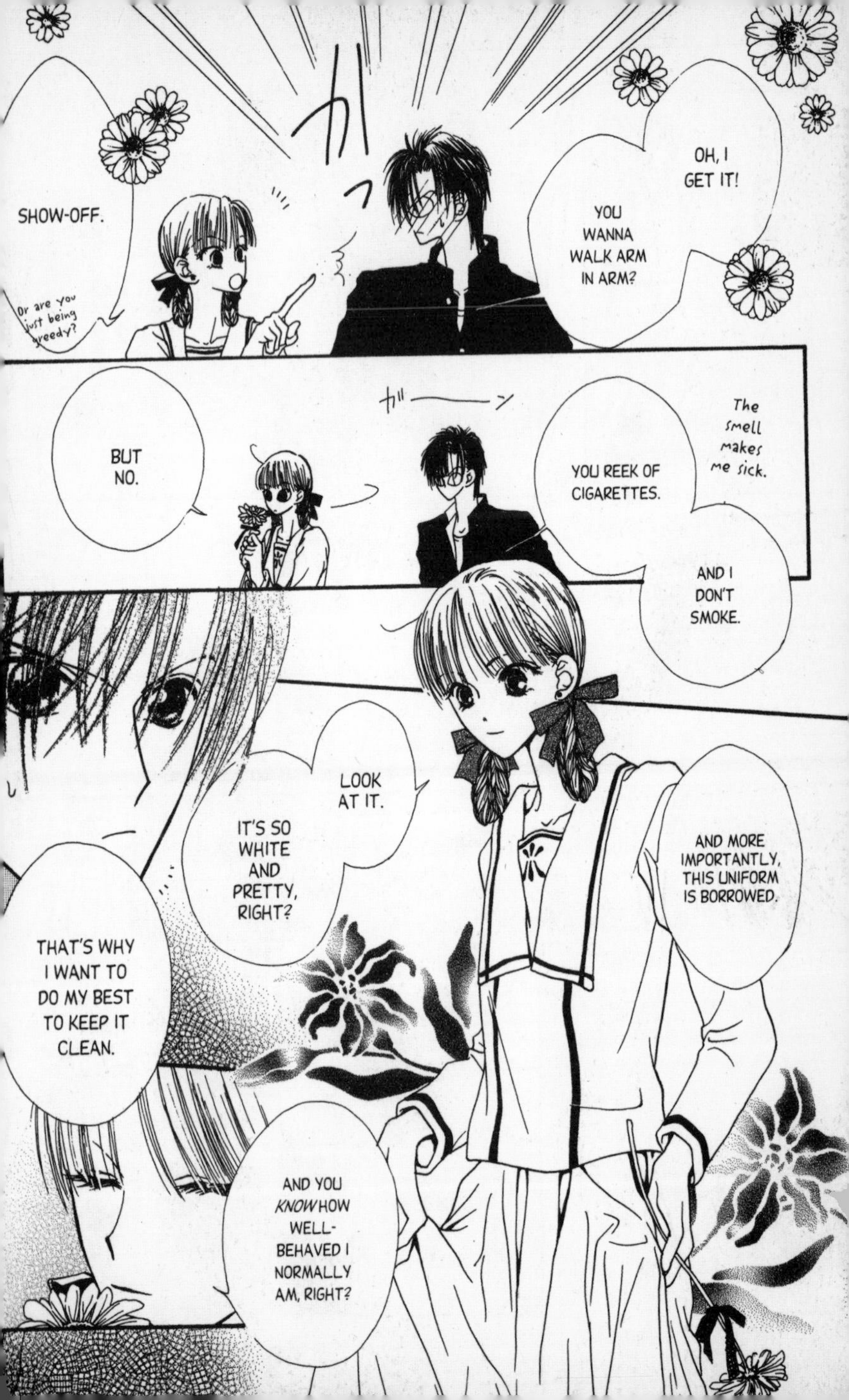
OH, I GET IT!
YOU WANNA WALK ARM IN ARM?
SHOW-OFF.
Or are you just being greedy?
YOU REEK OF CIGARETTES.
The smell makes me sick.
AND I DON'T SMOKE.
BUT NO.
AND MORE IMPORTANTLY, THIS UNIFORM IS BORROWED.
LOOK AT IT.
IT'S SO WHITE AND PRETTY, RIGHT?
THAT'S WHY I WANT TO DO MY BEST TO KEEP IT CLEAN.
AND YOU *KNOW* HOW WELL-BEHAVED I NORMALLY AM, RIGHT?

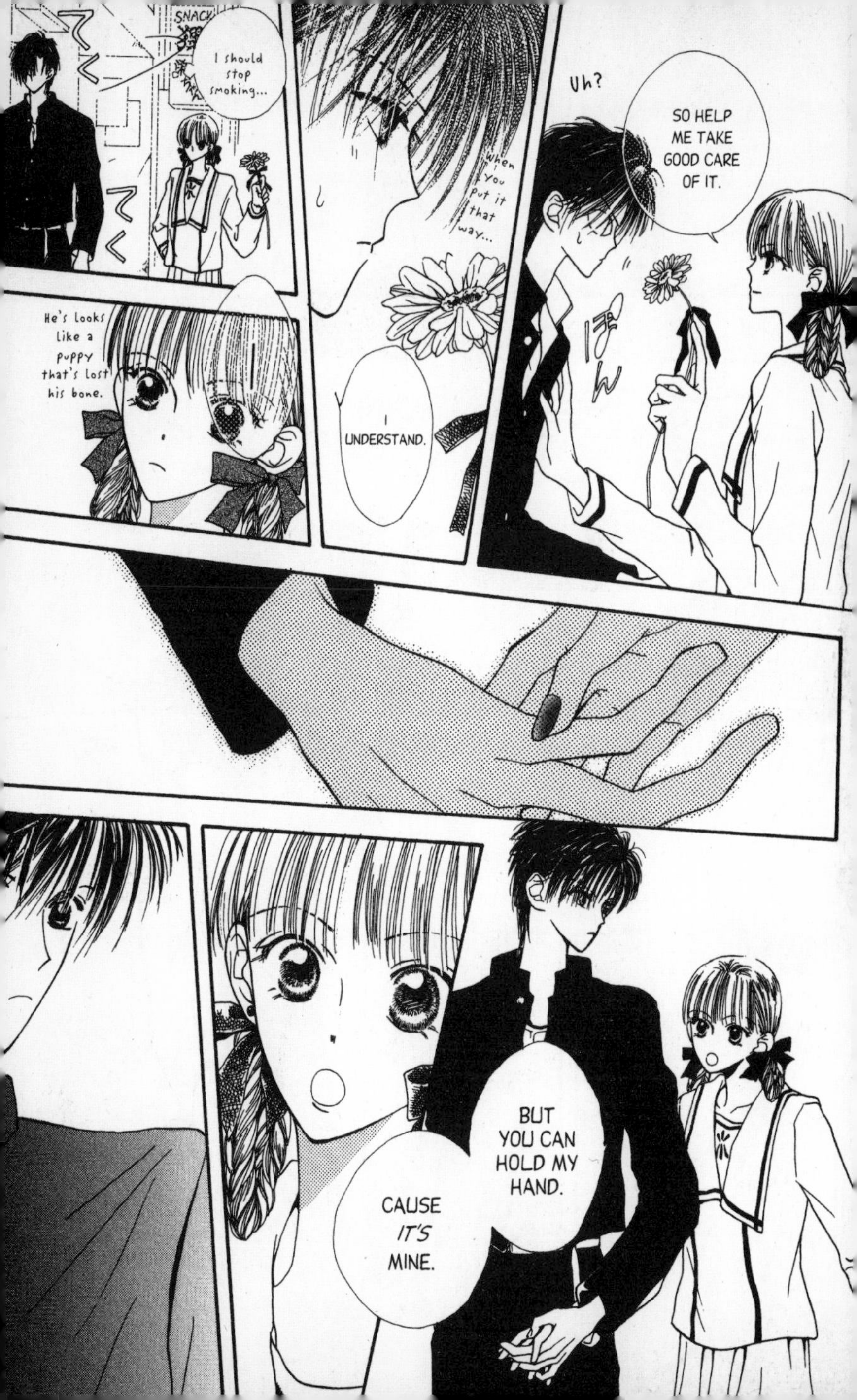
Uh?
SO HELP ME TAKE GOOD CARE OF IT.
ぽん
When you put it that way...
I UNDERSTAND.
SNACK
I should stop smoking...
てく てく
He's looks like a puppy that's lost his bone.
BUT YOU CAN HOLD MY HAND.
CAUSE *IT'S* MINE.

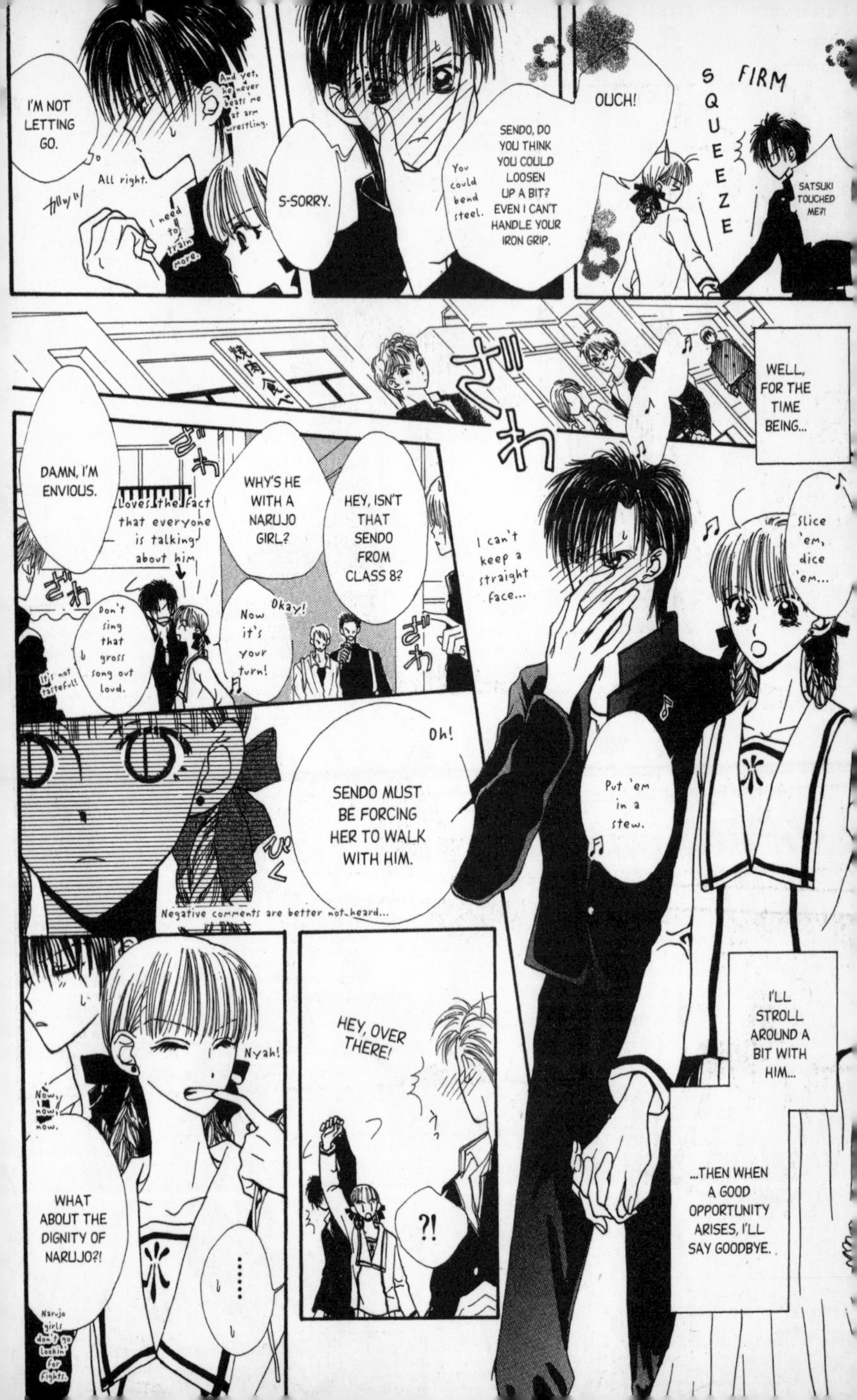
S Q U E E Z E
FIRM
SATSUKI TOUCHED ME?!
OUCH!
SENDO, DO YOU THINK YOU COULD LOOSEN UP A BIT? EVEN I CAN'T HANDLE YOUR IRON GRIP.
You could bend steel.
S-SORRY.
And yet, he never beats me at arm wrestling.
I'M NOT LETTING GO.
All right.
I need to train more.
WELL, FOR THE TIME BEING...
Slice 'em, dice 'em...
I can't keep a straight face...
Put 'em in a stew.
I'LL STROLL AROUND A BIT WITH HIM...
...THEN WHEN A GOOD OPPORTUNITY ARISES, I'LL SAY GOODBYE.
HEY, ISN'T THAT SENDO FROM CLASS 8?
WHY'S HE WITH A NARUJO GIRL?
DAMN, I'M ENVIOUS.
Loves the fact that everyone is talking about him
Okay!
Now it's your turn!
Don't sing that gross song out loud.
It's not tasteful!
Oh!
SENDO MUST BE FORCING HER TO WALK WITH HIM.
Negative comments are better not heard...
HEY, OVER THERE!
?!
......
Nyah!
Now, now, now.
WHAT ABOUT THE DIGNITY OF NARUJO?!
Narujo girls don't go lookin' for fights.

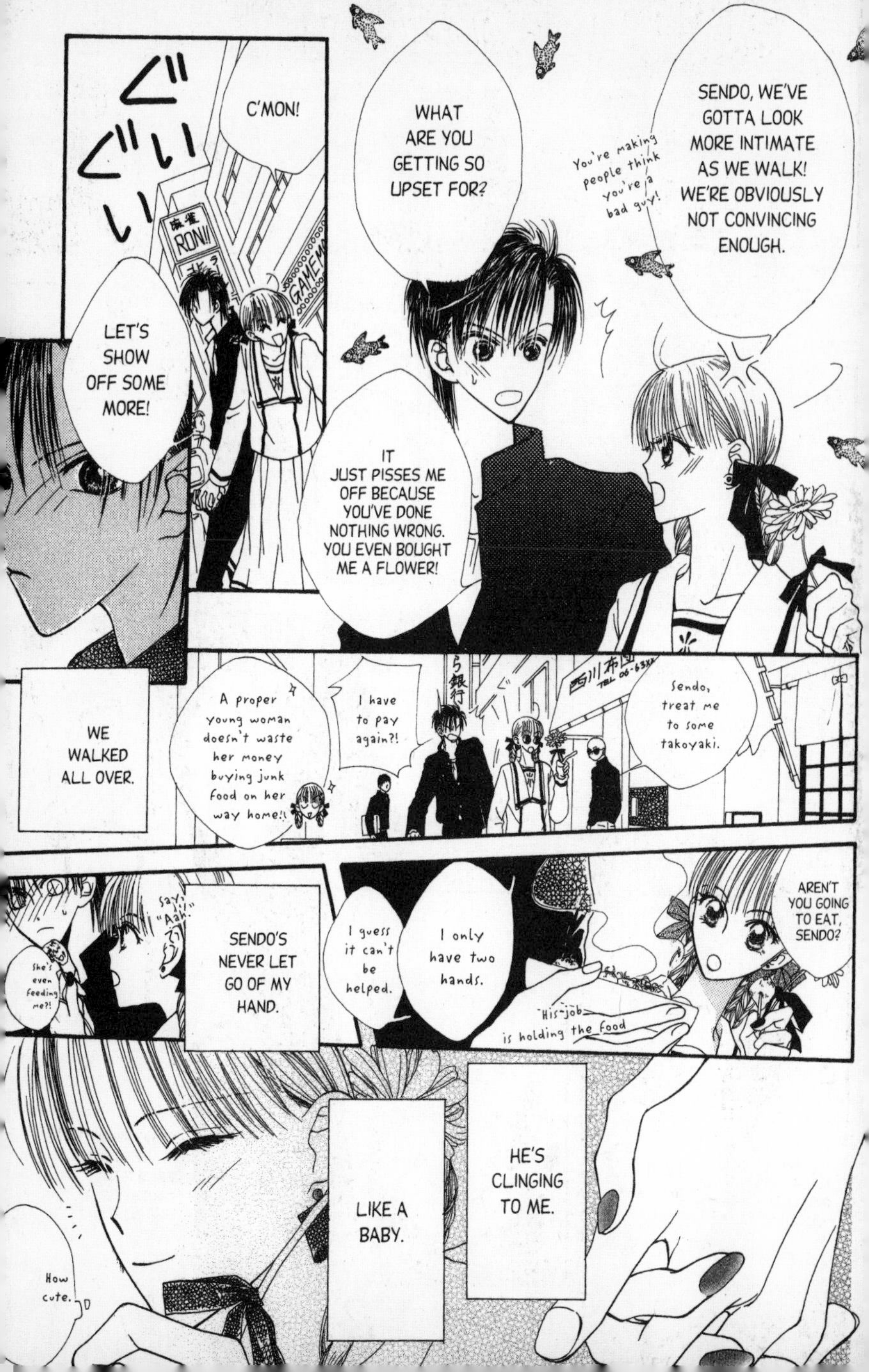
SENDO, WE'VE GOTTA LOOK MORE INTIMATE AS WE WALK! WE'RE OBVIOUSLY NOT CONVINCING ENOUGH.
You're making people think you're a bad guy!
WHAT ARE YOU GETTING SO UPSET FOR?
IT JUST PISSES ME OFF BECAUSE YOU'VE DONE NOTHING WRONG. YOU EVEN BOUGHT ME A FLOWER!
ぐいぐいい
C'MON!
麻雀 RON!!
GAME
LET'S SHOW OFF SOME MORE!
Sendo, treat me to some takoyaki.
I have to pay again?!
A proper young woman doesn't waste her money buying junk food on her way home!!
WE WALKED ALL OVER.
AREN'T YOU GOING TO EAT, SENDO?
I only have two hands.
I guess it can't be helped.
His job is holding the food
SENDO'S NEVER LET GO OF MY HAND.
Say, "Aah."
She's even feeding me?!
HE'S CLINGING TO ME.
LIKE A BABY.
...
How cute.

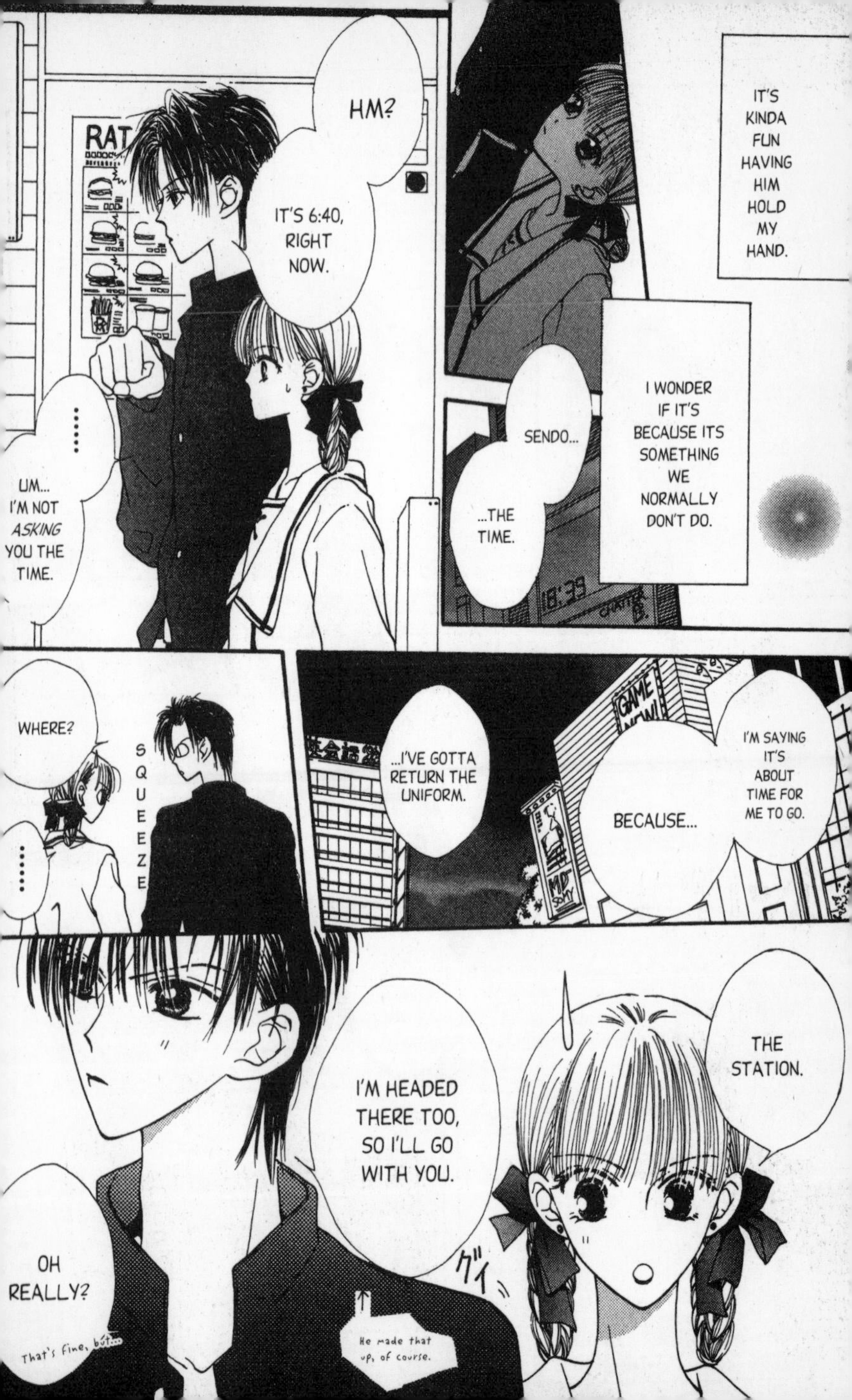
IT'S KINDA FUN HAVING HIM HOLD MY HAND.
I WONDER IF IT'S BECAUSE ITS SOMETHING WE NORMALLY DON'T DO.
SENDO...
...THE TIME.
18:39
HM?
IT'S 6:40, RIGHT NOW.
......
UM... I'M NOT *ASKING* YOU THE TIME.
I'M SAYING IT'S ABOUT TIME FOR ME TO GO.
BECAUSE...
...I'VE GOTTA RETURN THE UNIFORM.
GAME
WHERE?
SQUEEZE
......
THE STATION.
グイ
I'M HEADED THERE TOO, SO I'LL GO WITH YOU.
OH REALLY?
He made that up, of course.
That's fine, but...

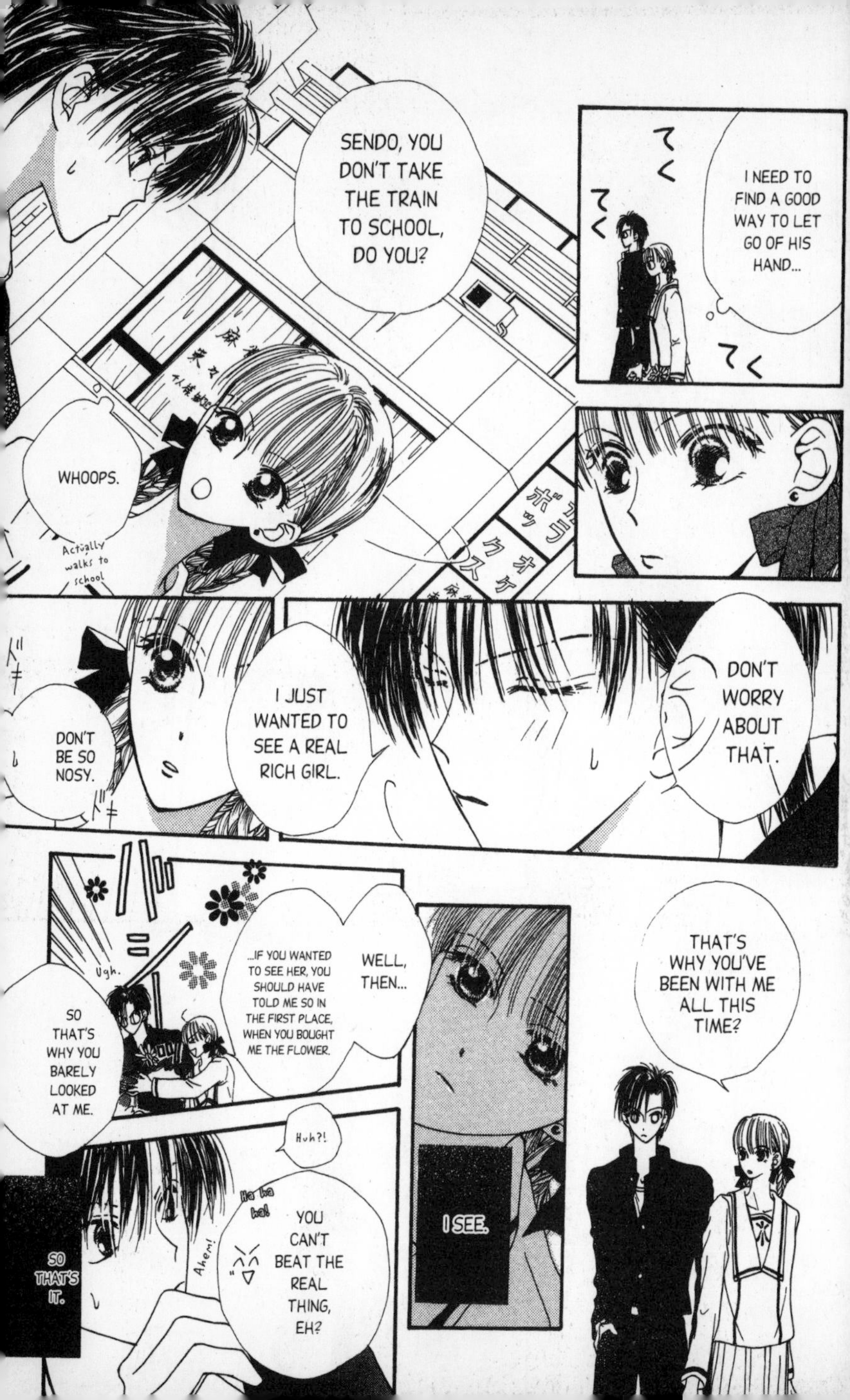
てく
てく
I NEED TO FIND A GOOD WAY TO LET GO OF HIS HAND...
てく
SENDO, YOU DON'T TAKE THE TRAIN TO SCHOOL, DO YOU?
WHOOPS.
Actually walks to school
DON'T WORRY ABOUT THAT.
I JUST WANTED TO SEE A REAL RICH GIRL.
ドキ
DON'T BE SO NOSY.
ドキ
THAT'S WHY YOU'VE BEEN WITH ME ALL THIS TIME?
I SEE.
WELL, THEN...
...IF YOU WANTED TO SEE HER, YOU SHOULD HAVE TOLD ME SO IN THE FIRST PLACE, WHEN YOU BOUGHT ME THE FLOWER.
Ugh.
SO THAT'S WHY YOU BARELY LOOKED AT ME.
Huh?!
YOU CAN'T BEAT THE REAL THING, EH?
Ha ha ha!
Ahem!
SO THAT'S IT.

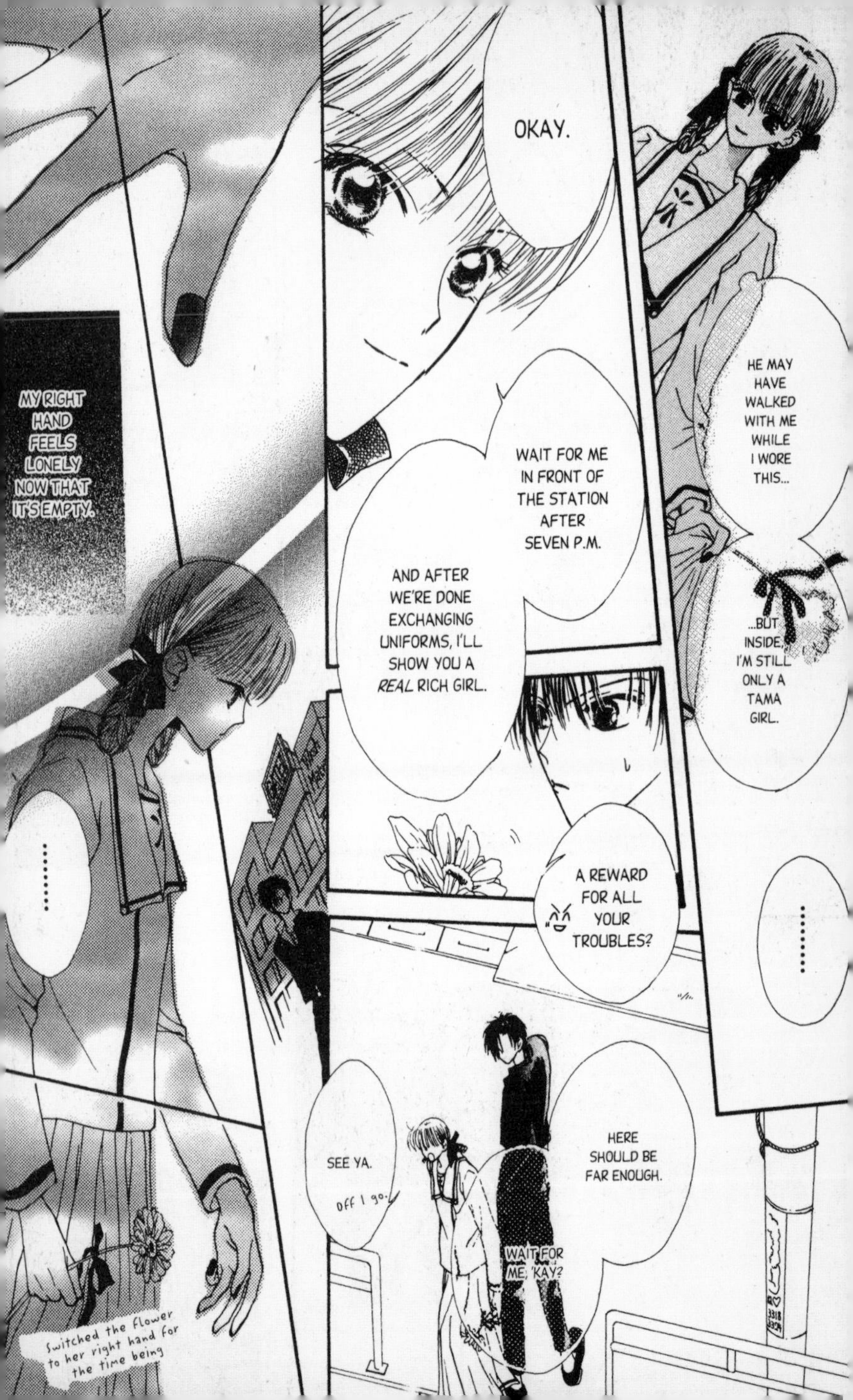
HE MAY HAVE WALKED WITH ME WHILE I WORE THIS...
...BUT INSIDE, I'M STILL ONLY A TAMA GIRL.
......
OKAY.
WAIT FOR ME IN FRONT OF THE STATION AFTER SEVEN P.M.
AND AFTER WE'RE DONE EXCHANGING UNIFORMS, I'LL SHOW YOU A *REAL* RICH GIRL.
A REWARD FOR ALL YOUR TROUBLES?
HERE SHOULD BE FAR ENOUGH.
SEE YA.
Off I go.
WAIT FOR ME, 'KAY?
MY RIGHT HAND FEELS LONELY NOW THAT IT'S EMPTY.
......
Switched the flower to her right hand for the time being

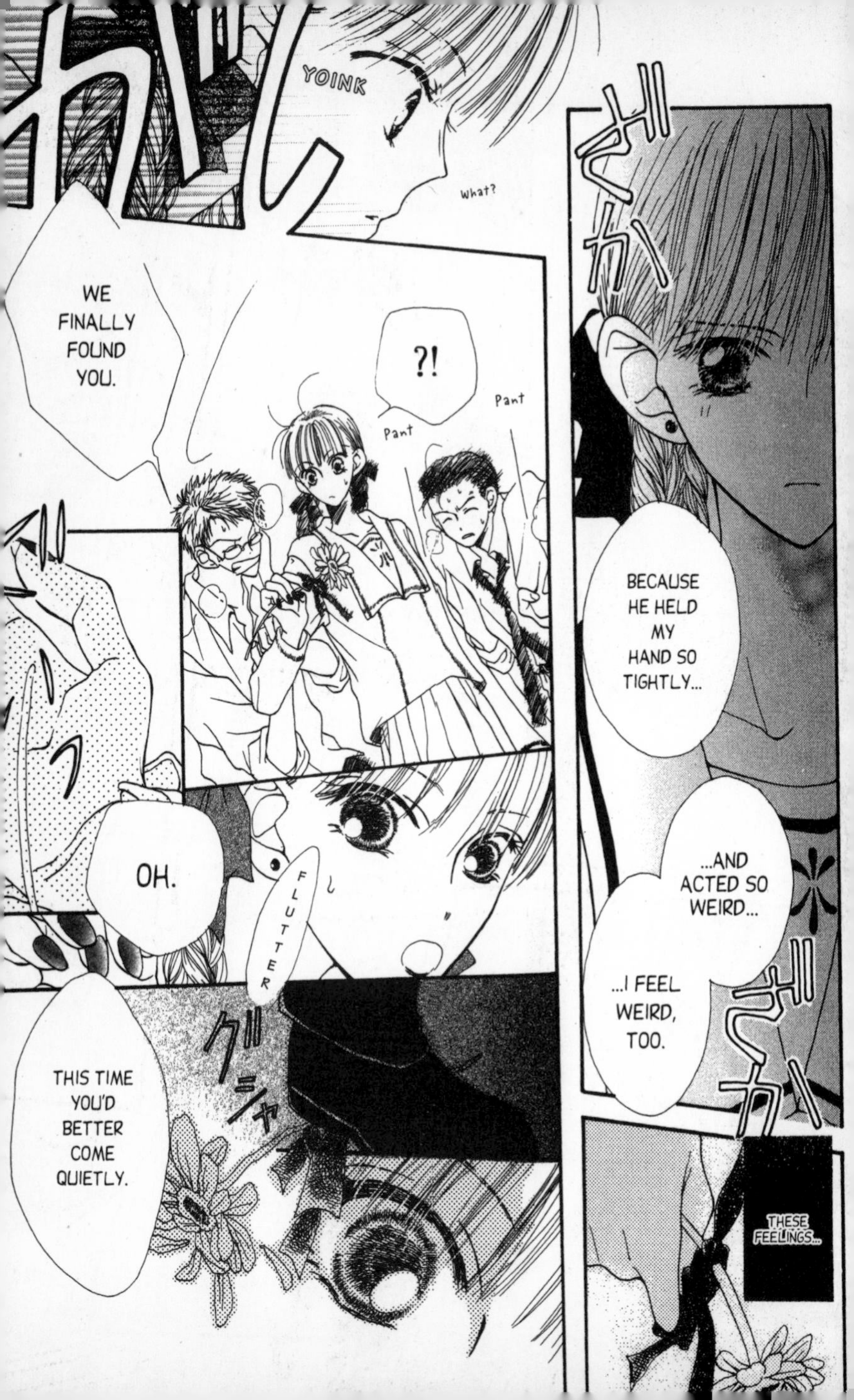
YOINK
What?
BECAUSE HE HELD MY HAND SO TIGHTLY...
...AND ACTED SO WEIRD...
...I FEEL WEIRD, TOO.
WE FINALLY FOUND YOU.
?!
Pant
Pant
OH.
FLUTTER
THESE FEELINGS...
THIS TIME YOU'D BETTER COME QUIETLY.

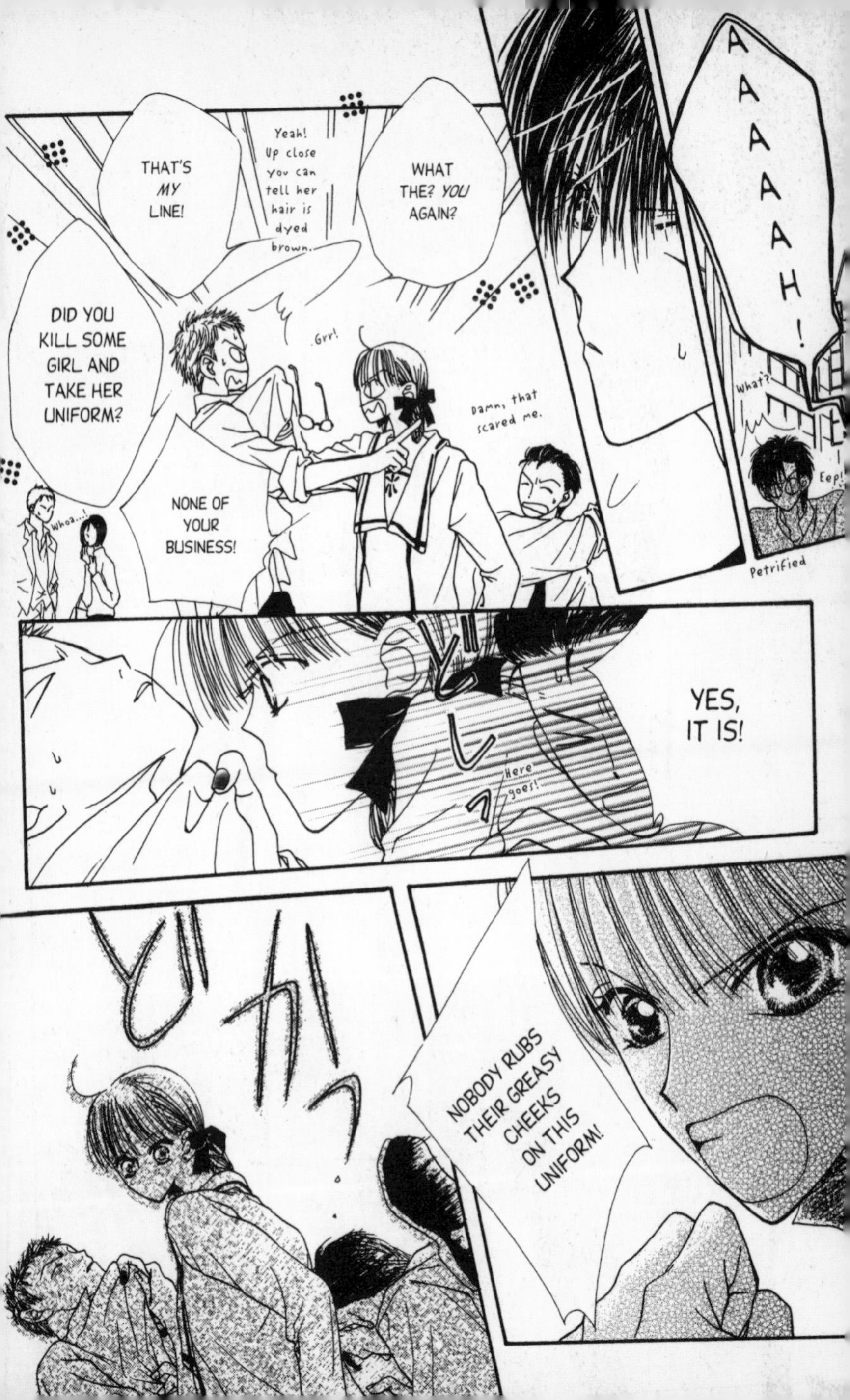
AAAAAH!
What?
Eep!
Petrified
WHAT THE? *YOU* AGAIN?
Yeah! Up close you can tell her hair is dyed brown.
THAT'S *MY* LINE!
Grr!
Damn, that scared me.
DID YOU KILL SOME GIRL AND TAKE HER UNIFORM?
NONE OF YOUR BUSINESS!
Whoa...!
YES, IT IS!
Here goes!
NOBODY RUBS THEIR GREASY CHEEKS ON THIS UNIFORM!

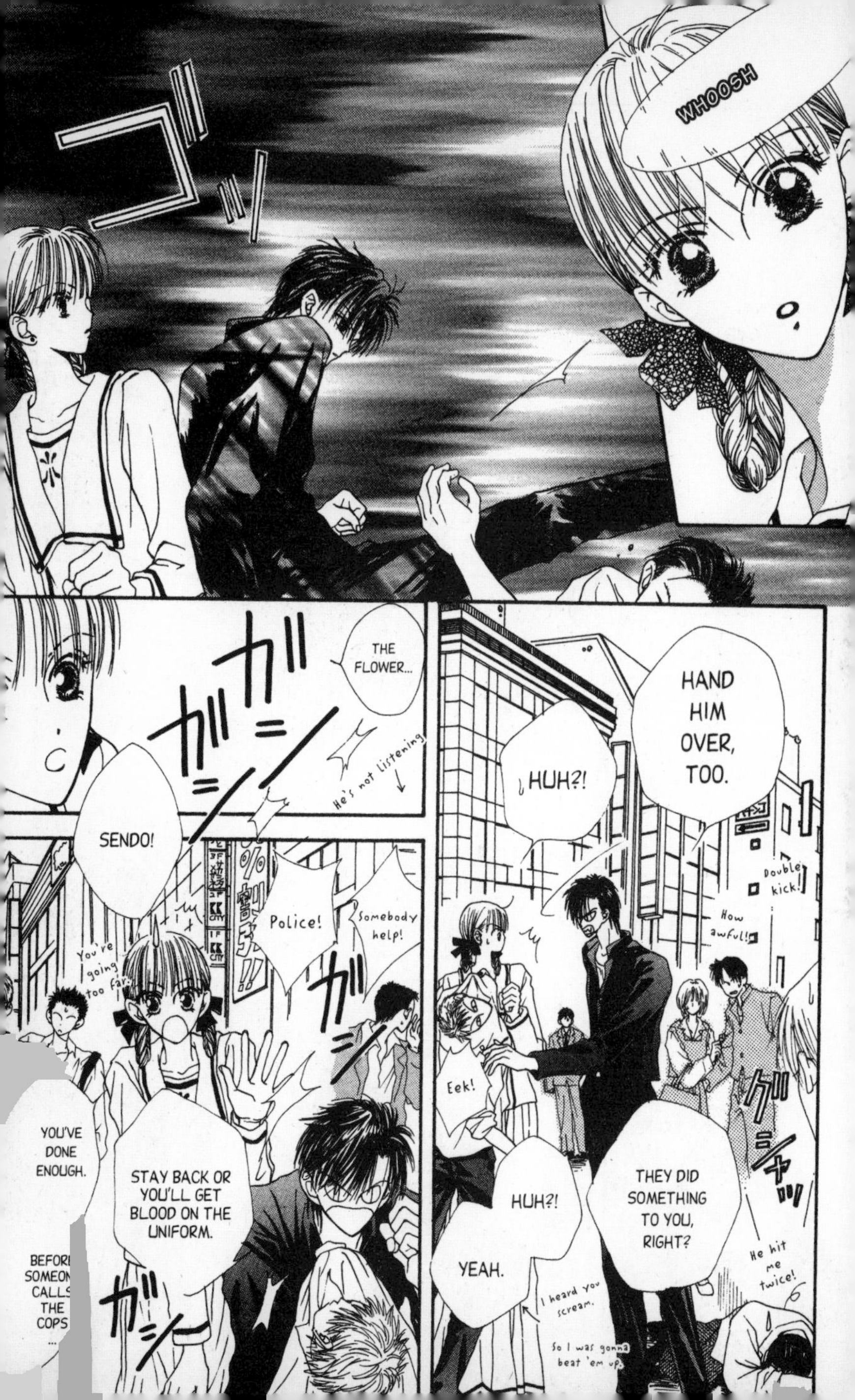
WHOOSH
HAND HIM OVER, TOO.
HUH?!
Double kick!
How awful!
THEY DID SOMETHING TO YOU, RIGHT?
He hit me twice!
HUH?!
Eek!
YEAH.
I heard you scream.
So I was gonna beat 'em up.
THE FLOWER...
He's not listening
SENDO!
Somebody help!
Police!
You're going too far.
STAY BACK OR YOU'LL GET BLOOD ON THE UNIFORM.
YOU'VE DONE ENOUGH.
BEFOR SOMEON CALLS THE COPS ...

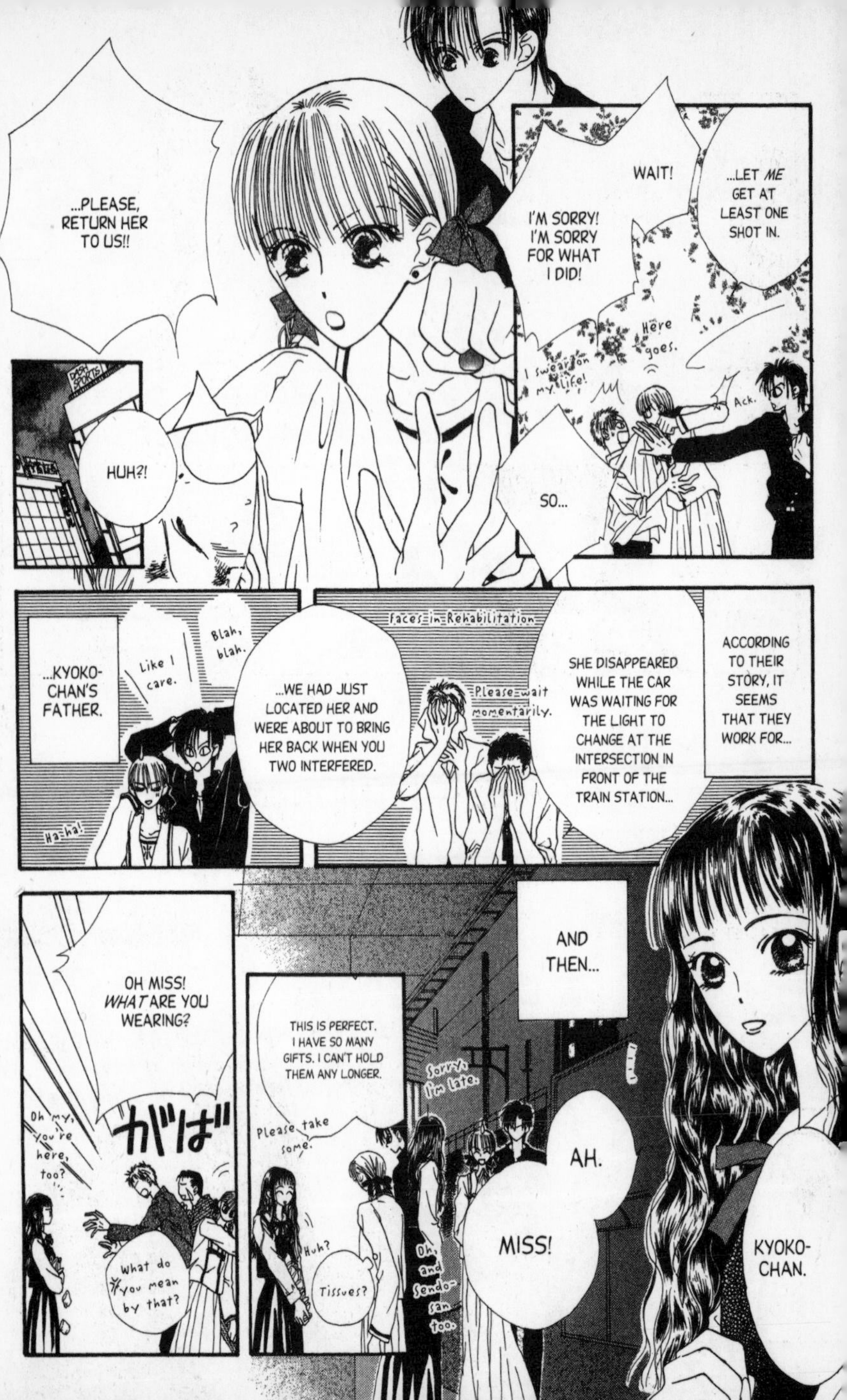
...LET *ME* GET AT LEAST ONE SHOT IN.
WAIT!
I'M SORRY! I'M SORRY FOR WHAT I DID!
Here goes.
Ack.
I swear on my life!
SO...
...PLEASE, RETURN HER TO US!!
HUH?!
ACCORDING TO THEIR STORY, IT SEEMS THAT THEY WORK FOR...
SHE DISAPPEARED WHILE THE CAR WAS WAITING FOR THE LIGHT TO CHANGE AT THE INTERSECTION IN FRONT OF THE TRAIN STATION...
Faces in Rehabilitation
Please wait momentarily.
...WE HAD JUST LOCATED HER AND WERE ABOUT TO BRING HER BACK WHEN YOU TWO INTERFERED.
Blah, blah.
Like I care.
...KYOKO-CHAN'S FATHER.
Ha-ha!
AND THEN...
KYOKO-CHAN.
AH.
MISS!
Sorry, I'm late.
Oh, and Sendo-san too.
THIS IS PERFECT. I HAVE SO MANY GIFTS. I CAN'T HOLD THEM ANY LONGER.
Please take some.
Huh?
Tissues?
OH MISS! *WHAT* ARE YOU WEARING?
がば
Oh my, you're here, too?
What do you mean by that?

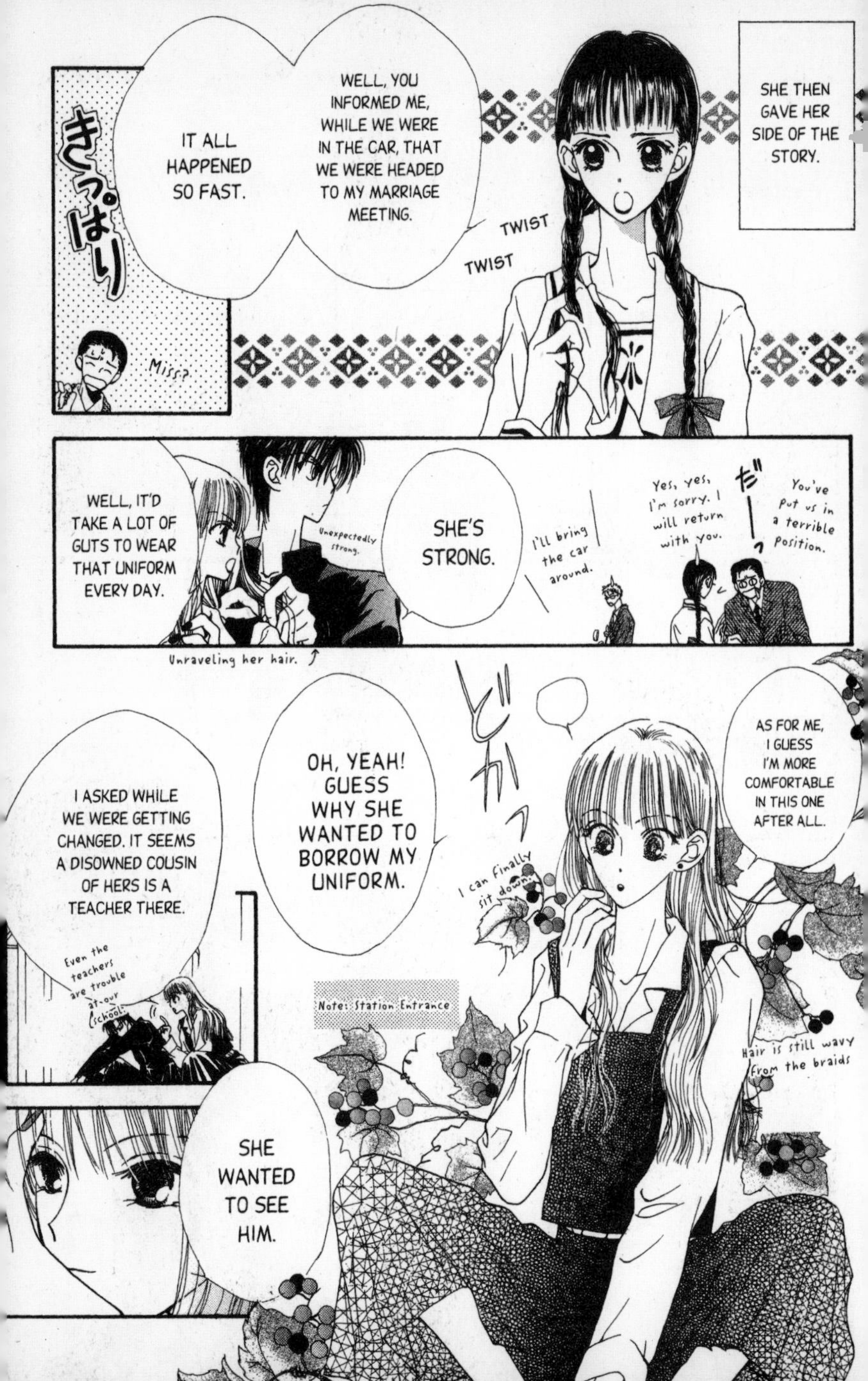
SHE THEN GAVE HER SIDE OF THE STORY.
TWIST
TWIST
WELL, YOU INFORMED ME, WHILE WE WERE IN THE CAR, THAT WE WERE HEADED TO MY MARRIAGE MEETING.
IT ALL HAPPENED SO FAST.
きっぱり
Miss?
You've put us in a terrible position.
だー
Yes, yes, I'm sorry. I will return with you.
I'll bring the car around.
SHE'S STRONG.
Unexpectedly strong.
WELL, IT'D TAKE A LOT OF GUTS TO WEAR THAT UNIFORM EVERY DAY.
Unraveling her hair.
AS FOR ME, I GUESS I'M MORE COMFORTABLE IN THIS ONE AFTER ALL.
Hair is still wavy from the braids
どかっ
I can finally sit down.
OH, YEAH! GUESS WHY SHE WANTED TO BORROW MY UNIFORM.
I ASKED WHILE WE WERE GETTING CHANGED. IT SEEMS A DISOWNED COUSIN OF HERS IS A TEACHER THERE.
Even the teachers are trouble at our school.
Note: Station Entrance
SHE WANTED TO SEE HIM.

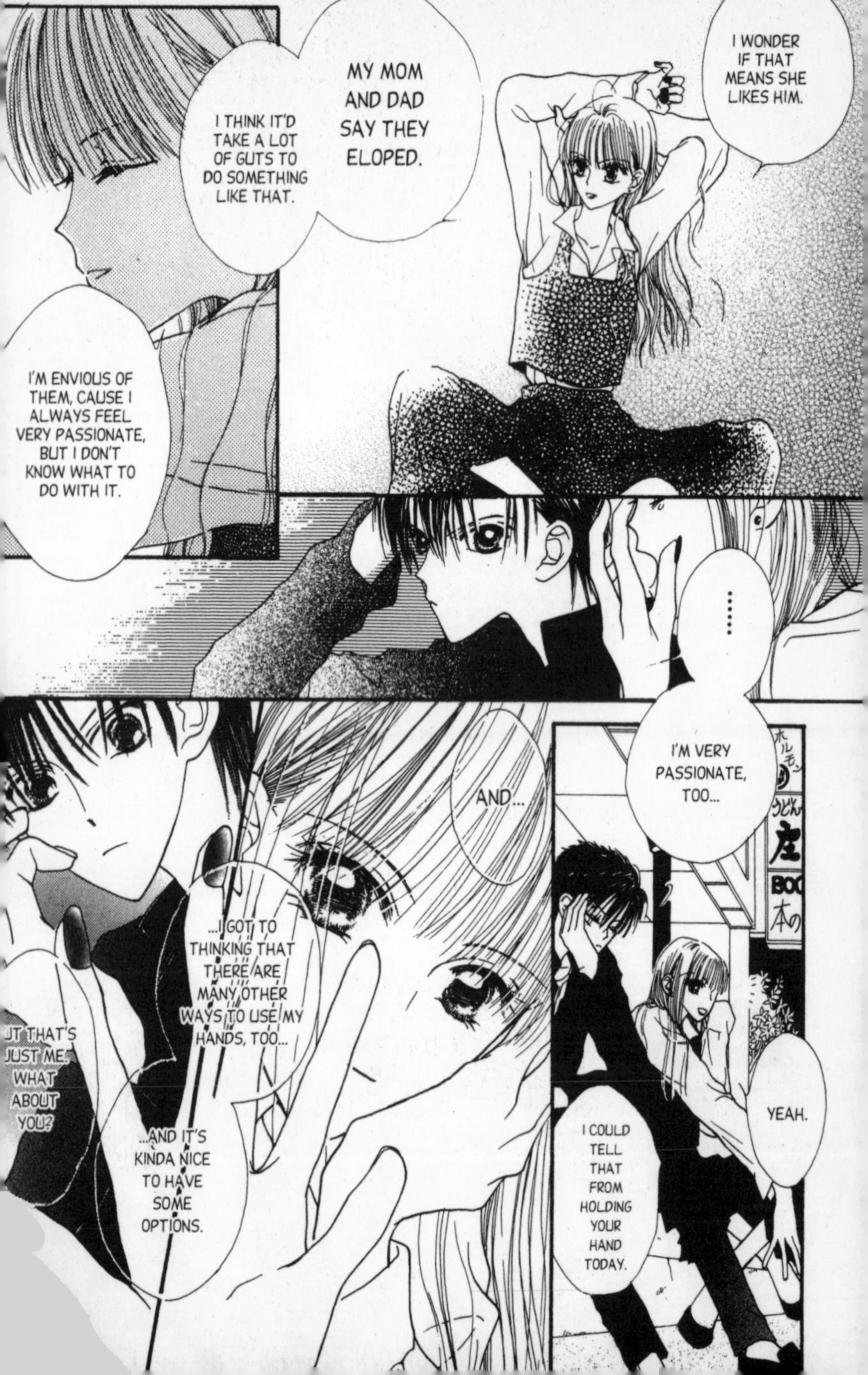
I WONDER IF THAT MEANS SHE LIKES HIM.
MY MOM AND DAD SAY THEY ELOPED.
I THINK IT'D TAKE A LOT OF GUTS TO DO SOMETHING LIKE THAT.
I'M ENVIOUS OF THEM, CAUSE I ALWAYS FEEL VERY PASSIONATE, BUT I DON'T KNOW WHAT TO DO WITH IT.
......
I'M VERY PASSIONATE, TOO...
YEAH.
I COULD TELL THAT FROM HOLDING YOUR HAND TODAY.
AND...
...I GOT TO THINKING THAT THERE ARE MANY OTHER WAYS TO USE MY HANDS, TOO...
...AND IT'S KINDA NICE TO HAVE SOME OPTIONS.
UT THAT'S JUST ME. WHAT ABOUT YOU?

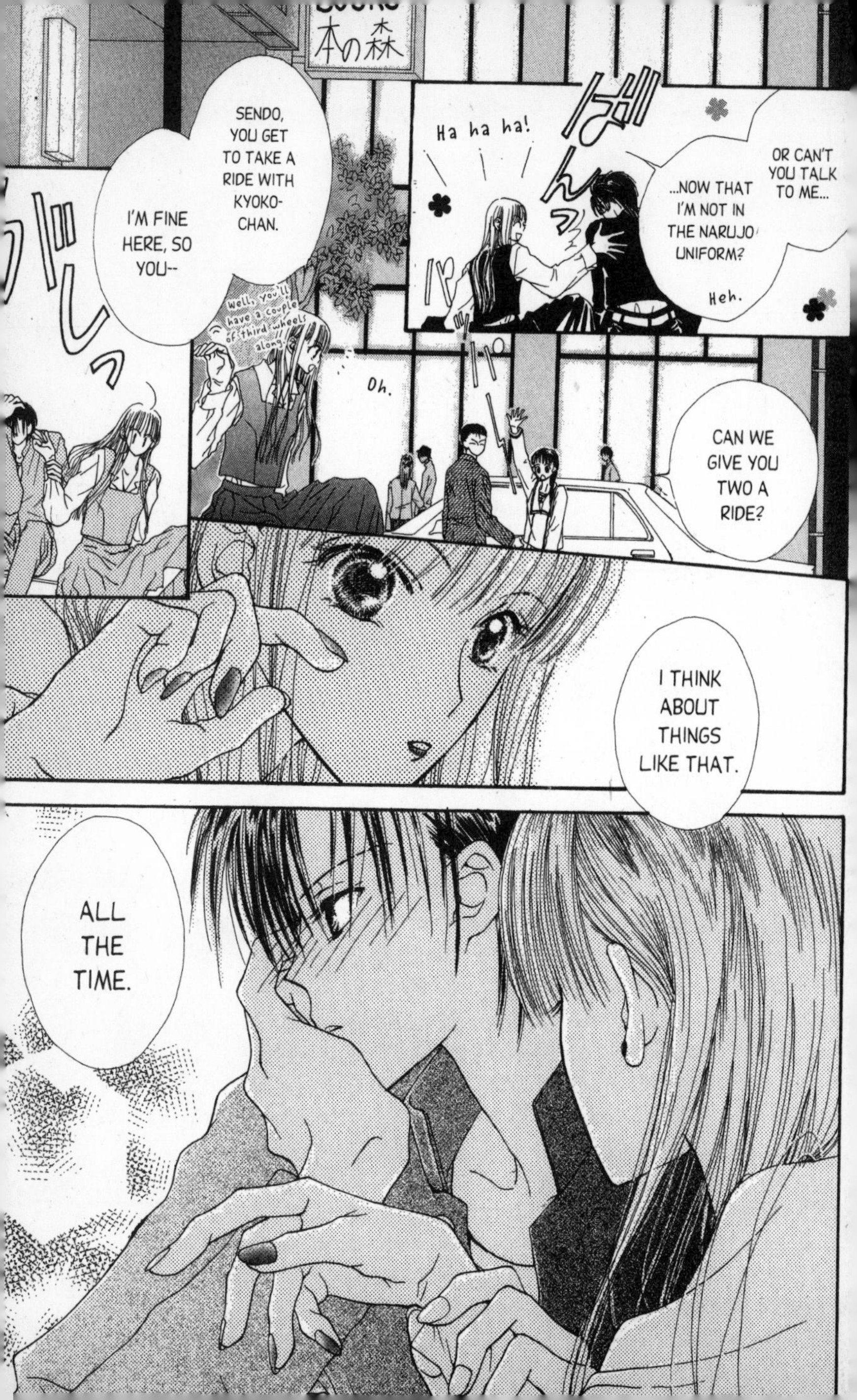
OR CAN'T YOU TALK TO ME...
...NOW THAT I'M NOT IN THE NARUJO UNIFORM?
Ha ha ha!
Heh.
本の森
CAN WE GIVE YOU TWO A RIDE?
Oh.
Well, you'll have a couple of third-wheels along.
SENDO, YOU GET TO TAKE A RIDE WITH KYOKO-CHAN.
I'M FINE HERE, SO YOU--
I THINK ABOUT THINGS LIKE THAT.
ALL THE TIME.

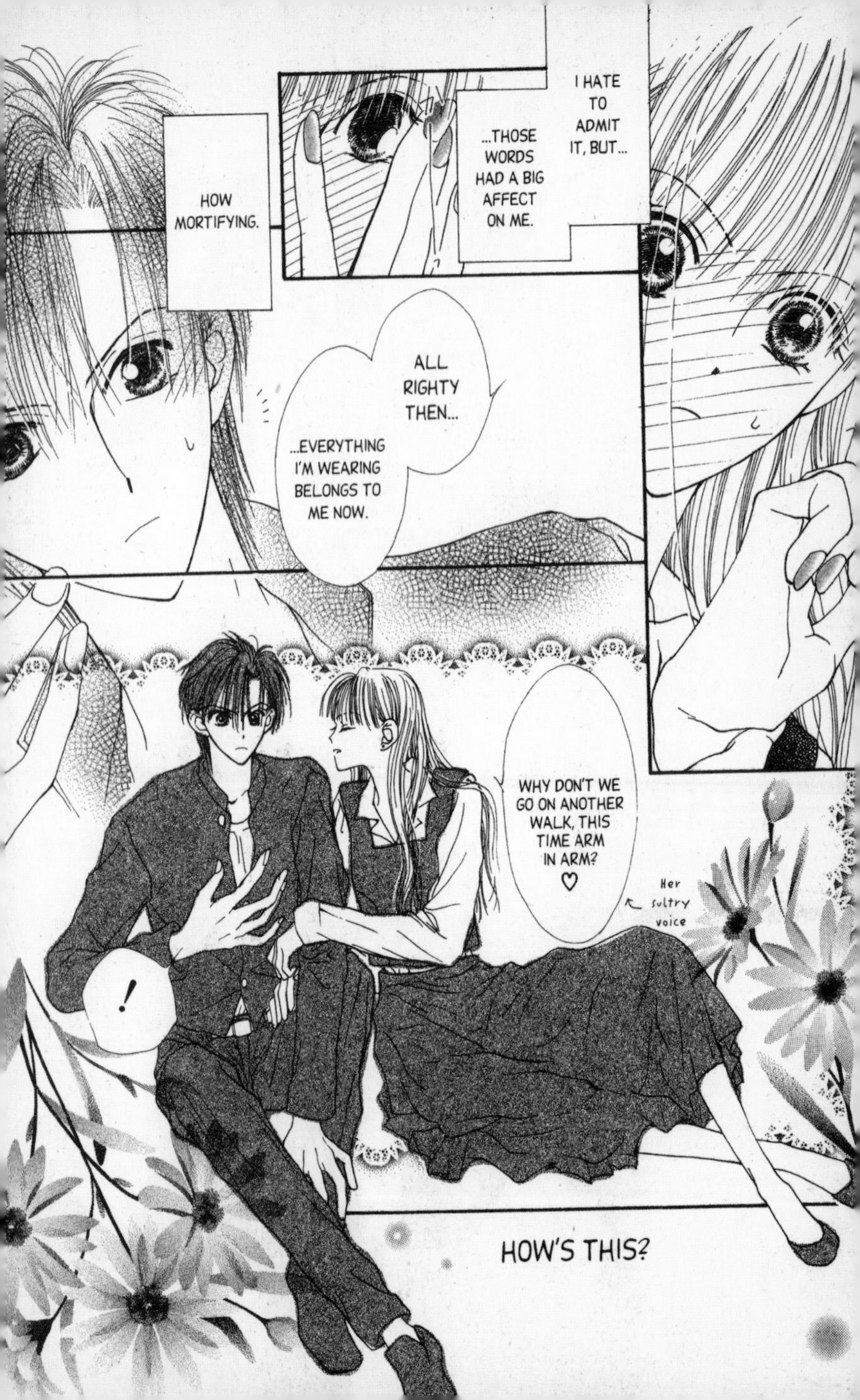
I HATE TO ADMIT IT, BUT...
...THOSE WORDS HAD A BIG AFFECT ON ME.
HOW MORTIFYING.
ALL RIGHTY THEN...
...EVERYTHING I'M WEARING BELONGS TO ME NOW.
WHY DON'T WE GO ON ANOTHER WALK, THIS TIME ARM IN ARM? ♡
Her sultry voice
!
HOW'S THIS?

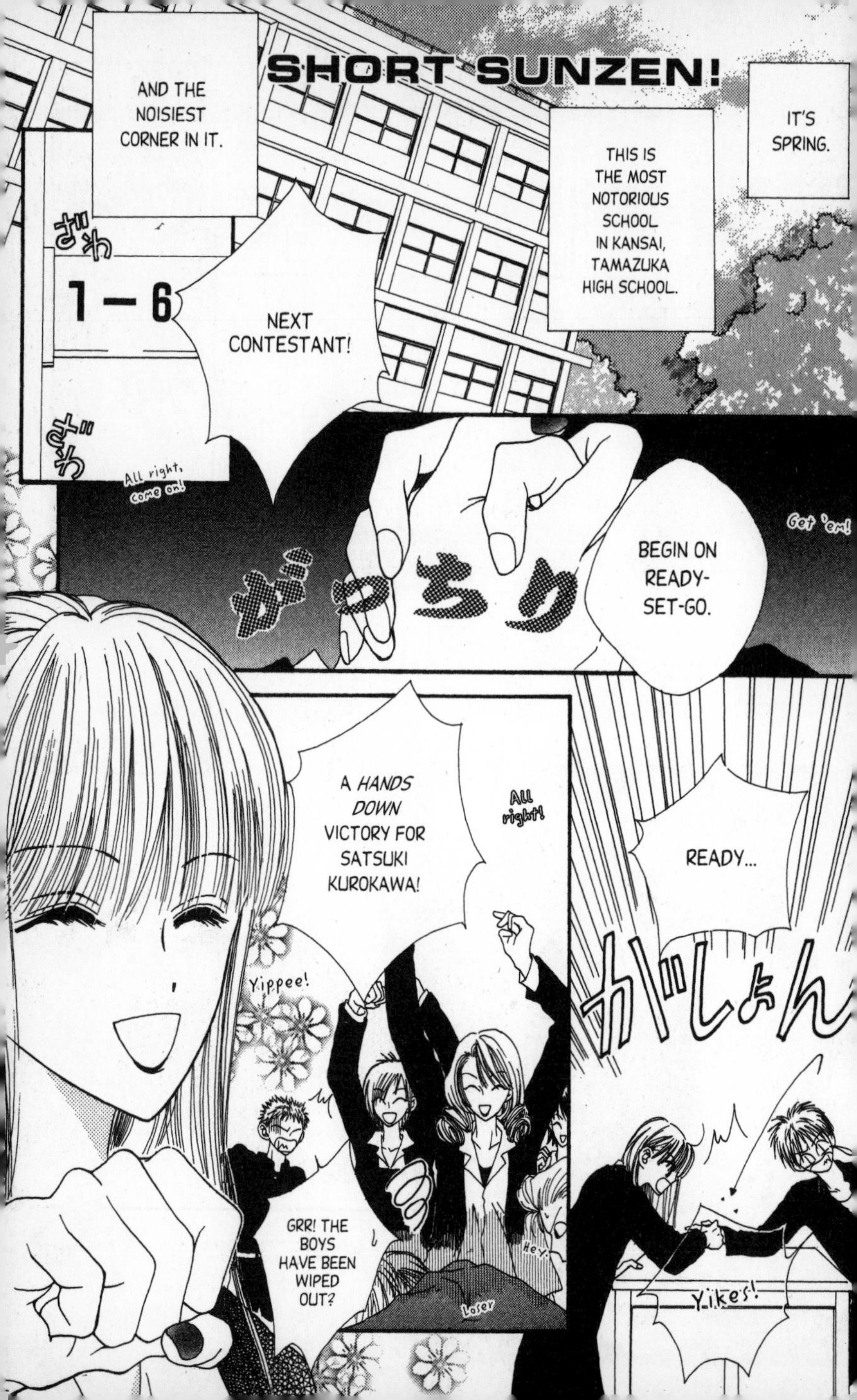
SHORT SUNZEN!
IT'S SPRING.
THIS IS THE MOST NOTORIOUS SCHOOL IN KANSAI, TAMAZUKA HIGH SCHOOL.
AND THE NOISIEST CORNER IN IT.
1 — 6
ざわ
ざわ
NEXT CONTESTANT!
All right, come on!
Get 'em!
BEGIN ON READY-SET-GO.
がっちり
READY...
がしょん
Yikes!
A HANDS DOWN VICTORY FOR SATSUKI KUROKAWA!
All right!
Yippee!
GRR! THE BOYS HAVE BEEN WIPED OUT?
Hey.
Loser

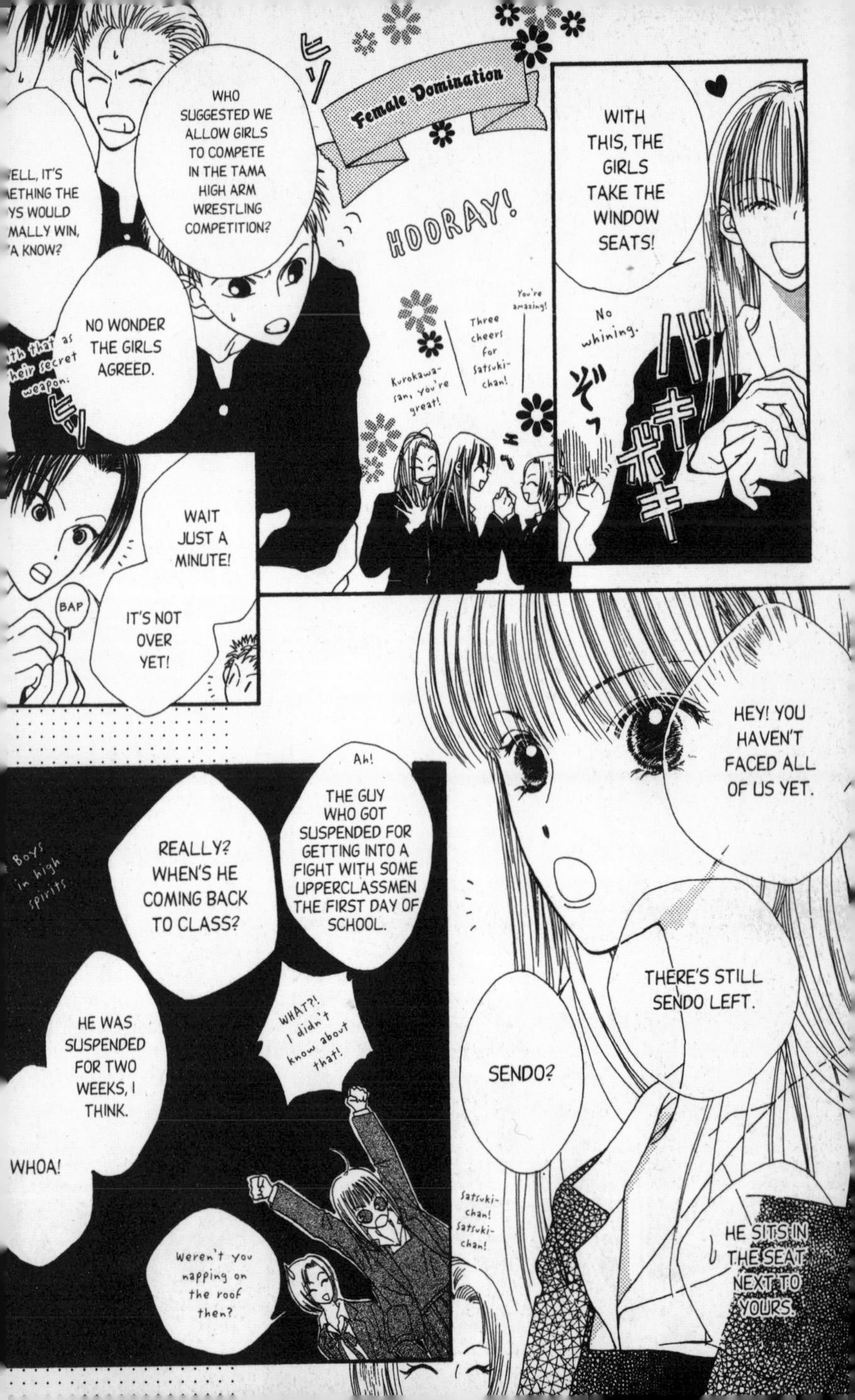
WITH THIS, THE GIRLS TAKE THE WINDOW SEATS!
No whining.
Female Domination
HOORAY!
You're amazing!
Three cheers for Satsuki-chan!
Kurokawa-san, you're great!
WHO SUGGESTED WE ALLOW GIRLS TO COMPETE IN THE TAMA HIGH ARM WRESTLING COMPETITION?
ELL, IT'S ETHING THE YS WOULD MALLY WIN, 'A KNOW?
NO WONDER THE GIRLS AGREED.
ith that as heir secret weapon.
WAIT JUST A MINUTE!
IT'S NOT OVER YET!
BAP
HEY! YOU HAVEN'T FACED ALL OF US YET.
THERE'S STILL SENDO LEFT.
SENDO?
HE SITS IN THE SEAT NEXT TO YOURS.
Satsuki-chan! Satsuki-chan!
Ah!
THE GUY WHO GOT SUSPENDED FOR GETTING INTO A FIGHT WITH SOME UPPERCLASSMEN THE FIRST DAY OF SCHOOL.
REALLY? WHEN'S HE COMING BACK TO CLASS?
Boys in high spirits
WHAT?! I didn't know about that!
HE WAS SUSPENDED FOR TWO WEEKS, I THINK.
WHOA!
Weren't you napping on the roof then?

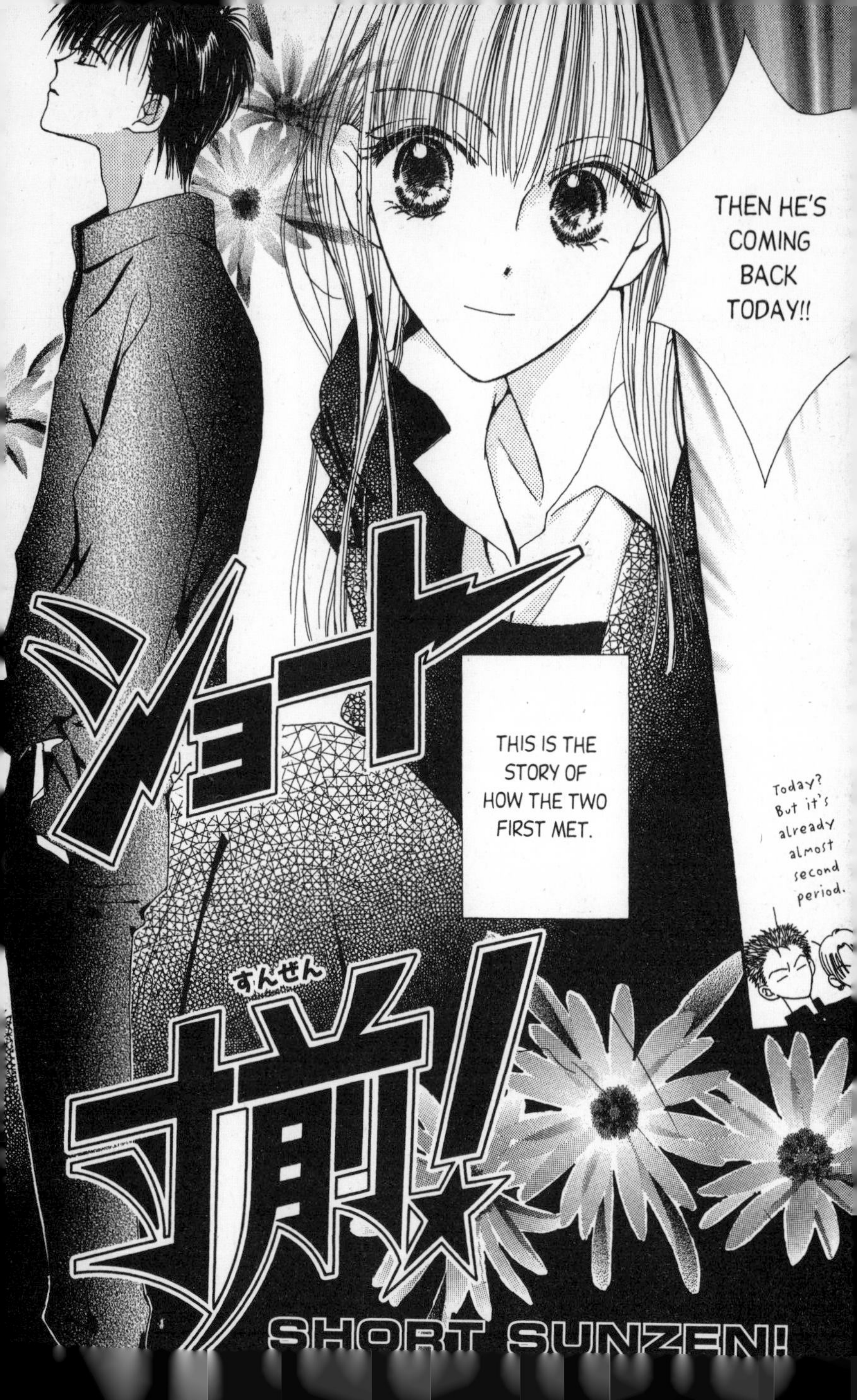
THEN HE'S COMING BACK TODAY!!
Today? But it's already almost second period.
THIS IS THE STORY OF HOW THE TWO FIRST MET.
ショート寸前!
SHORT SUNZEN!

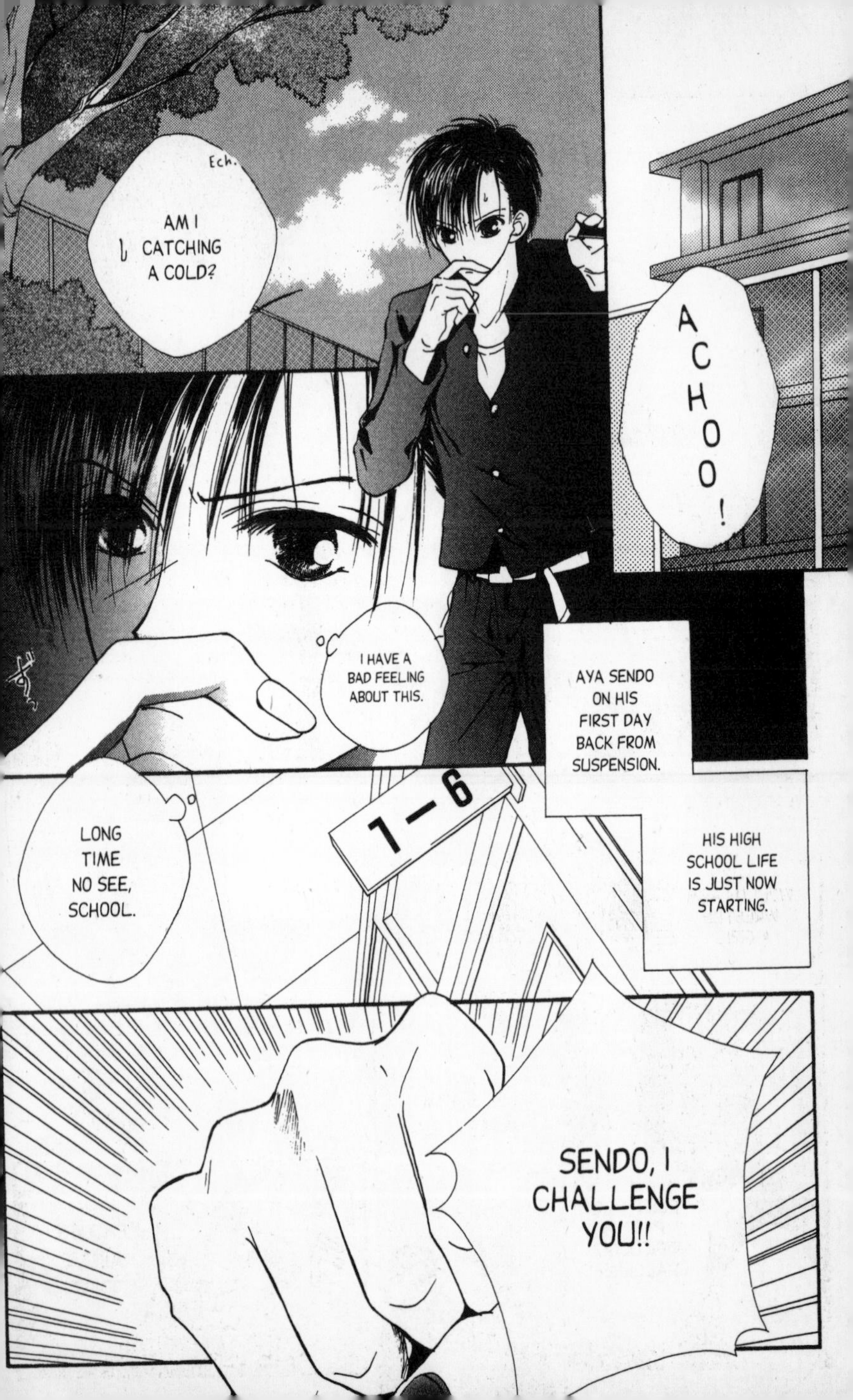
ACHOO!
Ech.
AM I CATCHING A COLD?
AYA SENDO ON HIS FIRST DAY BACK FROM SUSPENSION.
I HAVE A BAD FEELING ABOUT THIS.
HIS HIGH SCHOOL LIFE IS JUST NOW STARTING.
1-6
LONG TIME NO SEE, SCHOOL.
SENDO, I CHALLENGE YOU!!

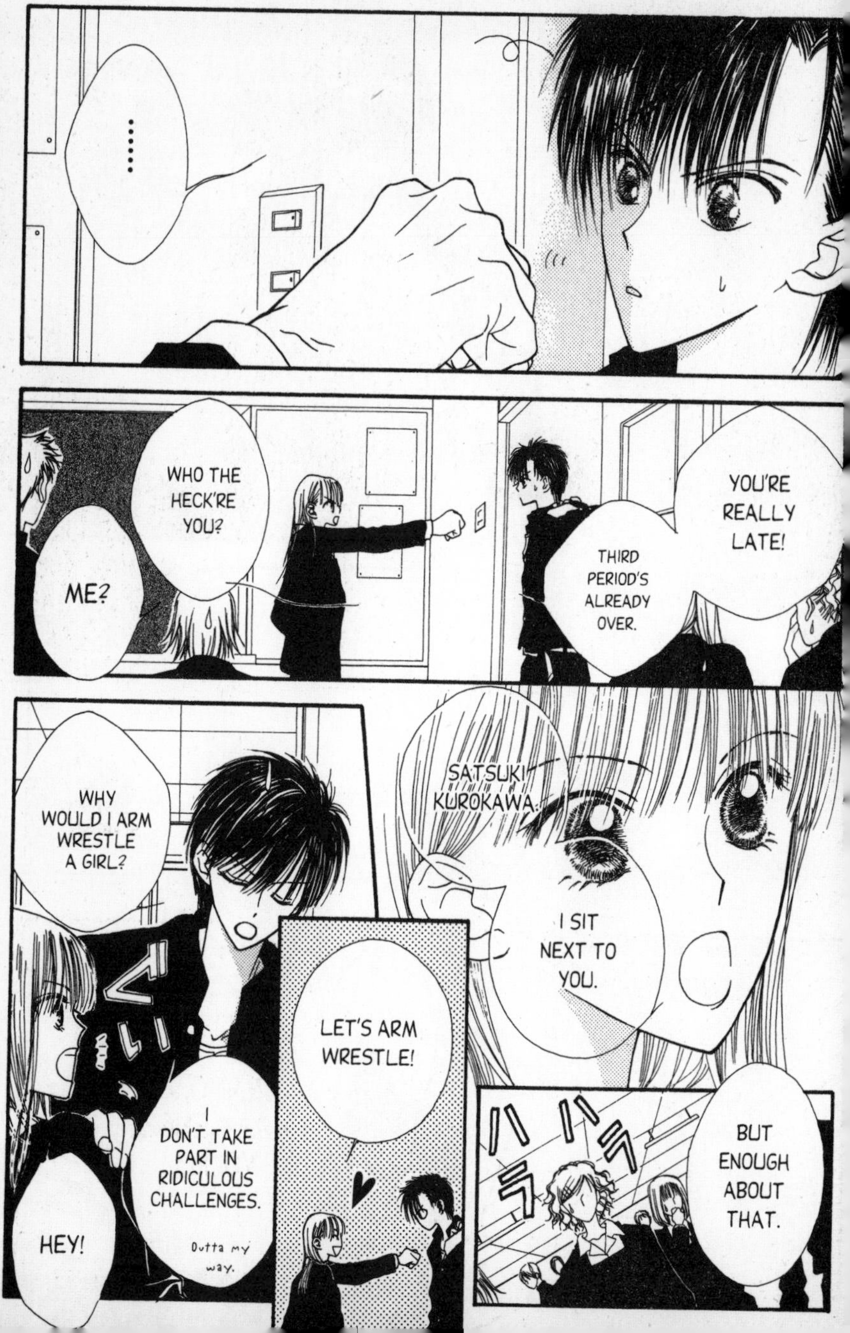
……
YOU'RE REALLY LATE!
THIRD PERIOD'S ALREADY OVER.
WHO THE HECK'RE YOU?
ME?
SATSUKI KUROKAWA.
I SIT NEXT TO YOU.
BUT ENOUGH ABOUT THAT.
LET'S ARM WRESTLE!
WHY WOULD I ARM WRESTLE A GIRL?
I DON'T TAKE PART IN RIDICULOUS CHALLENGES.
Outta my way.
HEY!

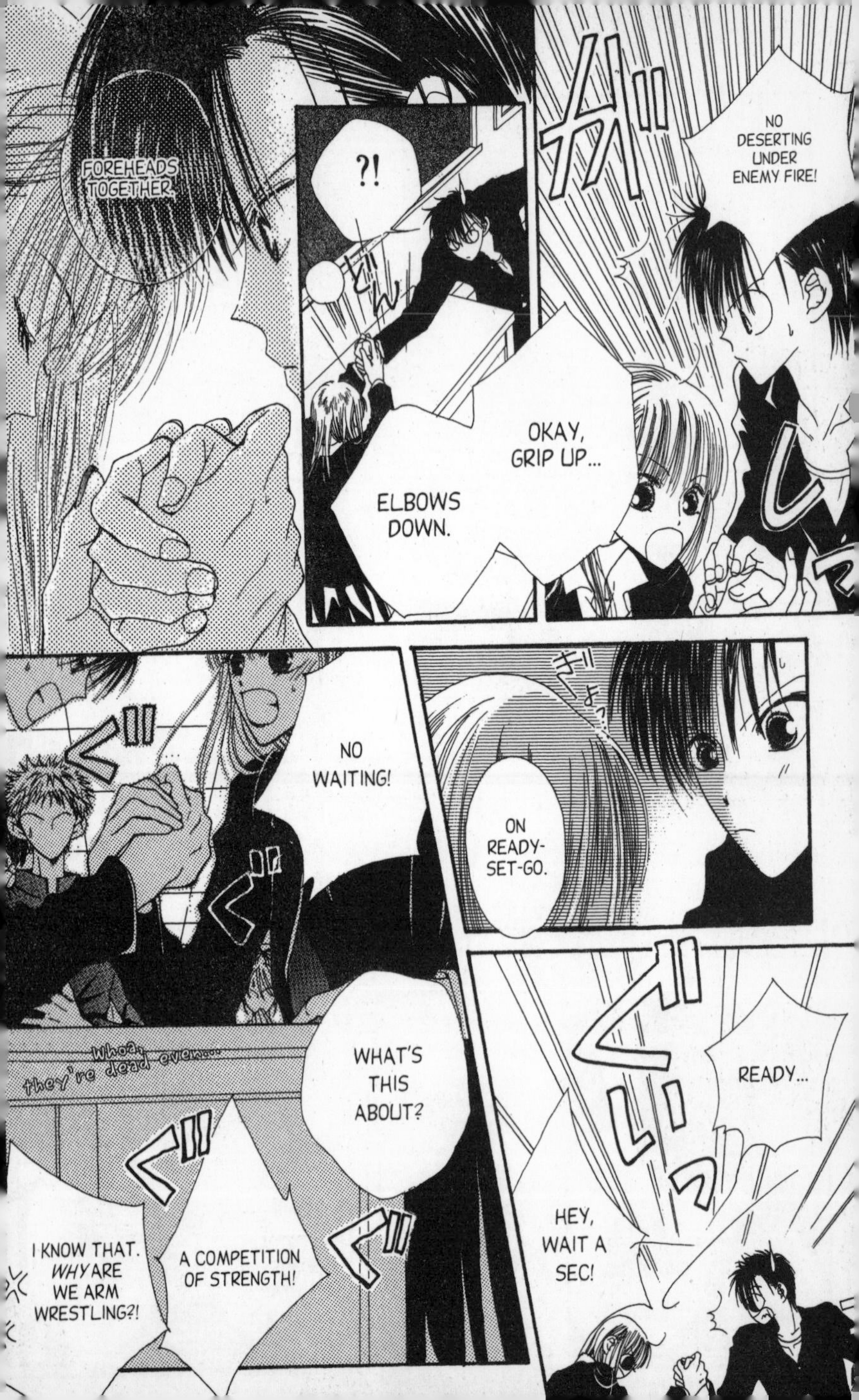
NO DESERTING UNDER ENEMY FIRE!
?!
OKAY, GRIP UP...
ELBOWS DOWN.
FOREHEADS TOGETHER.
ON READY-SET-GO.
READY...
HEY, WAIT A SEC!
NO WAITING!
WHAT'S THIS ABOUT?
Whoa, they're dead even...
A COMPETITION OF STRENGTH!
I KNOW THAT. *WHY* ARE WE ARM WRESTLING?!

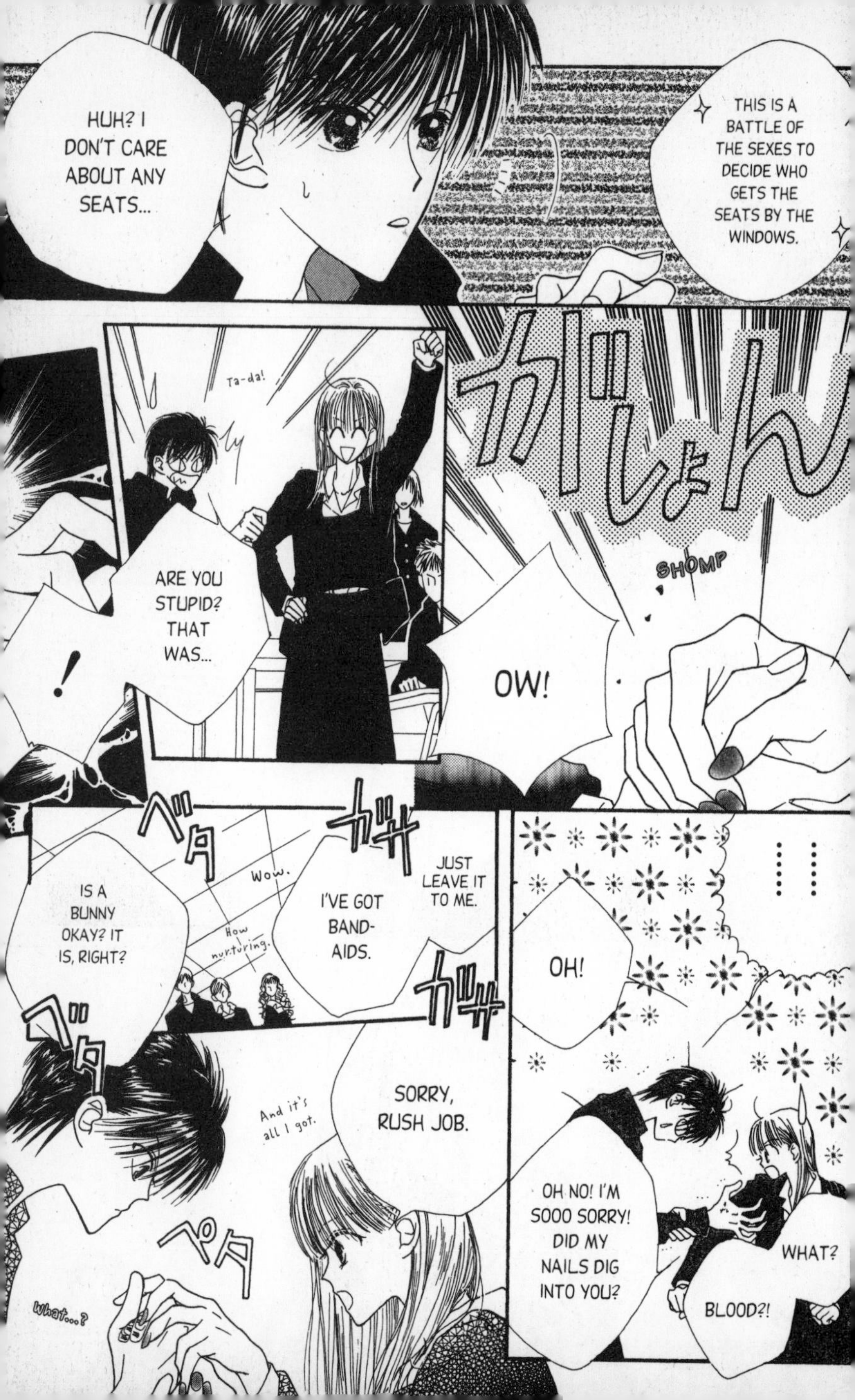
THIS IS A BATTLE OF THE SEXES TO DECIDE WHO GETS THE SEATS BY THE WINDOWS.
HUH? I DON'T CARE ABOUT ANY SEATS...
かじょん
SHOMP
OW!
Ta-da!
ARE YOU STUPID? THAT WAS...
!
......
OH!
WHAT?
BLOOD?!
OH NO! I'M SOOO SORRY! DID MY NAILS DIG INTO YOU?
ガサ
JUST LEAVE IT TO ME.
I'VE GOT BAND-AIDS.
Wow.
How nurturing.
ベタ
IS A BUNNY OKAY? IT IS, RIGHT?
ガサ
SORRY, RUSH JOB.
And it's all I got.
ベタ
ペタ
what...?

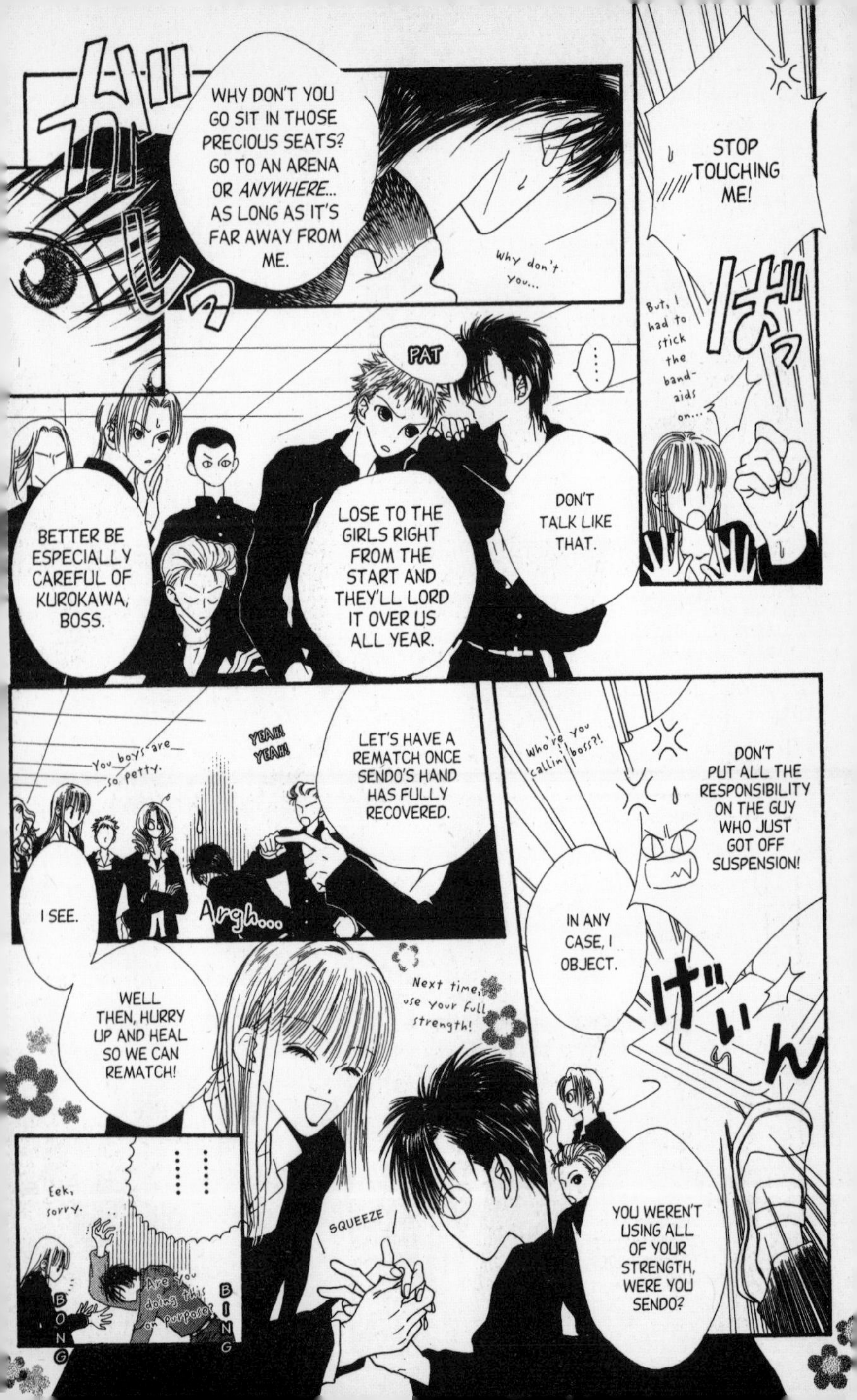
STOP TOUCHING ME!
ぱっ
But, I had to stick the band-aids on...
WHY DON'T YOU GO SIT IN THOSE PRECIOUS SEATS? GO TO AN ARENA OR *ANYWHERE*... AS LONG AS IT'S FAR AWAY FROM ME.
Why don't you...
PAT
...
DON'T TALK LIKE THAT.
LOSE TO THE GIRLS RIGHT FROM THE START AND THEY'LL LORD IT OVER US ALL YEAR.
BETTER BE ESPECIALLY CAREFUL OF KUROKAWA, BOSS.
DON'T PUT ALL THE RESPONSIBILITY ON THE GUY WHO JUST GOT OFF SUSPENSION!
Who're you callin' boss?!
IN ANY CASE, I OBJECT.
げいん
YOU WEREN'T USING ALL OF YOUR STRENGTH, WERE YOU SENDO?
LET'S HAVE A REMATCH ONCE SENDO'S HAND HAS FULLY RECOVERED.
YEAH! YEAH!
You boys are so petty.
I SEE.
Argh...
WELL THEN, HURRY UP AND HEAL SO WE CAN REMATCH!
Next time, use your full strength!
SQUEEZE
......
Eek, sorry.
Are you doing this on purpose?
BONG
BING

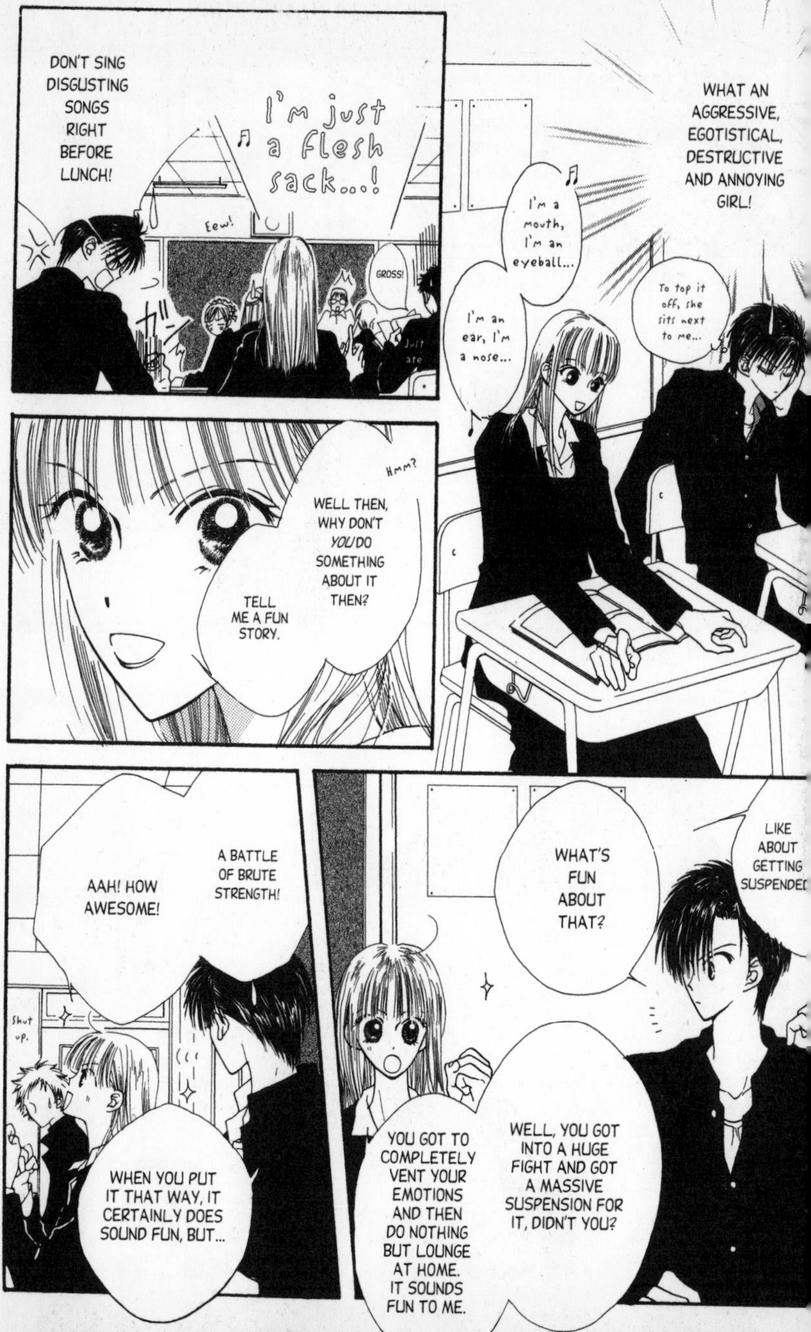
WHAT AN AGGRESSIVE, EGOTISTICAL, DESTRUCTIVE AND ANNOYING GIRL!
I'm a mouth, I'm an eyeball...
To top it off, she sits next to me...
I'm an ear, I'm a nose...
I'm just a flesh sack...!
DON'T SING DISGUSTING SONGS RIGHT BEFORE LUNCH!
GROSS!
Just ate
Eew!
Hmm?
WELL THEN, WHY DON'T *YOU* DO SOMETHING ABOUT IT THEN?
TELL ME A FUN STORY.
LIKE ABOUT GETTING SUSPENDE
WHAT'S FUN ABOUT THAT?
WELL, YOU GOT INTO A HUGE FIGHT AND GOT A MASSIVE SUSPENSION FOR IT, DIDN'T YOU?
YOU GOT TO COMPLETELY VENT YOUR EMOTIONS AND THEN DO NOTHING BUT LOUNGE AT HOME. IT SOUNDS FUN TO ME.
A BATTLE OF BRUTE STRENGTH!
AAH! HOW AWESOME!
Shut up.
WHEN YOU PUT IT THAT WAY, IT CERTAINLY DOES SOUND FUN, BUT...

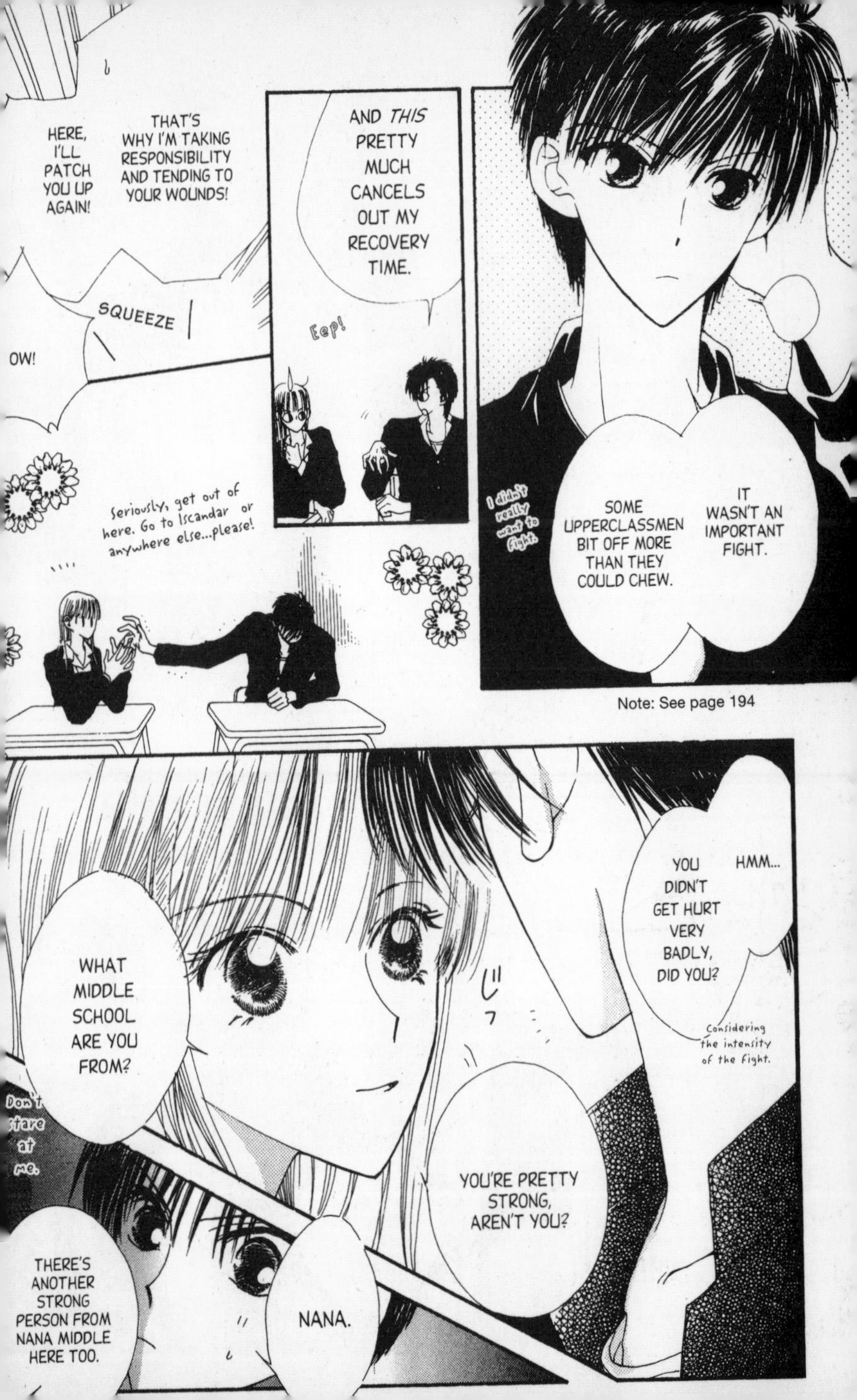
IT WASN'T AN IMPORTANT FIGHT.
SOME UPPERCLASSMEN BIT OFF MORE THAN THEY COULD CHEW.
I didn't really want to fight.
AND THIS PRETTY MUCH CANCELS OUT MY RECOVERY TIME.
Eep!
THAT'S WHY I'M TAKING RESPONSIBILITY AND TENDING TO YOUR WOUNDS!
HERE, I'LL PATCH YOU UP AGAIN!
SQUEEZE
OW!
Seriously, get out of here. Go to Iscandar or anywhere else...please!
HMM...
YOU DIDN'T GET HURT VERY BADLY, DID YOU?
Considering the intensity of the fight.
YOU'RE PRETTY STRONG, AREN'T YOU?
WHAT MIDDLE SCHOOL ARE YOU FROM?
Don't stare at me.
NANA.
THERE'S ANOTHER STRONG PERSON FROM NANA MIDDLE HERE TOO.

Note: See page 194

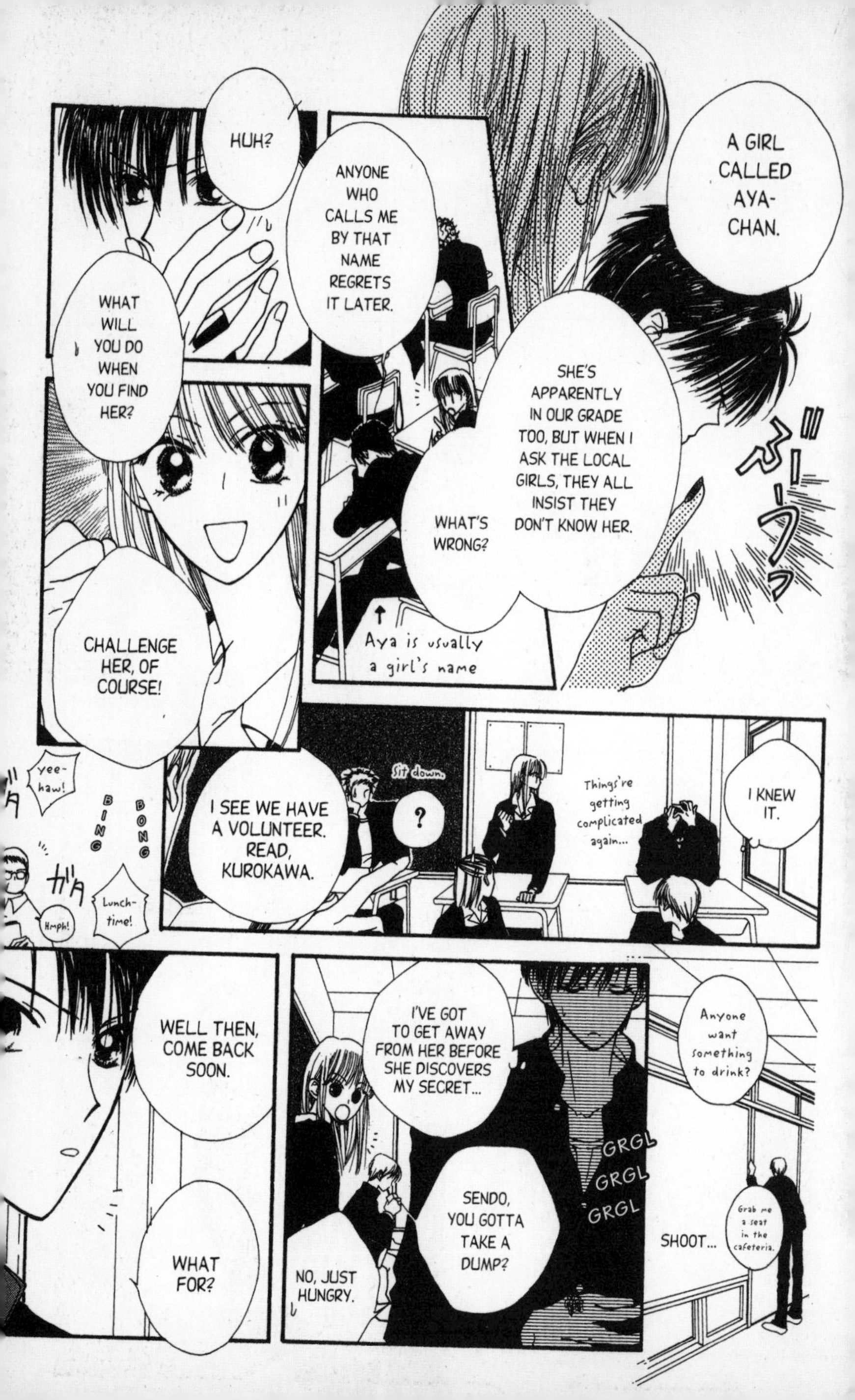
A GIRL CALLED AYA-CHAN.
SHE'S APPARENTLY IN OUR GRADE TOO, BUT WHEN I ASK THE LOCAL GIRLS, THEY ALL INSIST THEY DON'T KNOW HER.
WHAT'S WRONG?
ANYONE WHO CALLS ME BY THAT NAME REGRETS IT LATER.
Aya is usually a girl's name
HUH?
WHAT WILL YOU DO WHEN YOU FIND HER?
CHALLENGE HER, OF COURSE!
I KNEW IT.
Things're getting complicated again...
Sit down.
?
I SEE WE HAVE A VOLUNTEER. READ, KUROKAWA.
yee-haw!
BING BONG
Lunch-time!
Hmph!
Anyone want something to drink?
Grab me a seat in the cafeteria.
SHOOT...
I'VE GOT TO GET AWAY FROM HER BEFORE SHE DISCOVERS MY SECRET...
GRGL GRGL GRGL
SENDO, YOU GOTTA TAKE A DUMP?
NO, JUST HUNGRY.
WELL THEN, COME BACK SOON.
WHAT FOR?

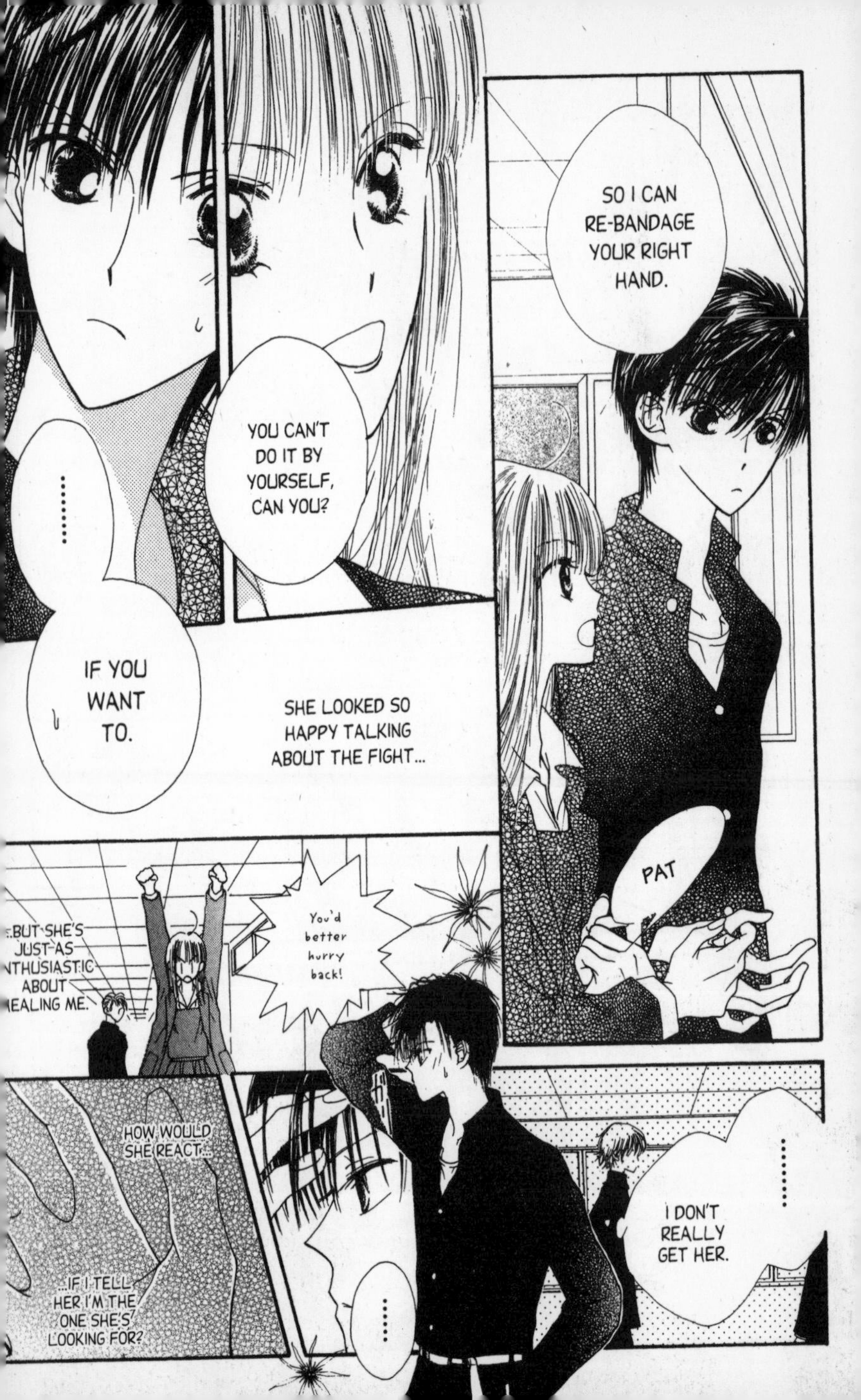

SO I CAN RE-BANDAGE YOUR RIGHT HAND.
PAT
YOU CAN'T DO IT BY YOURSELF, CAN YOU?
....
IF YOU WANT TO.
SHE LOOKED SO HAPPY TALKING ABOUT THE FIGHT...
You'd better hurry back!
.BUT SHE'S JUST AS NTHUSIASTIC ABOUT EALING ME.
......
I DON'T REALLY GET HER.
.....
HOW WOULD SHE REACT...
...IF I TELL HER I'M THE ONE SHE'S LOOKING FOR?

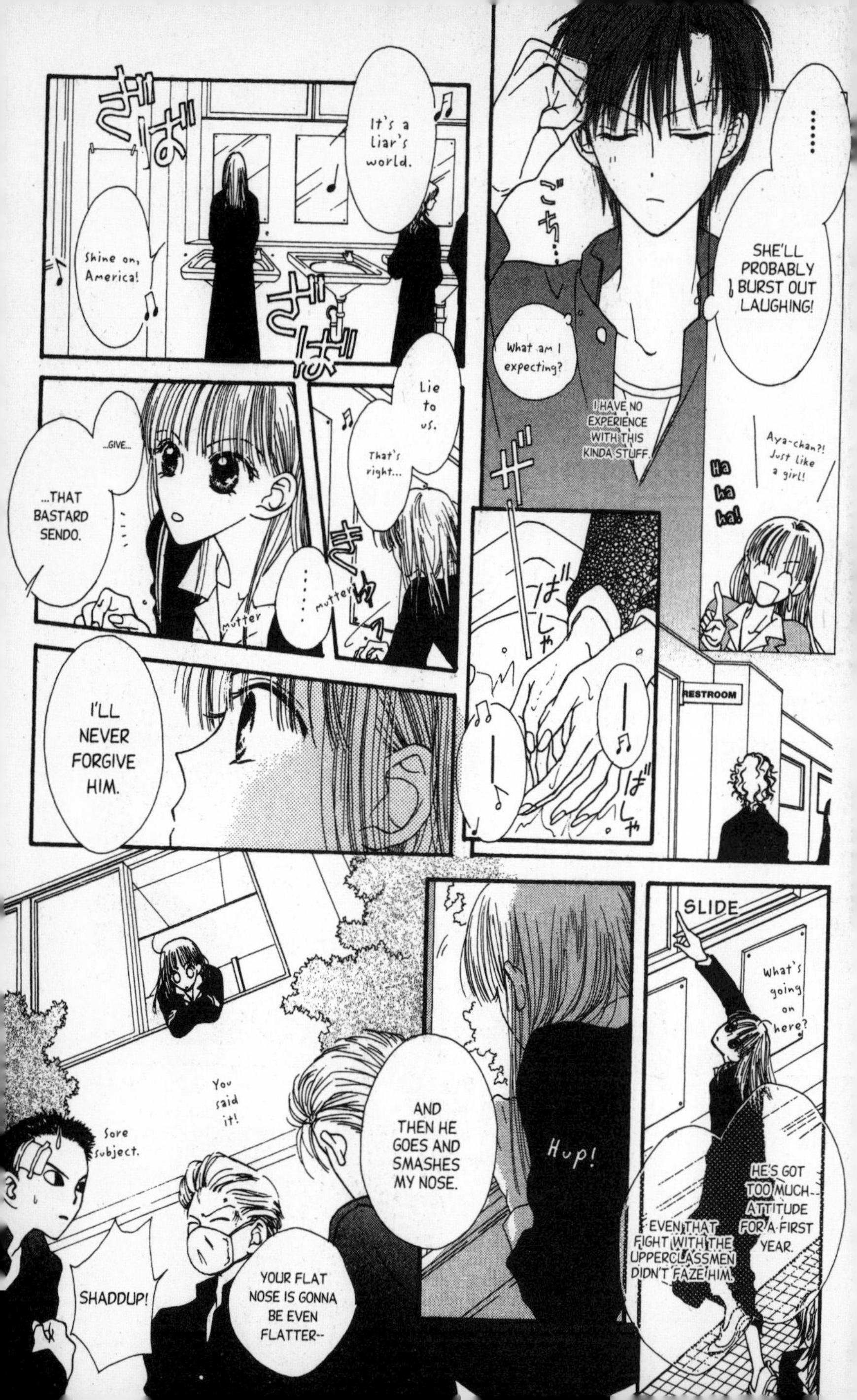
......
SHE'LL PROBABLY BURST OUT LAUGHING!
What am I expecting?
I HAVE NO EXPERIENCE WITH THIS KINDA STUFF.
Aya-chan?! Just like a girl!
Ha ha ha!
RESTROOM
!
!
It's a liar's world.
Shine on, America!
Lie to us.
That's right...
...GIVE...
...THAT BASTARD SENDO.
......
mutter
mutter
I'LL NEVER FORGIVE HIM.
SLIDE
What's going on here?
HE'S GOT TOO MUCH ATTITUDE FOR A FIRST YEAR.
EVEN THAT FIGHT WITH THE UPPERCLASSMEN DIDN'T FAZE HIM.
Hup!
AND THEN HE GOES AND SMASHES MY NOSE.
You said it!
Sore subject.
YOUR FLAT NOSE IS GONNA BE EVEN FLATTER--
SHADDUP!

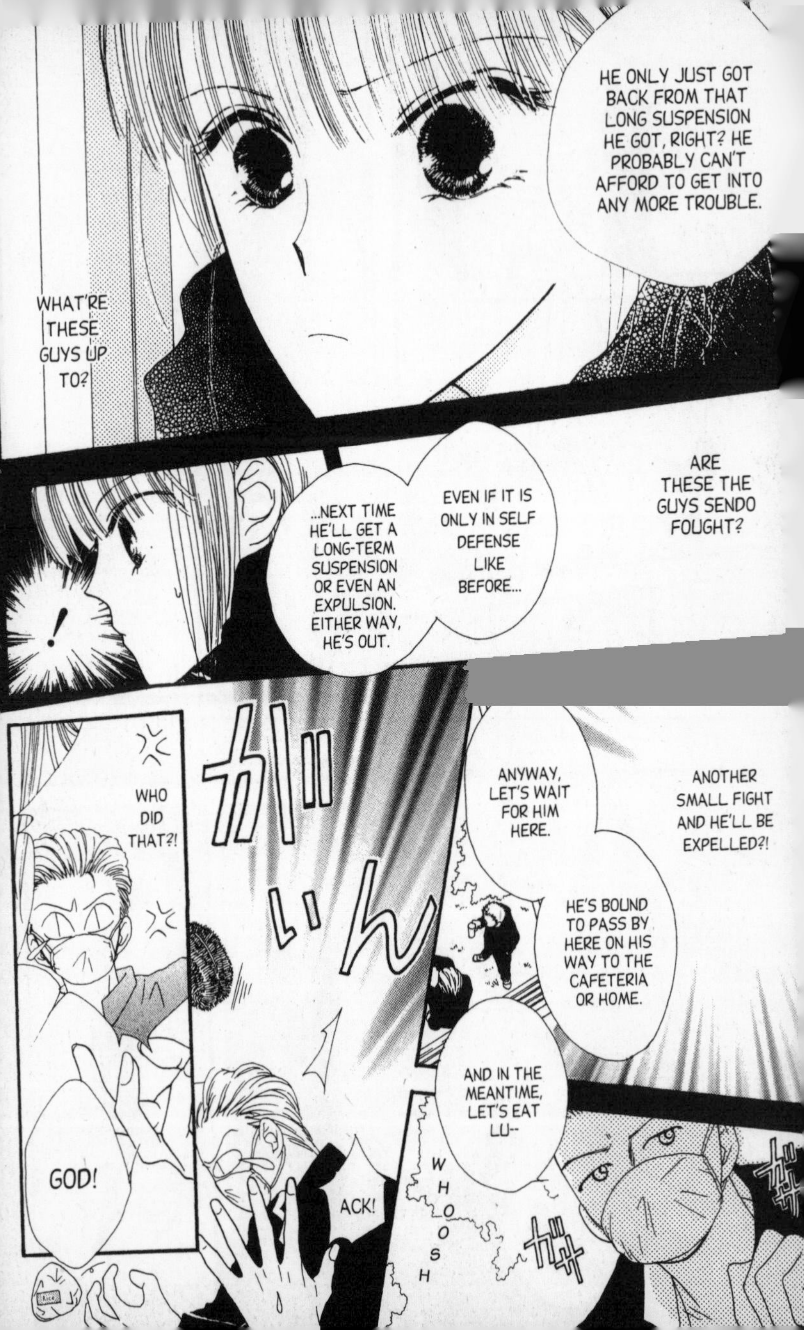
HE ONLY JUST GOT BACK FROM THAT LONG SUSPENSION HE GOT, RIGHT? HE PROBABLY CAN'T AFFORD TO GET INTO ANY MORE TROUBLE.
WHAT'RE THESE GUYS UP TO?
ARE THESE THE GUYS SENDO FOUGHT?
EVEN IF IT IS ONLY IN SELF DEFENSE LIKE BEFORE...
...NEXT TIME HE'LL GET A LONG-TERM SUSPENSION OR EVEN AN EXPULSION. EITHER WAY, HE'S OUT.
!
ANOTHER SMALL FIGHT AND HE'LL BE EXPELLED?!
ANYWAY, LET'S WAIT FOR HIM HERE.
HE'S BOUND TO PASS BY HERE ON HIS WAY TO THE CAFETERIA OR HOME.
AND IN THE MEANTIME, LET'S EAT LU--
WHOOSH
ACK!
WHO DID THAT?!
GOD!

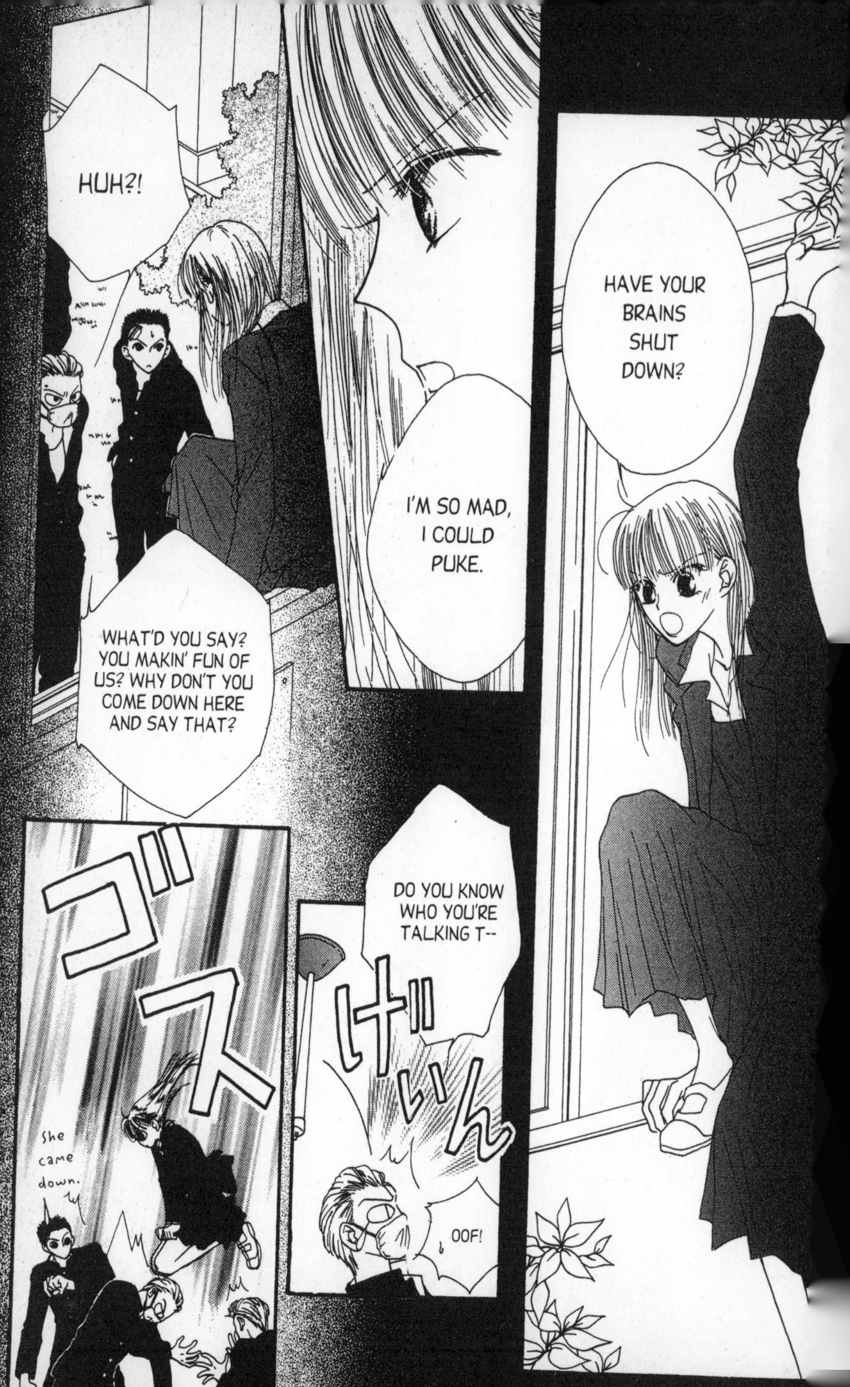

HAVE YOUR BRAINS SHUT DOWN?
I'M SO MAD, I COULD PUKE.
HUH?!
WHAT'D YOU SAY? YOU MAKIN' FUN OF US? WHY DON'T YOU COME DOWN HERE AND SAY THAT?
DO YOU KNOW WHO YOU'RE TALKING T--
げいん
OOF!
ゴス
She came down.

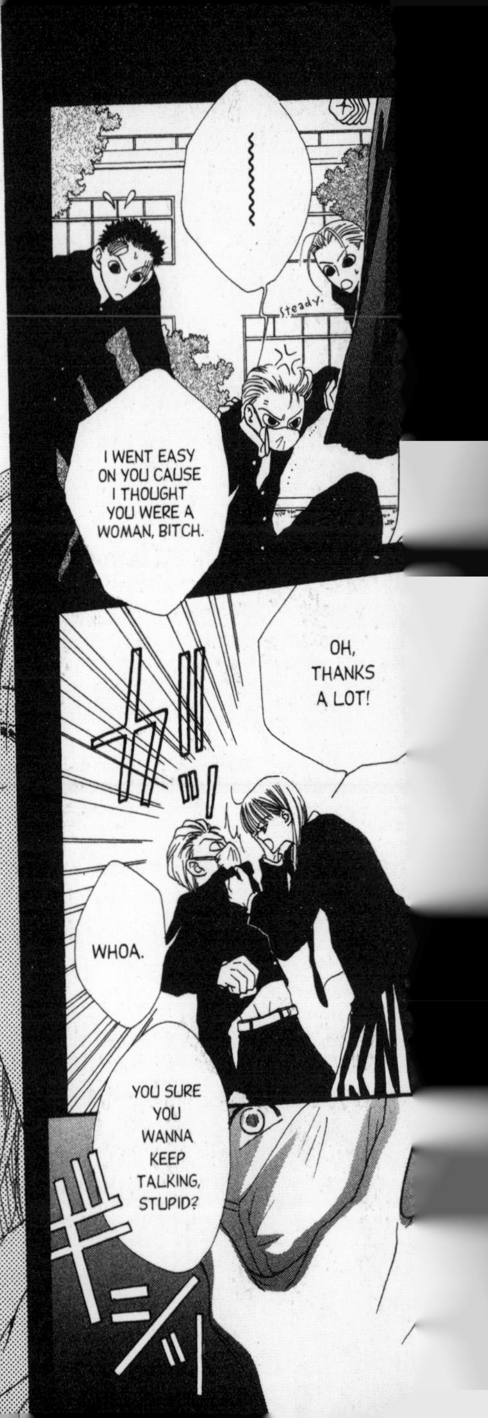
steady.
I WENT EASY ON YOU CAUSE I THOUGHT YOU WERE A WOMAN, BITCH.
OH, THANKS A LOT!
WHOA.
YOU SURE YOU WANNA KEEP TALKING, STUPID?

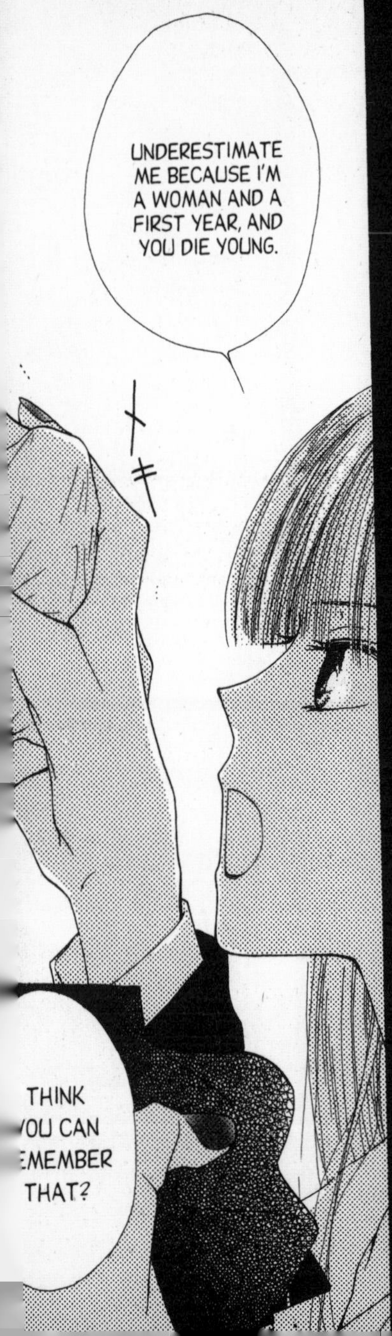
UNDERESTIMATE ME BECAUSE I'M A WOMAN AND A FIRST YEAR, AND YOU DIE YOUNG.
THINK YOU CAN EMEMBER THAT?

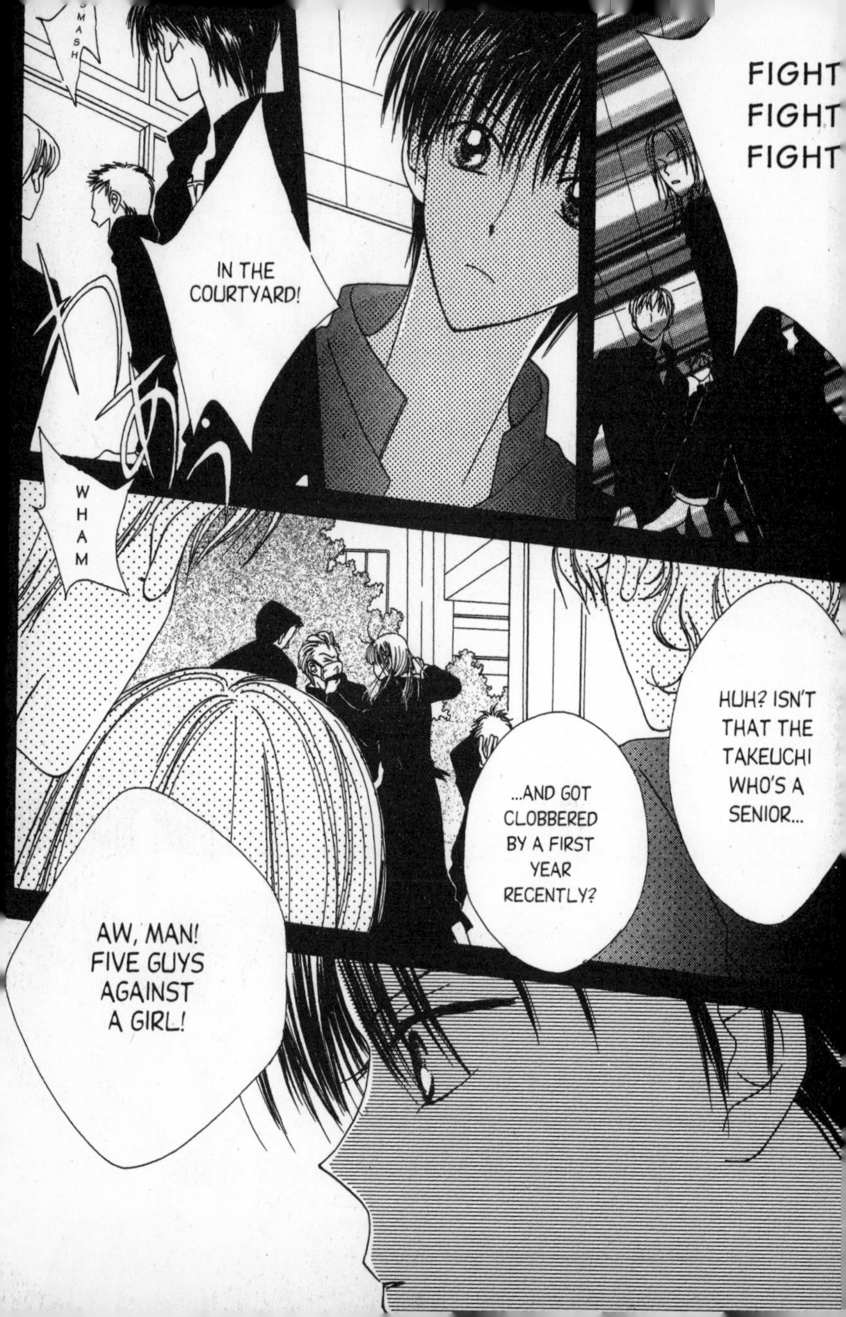

FIGHT FIGHT FIGHT
SMASH
IN THE COURTYARD!
WHAM
HUH? ISN'T THAT THE TAKEUCHI WHO'S A SENIOR...
...AND GOT CLOBBERED BY A FIRST YEAR RECENTLY?
AW, MAN! FIVE GUYS AGAINST A GIRL!

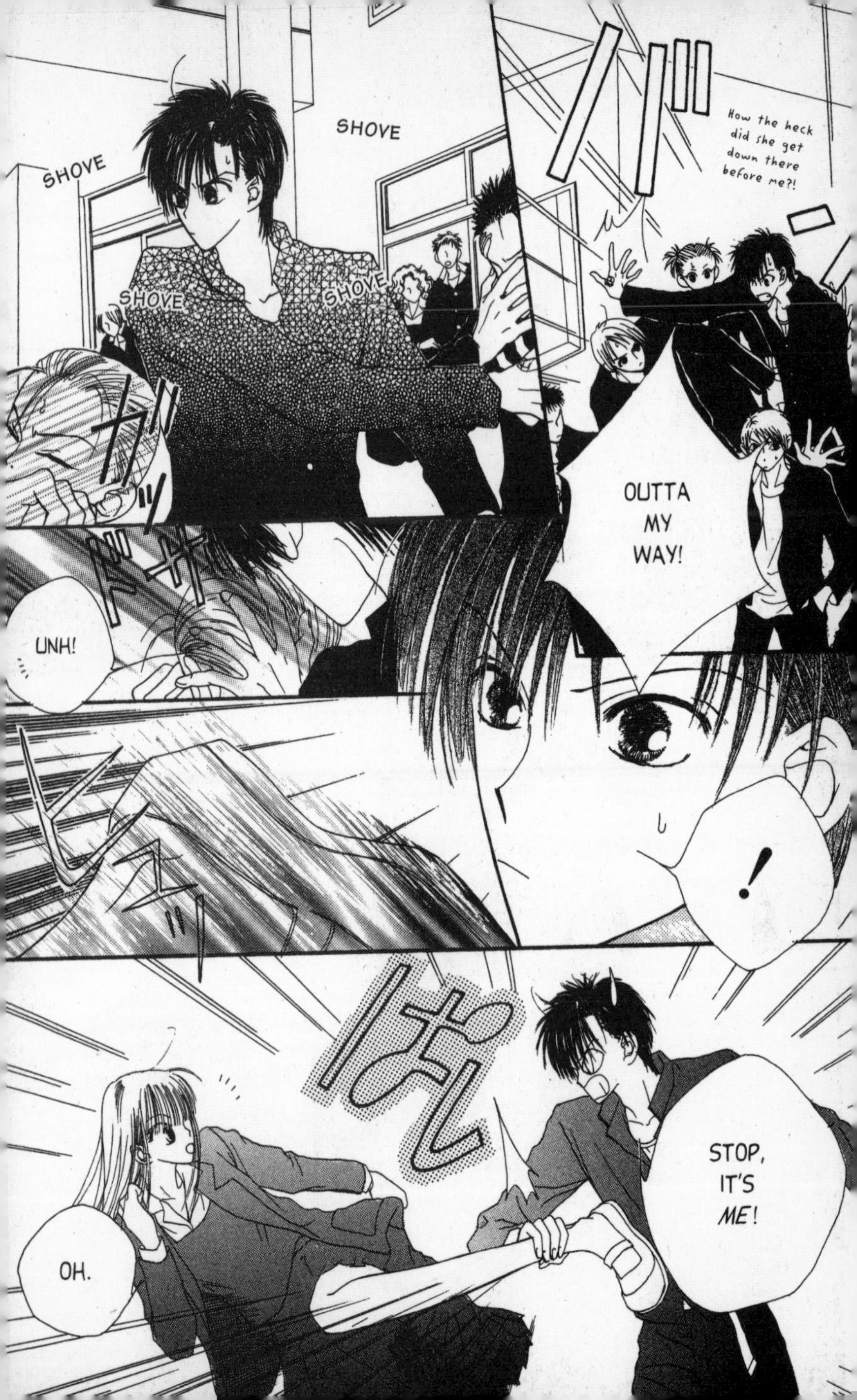
How the heck did she get down there before me?!
OUTTA MY WAY!
SHOVE
SHOVE
SHOVE
SHOVE
!
UNH!
STOP, IT'S *ME*!
OH.

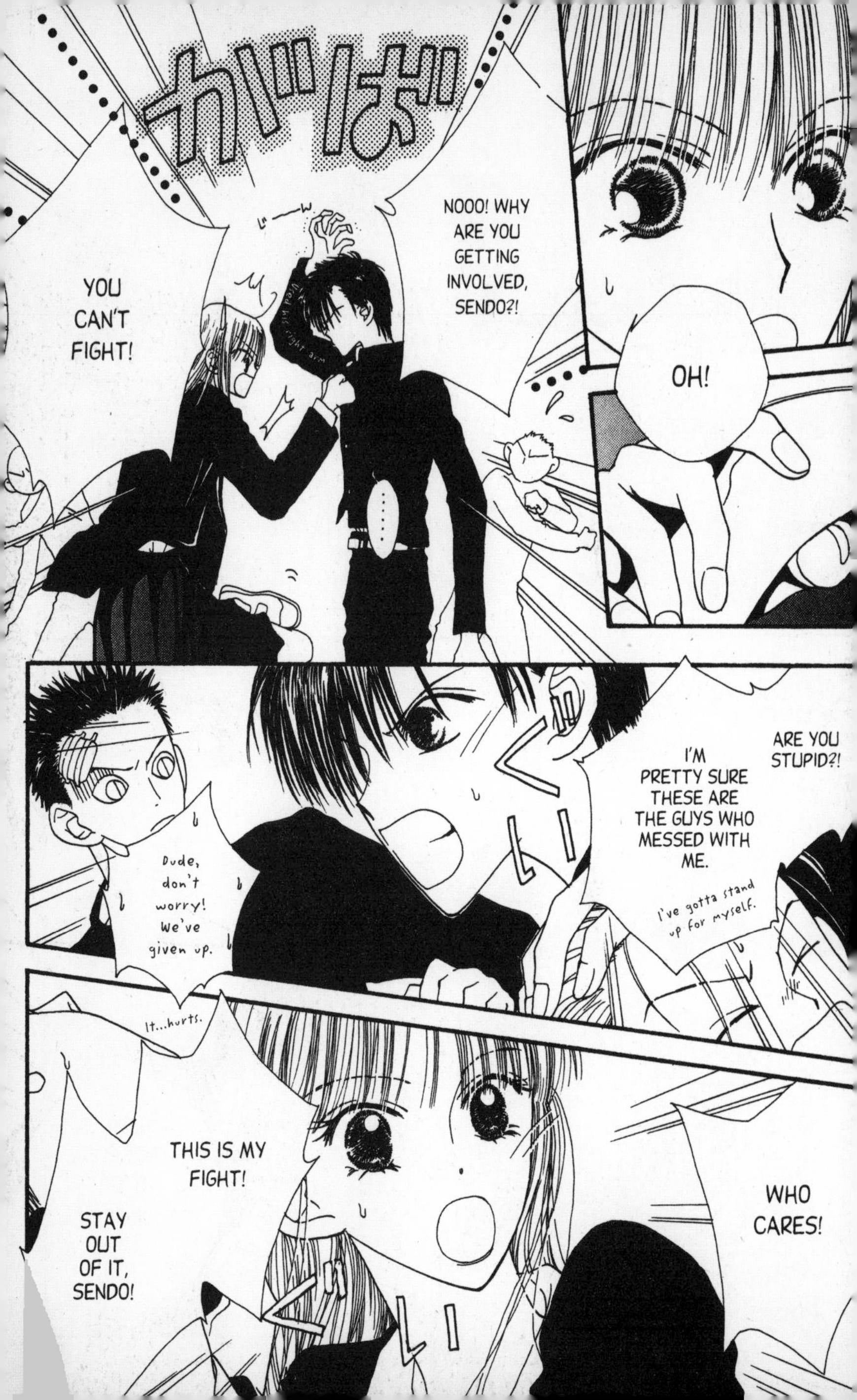
OH!
カバッ
じーw
Used his right arm
NOOO! WHY ARE YOU GETTING INVOLVED, SENDO?!
YOU CAN'T FIGHT!
ARE YOU STUPID?!
I'M PRETTY SURE THESE ARE THE GUYS WHO MESSED WITH ME.
I've gotta stand up for myself.
Dude, don't worry! We've given up.
It...hurts.
WHO CARES!
THIS IS MY FIGHT!
STAY OUT OF IT, SENDO!

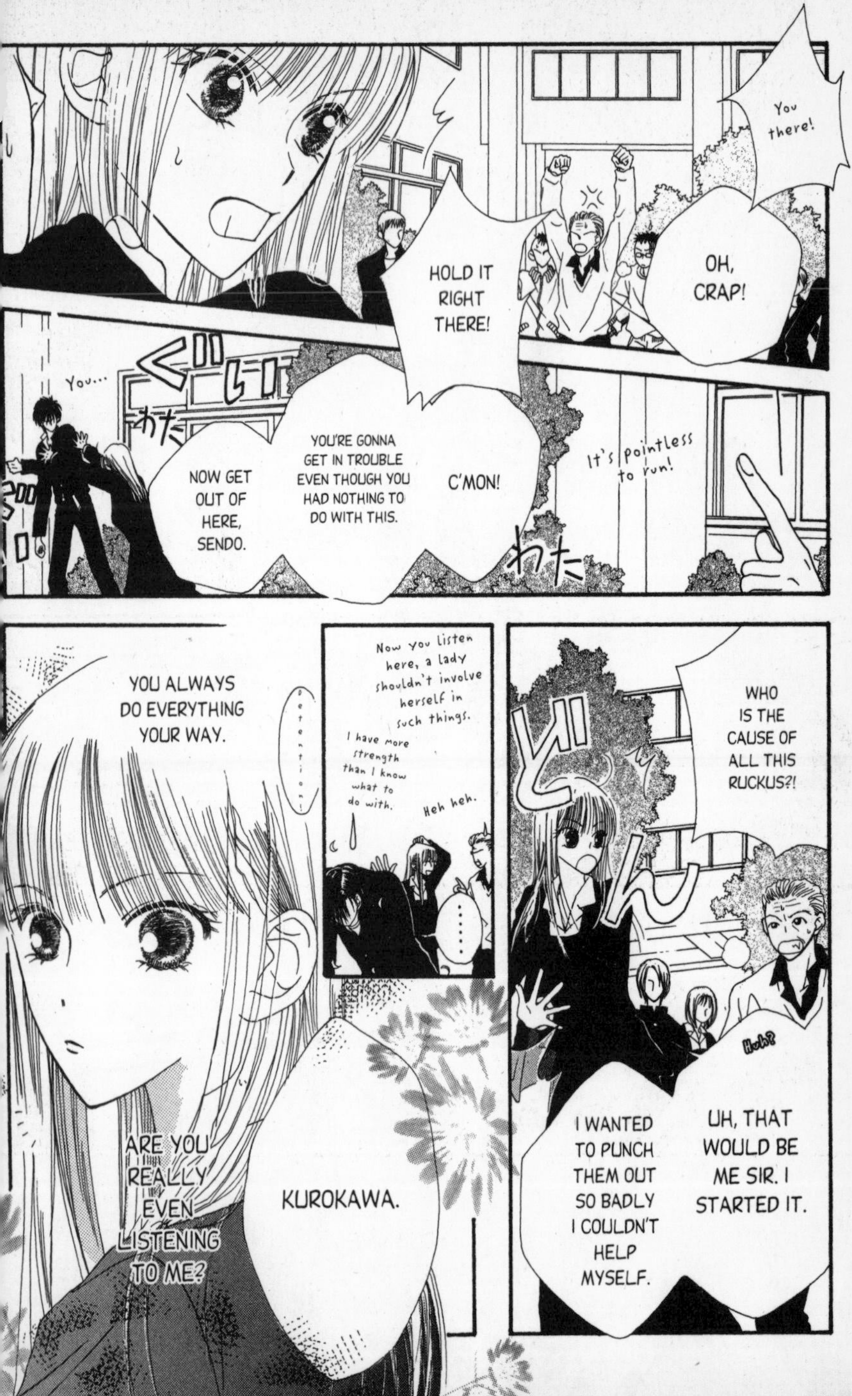
You there!
OH, CRAP!
HOLD IT RIGHT THERE!
It's pointless to run!
わた
C'MON!
YOU'RE GONNA GET IN TROUBLE EVEN THOUGH YOU HAD NOTHING TO DO WITH THIS.
NOW GET OUT OF HERE, SENDO.
You...
わた
WHO IS THE CAUSE OF ALL THIS RUCKUS?!
UH, THAT WOULD BE ME SIR. I STARTED IT.
Huh?
I WANTED TO PUNCH THEM OUT SO BADLY I COULDN'T HELP MYSELF.
Now you listen here, a lady shouldn't involve herself in such things.
I have more strength than I know what to do with.
Heh heh.
Detention!
......
YOU ALWAYS DO EVERYTHING YOUR WAY.
KUROKAWA.
ARE YOU REALLY EVEN LISTENING TO ME?

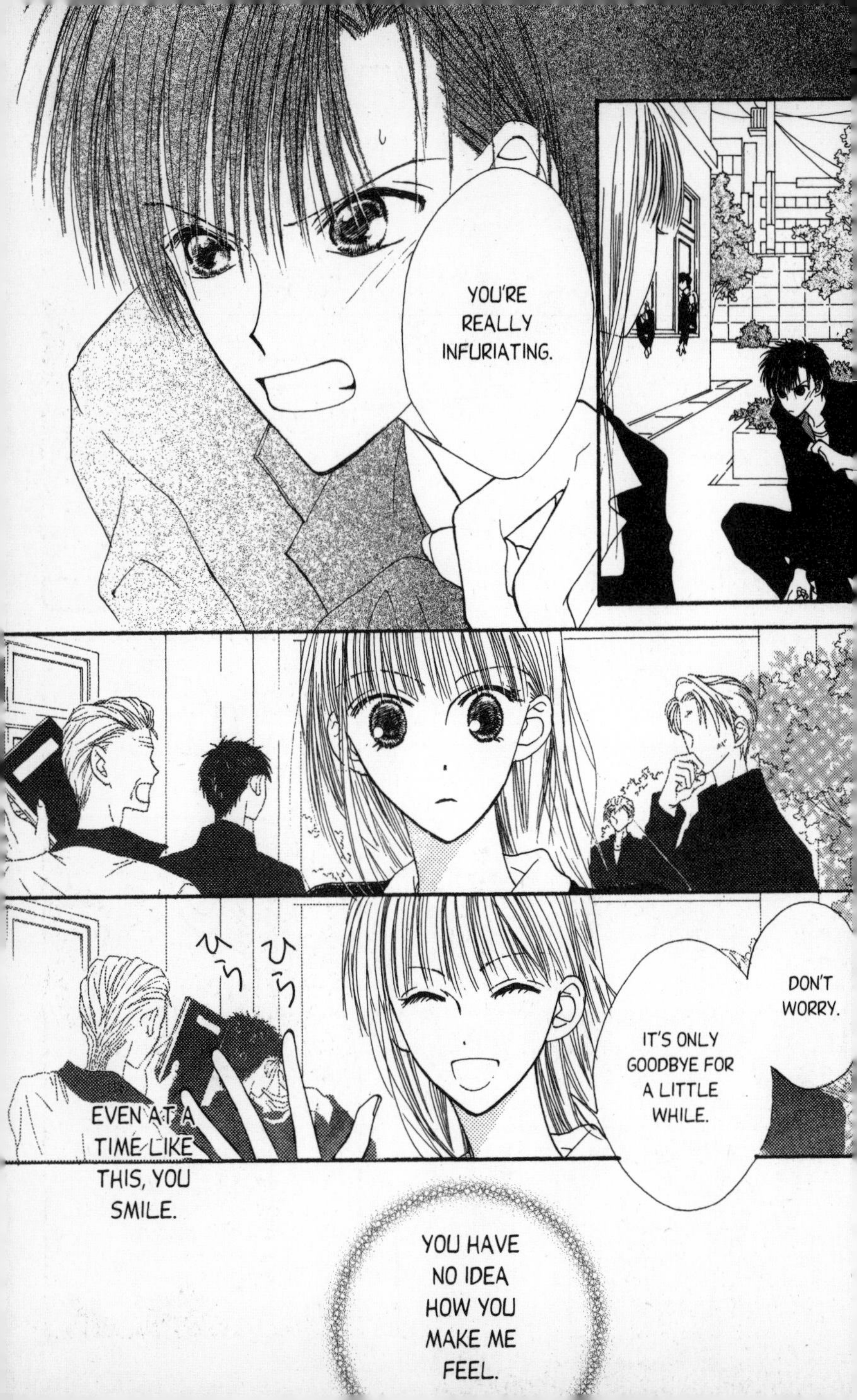
YOU'RE REALLY INFURIATING.
DON'T WORRY.
IT'S ONLY GOODBYE FOR A LITTLE WHILE.
ひら
ひら
EVEN AT A TIME LIKE THIS, YOU SMILE.
YOU HAVE NO IDEA HOW YOU MAKE ME FEEL.

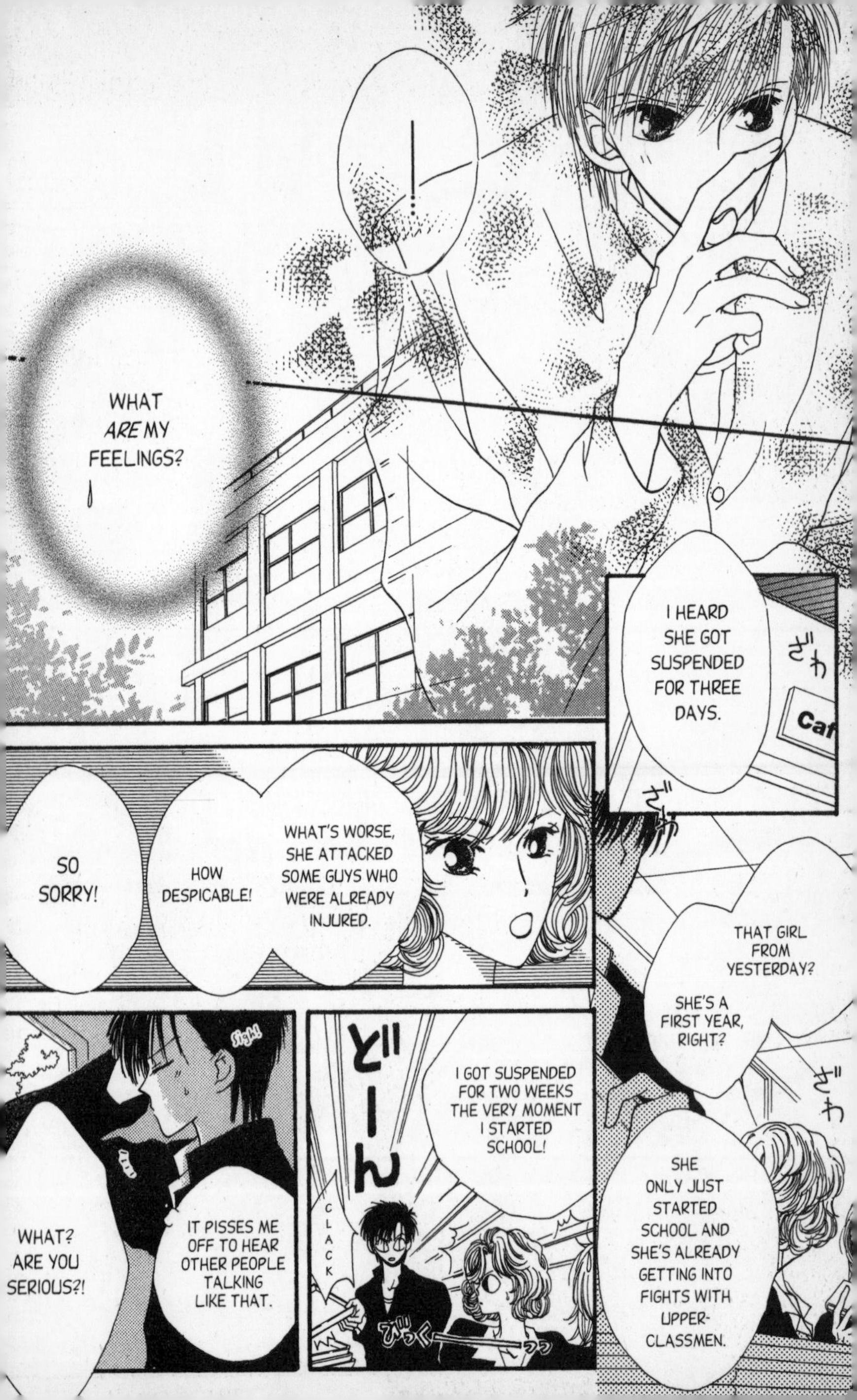
!
WHAT ARE MY FEELINGS?
I HEARD SHE GOT SUSPENDED FOR THREE DAYS.
ざわ
ざわ
Caf
THAT GIRL FROM YESTERDAY?
SHE'S A FIRST YEAR, RIGHT?
ざわ
SHE ONLY JUST STARTED SCHOOL AND SHE'S ALREADY GETTING INTO FIGHTS WITH UPPER-CLASSMEN.
WHAT'S WORSE, SHE ATTACKED SOME GUYS WHO WERE ALREADY INJURED.
HOW DESPICABLE!
SO SORRY!
どーん
I GOT SUSPENDED FOR TWO WEEKS THE VERY MOMENT I STARTED SCHOOL!
CLACK
びっく
Sigh!
IT PISSES ME OFF TO HEAR OTHER PEOPLE TALKING LIKE THAT.
WHAT? ARE YOU SERIOUS?!

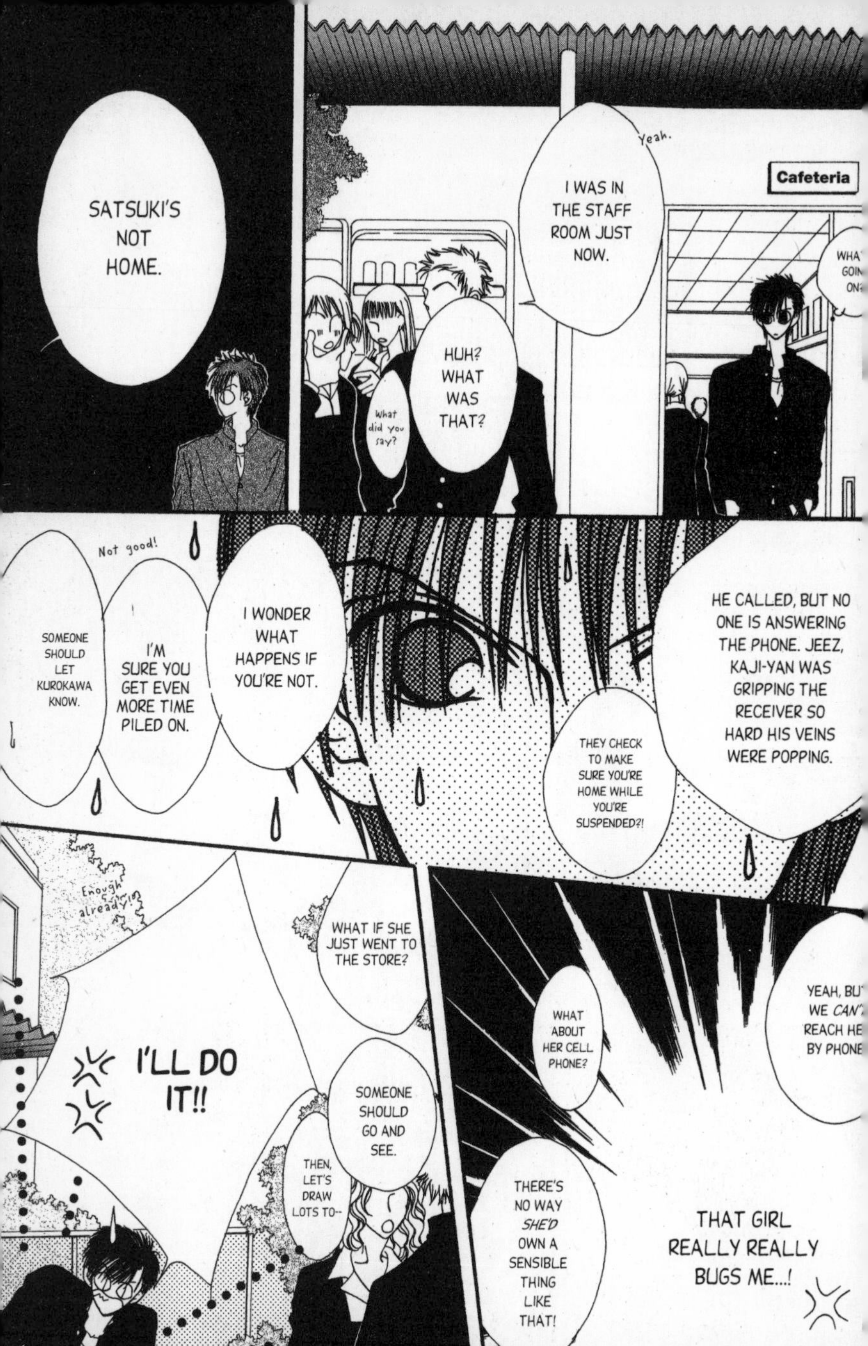
Yeah.
I WAS IN THE STAFF ROOM JUST NOW.
Cafeteria
WHA GOIN ON?
HUH? WHAT WAS THAT?
What did you say?
SATSUKI'S NOT HOME.
HE CALLED, BUT NO ONE IS ANSWERING THE PHONE. JEEZ, KAJI-YAN WAS GRIPPING THE RECEIVER SO HARD HIS VEINS WERE POPPING.
THEY CHECK TO MAKE SURE YOU'RE HOME WHILE YOU'RE SUSPENDED?!
I WONDER WHAT HAPPENS IF YOU'RE NOT.
I'M SURE YOU GET EVEN MORE TIME PILED ON.
Not good!
SOMEONE SHOULD LET KUROKAWA KNOW.
YEAH, BUT WE *CAN'* REACH HE BY PHONE
WHAT ABOUT HER CELL PHONE?
THERE'S NO WAY *SHE'D* OWN A SENSIBLE THING LIKE THAT!
THAT GIRL REALLY REALLY BUGS ME...!
WHAT IF SHE JUST WENT TO THE STORE?
SOMEONE SHOULD GO AND SEE.
THEN, LET'S DRAW LOTS TO--
I'LL DO IT!!
Enough already!!

Note: See page 194

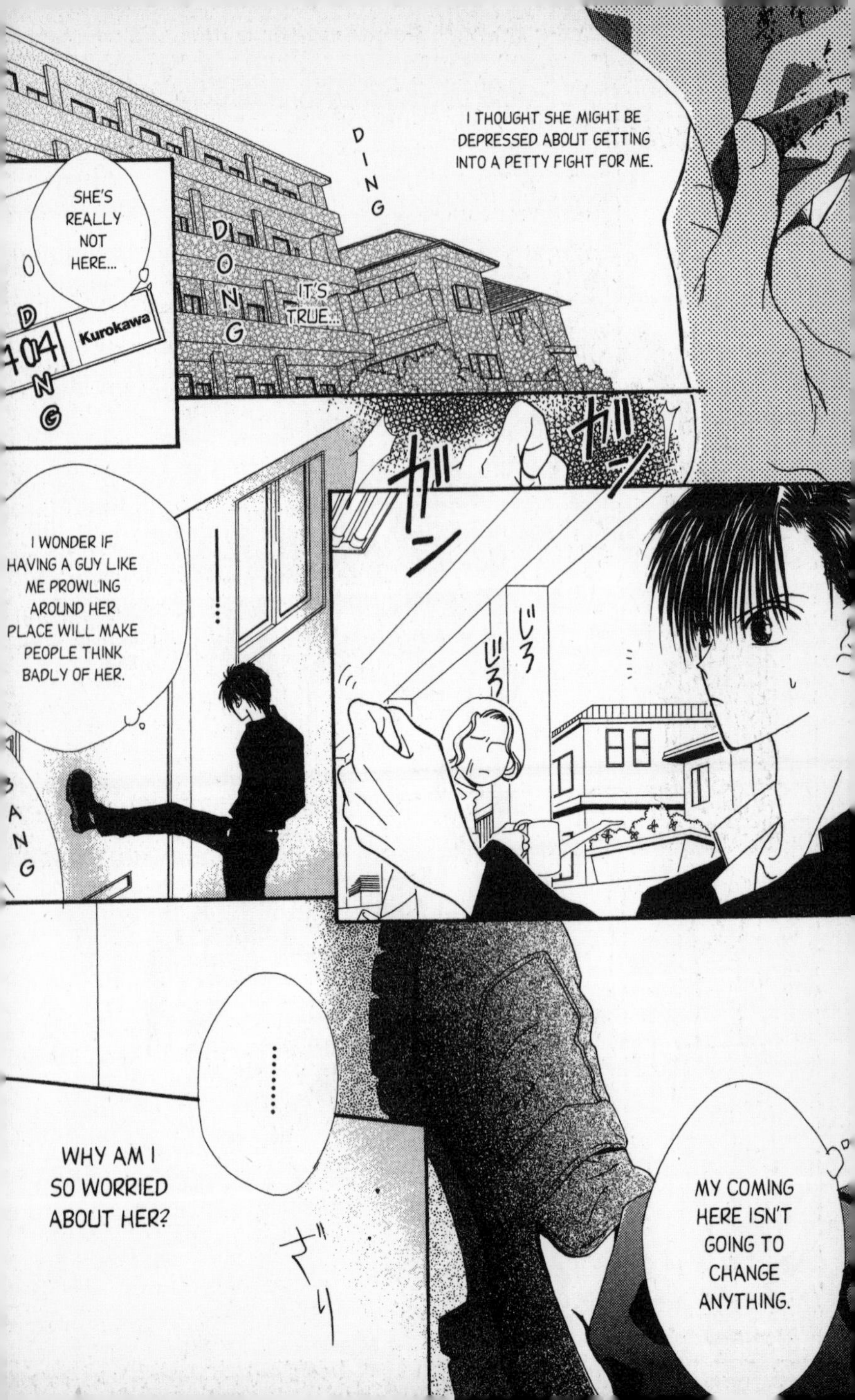
I THOUGHT SHE MIGHT BE DEPRESSED ABOUT GETTING INTO A PETTY FIGHT FOR ME.
DING
DONG
IT'S TRUE...
SHE'S REALLY NOT HERE...
404 Kurokawa
DING DONG
ガーン
ガーン
じろ
じろ
!
I WONDER IF HAVING A GUY LIKE ME PROWLING AROUND HER PLACE WILL MAKE PEOPLE THINK BADLY OF HER.
BANG
MY COMING HERE ISN'T GOING TO CHANGE ANYTHING.
ざり
......
WHY AM I SO WORRIED ABOUT HER?

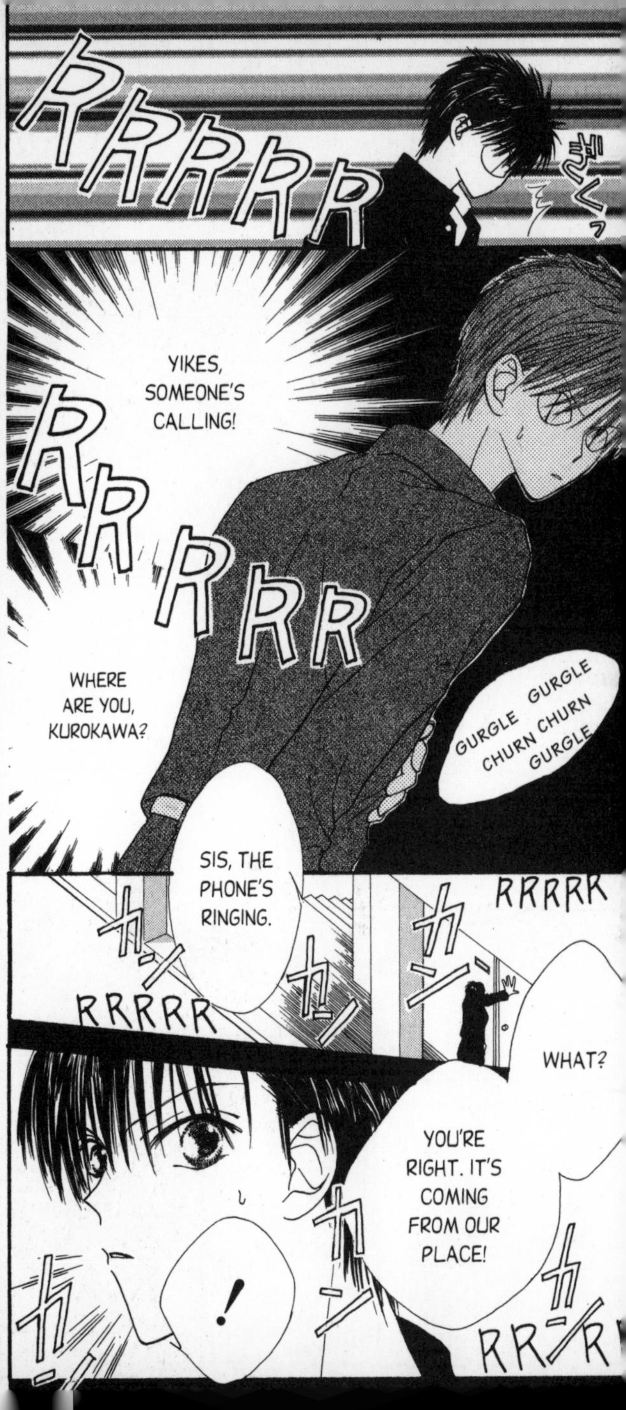
RRRRRR
YIKES, SOMEONE'S CALLING!
RRRRRR
GURGLE GURGLE CHURN CHURN GURGLE
WHERE ARE YOU, KUROKAWA?
SIS, THE PHONE'S RINGING.
RRRRR
RRRRR
WHAT?
YOU'RE RIGHT. IT'S COMING FROM OUR PLACE!
!
RR-R

WARDROBE

You see, it was nothing spectacular, just paper dolls. I've loved paper dolls since way back when. How about all of you?

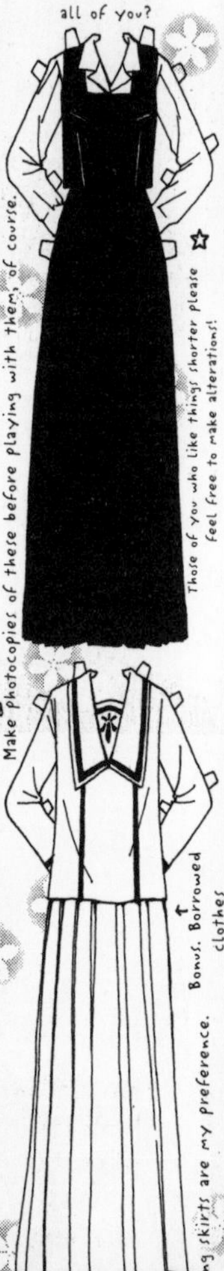
Make photocopies of these before playing with them, of course.
Those of You who like things shorter please feel free to make alterations!
Long skirts are my preference.
Bonus. Borrowed clothes

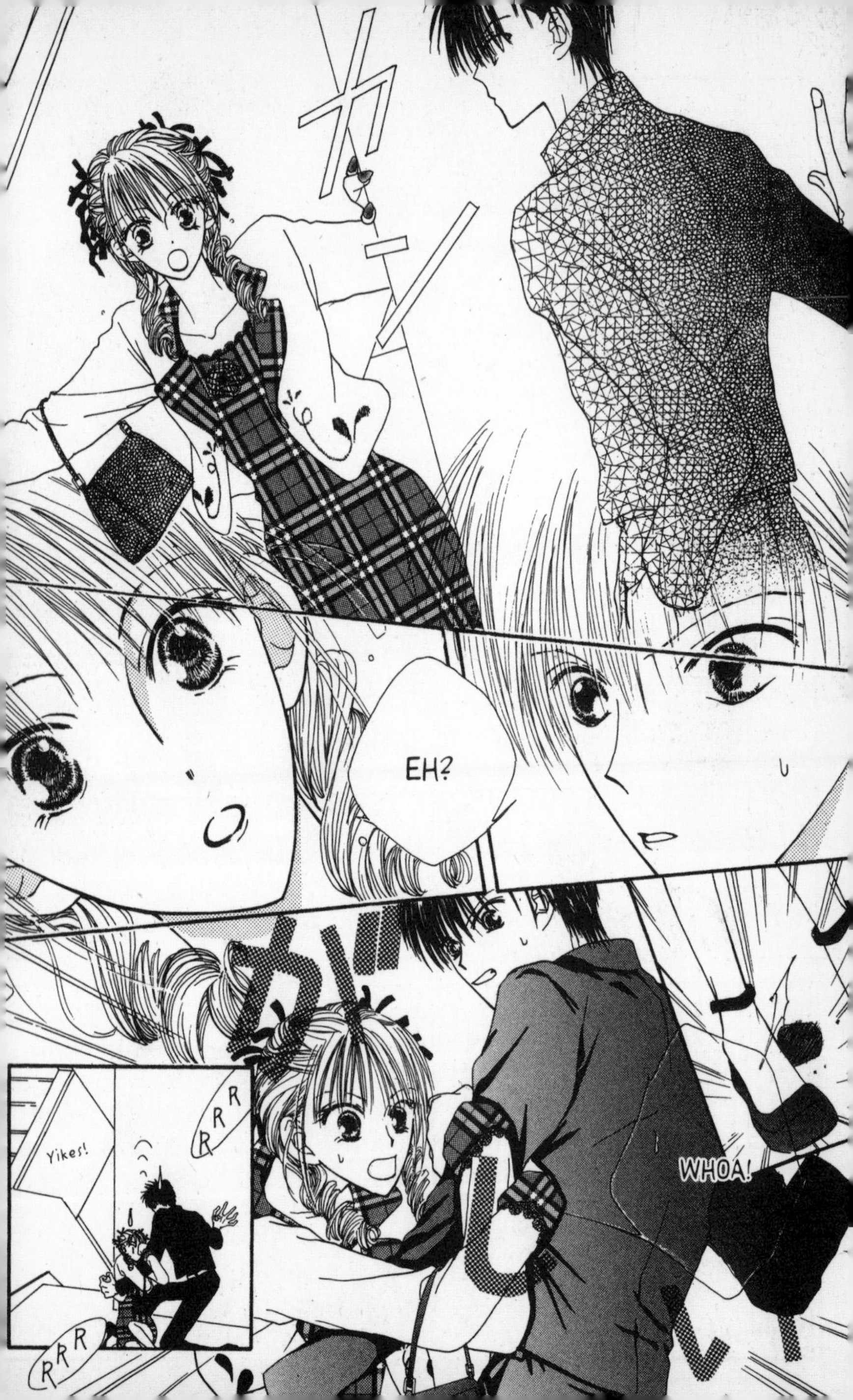

EH?
WHOA!
RRRR
Yikes!
RRRR

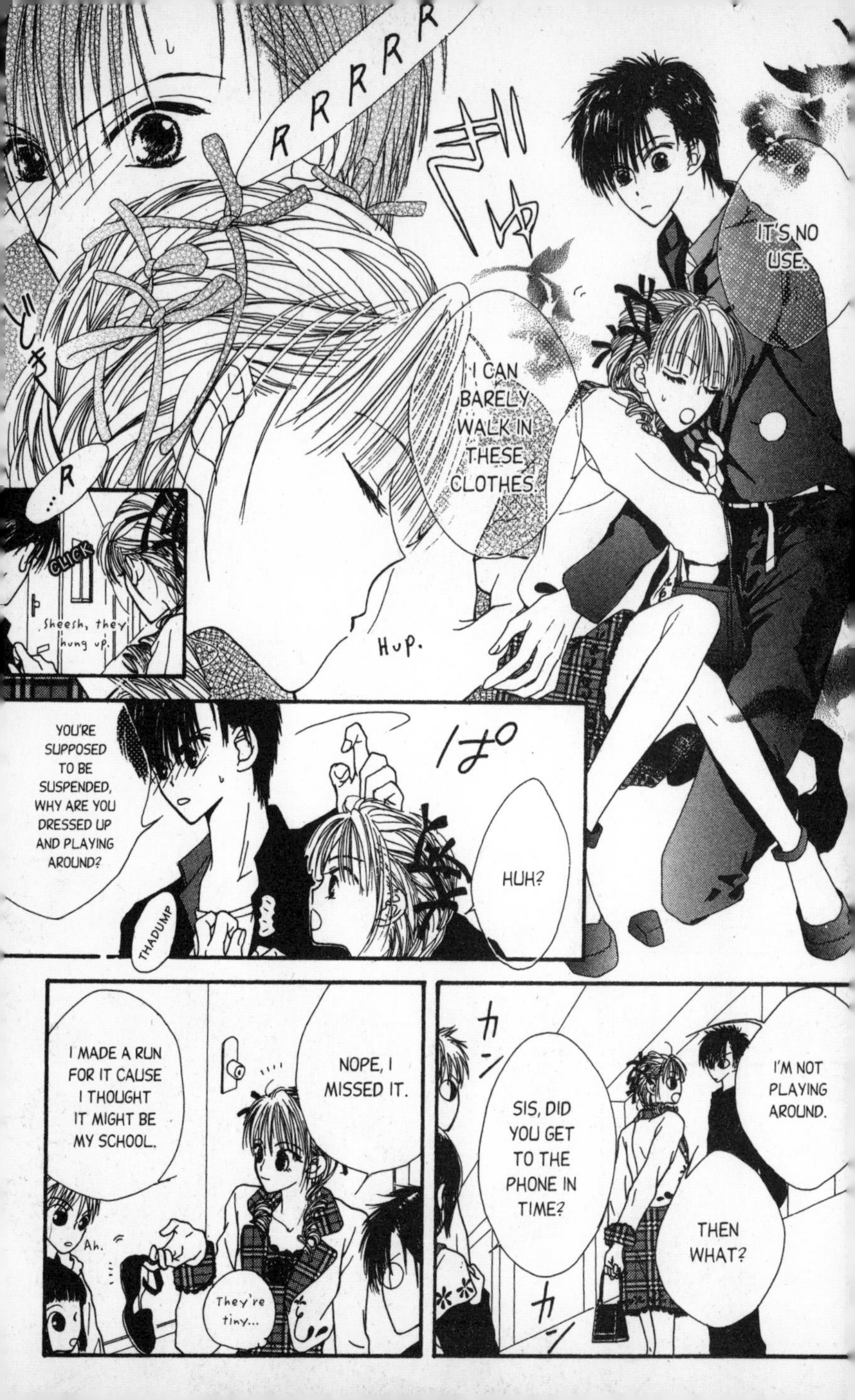

RRRRRRR
きゅ
IT'S NO USE.
I CAN BARELY WALK IN THESE CLOTHES.
Hup.
...R
CLICK
Sheesh, they hung up.
ぱ
HUH?
YOU'RE SUPPOSED TO BE SUSPENDED, WHY ARE YOU DRESSED UP AND PLAYING AROUND?
THADUMP
I'M NOT PLAYING AROUND.
THEN WHAT?
カン
SIS, DID YOU GET TO THE PHONE IN TIME?
カン
NOPE, I MISSED IT.
I MADE A RUN FOR IT CAUSE I THOUGHT IT MIGHT BE MY SCHOOL.
Ah.
They're tiny...

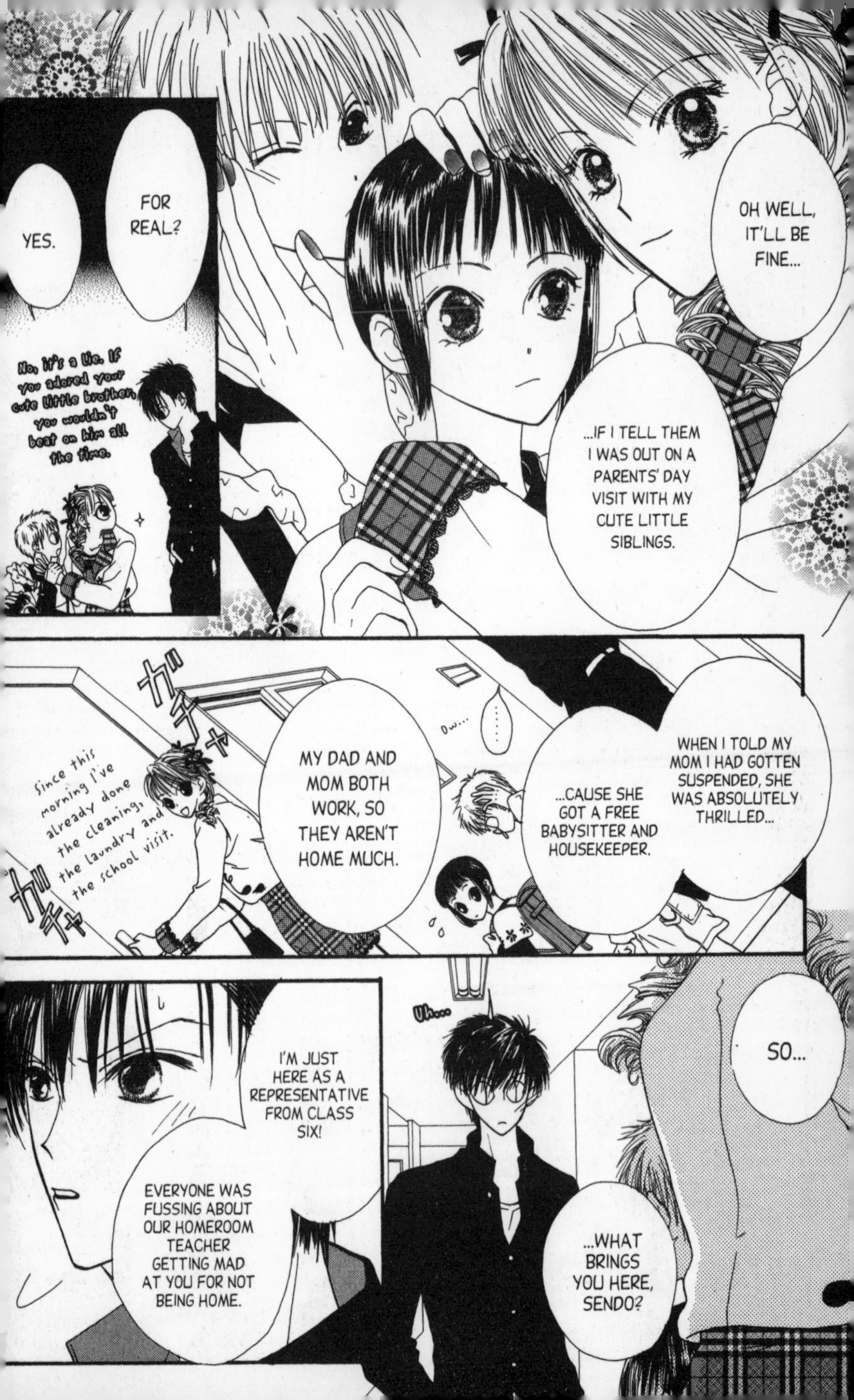
OH WELL, IT'LL BE FINE...
...IF I TELL THEM I WAS OUT ON A PARENTS' DAY VISIT WITH MY CUTE LITTLE SIBLINGS.
FOR REAL?
YES.
No, it's a lie. If you adored your cute little brother, you wouldn't beat on him all the time.
WHEN I TOLD MY MOM I HAD GOTTEN SUSPENDED, SHE WAS ABSOLUTELY THRILLED...
...CAUSE SHE GOT A FREE BABYSITTER AND HOUSEKEEPER.
......
Ow...
MY DAD AND MOM BOTH WORK, SO THEY AREN'T HOME MUCH.
ガチャ
Since this morning I've already done the cleaning, the laundry and the school visit.
ガチャ
SO...
...WHAT BRINGS YOU HERE, SENDO?
Uh...
I'M JUST HERE AS A REPRESENTATIVE FROM CLASS SIX!
EVERYONE WAS FUSSING ABOUT OUR HOMEROOM TEACHER GETTING MAD AT YOU FOR NOT BEING HOME.

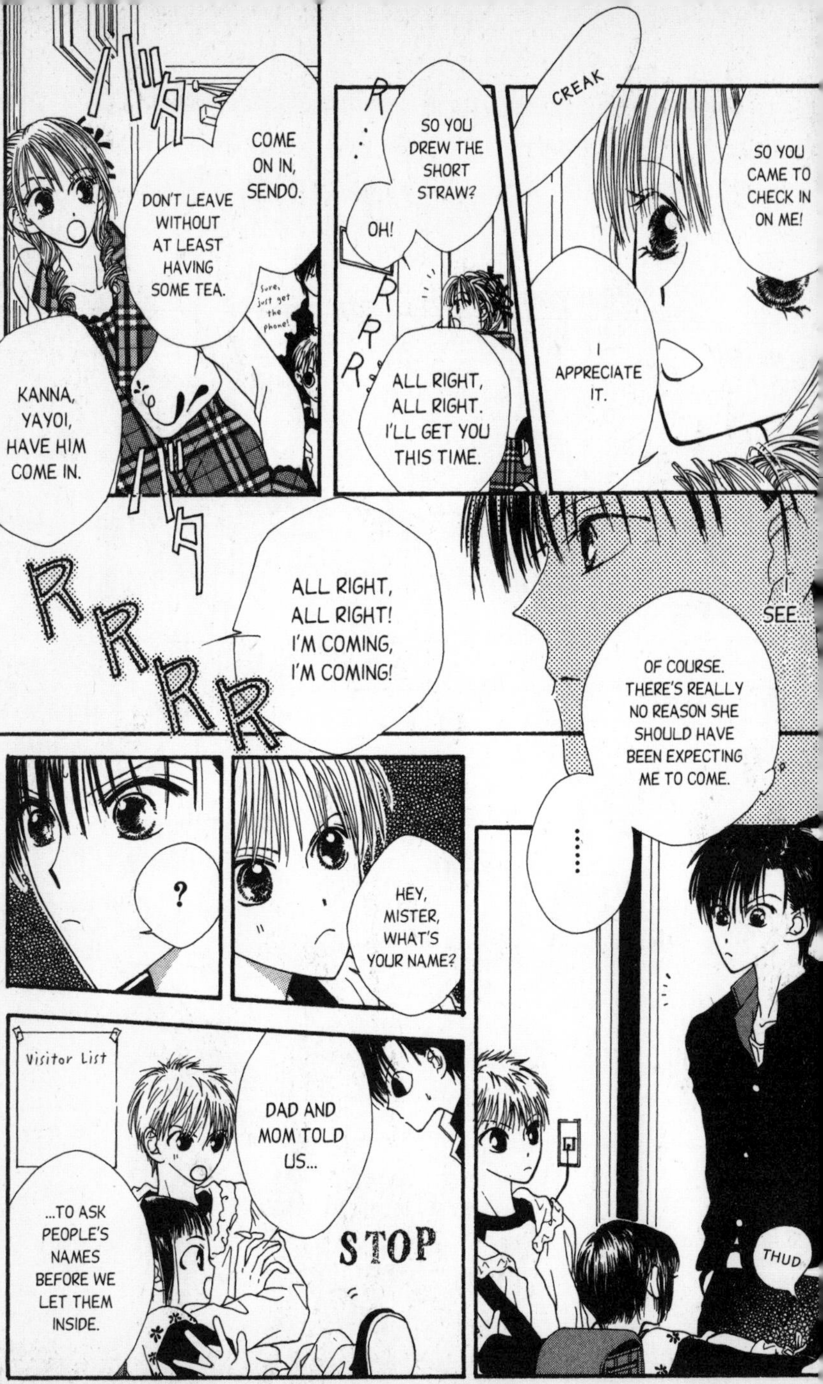
CREAK
SO YOU CAME TO CHECK IN ON ME!
I APPRECIATE IT.
SO YOU DREW THE SHORT STRAW?
OH!
RRRR
ALL RIGHT, ALL RIGHT. I'LL GET YOU THIS TIME.
COME ON IN, SENDO.
DON'T LEAVE WITHOUT AT LEAST HAVING SOME TEA.
Sure, just get the phone!
KANNA, YAYOI, HAVE HIM COME IN.
I SEE...
OF COURSE. THERE'S REALLY NO REASON SHE SHOULD HAVE BEEN EXPECTING ME TO COME.
RRRR
ALL RIGHT, ALL RIGHT! I'M COMING, I'M COMING!
......
THUD
HEY, MISTER, WHAT'S YOUR NAME?
?
Visitor List
DAD AND MOM TOLD US...
...TO ASK PEOPLE'S NAMES BEFORE WE LET THEM INSIDE.
STOP

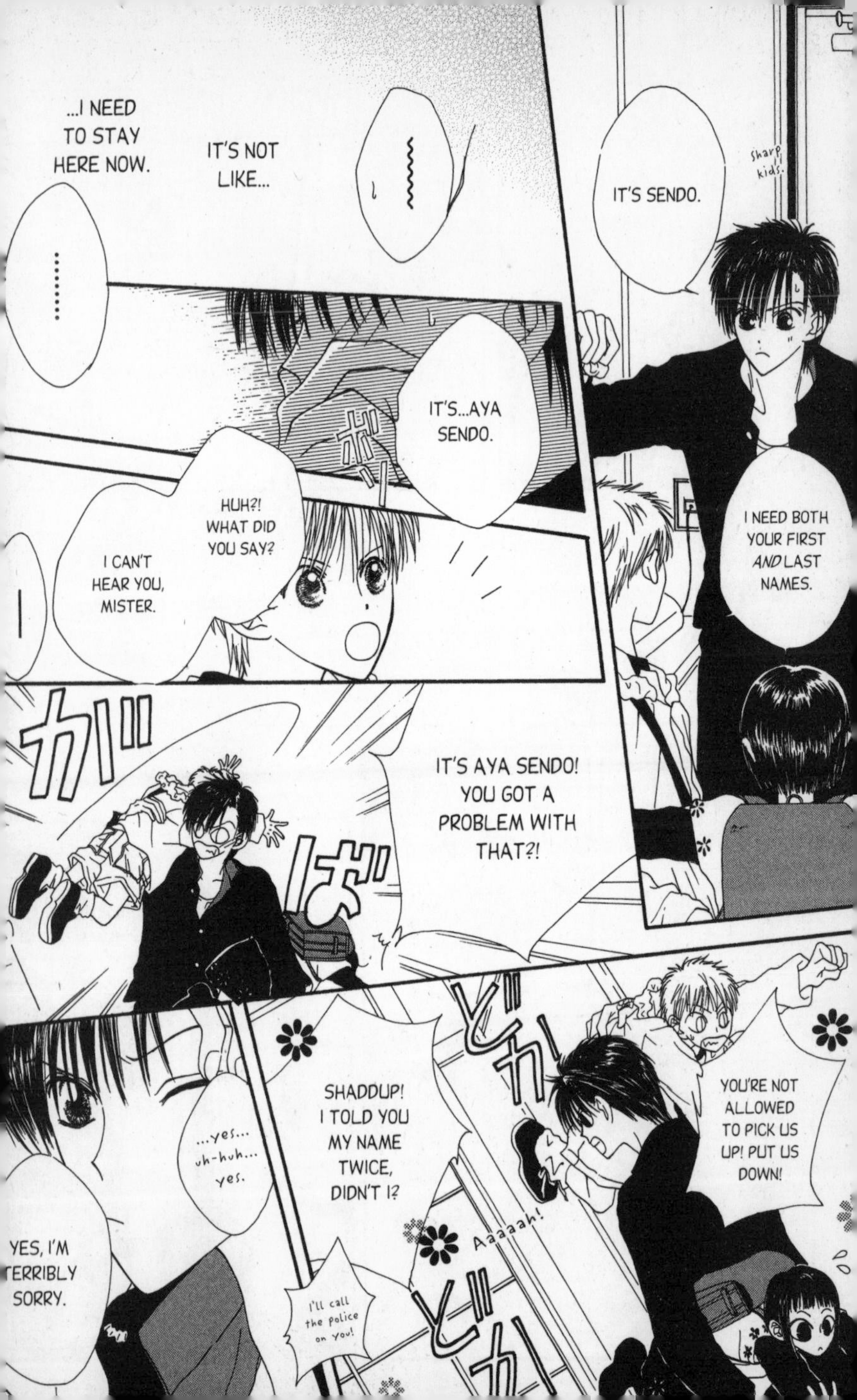
IT'S SENDO.
Sharp kids!
I NEED BOTH YOUR FIRST AND LAST NAMES.
IT'S NOT LIKE...
...I NEED TO STAY HERE NOW.
......
IT'S...AYA SENDO.
ポッ
HUH?! WHAT DID YOU SAY?
I CAN'T HEAR YOU, MISTER.
!
IT'S AYA SENDO! YOU GOT A PROBLEM WITH THAT?!
ばっ
ガッ
YOU'RE NOT ALLOWED TO PICK US UP! PUT US DOWN!
どかっ
Aaaaah!
どかっ
SHADDUP! I TOLD YOU MY NAME TWICE, DIDN'T I?
I'll call the police on you!
...yes... uh-huh... yes.
YES, I'M TERRIBLY SORRY.

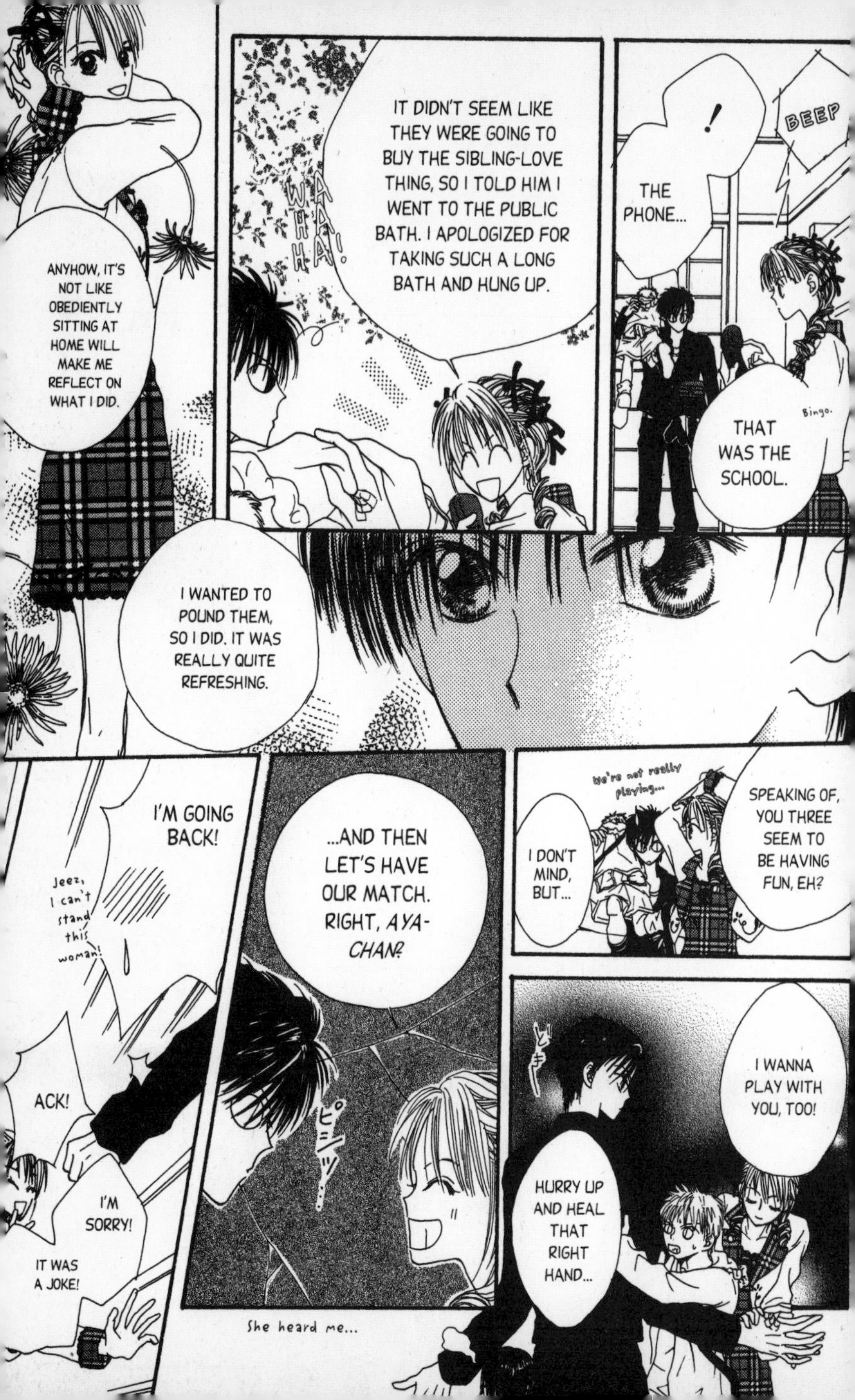
!
BEEP
THE PHONE...
THAT WAS THE SCHOOL.
Bingo.
WA HA HA!
IT DIDN'T SEEM LIKE THEY WERE GOING TO BUY THE SIBLING-LOVE THING, SO I TOLD HIM I WENT TO THE PUBLIC BATH. I APOLOGIZED FOR TAKING SUCH A LONG BATH AND HUNG UP.
I WANTED TO POUND THEM, SO I DID. IT WAS REALLY QUITE REFRESHING.
ANYHOW, IT'S NOT LIKE OBEDIENTLY SITTING AT HOME WILL MAKE ME REFLECT ON WHAT I DID.
SPEAKING OF, YOU THREE SEEM TO BE HAVING FUN, EH?
We're not really playing...
I DON'T MIND, BUT...
I WANNA PLAY WITH YOU, TOO!
HURRY UP AND HEAL THAT RIGHT HAND...
...AND THEN LET'S HAVE OUR MATCH. RIGHT, AYA-CHAN?
I'M GOING BACK!
Jeez, I can't stand this woman!
ACK!
I'M SORRY!
IT WAS A JOKE!
She heard me...

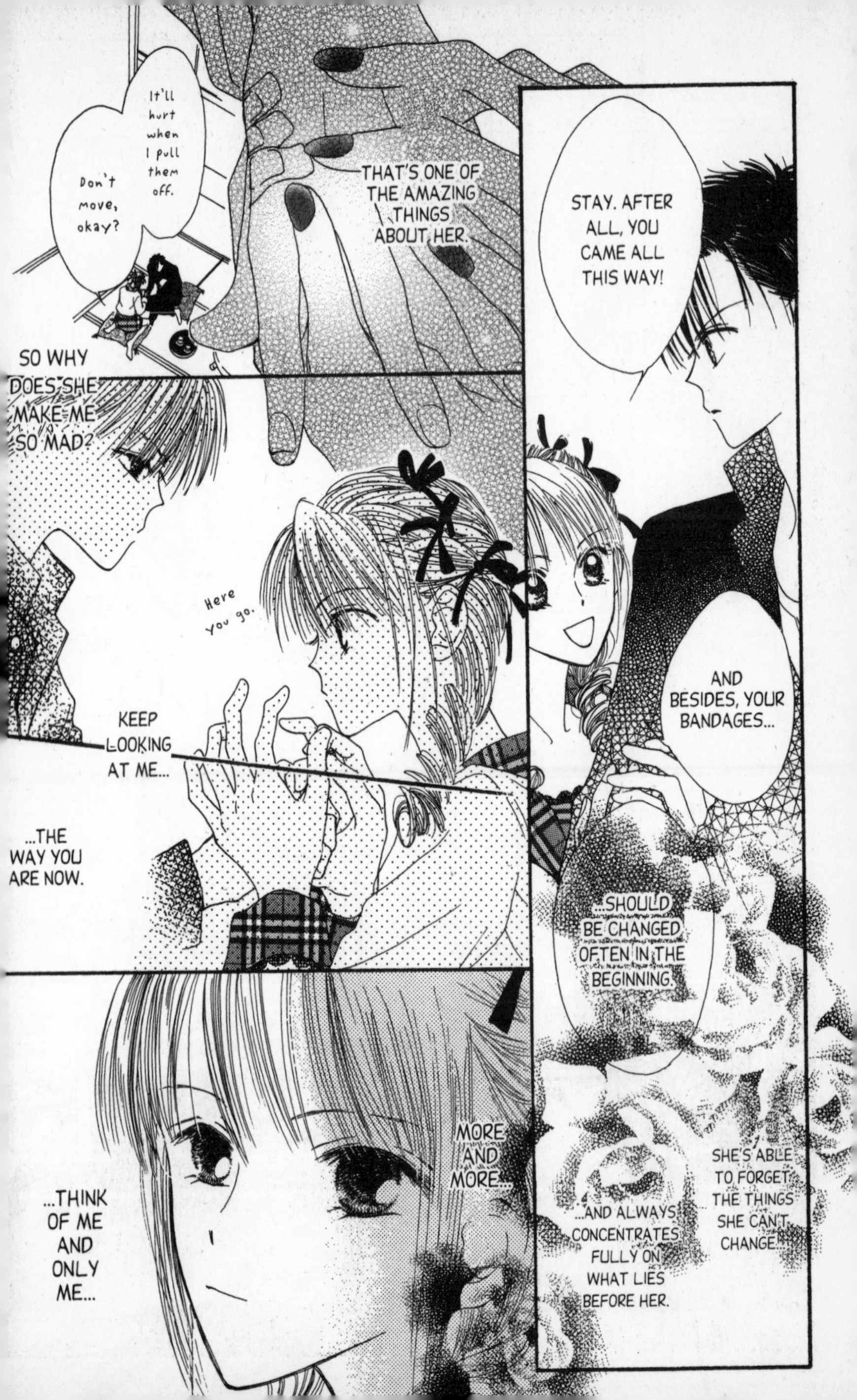
STAY. AFTER ALL, YOU CAME ALL THIS WAY!
AND BESIDES, YOUR BANDAGES...
...SHOULD BE CHANGED OFTEN IN THE BEGINNING.
SHE'S ABLE TO FORGET THE THINGS SHE CAN'T CHANGE...
...AND ALWAYS CONCENTRATES FULLY ON WHAT LIES BEFORE HER.
It'll hurt when I pull them off.
Don't move, okay?
THAT'S ONE OF THE AMAZING THINGS ABOUT HER.
SO WHY DOES SHE MAKE ME SO MAD?
Here you go.
KEEP LOOKING AT ME...
...THE WAY YOU ARE NOW.
MORE AND MORE...
...THINK OF ME AND ONLY ME...

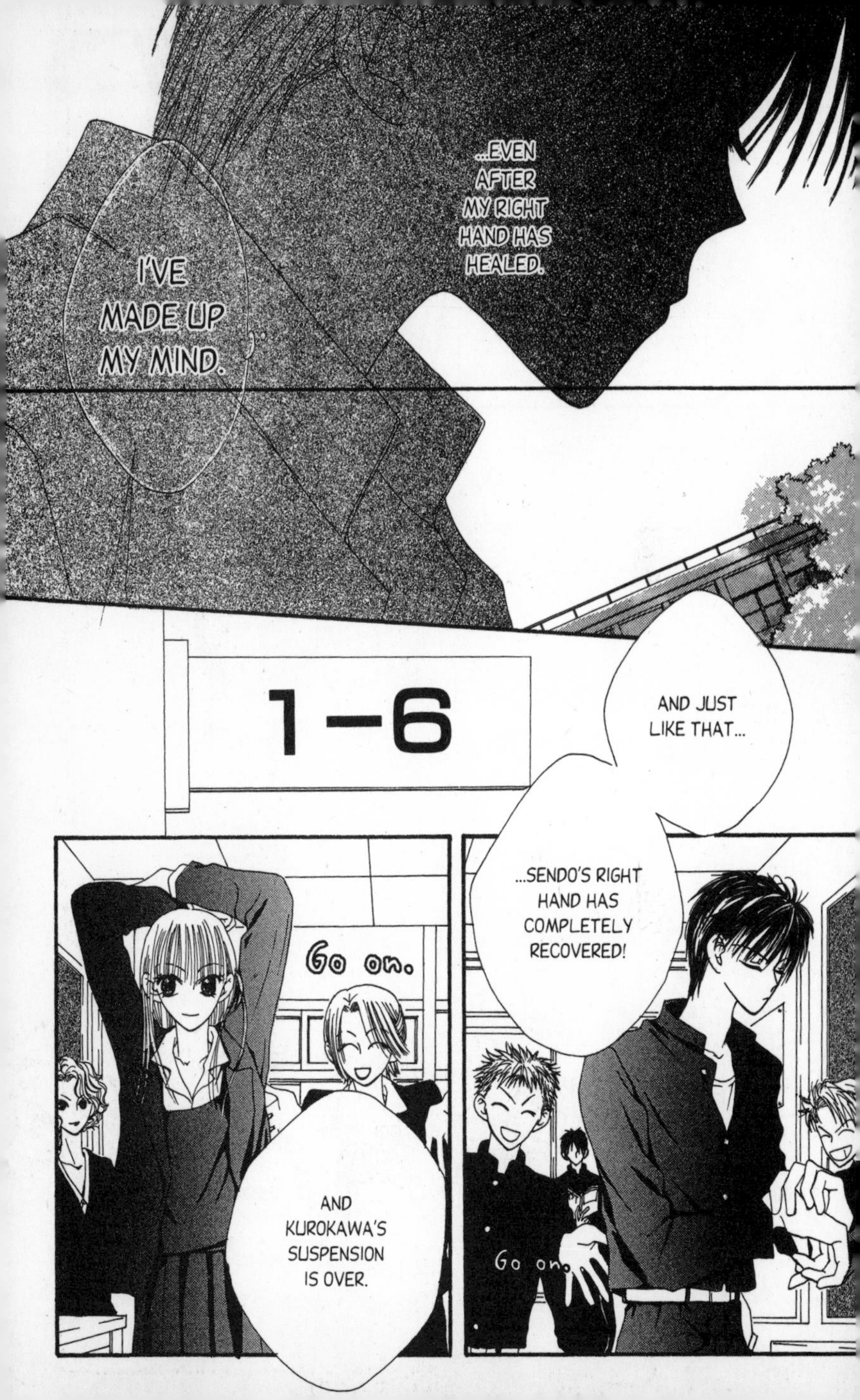
...EVEN AFTER MY RIGHT HAND HAS HEALED.
I'VE MADE UP MY MIND.
1-6
AND JUST LIKE THAT...
...SENDO'S RIGHT HAND HAS COMPLETELY RECOVERED!
Go on.
Go on.
AND KUROKAWA'S SUSPENSION IS OVER.

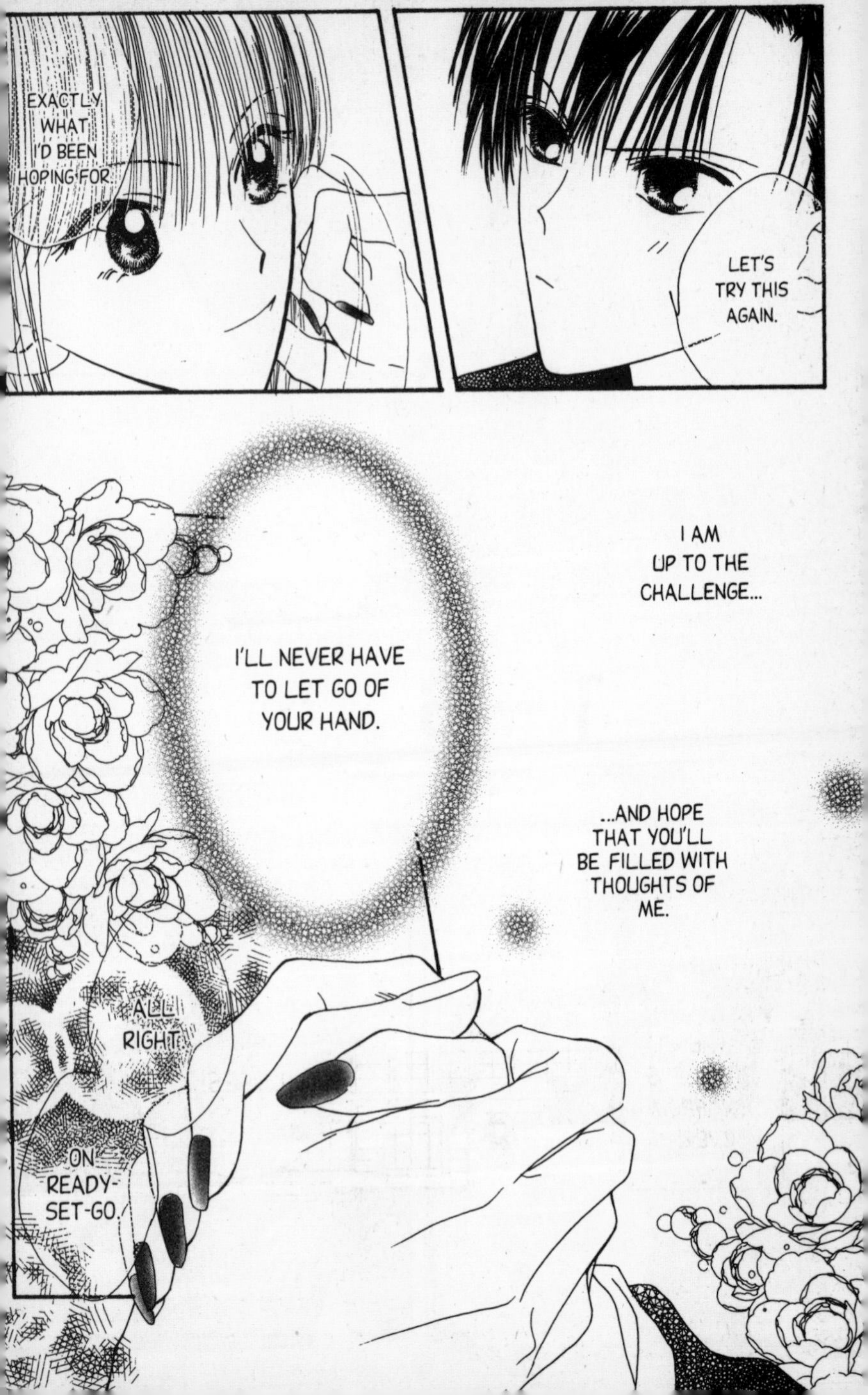
LET'S TRY THIS AGAIN.
EXACTLY WHAT I'D BEEN HOPING FOR.
I AM UP TO THE CHALLENGE...
...AND HOPE THAT YOU'LL BE FILLED WITH THOUGHTS OF ME.
I'LL NEVER HAVE TO LET GO OF YOUR HAND.
ALL RIGHT
ON READY-SET-GO.

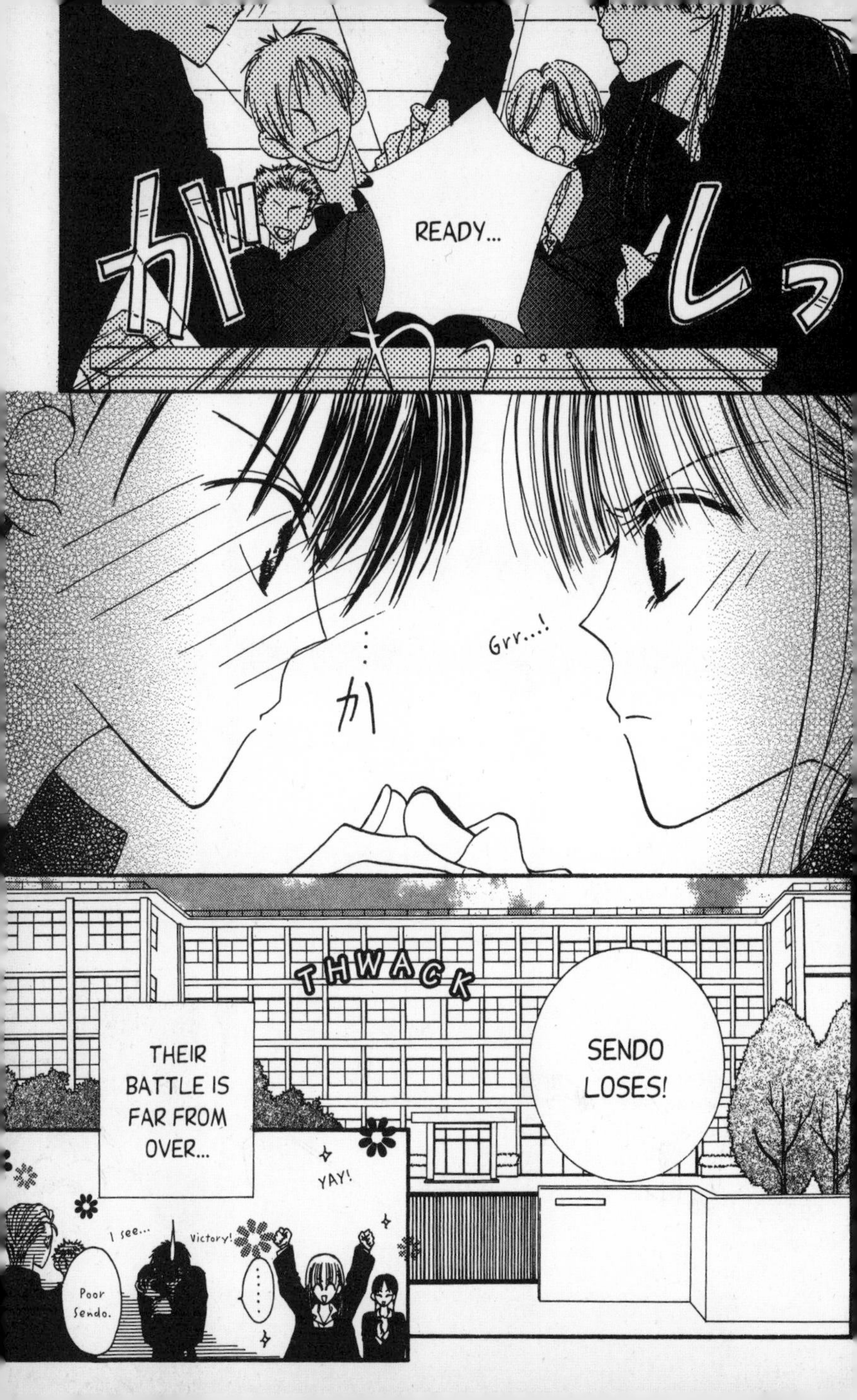
しっ
カッ
READY...
Grr...!
...
THWACK
SENDO LOSES!
THEIR BATTLE IS FAR FROM OVER...
YAY!
Victory!
......
I see...
Poor Sendo.

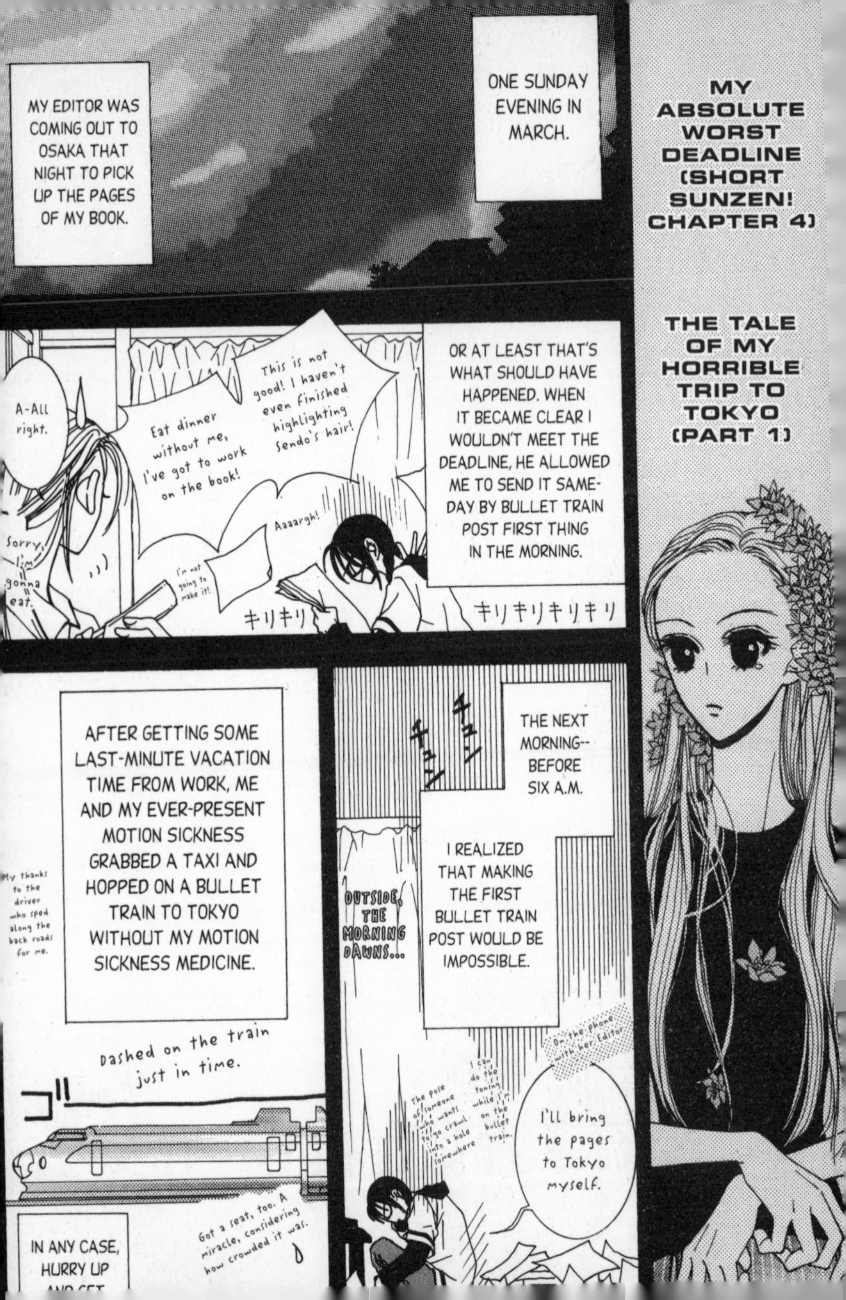
MY ABSOLUTE WORST DEADLINE (SHORT SUNZEN! CHAPTER 4)
THE TALE OF MY HORRIBLE TRIP TO TOKYO (PART 1)
ONE SUNDAY EVENING IN MARCH.
MY EDITOR WAS COMING OUT TO OSAKA THAT NIGHT TO PICK UP THE PAGES OF MY BOOK.
OR AT LEAST THAT'S WHAT SHOULD HAVE HAPPENED. WHEN IT BECAME CLEAR I WOULDN'T MEET THE DEADLINE, HE ALLOWED ME TO SEND IT SAME-DAY BY BULLET TRAIN POST FIRST THING IN THE MORNING.
キリキリキリキリ
This is not good! I haven't even finished highlighting Sendo's hair!
Eat dinner without me, I've got to work on the book!
Aaaargh!
I'm not going to make it!
キリキリ
A-All right.
Sorry, I'm gonna eat.
THE NEXT MORNING-- BEFORE SIX A.M.
I REALIZED THAT MAKING THE FIRST BULLET TRAIN POST WOULD BE IMPOSSIBLE.
OUTSIDE, THE MORNING DAWNS...
On the phone with her Editor
I'll bring the pages to Tokyo myself.
I can do the toning while I'm on the bullet train.
The pose of someone who wants to go crawl into a hole somewhere
AFTER GETTING SOME LAST-MINUTE VACATION TIME FROM WORK, ME AND MY EVER-PRESENT MOTION SICKNESS GRABBED A TAXI AND HOPPED ON A BULLET TRAIN TO TOKYO WITHOUT MY MOTION SICKNESS MEDICINE.
My thanks to the driver who sped along the back roads for me.
Dashed on the train just in time.
Got a seat, too. A miracle, considering how crowded it was.
IN ANY CASE, HURRY UP

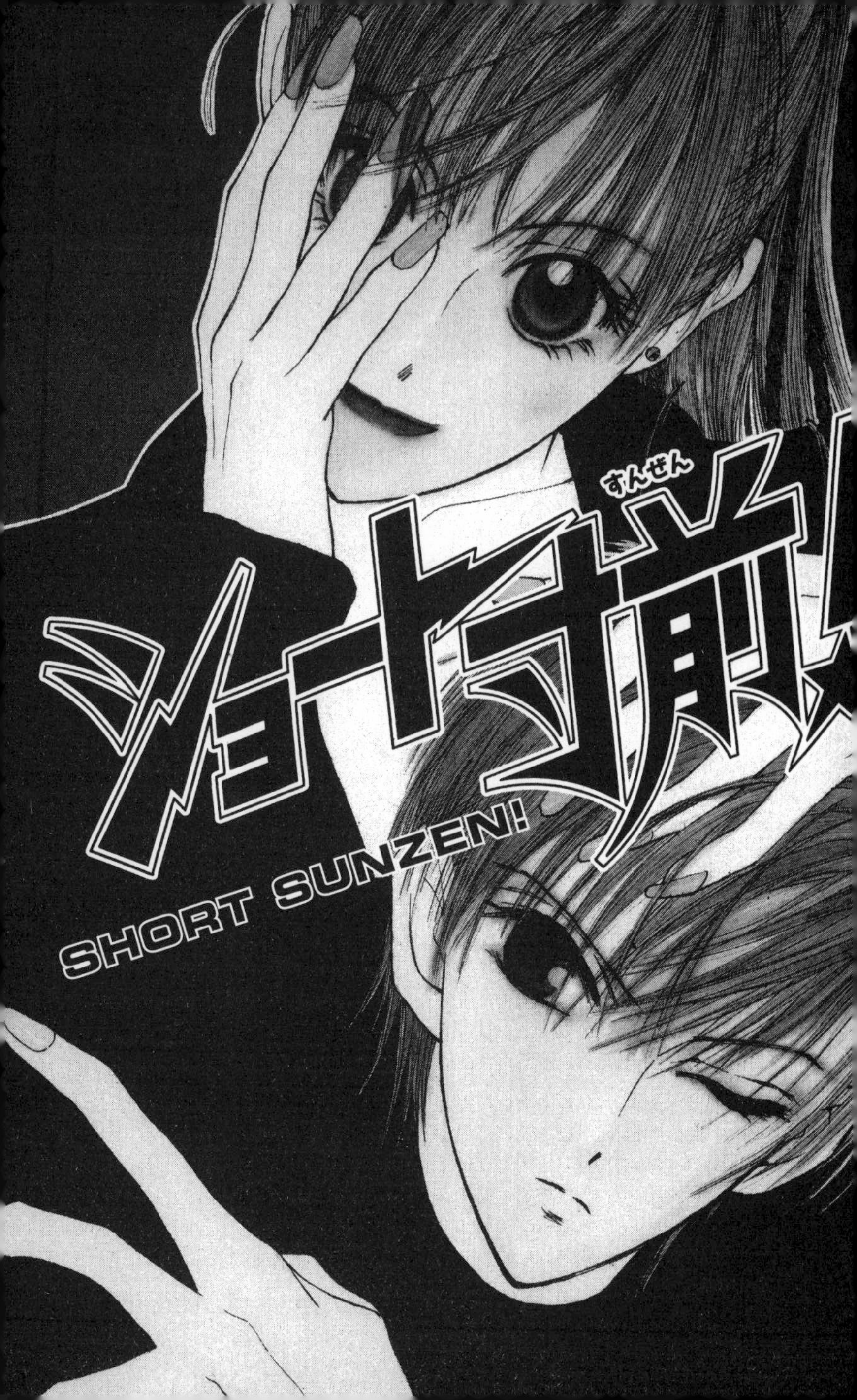
すんぜん
ショート寸前!
SHORT SUNZEN!

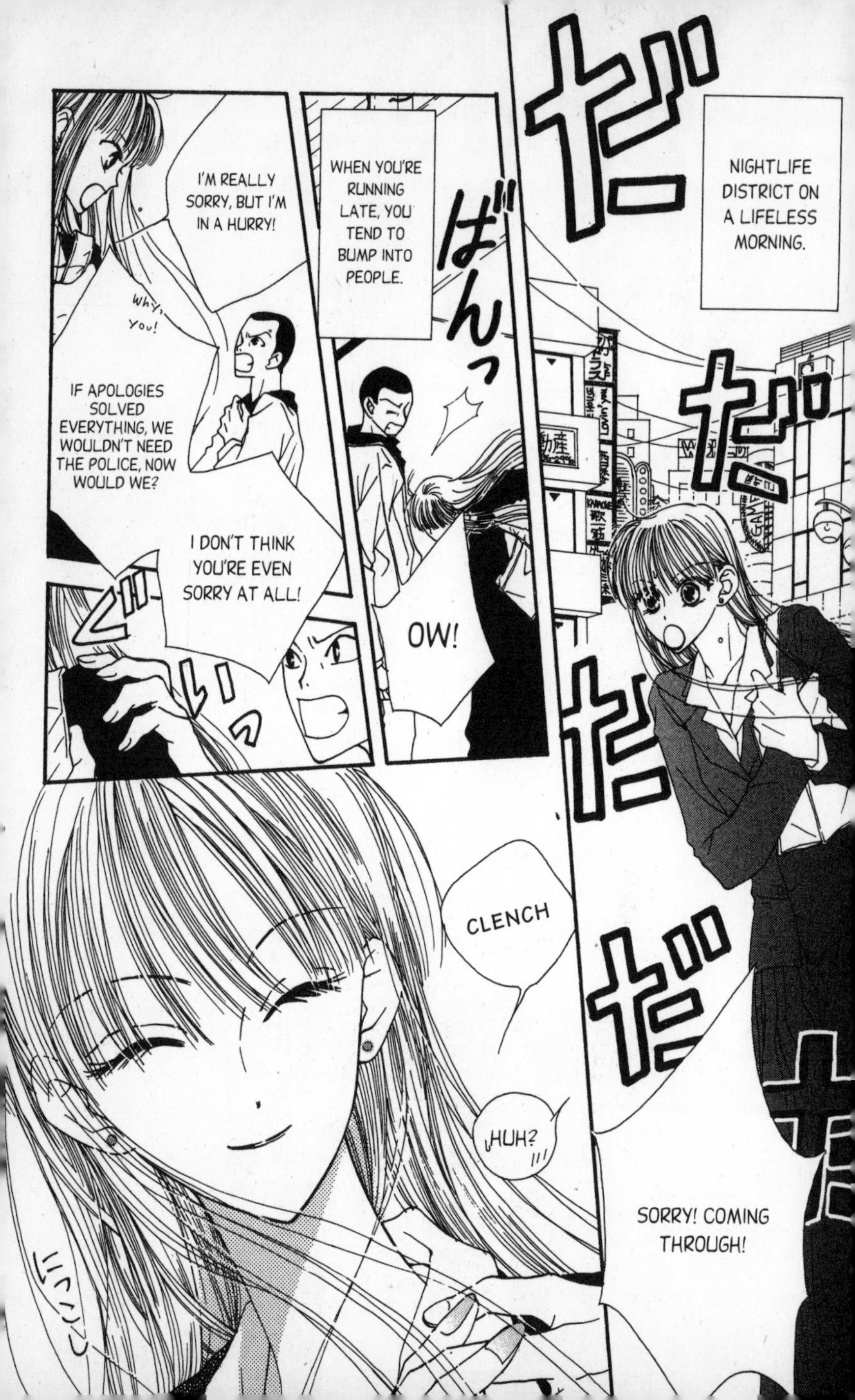
NIGHTLIFE DISTRICT ON A LIFELESS MORNING.
SORRY! COMING THROUGH!
WHEN YOU'RE RUNNING LATE, YOU TEND TO BUMP INTO PEOPLE.
ばんっ
OW!
I'M REALLY SORRY, BUT I'M IN A HURRY!
Why, you!
IF APOLOGIES SOLVED EVERYTHING, WE WOULDN'T NEED THE POLICE, NOW WOULD WE?
I DON'T THINK YOU'RE EVEN SORRY AT ALL!
CLENCH
HUH?

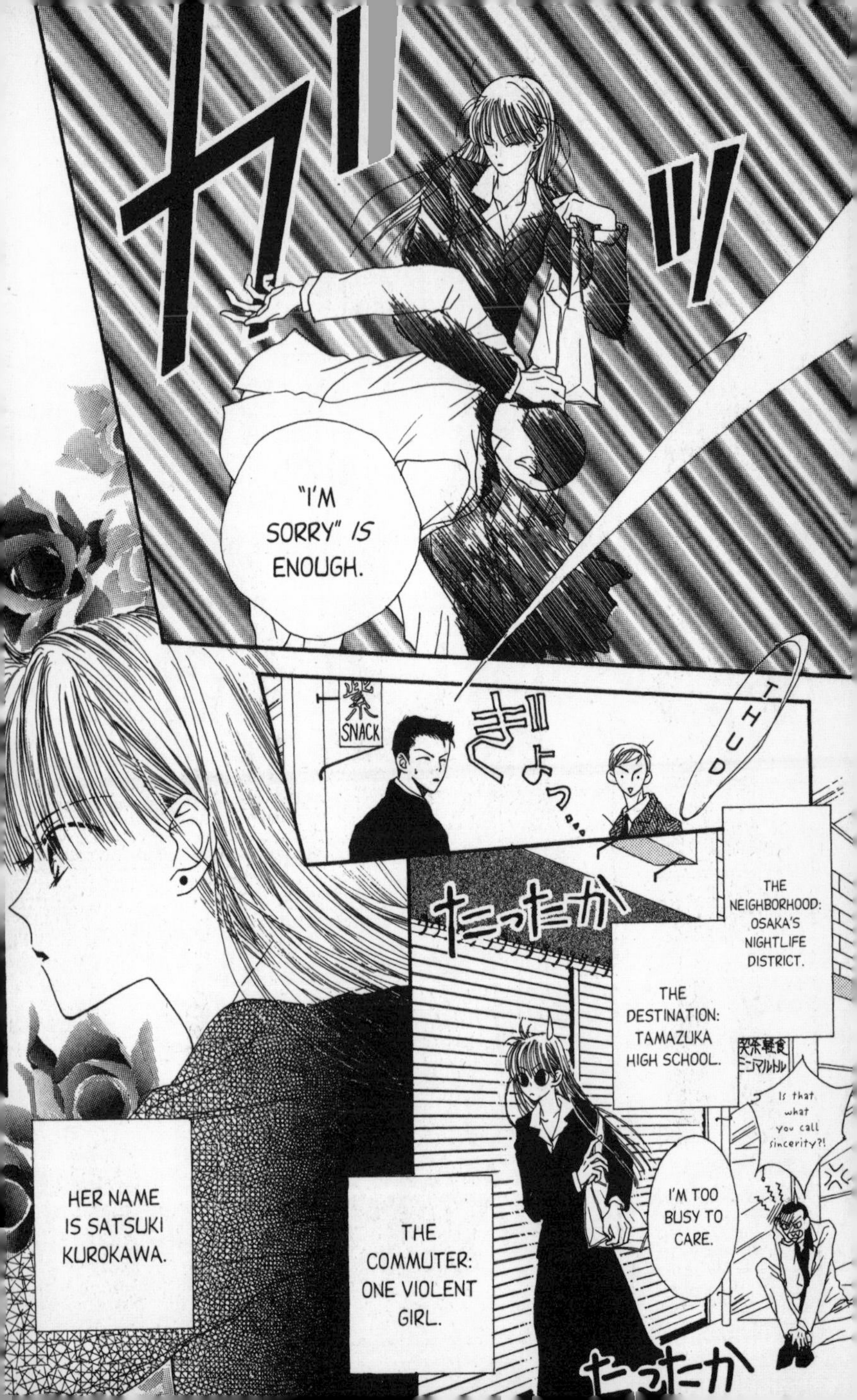
"I'M SORRY" IS ENOUGH.
SNACK
THUD
ぎょっ...
たったか
THE NEIGHBORHOOD: OSAKA'S NIGHTLIFE DISTRICT.
THE DESTINATION: TAMAZUKA HIGH SCHOOL.
Is that what you call sincerity?!
I'M TOO BUSY TO CARE.
THE COMMUTER: ONE VIOLENT GIRL.
HER NAME IS SATSUKI KUROKAWA.
たったか

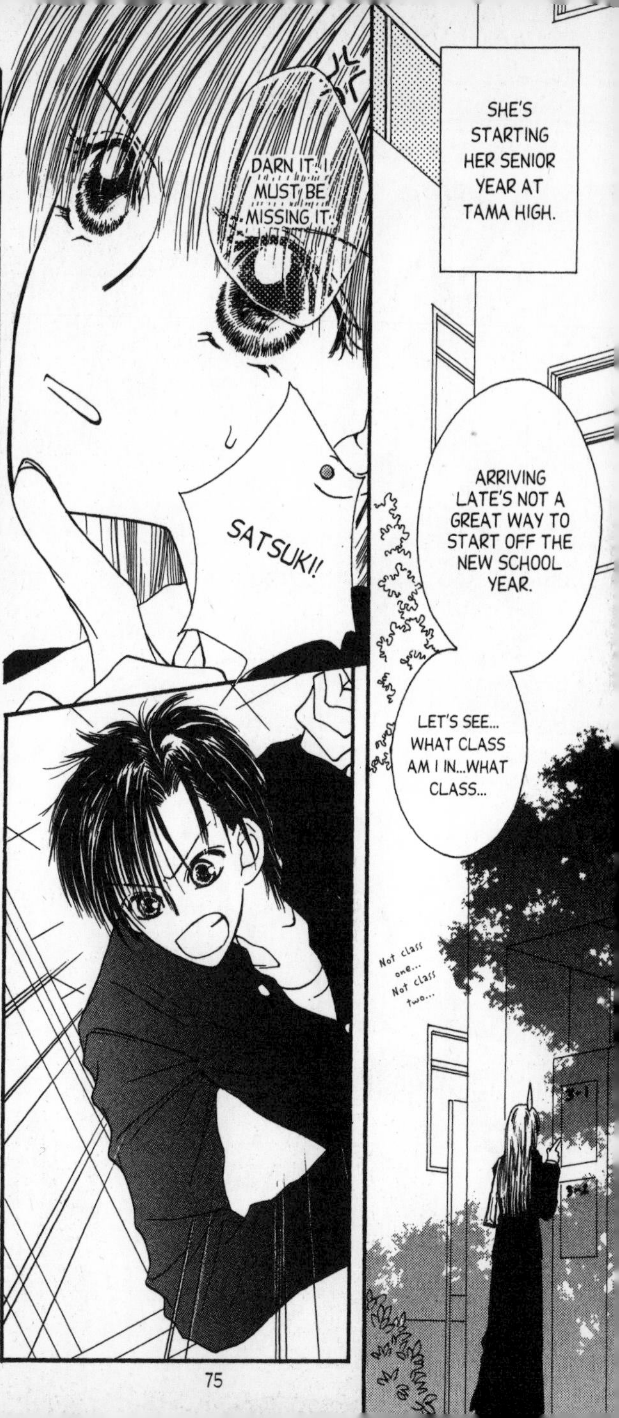
SHE'S STARTING HER SENIOR YEAR AT TAMA HIGH.
ARRIVING LATE'S NOT A GREAT WAY TO START OFF THE NEW SCHOOL YEAR.
LET'S SEE... WHAT CLASS AM I IN...WHAT CLASS...
Not class one... Not class two...
DARN IT. I MUST BE MISSING IT.
SATSUKI!!

WARDROBE

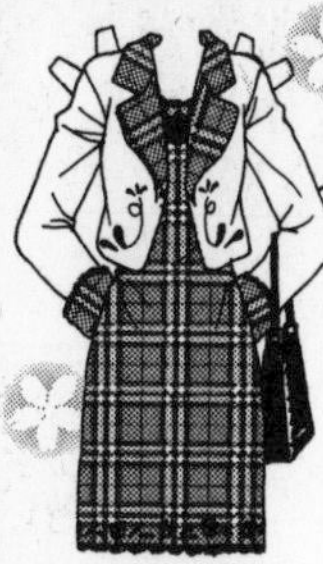

I love plaid and flower patterns! It's fun dressing Satsuki up all cute.

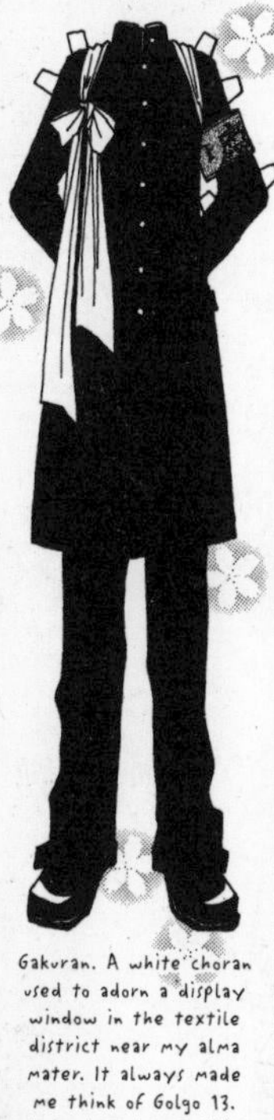

Gakuran. A white choran used to adorn a display window in the textile district near my alma mater. It always made me think of Golgo 13. I wonder why. To this day, I've still never seen a uniform more striking than that one.

Note: See Page 194

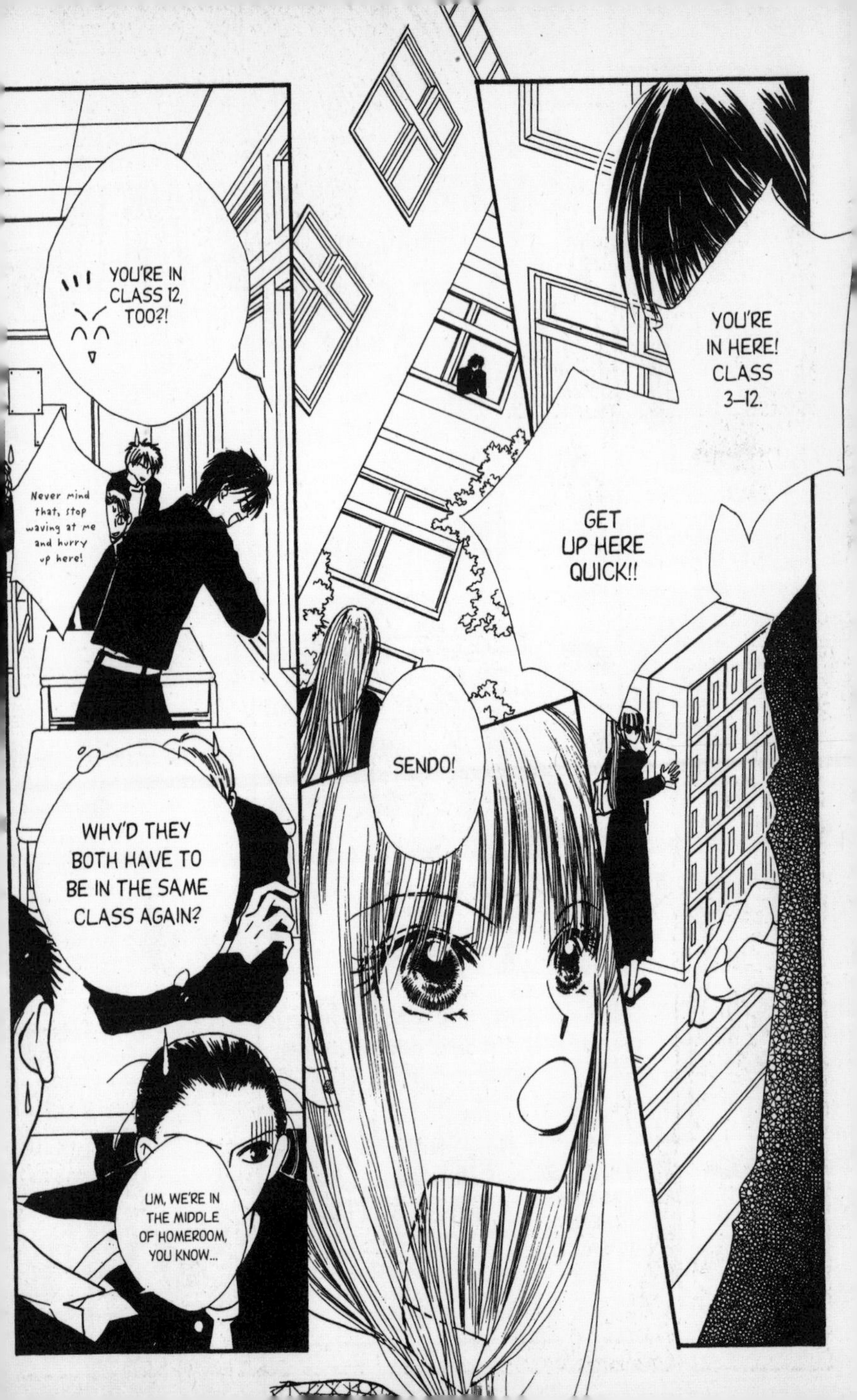
YOU'RE IN HERE! CLASS 3–12.
GET UP HERE QUICK!!
SENDO!
YOU'RE IN CLASS 12, TOO?!
Never mind that, stop waving at me and hurry up here!
WHY'D THEY BOTH HAVE TO BE IN THE SAME CLASS AGAIN?
UM, WE'RE IN THE MIDDLE OF HOMEROOM, YOU KNOW...

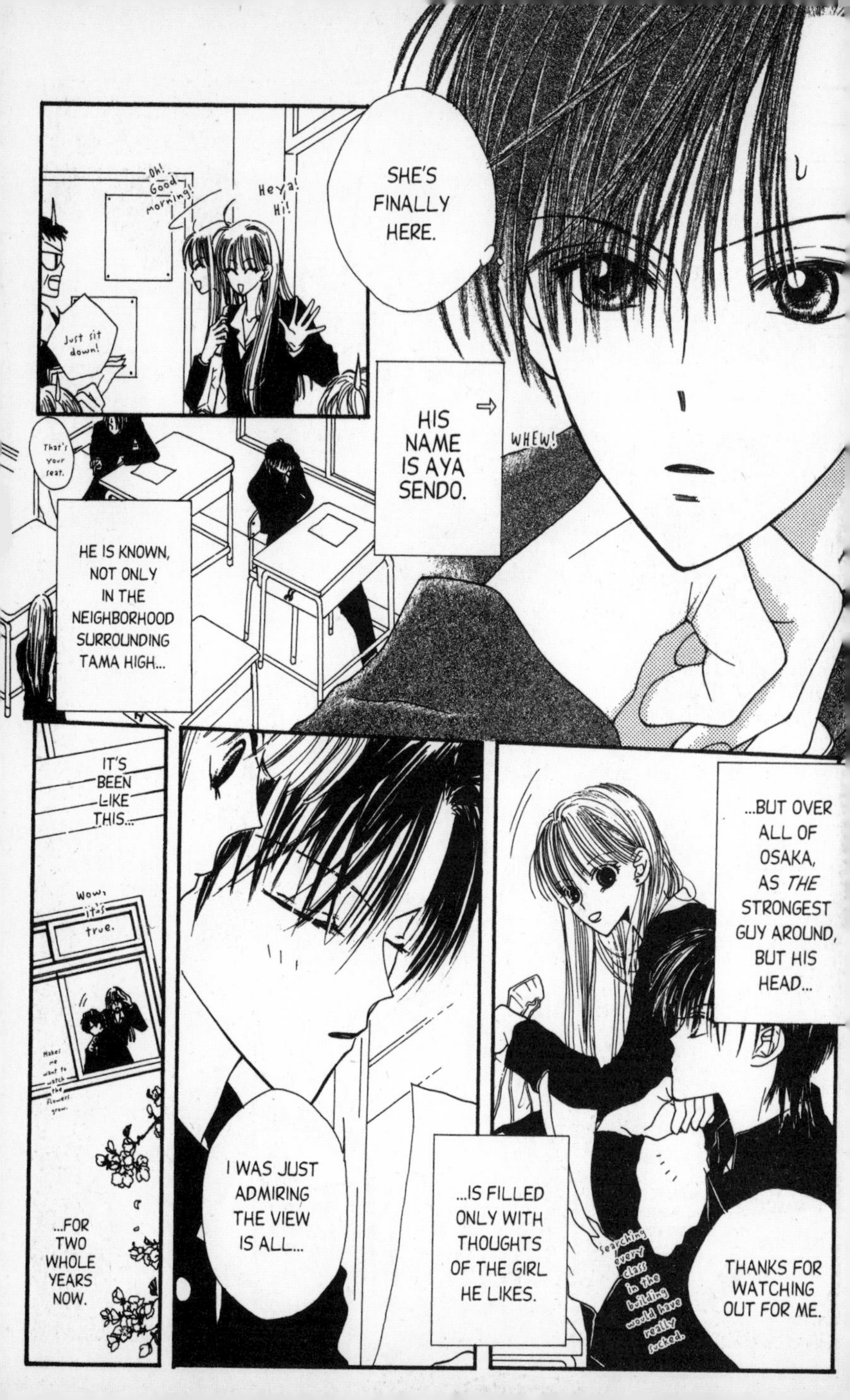
SHE'S FINALLY HERE.
HIS NAME IS AYA SENDO.
WHEW!
Oh! Good morning!
Heya! Hi!
Just sit down!
That's your seat.
HE IS KNOWN, NOT ONLY IN THE NEIGHBORHOOD SURROUNDING TAMA HIGH...
...BUT OVER ALL OF OSAKA, AS *THE* STRONGEST GUY AROUND, BUT HIS HEAD...
THANKS FOR WATCHING OUT FOR ME.
Searching every class in the building would have really sucked.
...IS FILLED ONLY WITH THOUGHTS OF THE GIRL HE LIKES.
I WAS JUST ADMIRING THE VIEW IS ALL...
IT'S BEEN LIKE THIS...
Wow, it's true.
Makes me want to watch the flowers grow.
...FOR TWO WHOLE YEARS NOW.

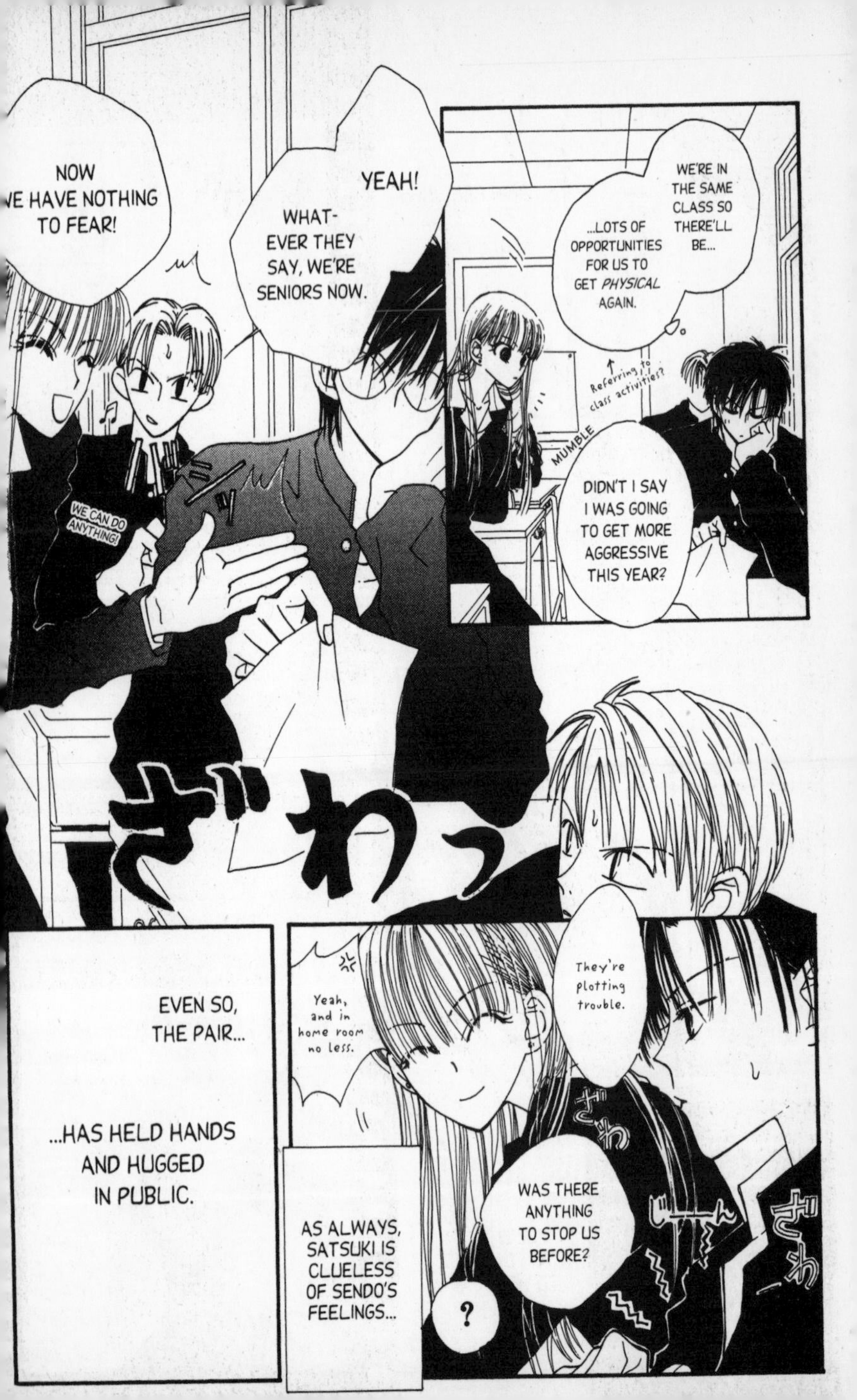
WE'RE IN THE SAME CLASS SO THERE'LL BE...
...LOTS OF OPPORTUNITIES FOR US TO GET *PHYSICAL* AGAIN.
Referring to class activities?
MUMBLE
DIDN'T I SAY I WAS GOING TO GET MORE AGGRESSIVE THIS YEAR?
YEAH!
WHATEVER THEY SAY, WE'RE SENIORS NOW.
NOW WE HAVE NOTHING TO FEAR!
WE CAN DO ANYTHING!
ざわっ
They're plotting trouble.
Yeah, and in home room no less.
WAS THERE ANYTHING TO STOP US BEFORE?
?
AS ALWAYS, SATSUKI IS CLUELESS OF SENDO'S FEELINGS...
EVEN SO, THE PAIR...
...HAS HELD HANDS AND HUGGED IN PUBLIC.

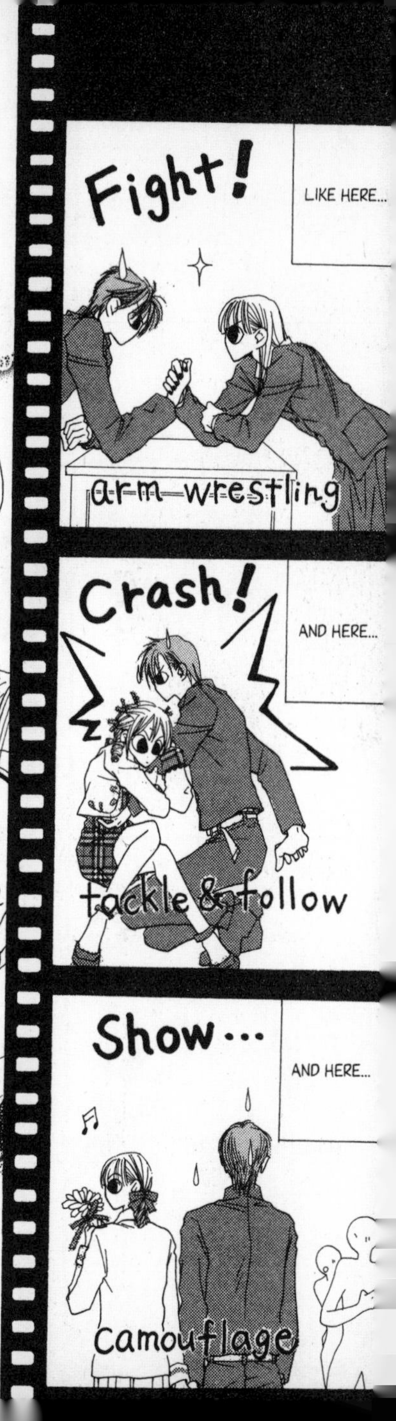
LIKE HERE...
Fight!
arm wrestling
AND HERE...
Crash!
tackle & follow
AND HERE...
Show...
camouflage

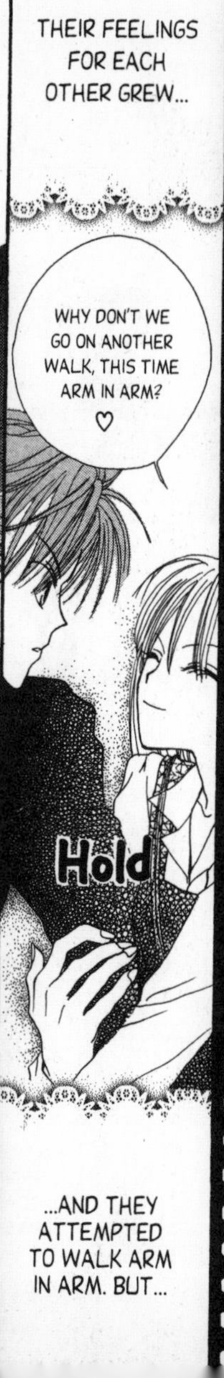
THEIR FEELINGS FOR EACH OTHER GREW...
WHY DON'T WE GO ON ANOTHER WALK, THIS TIME ARM IN ARM? ♡
Hold
...AND THEY ATTEMPTED TO WALK ARM IN ARM. BUT...

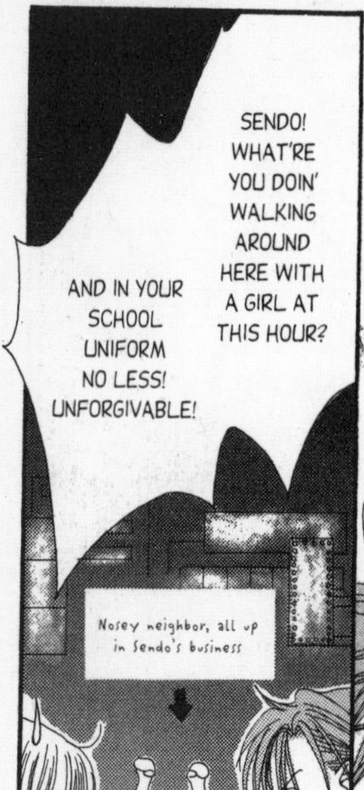
SENDO! WHAT'RE YOU DOIN' WALKING AROUND HERE WITH A GIRL AT THIS HOUR?
AND IN YOUR SCHOOL UNIFORM NO LESS! UNFORGIVABLE!
Nosey neighbor, all up in Sendo's business
What?!
ARGH!
That old fogey!

Note: See page 194

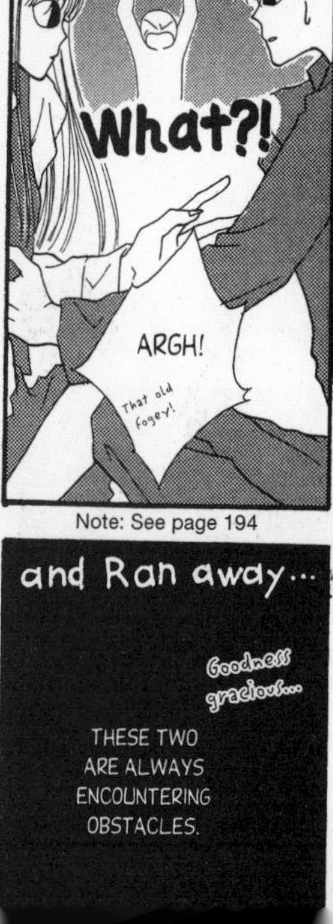
and Ran away...
Goodness gracious...
THESE TWO ARE ALWAYS ENCOUNTERING OBSTACLES.

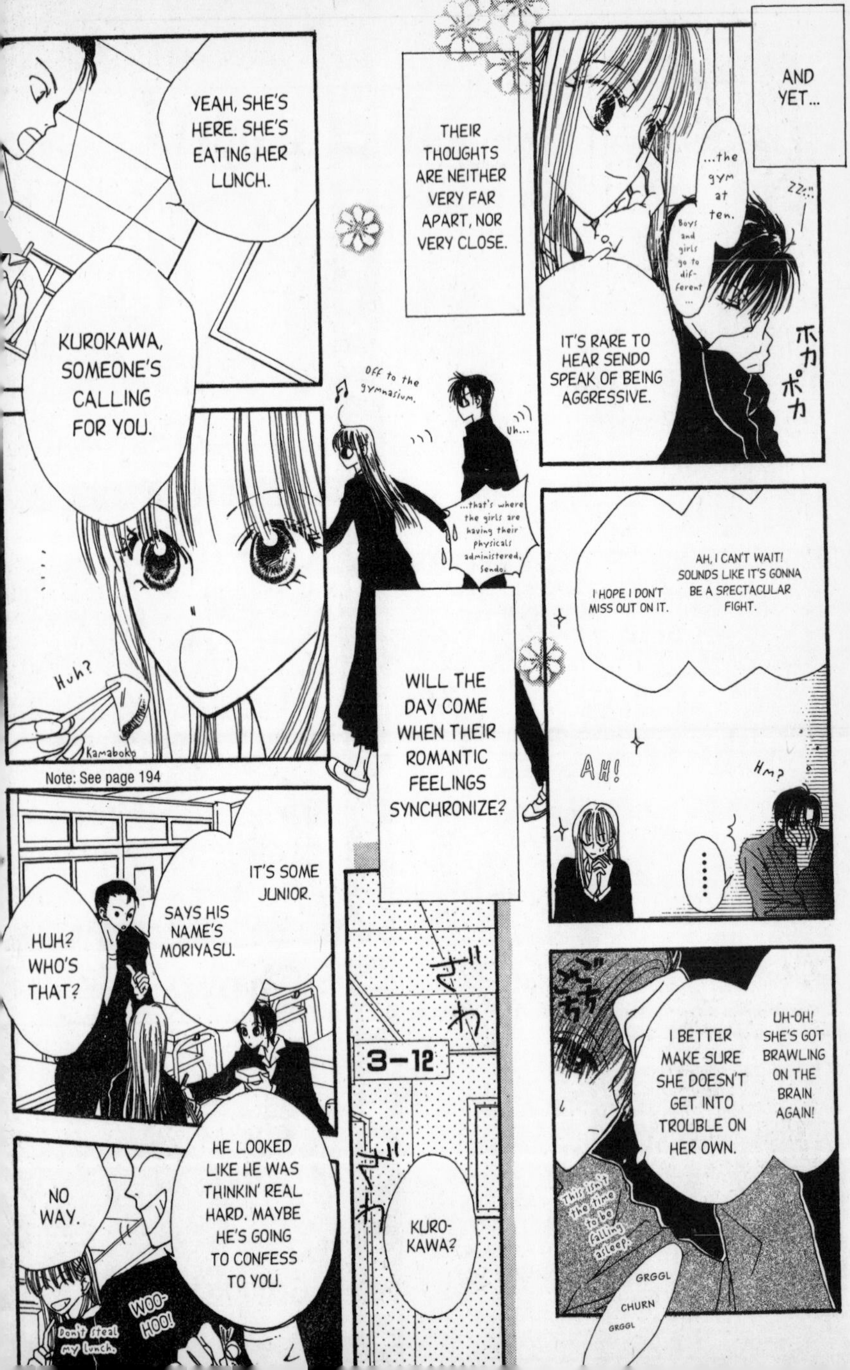
AND YET...
...the gym at ten.
Boys and girls go to different...
ZZZ...
IT'S RARE TO HEAR SENDO SPEAK OF BEING AGGRESSIVE.
ホカポカ
AH, I CAN'T WAIT! SOUNDS LIKE IT'S GONNA BE A SPECTACULAR FIGHT.
I HOPE I DON'T MISS OUT ON IT.
AH!
Hm?
......
UH-OH! SHE'S GOT BRAWLING ON THE BRAIN AGAIN!
I BETTER MAKE SURE SHE DOESN'T GET INTO TROUBLE ON HER OWN.
This isn't the time to be falling asleep.
GRGGL
CHURN
GRGGL
THEIR THOUGHTS ARE NEITHER VERY FAR APART, NOR VERY CLOSE.
Off to the gymnasium.
Uh...
...that's where the girls are having their physicals administered, Sendo.
WILL THE DAY COME WHEN THEIR ROMANTIC FEELINGS SYNCHRONIZE?
ざわ
ざわ
3-12
KURO-KAWA?
YEAH, SHE'S HERE. SHE'S EATING HER LUNCH.
KUROKAWA, SOMEONE'S CALLING FOR YOU.
Huh?
Kamaboko
IT'S SOME JUNIOR.
SAYS HIS NAME'S MORIYASU.
HUH? WHO'S THAT?
HE LOOKED LIKE HE WAS THINKIN' REAL HARD. MAYBE HE'S GOING TO CONFESS TO YOU.
NO WAY.
WOO-HOO!
Don't steal my lunch.

Note: See page 194

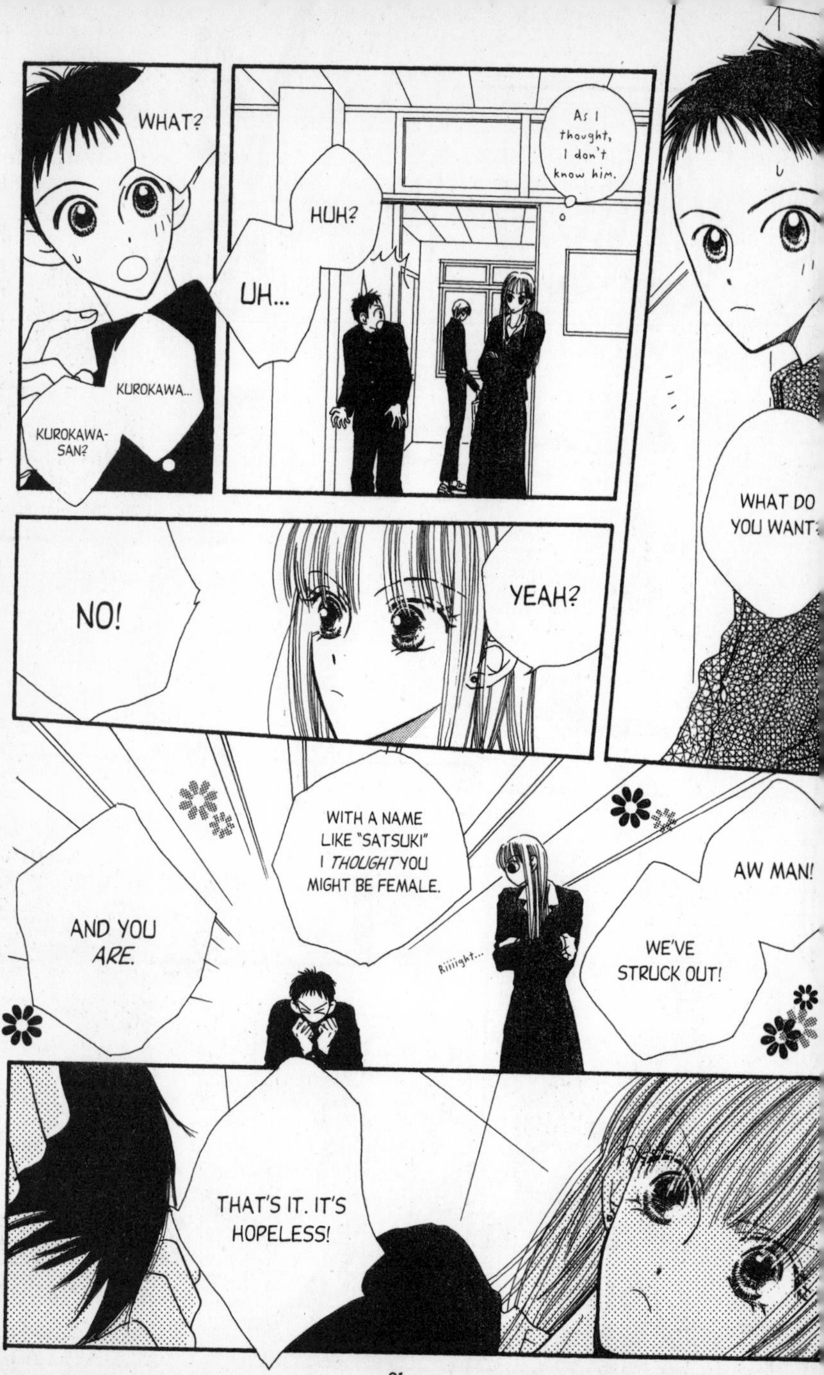
WHAT DO YOU WANT?
As I thought, I don't know him.
HUH?
UH...
WHAT?
KUROKAWA...
KUROKAWA-SAN?
YEAH?
NO!
AW MAN!
WE'VE STRUCK OUT!
Riiiight...
WITH A NAME LIKE "SATSUKI" I *THOUGHT* YOU MIGHT BE FEMALE.
AND YOU *ARE*.
THAT'S IT. IT'S HOPELESS!

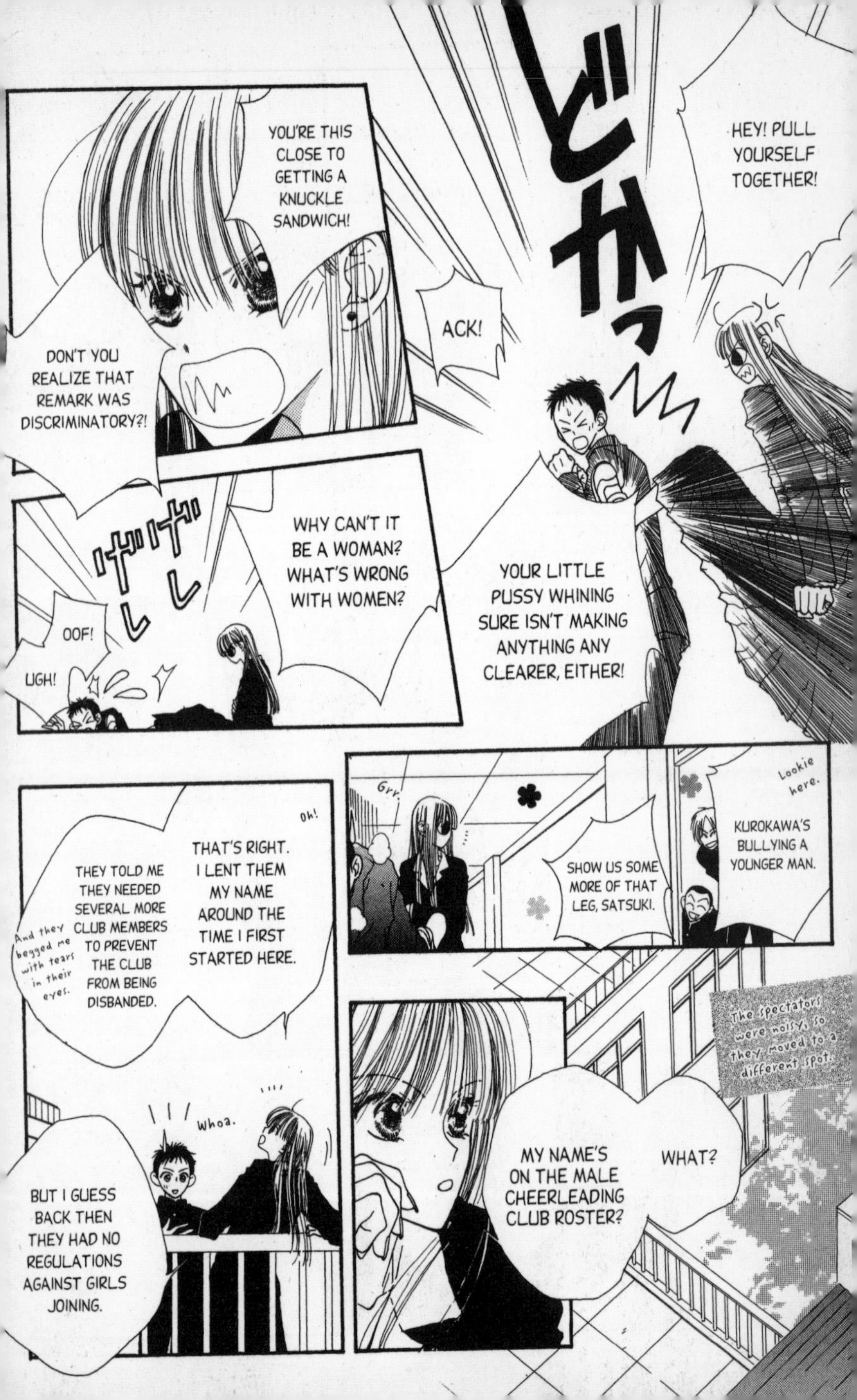
HEY! PULL YOURSELF TOGETHER!
どかっ
ACK!
YOUR LITTLE PUSSY WHINING SURE ISN'T MAKING ANYTHING ANY CLEARER, EITHER!
YOU'RE THIS CLOSE TO GETTING A KNUCKLE SANDWICH!
DON'T YOU REALIZE THAT REMARK WAS DISCRIMINATORY?!
WHY CAN'T IT BE A WOMAN? WHAT'S WRONG WITH WOMEN?
げしげし
OOF!
UGH!
Lookie here.
KUROKAWA'S BULLYING A YOUNGER MAN.
SHOW US SOME MORE OF THAT LEG, SATSUKI.
Grr.
The spectators were noisy, so they moved to a different spot.
WHAT?
MY NAME'S ON THE MALE CHEERLEADING CLUB ROSTER?
Oh!
THAT'S RIGHT. I LENT THEM MY NAME AROUND THE TIME I FIRST STARTED HERE.
THEY TOLD ME THEY NEEDED SEVERAL MORE CLUB MEMBERS TO PREVENT THE CLUB FROM BEING DISBANDED.
And they begged me with tears in their eyes.
Whoa.
BUT I GUESS BACK THEN THEY HAD NO REGULATIONS AGAINST GIRLS JOINING.

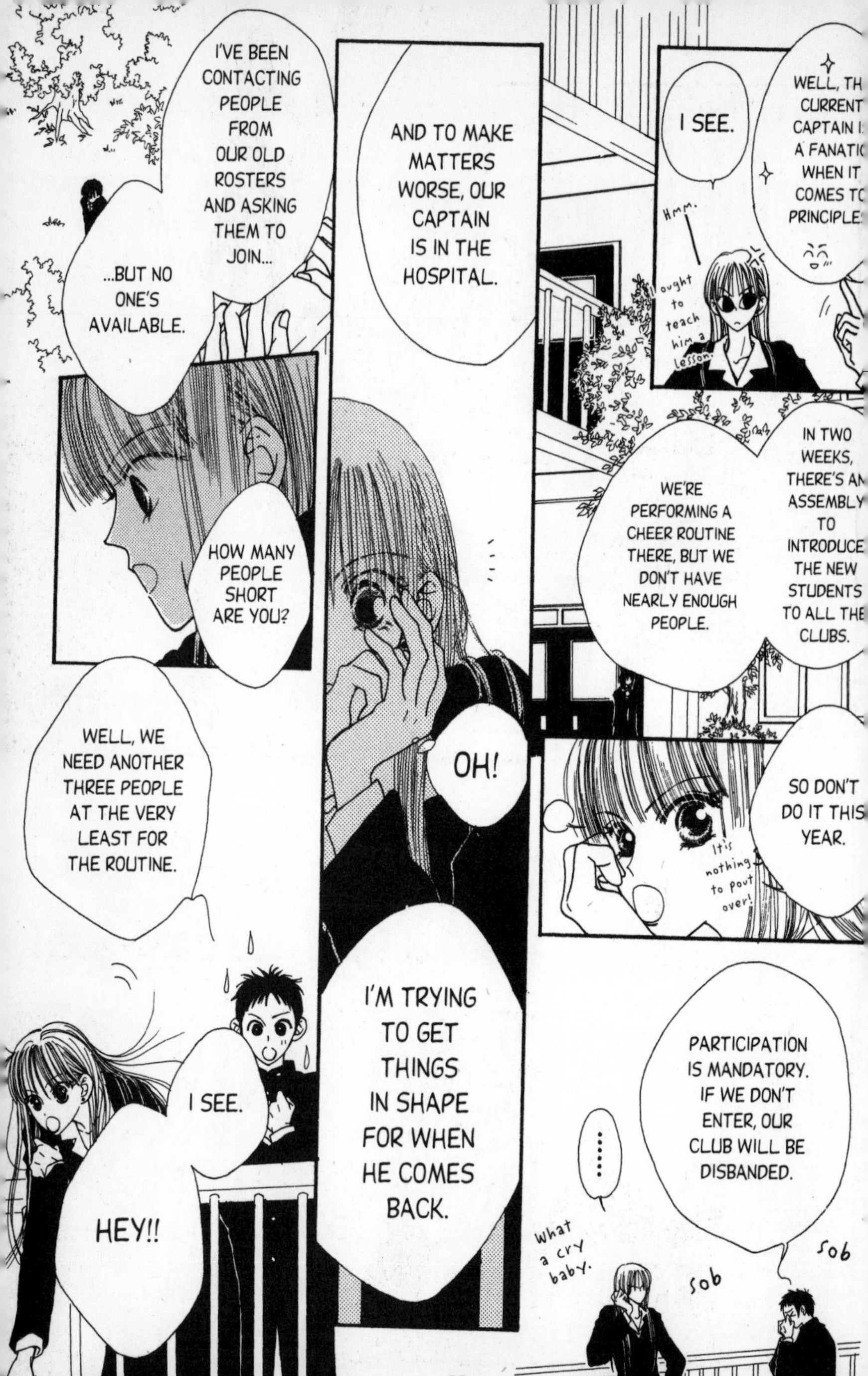
WELL, TH CURRENT CAPTAIN I A FANATI WHEN IT COMES T PRINCIPLE
I SEE.
Hmm.
I ought to teach him a lesson.
IN TWO WEEKS, THERE'S A ASSEMBLY TO INTRODUCE THE NEW STUDENTS TO ALL THE CLUBS.
WE'RE PERFORMING A CHEER ROUTINE THERE, BUT WE DON'T HAVE NEARLY ENOUGH PEOPLE.
SO DON'T DO IT THIS YEAR.
It's nothing to pout over!
PARTICIPATION IS MANDATORY. IF WE DON'T ENTER, OUR CLUB WILL BE DISBANDED.
……
sob
sob
What a cry baby.
AND TO MAKE MATTERS WORSE, OUR CAPTAIN IS IN THE HOSPITAL.
OH!
I'M TRYING TO GET THINGS IN SHAPE FOR WHEN HE COMES BACK.
I'VE BEEN CONTACTING PEOPLE FROM OUR OLD ROSTERS AND ASKING THEM TO JOIN...
...BUT NO ONE'S AVAILABLE.
HOW MANY PEOPLE SHORT ARE YOU?
WELL, WE NEED ANOTHER THREE PEOPLE AT THE VERY LEAST FOR THE ROUTINE.
I SEE.
HEY!!

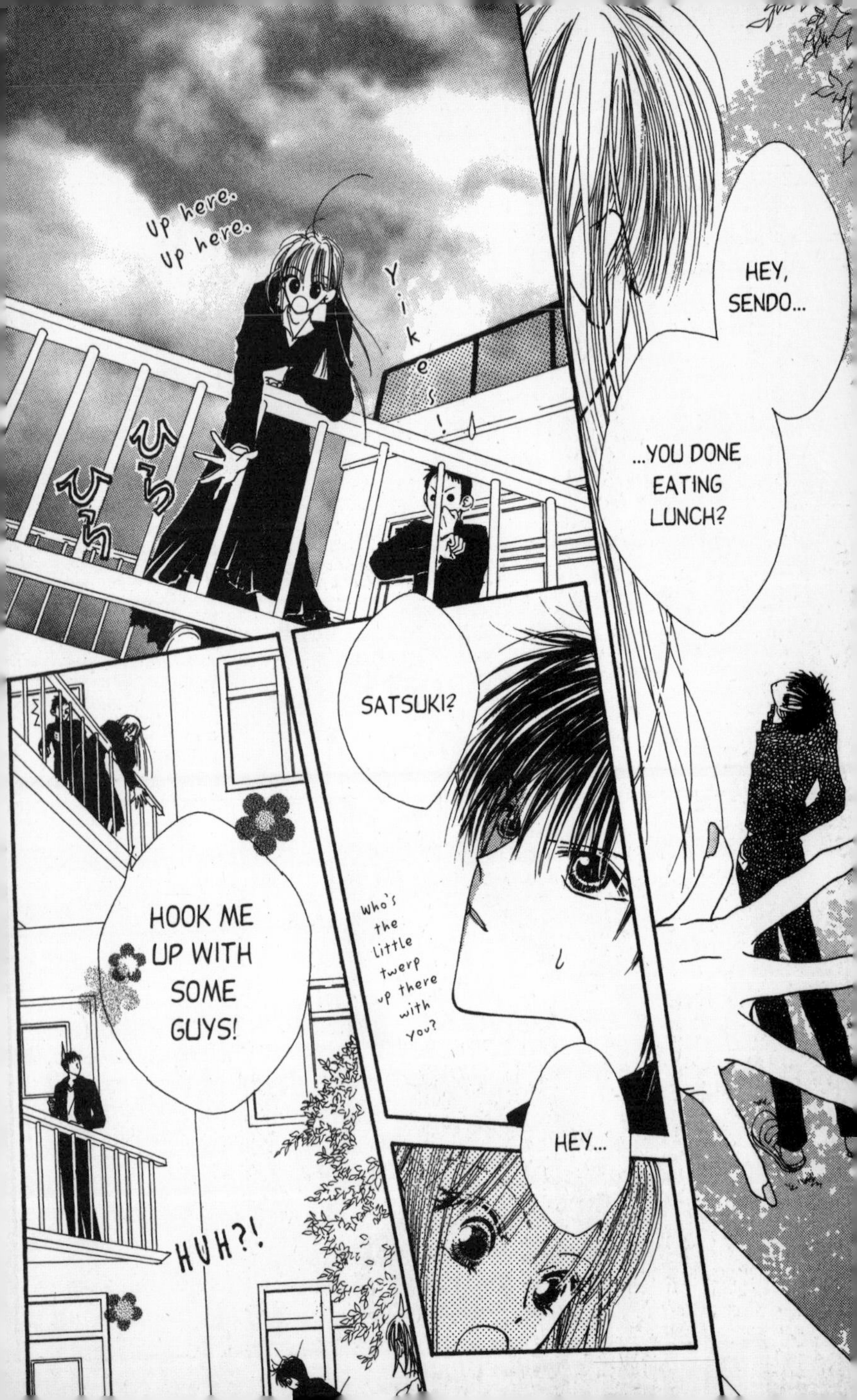
HEY, SENDO...
...YOU DONE EATING LUNCH?
up here. up here.
ひら ひら
Yikes!
SATSUKI?
who's the little twerp up there with you?
HEY...
HOOK ME UP WITH SOME GUYS!
HUH?!

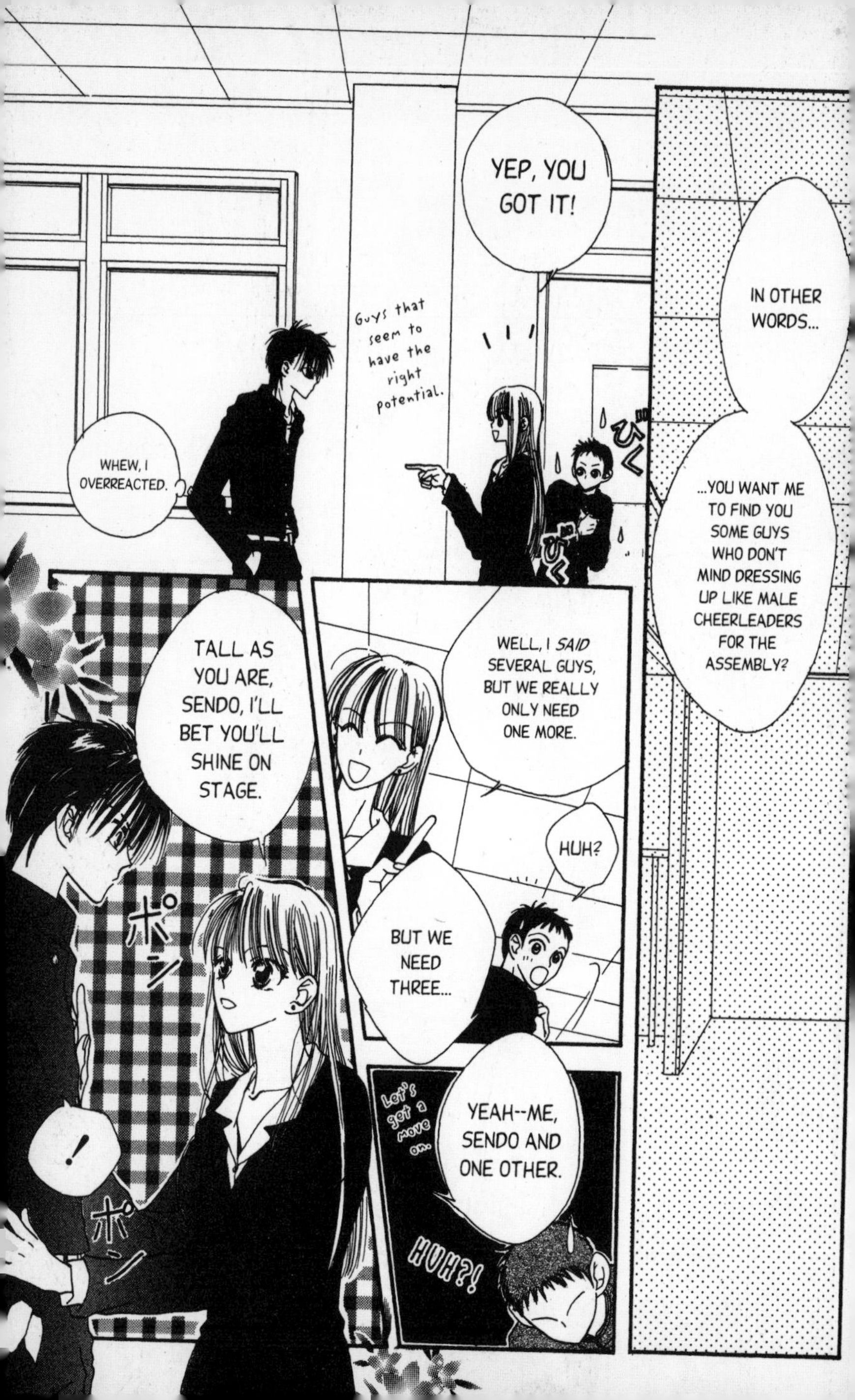

IN OTHER WORDS...
...YOU WANT ME TO FIND YOU SOME GUYS WHO DON'T MIND DRESSING UP LIKE MALE CHEERLEADERS FOR THE ASSEMBLY?
YEP, YOU GOT IT!
Guys that seem to have the right potential.
びく
びく
WHEW, I OVERREACTED.
WELL, I *SAID* SEVERAL GUYS, BUT WE REALLY ONLY NEED ONE MORE.
HUH?
BUT WE NEED THREE...
YEAH--ME, SENDO AND ONE OTHER.
Let's get a move on.
HUH?!
TALL AS YOU ARE, SENDO, I'LL BET YOU'LL SHINE ON STAGE.
ポーン
!
ポーン

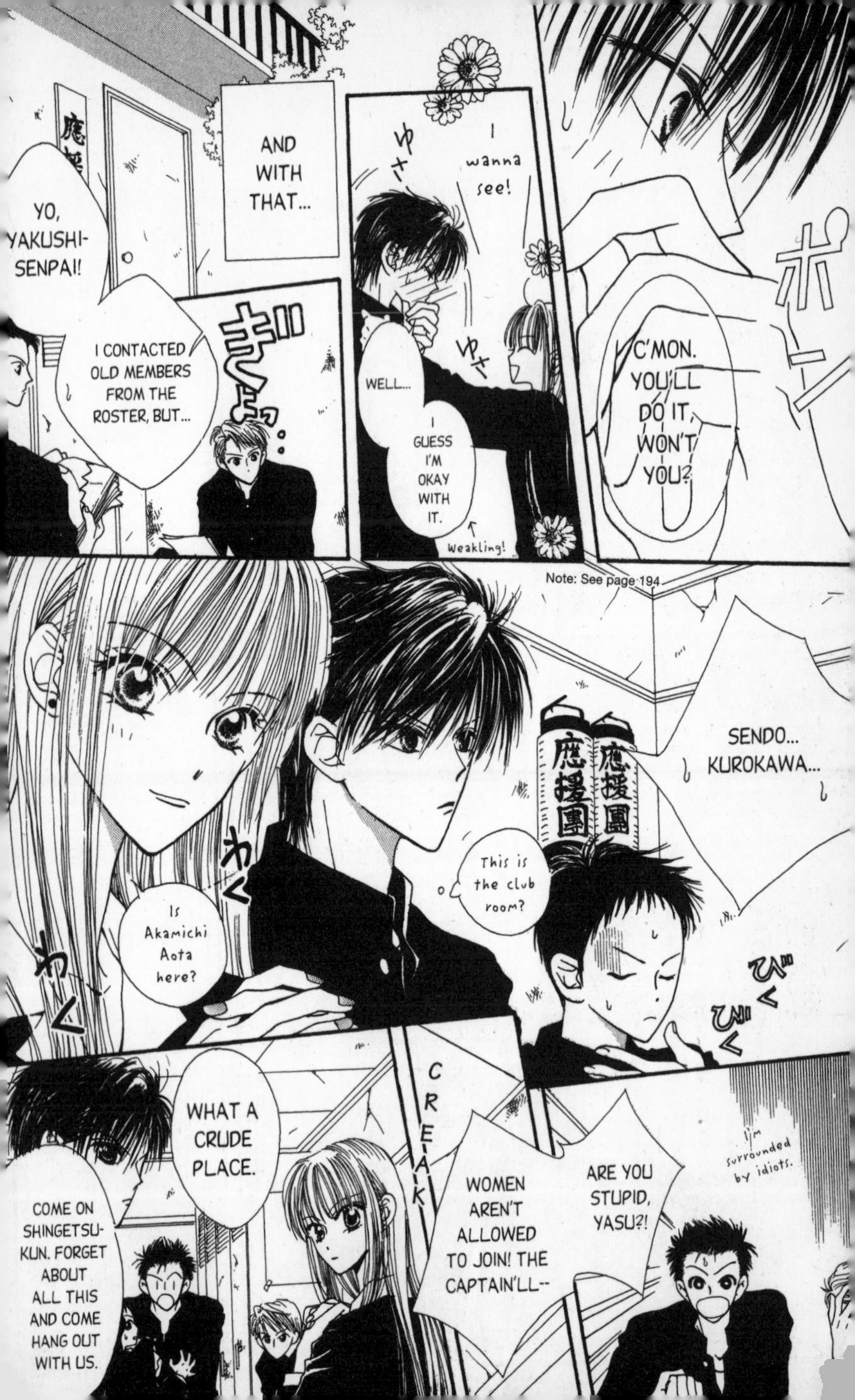
ポー
C'MON. YOU'LL DO IT, WON'T YOU?
I wanna see!
ゆさ
ゆさ
WELL...
I GUESS I'M OKAY WITH IT.
Weakling!
AND WITH THAT...
應援
YO, YAKUSHI-SENPAI!
I CONTACTED OLD MEMBERS FROM THE ROSTER, BUT...
きょ
Note: See page 194
SENDO... KUROKAWA...
びく
びく
應援團
應援團
This is the club room?
Is Akamichi Aota here?
わく
わく
I'm surrounded by idiots.
ARE YOU STUPID, YASU?!
WOMEN AREN'T ALLOWED TO JOIN! THE CAPTAIN'LL--
CREAK
WHAT A CRUDE PLACE.
COME ON SHINGETSU-KUN. FORGET ABOUT ALL THIS AND COME HANG OUT WITH US.

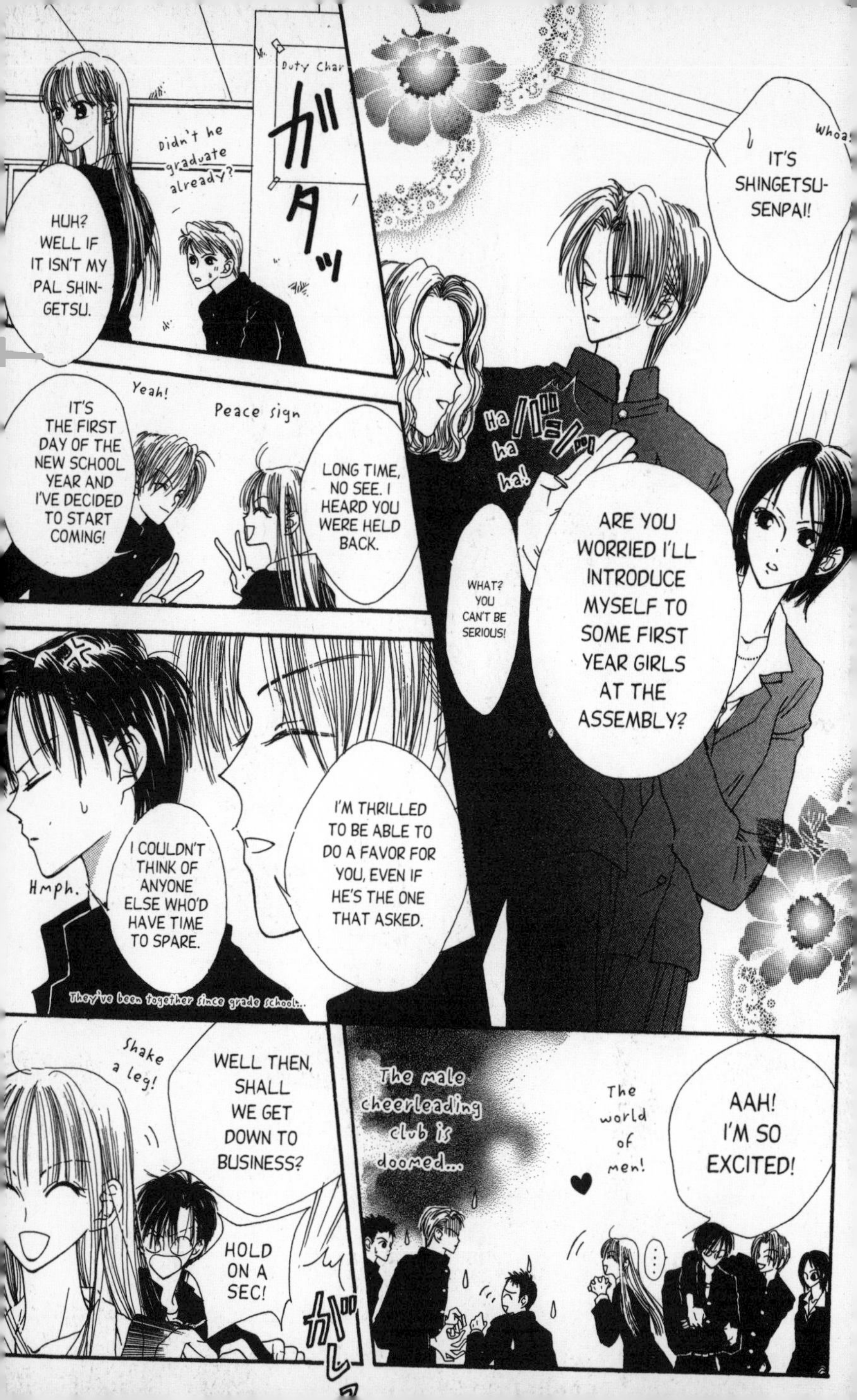
Whoa!
IT'S SHINGETSU-SENPAI!
Ha ha ha!
ARE YOU WORRIED I'LL INTRODUCE MYSELF TO SOME FIRST YEAR GIRLS AT THE ASSEMBLY?
WHAT? YOU CAN'T BE SERIOUS!
Duty Char
ガタッ
Didn't he graduate already?
HUH? WELL IF IT ISN'T MY PAL SHIN-GETSU.
LONG TIME, NO SEE. I HEARD YOU WERE HELD BACK.
Peace sign
Yeah!
IT'S THE FIRST DAY OF THE NEW SCHOOL YEAR AND I'VE DECIDED TO START COMING!
I'M THRILLED TO BE ABLE TO DO A FAVOR FOR YOU, EVEN IF HE'S THE ONE THAT ASKED.
I COULDN'T THINK OF ANYONE ELSE WHO'D HAVE TIME TO SPARE.
Hmph.
They've been together since grade school...
AAH! I'M SO EXCITED!
The world of men!
The male cheerleading club is doomed...
WELL THEN, SHALL WE GET DOWN TO BUSINESS?
Shake a leg!
HOLD ON A SEC!

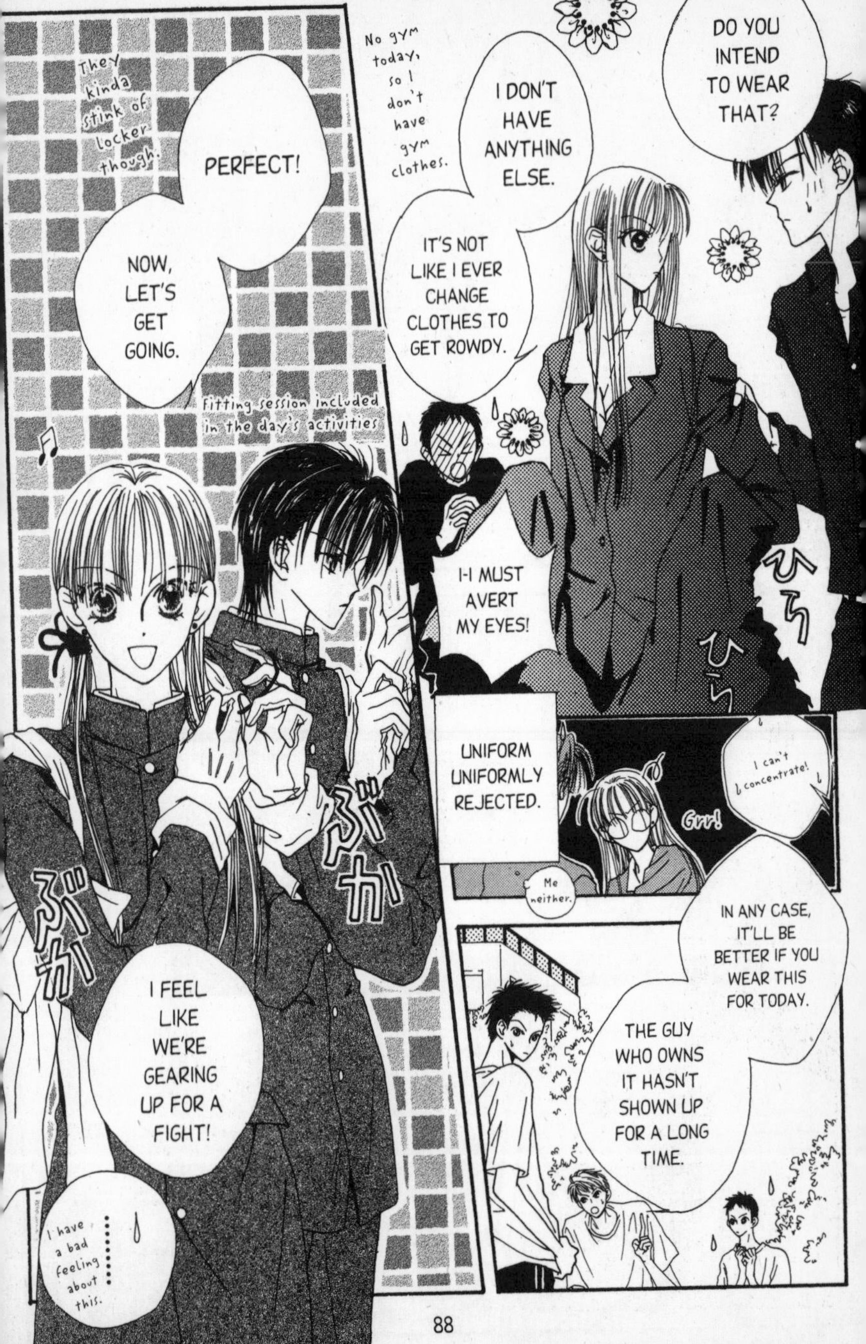
DO YOU INTEND TO WEAR THAT?
I DON'T HAVE ANYTHING ELSE.
No gym today, so I don't have gym clothes.
IT'S NOT LIKE I EVER CHANGE CLOTHES TO GET ROWDY.
I-I MUST AVERT MY EYES!
ひら
ひら
UNIFORM UNIFORMLY REJECTED.
I can't concentrate!
Grr!
Me neither.
IN ANY CASE, IT'LL BE BETTER IF YOU WEAR THIS FOR TODAY.
THE GUY WHO OWNS IT HASN'T SHOWN UP FOR A LONG TIME.
They kinda stink of locker though.
PERFECT!
NOW, LET'S GET GOING.
Fitting session included in the day's activities
ぶか
ぶか
I FEEL LIKE WE'RE GEARING UP FOR A FIGHT!
I have a bad feeling about this......

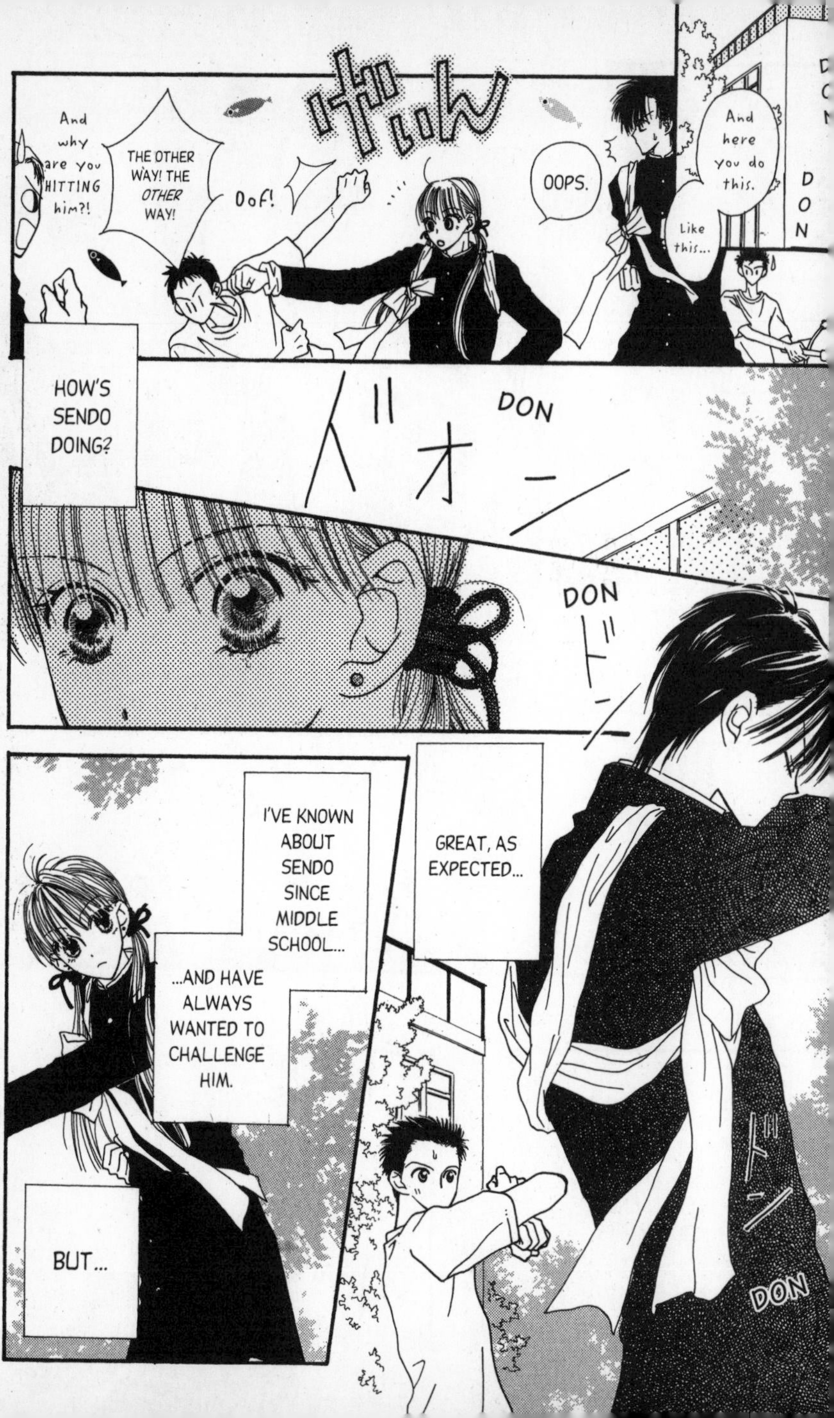
DON
And here you do this.
Like this...
OOPS.
Oof!
THE OTHER WAY! THE OTHER WAY!
And why are you HITTING him?!
HOW'S SENDO DOING?
DON
DON
GREAT, AS EXPECTED...
I'VE KNOWN ABOUT SENDO SINCE MIDDLE SCHOOL...
...AND HAVE ALWAYS WANTED TO CHALLENGE HIM.
DON
BUT...

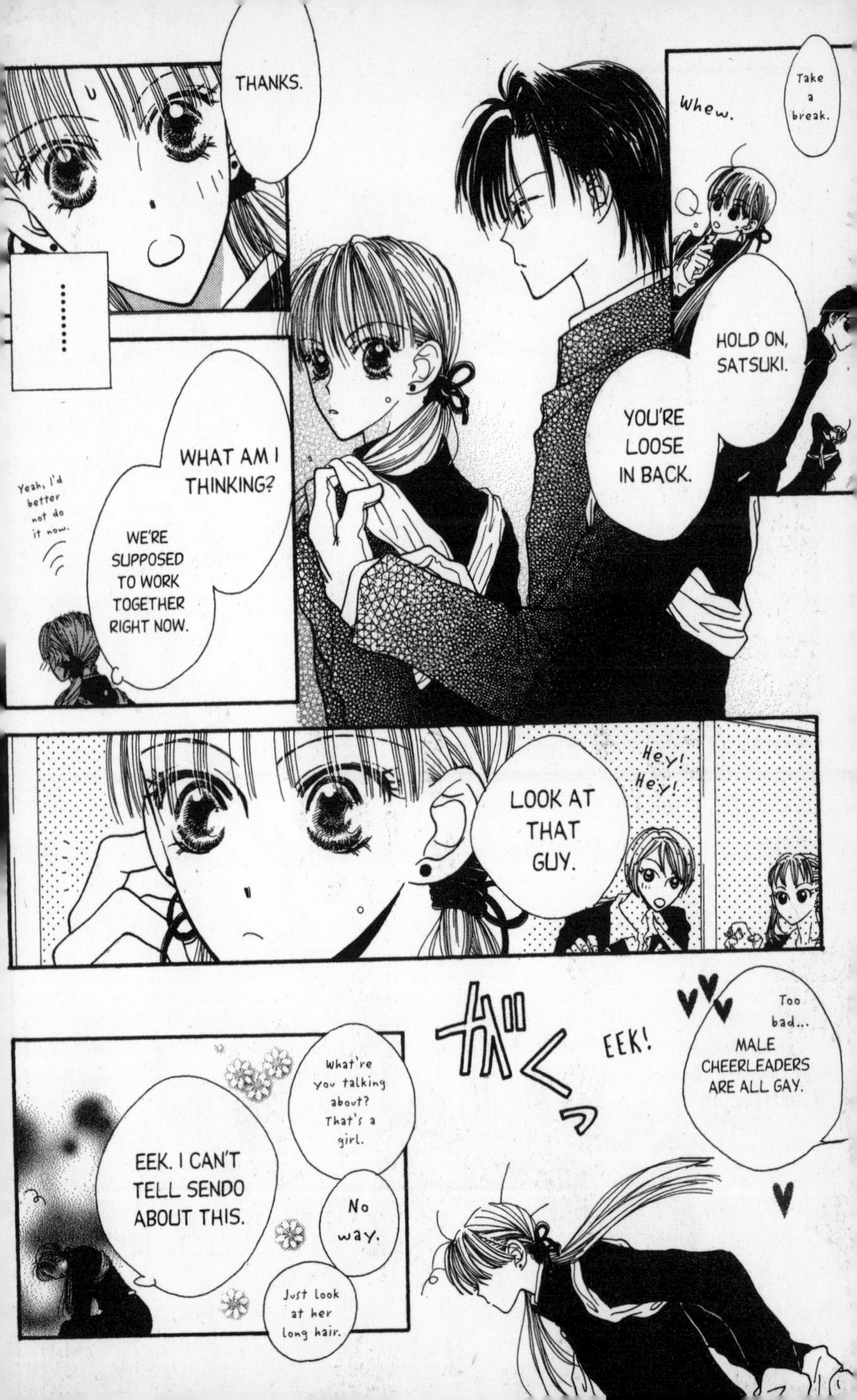
Take a break.
Whew.
HOLD ON, SATSUKI.
YOU'RE LOOSE IN BACK.
THANKS.
....
WHAT AM I THINKING?
WE'RE SUPPOSED TO WORK TOGETHER RIGHT NOW.
Yeah, I'd better not do it now.
Hey! Hey!
LOOK AT THAT GUY.
Too bad... MALE CHEERLEADERS ARE ALL GAY.
EEK!
ガくっ
What're you talking about? That's a girl.
No way.
Just look at her long hair.
EEK. I CAN'T TELL SENDO ABOUT THIS.

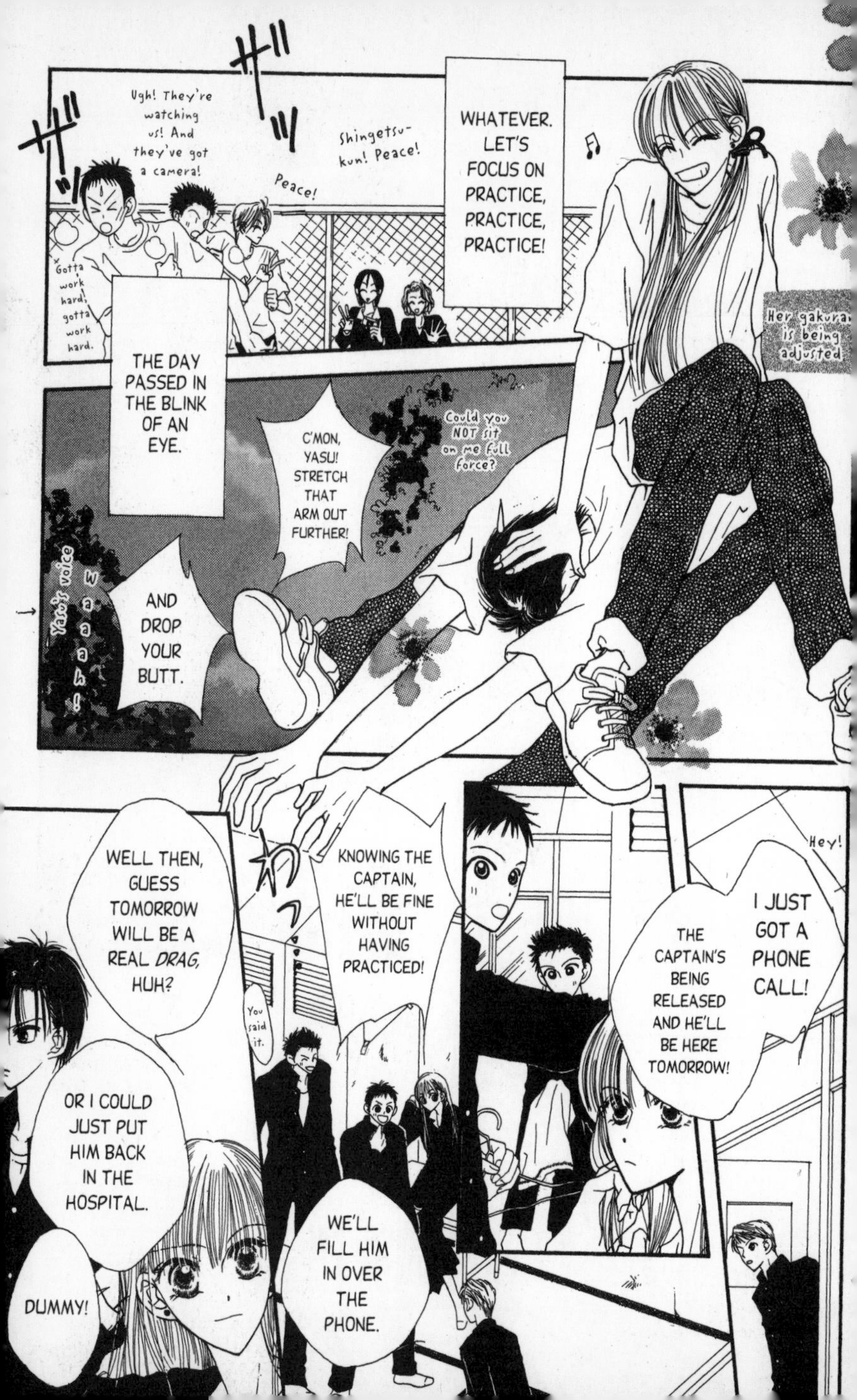
WHATEVER. LET'S FOCUS ON PRACTICE, PRACTICE, PRACTICE!
Her gakuran is being adjusted
Shingetsu-kun! Peace!
Peace!
Ugh! They're watching us! And they've got a camera!
Gotta work hard, gotta work hard.
THE DAY PASSED IN THE BLINK OF AN EYE.
Could you NOT sit on me full force?
C'MON, YASU! STRETCH THAT ARM OUT FURTHER!
AND DROP YOUR BUTT.
Waaaah!
Yasu's voice
Hey!
I JUST GOT A PHONE CALL!
THE CAPTAIN'S BEING RELEASED AND HE'LL BE HERE TOMORROW!
KNOWING THE CAPTAIN, HE'LL BE FINE WITHOUT HAVING PRACTICED!
WELL THEN, GUESS TOMORROW WILL BE A REAL *DRAG*, HUH?
You said it.
WE'LL FILL HIM IN OVER THE PHONE.
OR I COULD JUST PUT HIM BACK IN THE HOSPITAL.
DUMMY!

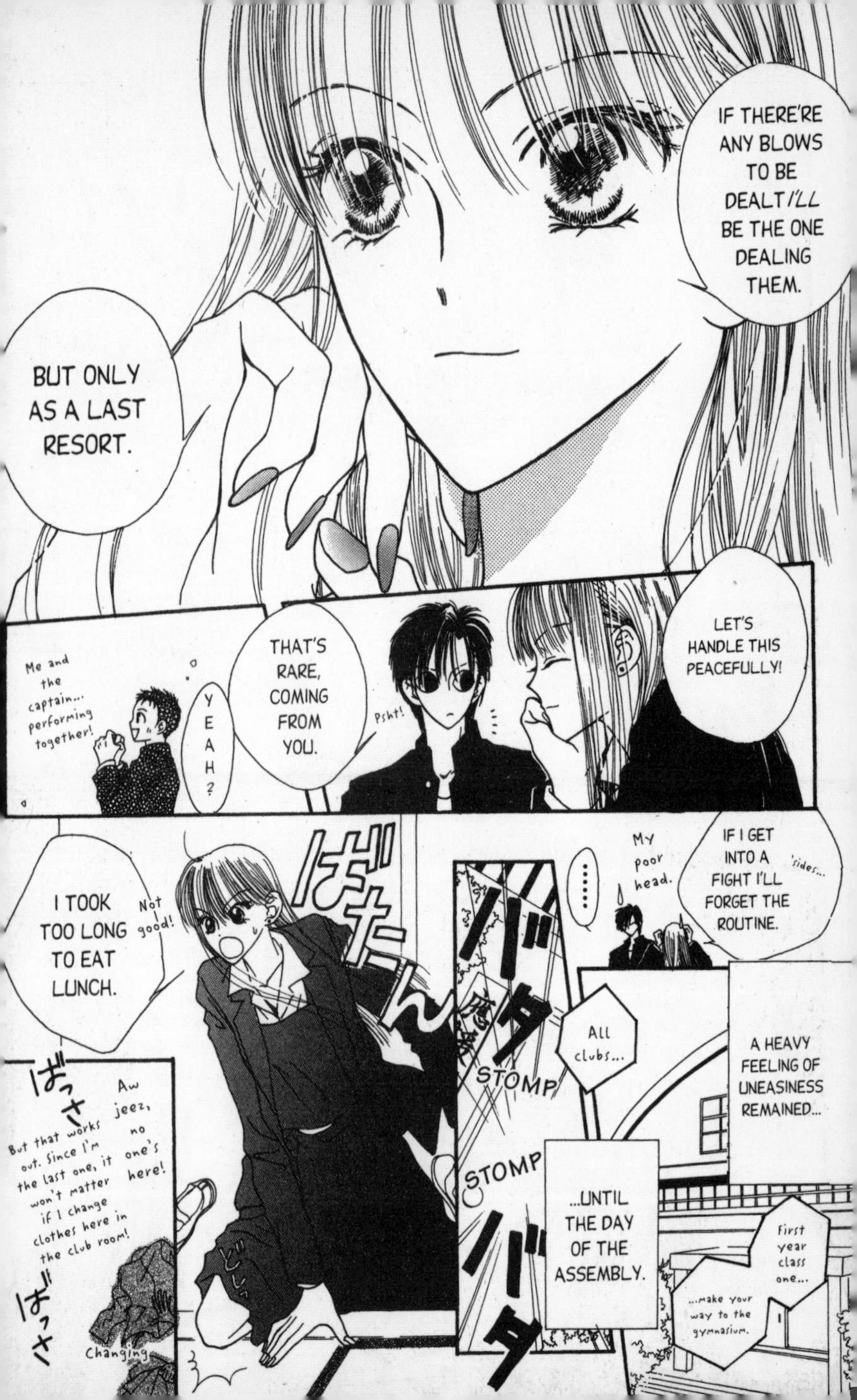
IF THERE'RE ANY BLOWS TO BE DEALT I'LL BE THE ONE DEALING THEM.
BUT ONLY AS A LAST RESORT.
LET'S HANDLE THIS PEACEFULLY!
Psht!
THAT'S RARE, COMING FROM YOU.
YEAH?
Me and the captain... performing together!
'sides...
IF I GET INTO A FIGHT I'LL FORGET THE ROUTINE.
My poor head.
......
A HEAVY FEELING OF UNEASINESS REMAINED...
...UNTIL THE DAY OF THE ASSEMBLY.
All clubs...
First year class one...
...make your way to the gymnasium.
バタ
STOMP
STOMP
バタ
ばたん
I TOOK TOO LONG TO EAT LUNCH.
Not good!
Aw jeez, no one's here!
But that works out. Since I'm the last one, it won't matter if I change clothes here in the club room!
ばっさ
ばっさ
Changing

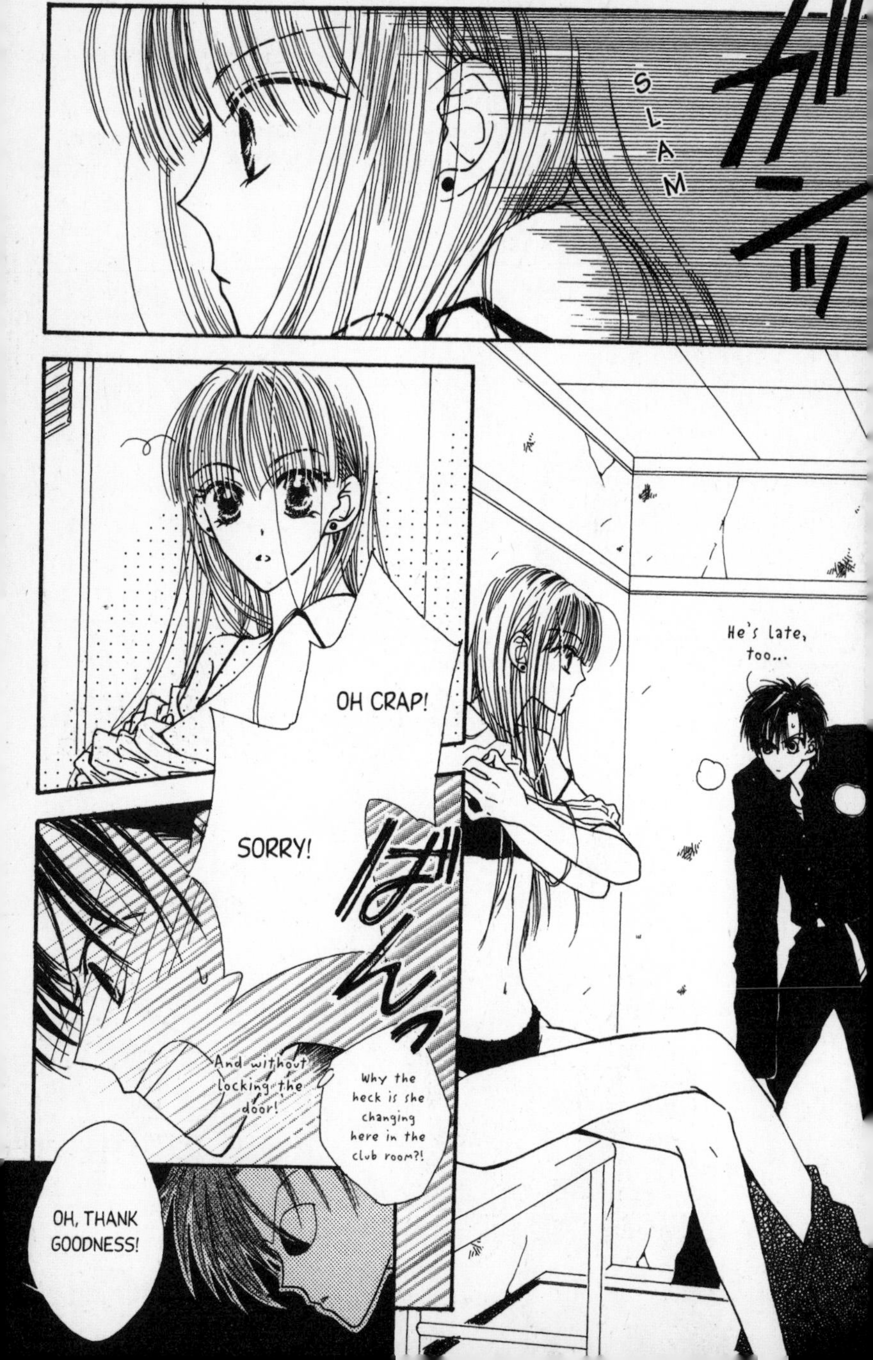
SLAM
He's late, too...
Why the heck is she changing here in the club room?!
And without locking the door!
OH CRAP!
SORRY!
OH, THANK GOODNESS!

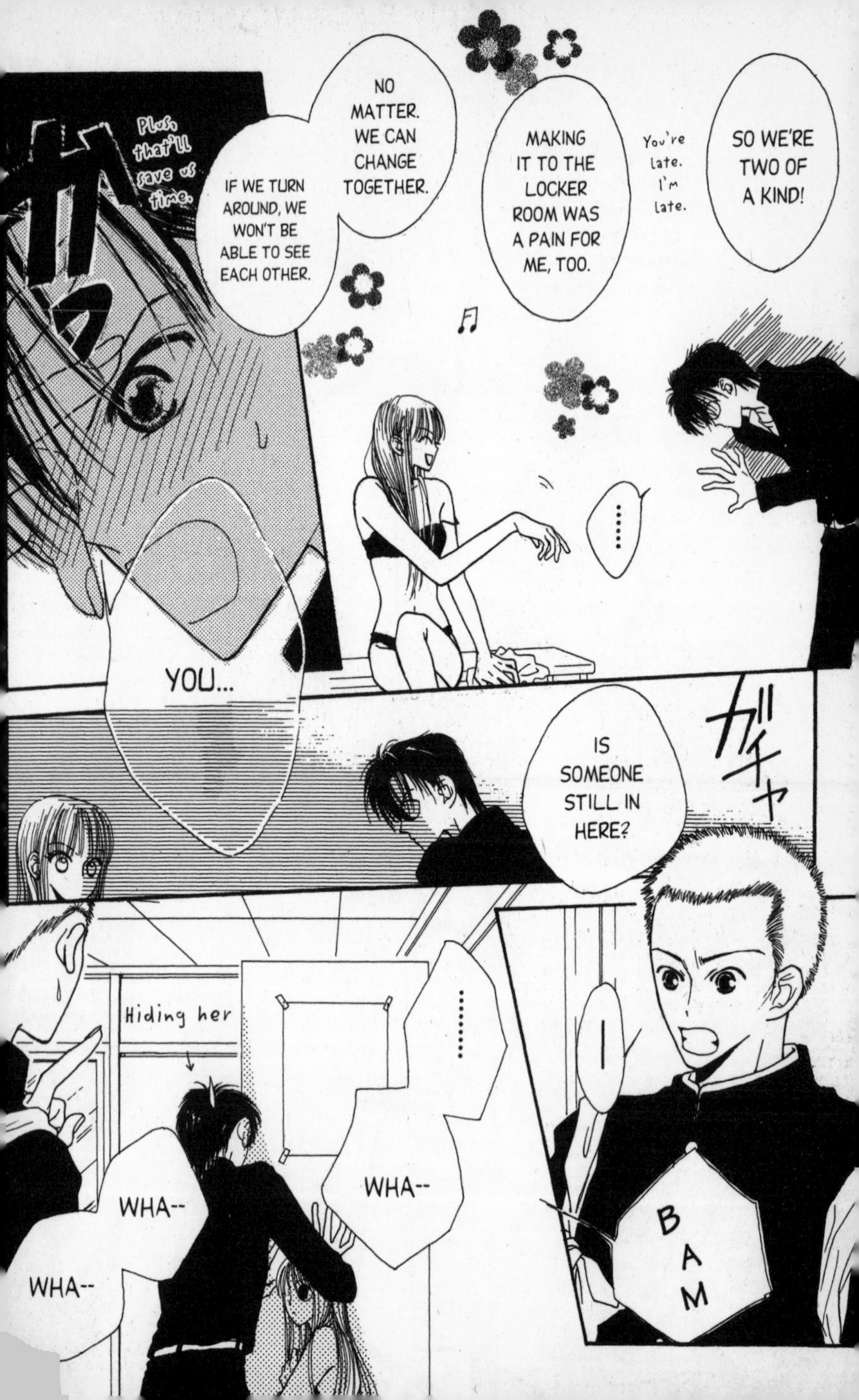
SO WE'RE TWO OF A KIND!
You're late. I'm late.
MAKING IT TO THE LOCKER ROOM WAS A PAIN FOR ME, TOO.
NO MATTER. WE CAN CHANGE TOGETHER.
IF WE TURN AROUND, WE WON'T BE ABLE TO SEE EACH OTHER.
......
Plus, that'll save us time.
YOU...
ガチャ
IS SOMEONE STILL IN HERE?
!
BAM
....
WHA--
WHA--
Hiding her
WHA--

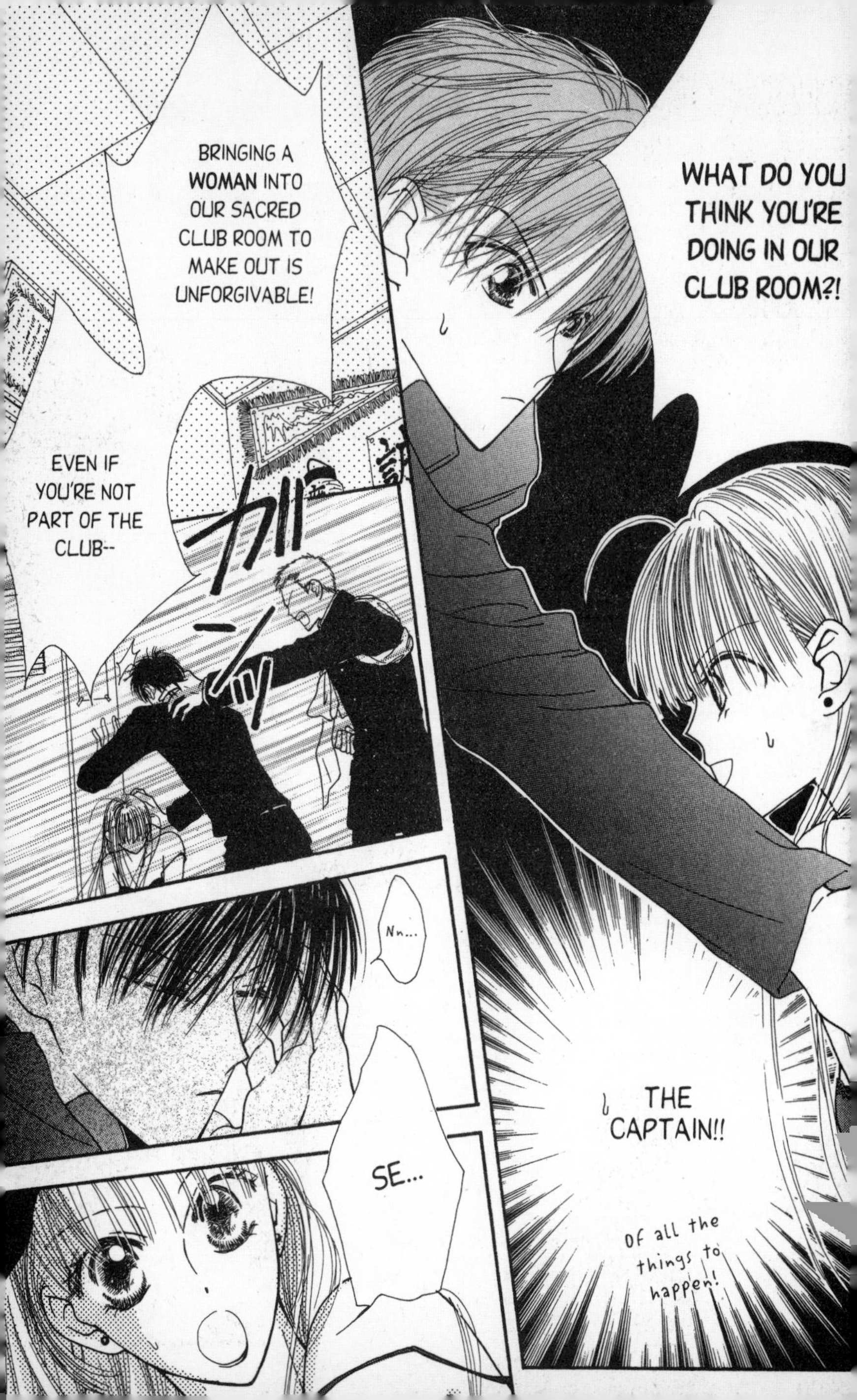
WHAT DO YOU THINK YOU'RE DOING IN OUR CLUB ROOM?!
THE CAPTAIN!!
Of all the things to happen!
BRINGING A WOMAN INTO OUR SACRED CLUB ROOM TO MAKE OUT IS UNFORGIVABLE!
EVEN IF YOU'RE NOT PART OF THE CLUB--
カ!!
Nn...
SE...

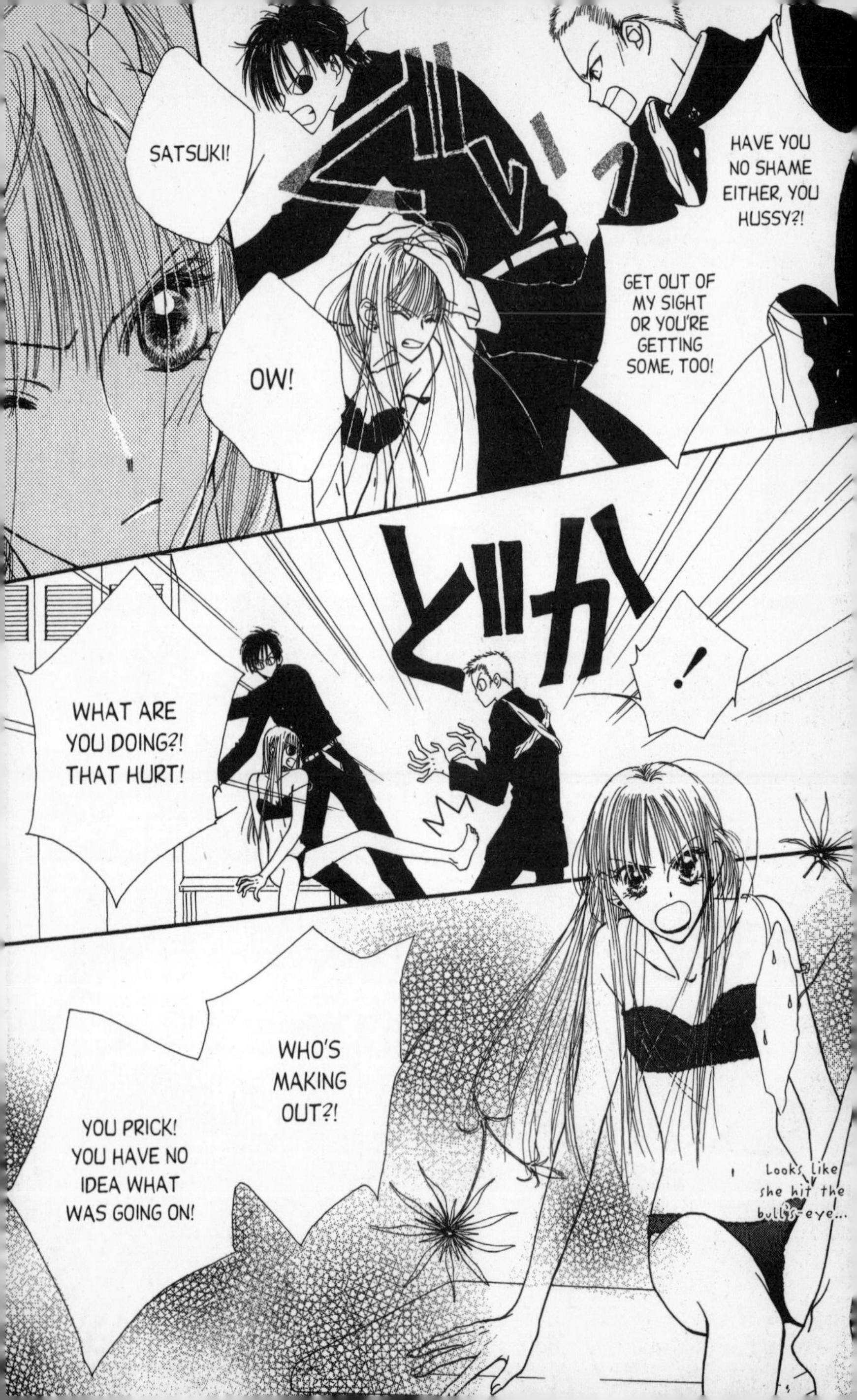
HAVE YOU NO SHAME EITHER, YOU HUSSY?!
GET OUT OF MY SIGHT OR YOU'RE GETTING SOME, TOO!
SATSUKI!
OW!
ドカッ
!
WHAT ARE YOU DOING?! THAT HURT!
WHO'S MAKING OUT?!
YOU PRICK! YOU HAVE NO IDEA WHAT WAS GOING ON!
Looks like she hit the bull's-eye...

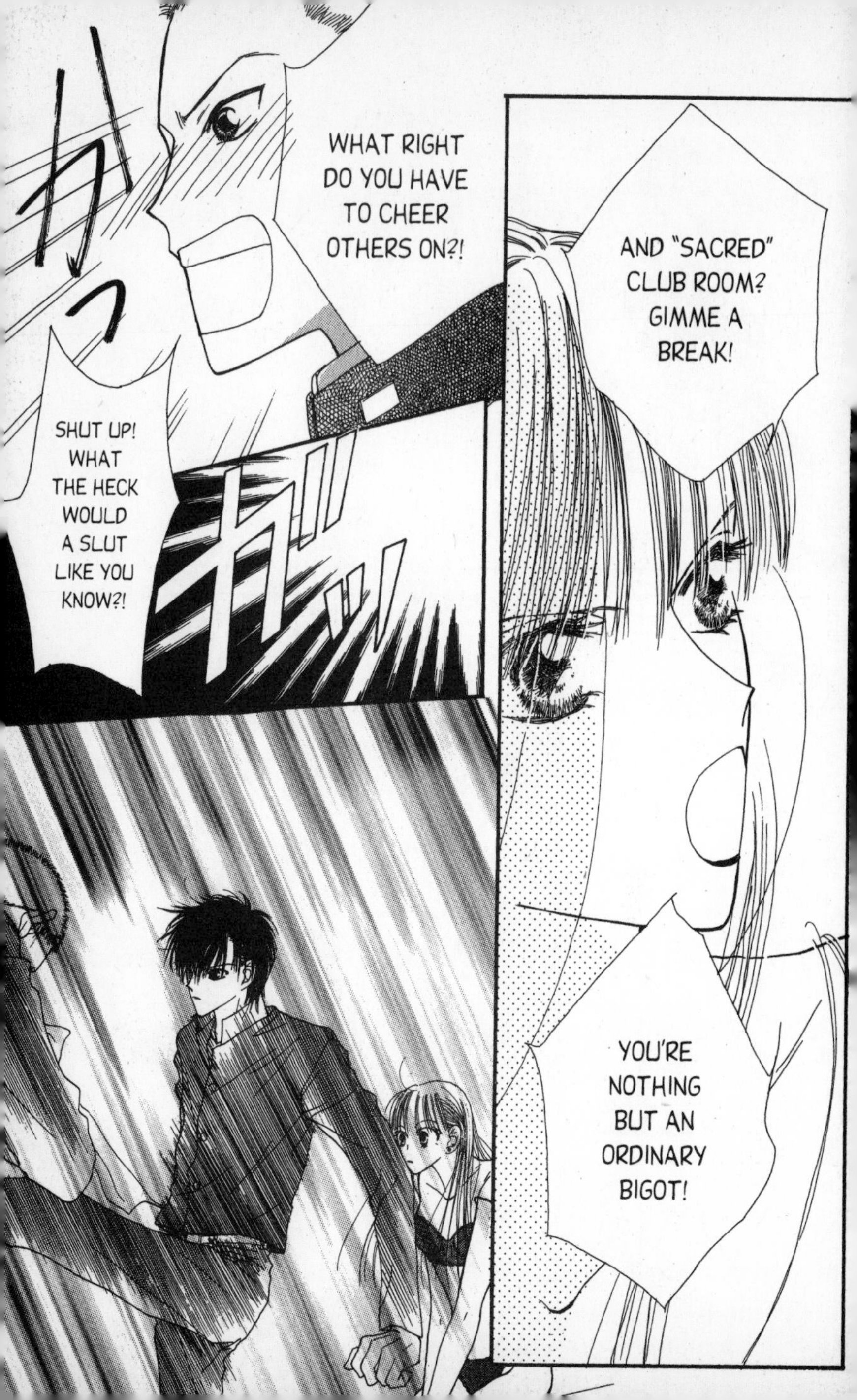
AND "SACRED" CLUB ROOM? GIMME A BREAK!
YOU'RE NOTHING BUT AN ORDINARY BIGOT!
WHAT RIGHT DO YOU HAVE TO CHEER OTHERS ON?!
SHUT UP! WHAT THE HECK WOULD A SLUT LIKE YOU KNOW?!

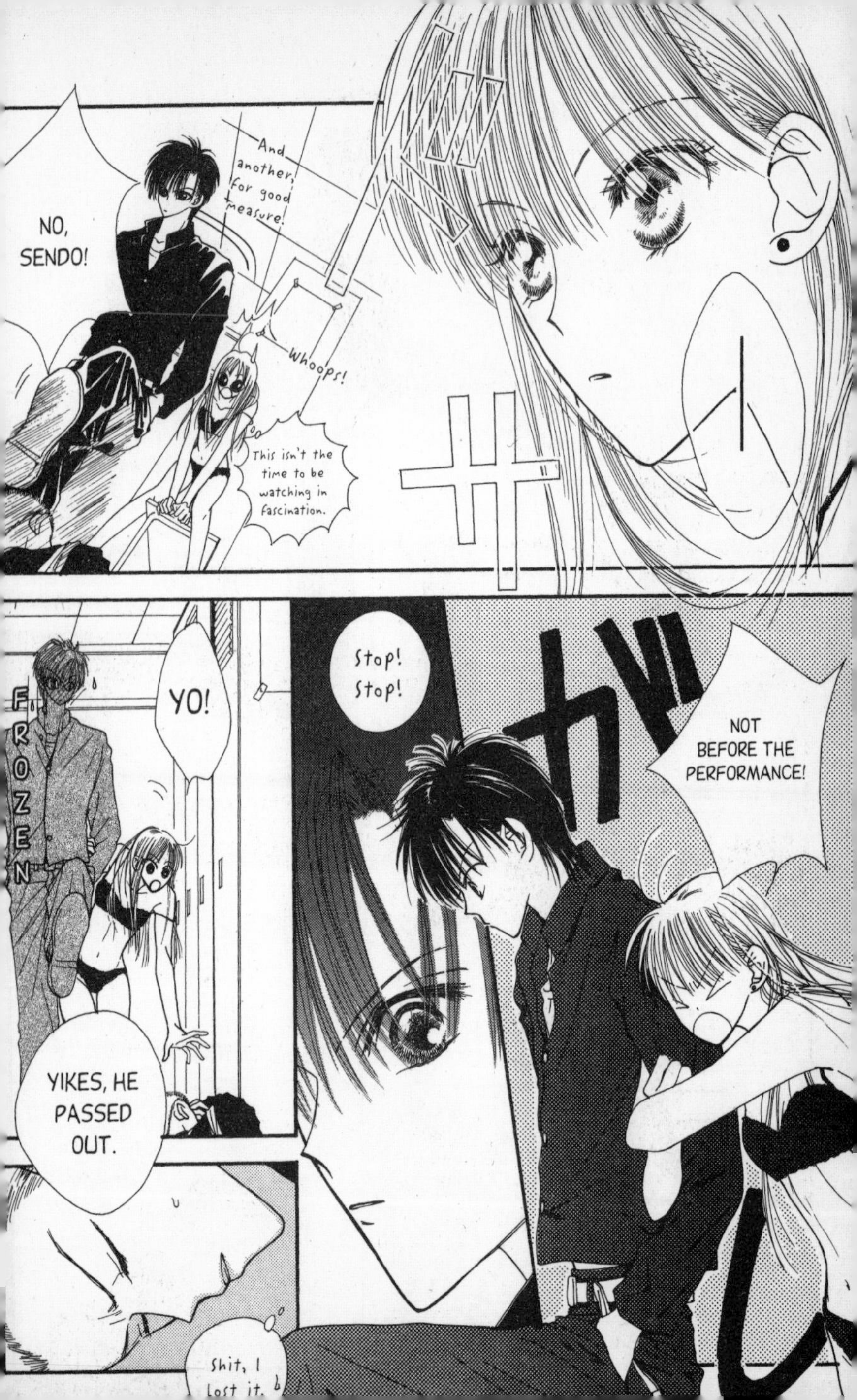
ザ
And another, for good measure!
NO, SENDO!
Whoops!
This isn't the time to be watching in fascination.
ガ
NOT BEFORE THE PERFORMANCE!
Stop! Stop!
YO!
FROZEN
YIKES, HE PASSED OUT.
Shit, I lost it.

Note: See page 194

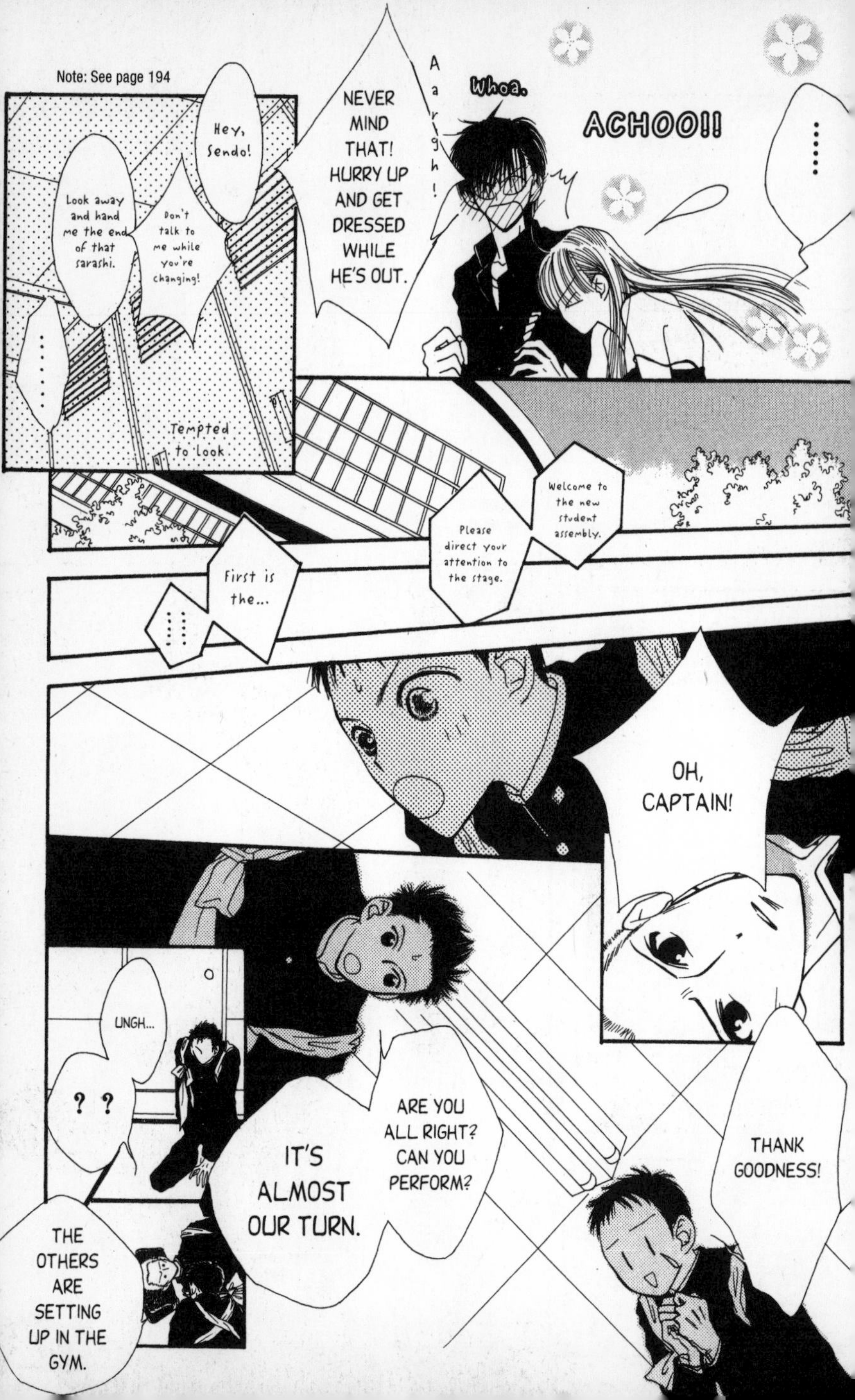
......
ACHOO!!
Whoa.
Aargh!
NEVER MIND THAT! HURRY UP AND GET DRESSED WHILE HE'S OUT.
Hey, Sendo!
Don't talk to me while you're changing!
Look away and hand me the end of that sarashi.
......
Tempted to look.
Welcome to the new student assembly.
Please direct your attention to the stage.
First is the...
......
OH, CAPTAIN!
THANK GOODNESS!
ARE YOU ALL RIGHT? CAN YOU PERFORM?
IT'S ALMOST OUR TURN.
UNGH...
? ?
THE OTHERS ARE SETTING UP IN THE GYM.

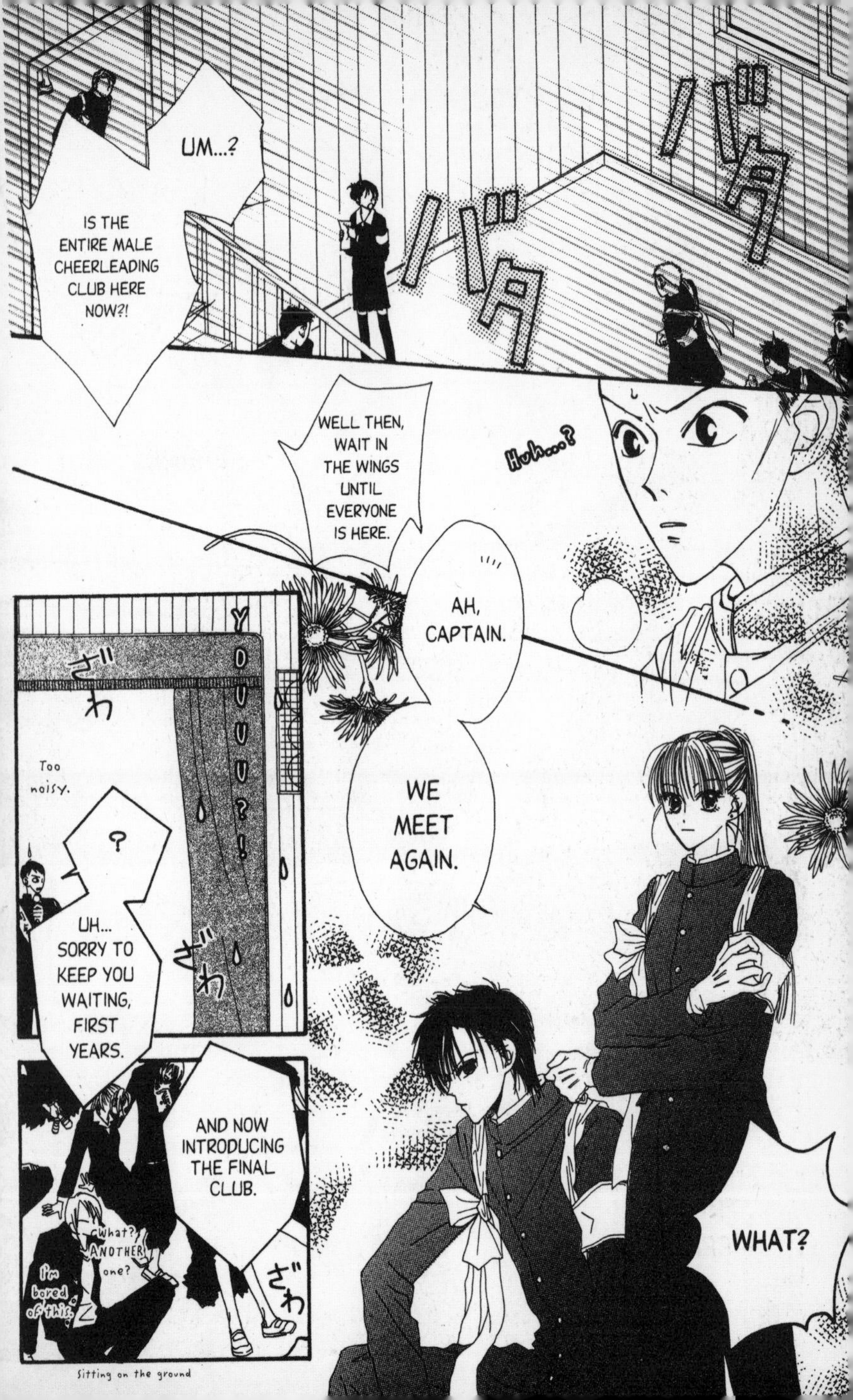
バタ
バタ
UM...?
IS THE ENTIRE MALE CHEERLEADING CLUB HERE NOW?!
Huh...?
WELL THEN, WAIT IN THE WINGS UNTIL EVERYONE IS HERE.
AH, CAPTAIN.
WE MEET AGAIN.
WHAT?
YOUUUU?!
ざわ
ざわ
Too noisy.
?
UH... SORRY TO KEEP YOU WAITING, FIRST YEARS.
AND NOW INTRODUCING THE FINAL CLUB.
What? ANOTHER one?
I'm bored of this.
ざわ
Sitting on the ground

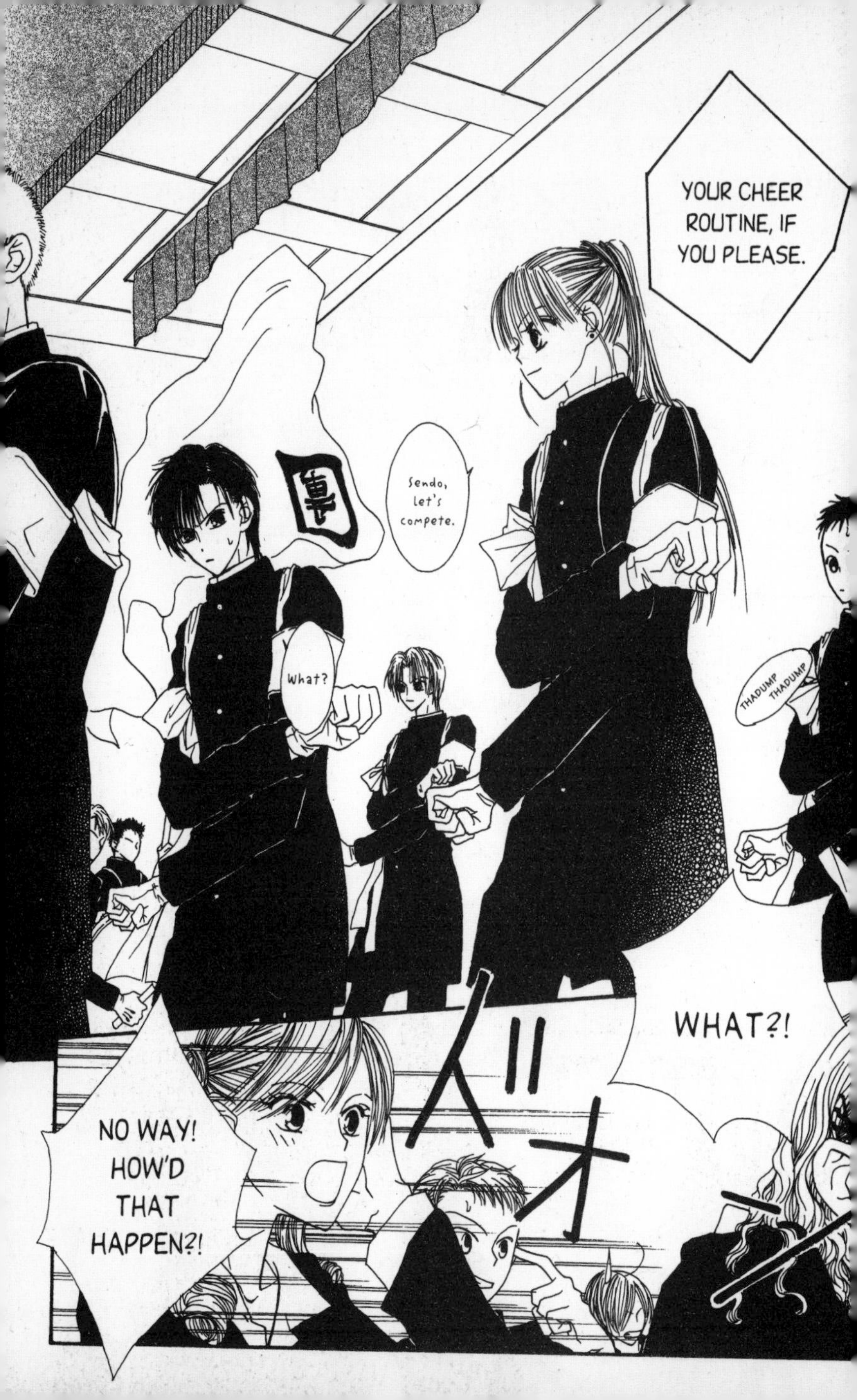
YOUR CHEER ROUTINE, IF YOU PLEASE.
Sendo, let's compete.
What?
THADUMP THADUMP
WHAT?!
NO WAY! HOW'D THAT HAPPEN?!

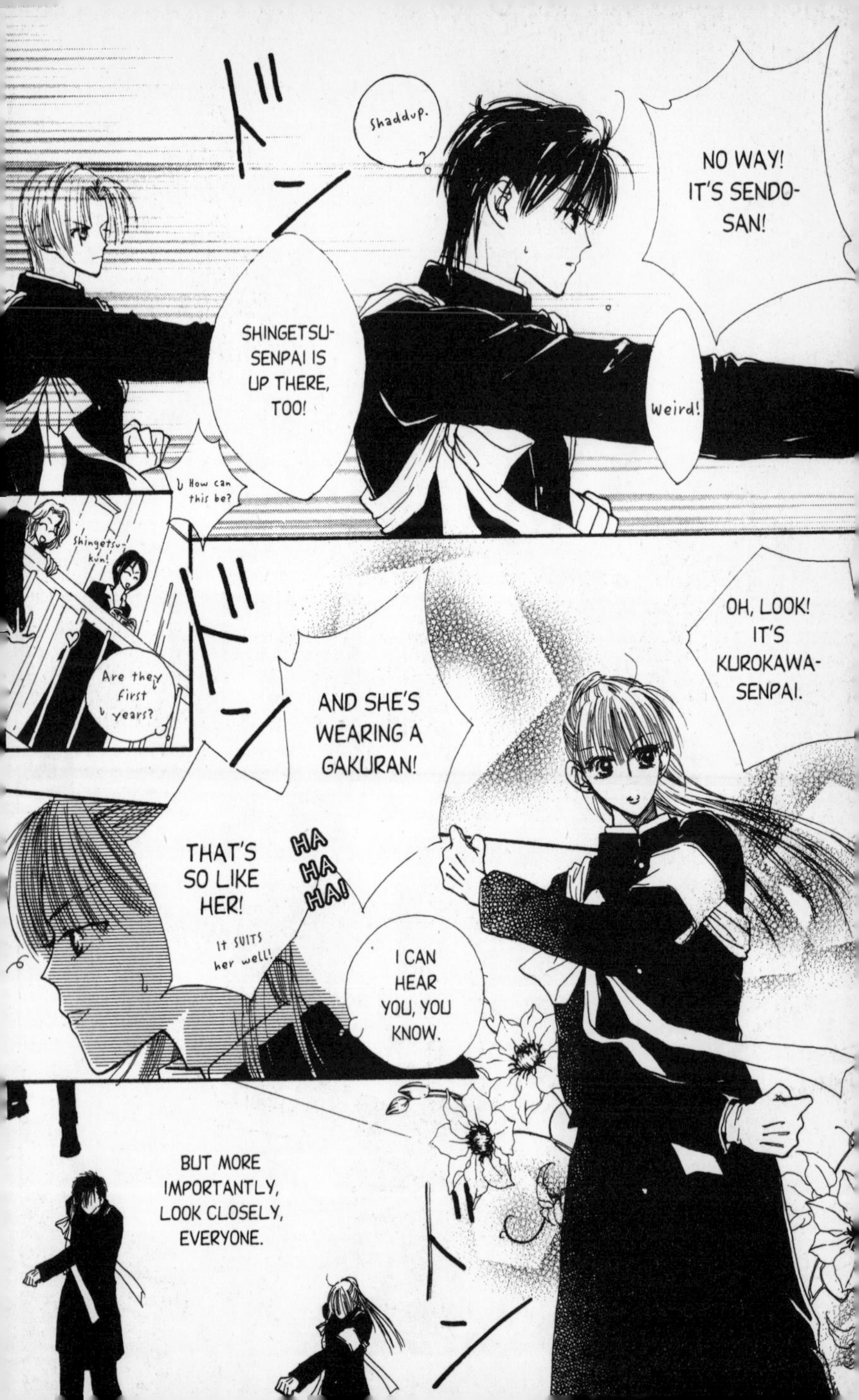

NO WAY! IT'S SENDO-SAN!
Shaddup.
ドー
Weird!
SHINGETSU-SENPAI IS UP THERE, TOO!
How can this be?
OH, LOOK! IT'S KUROKAWA-SENPAI.
AND SHE'S WEARING A GAKURAN!
ドー
Shingetsu-kun!
Are they first years?
I CAN HEAR YOU, YOU KNOW.
HA HA HA!
THAT'S SO LIKE HER!
It suits her well!
ドー
BUT MORE IMPORTANTLY, LOOK CLOSELY, EVERYONE.

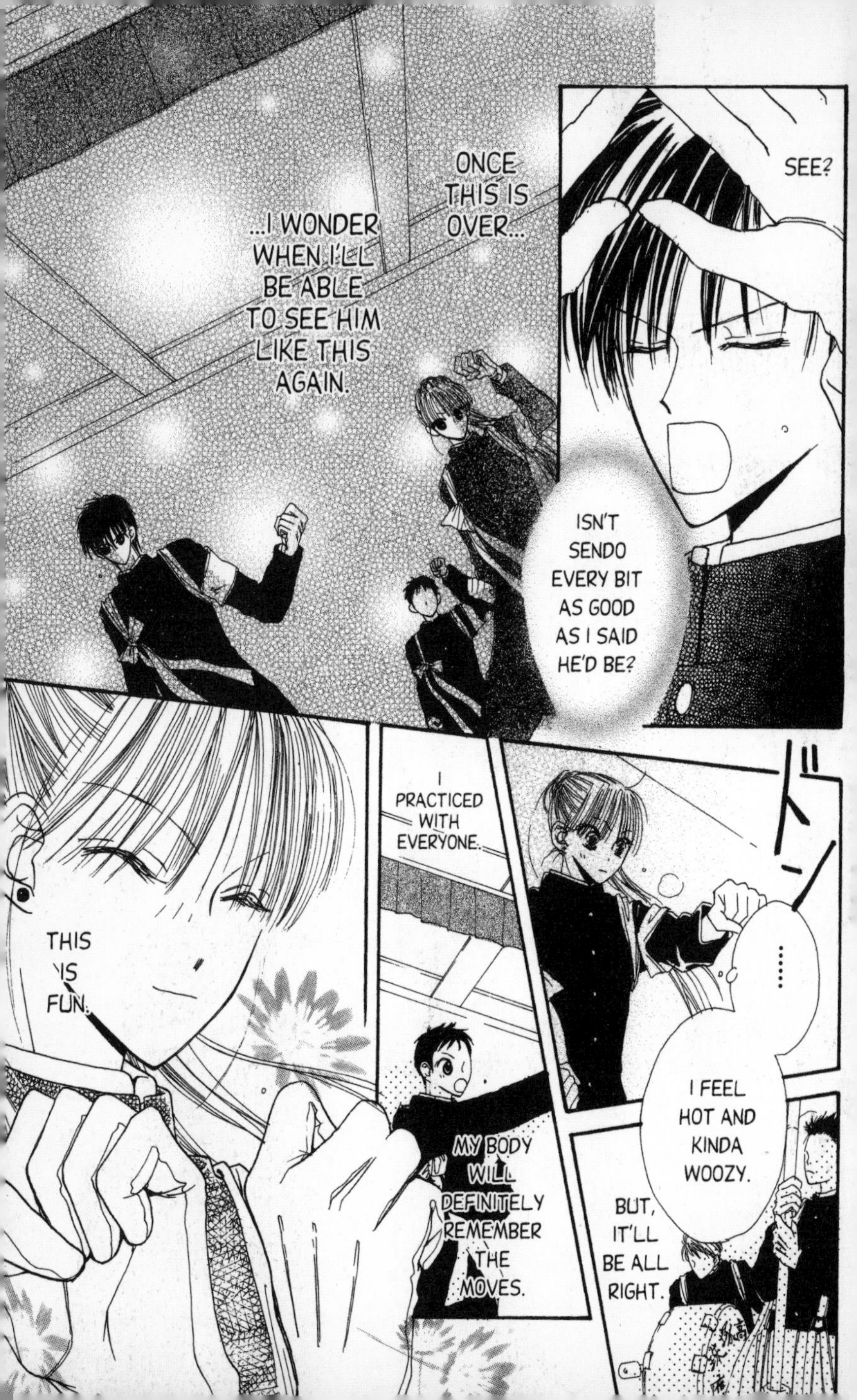
SEE?
ISN'T SENDO EVERY BIT AS GOOD AS I SAID HE'D BE?
ONCE THIS IS OVER...
...I WONDER WHEN I'LL BE ABLE TO SEE HIM LIKE THIS AGAIN.
ドーン
......
I FEEL HOT AND KINDA WOOZY.
BUT, IT'LL BE ALL RIGHT.
I PRACTICED WITH EVERYONE.
MY BODY WILL DEFINITELY REMEMBER THE MOVES.
THIS IS FUN.

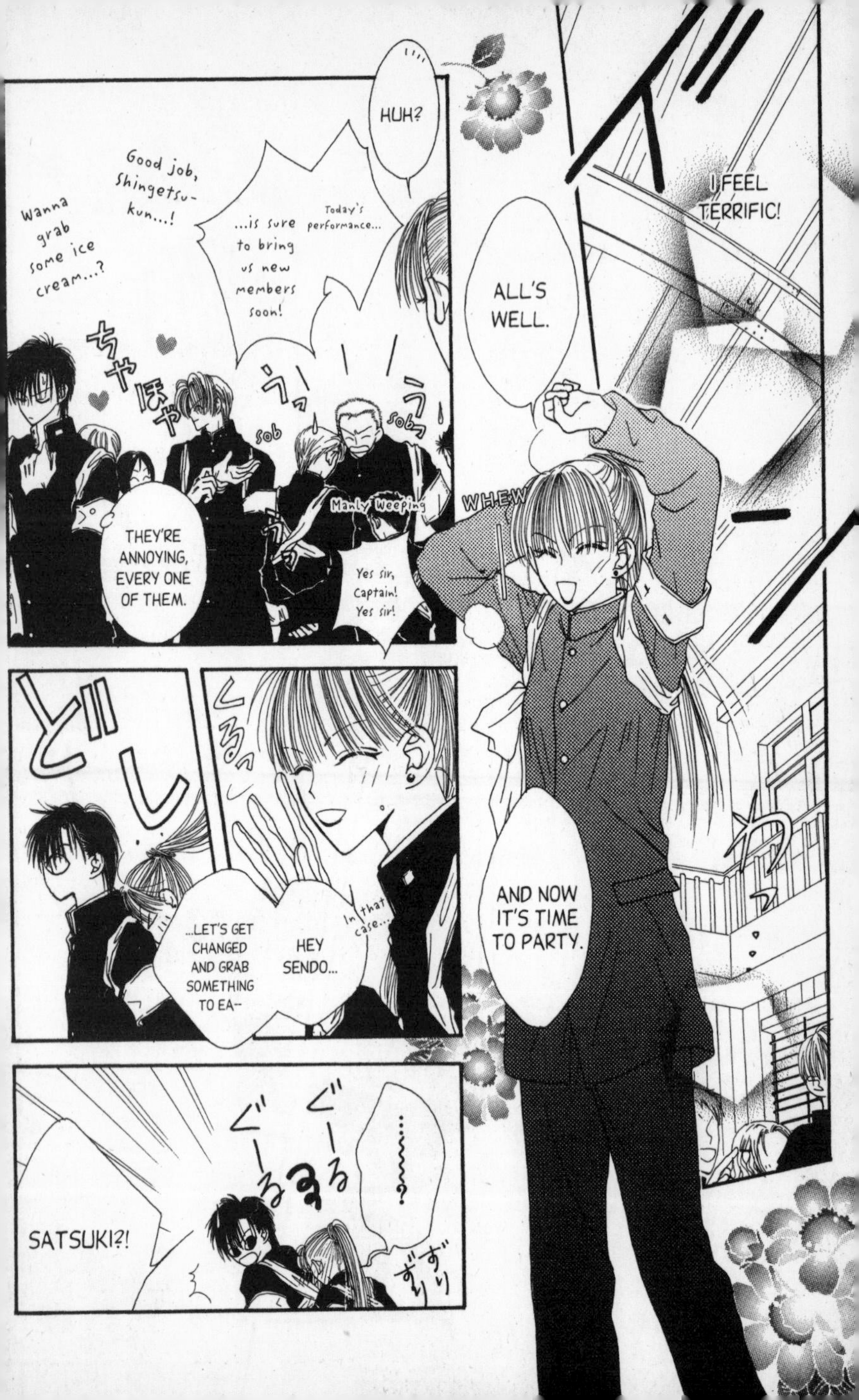
I FEEL TERRIFIC!
ALL'S WELL.
WHEW
AND NOW IT'S TIME TO PARTY.
HUH?
Today's performance...
...is sure to bring us new members soon!
Good job, Shingetsu-kun...!
Wanna grab some ice cream...?
ちやほや
sob
sob
Manly Weeping
Yes sir, Captain! Yes sir!
THEY'RE ANNOYING, EVERY ONE OF THEM.
くるっ
In that case...
HEY SENDO...
...LET'S GET CHANGED AND GRAB SOMETHING TO EA--
どしっ
......?
SATSUKI?!
ずりずり

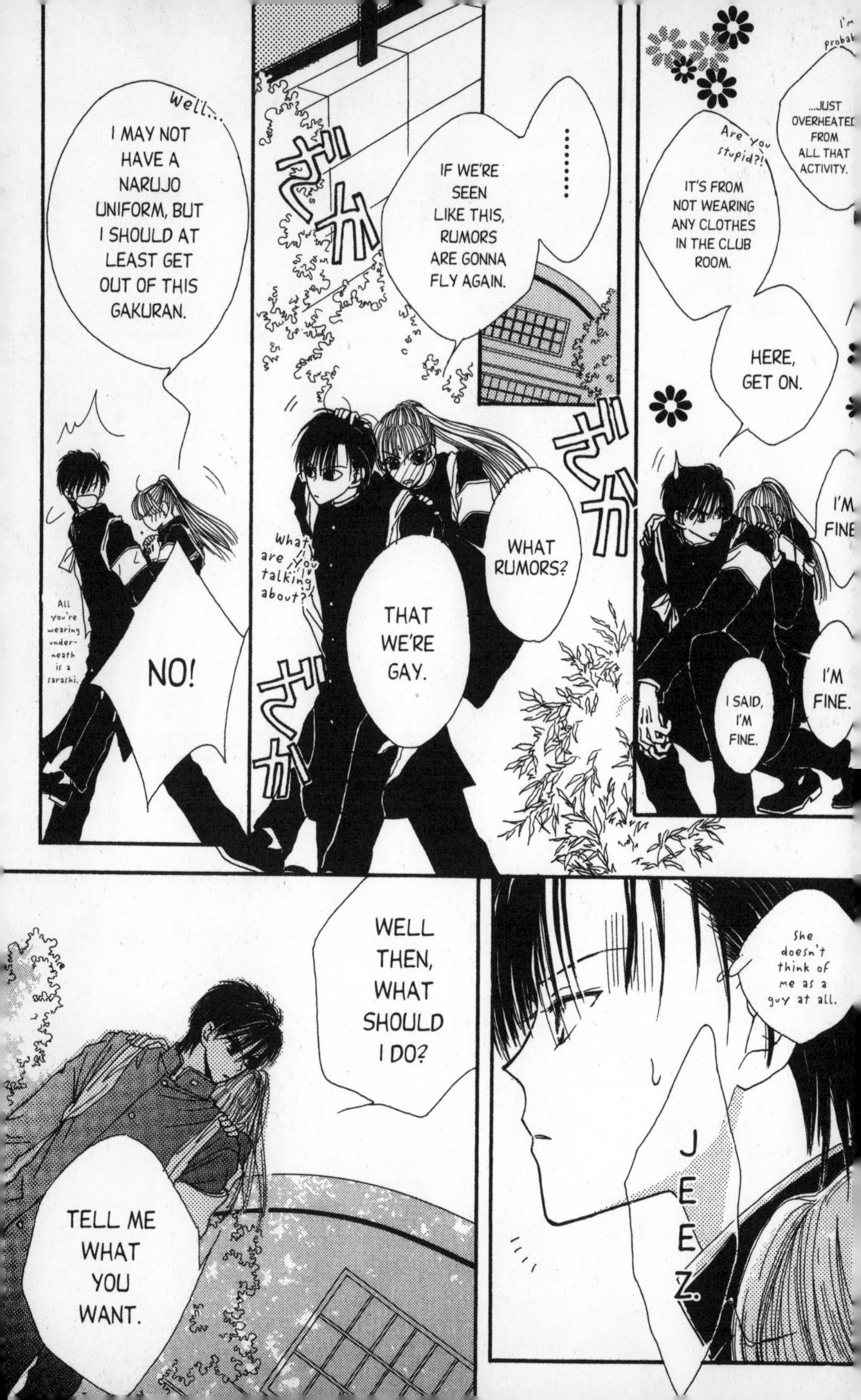
...JUST OVERHEATED FROM ALL THAT ACTIVITY.
Are you stupid?!
IT'S FROM NOT WEARING ANY CLOTHES IN THE CLUB ROOM.
HERE, GET ON.
I'M FINE
I'M FINE.
I SAID, I'M FINE.
......
ざか
IF WE'RE SEEN LIKE THIS, RUMORS ARE GONNA FLY AGAIN.
ざか
WHAT RUMORS?
What are you talking about?
THAT WE'RE GAY.
ざか
Well...
I MAY NOT HAVE A NARUJO UNIFORM, BUT I SHOULD AT LEAST GET OUT OF THIS GAKURAN.
All you're wearing underneath is a sarashi.
NO!
She doesn't think of me as a guy at all.
JEEZ.
WELL THEN, WHAT SHOULD I DO?
TELL ME WHAT YOU WANT.

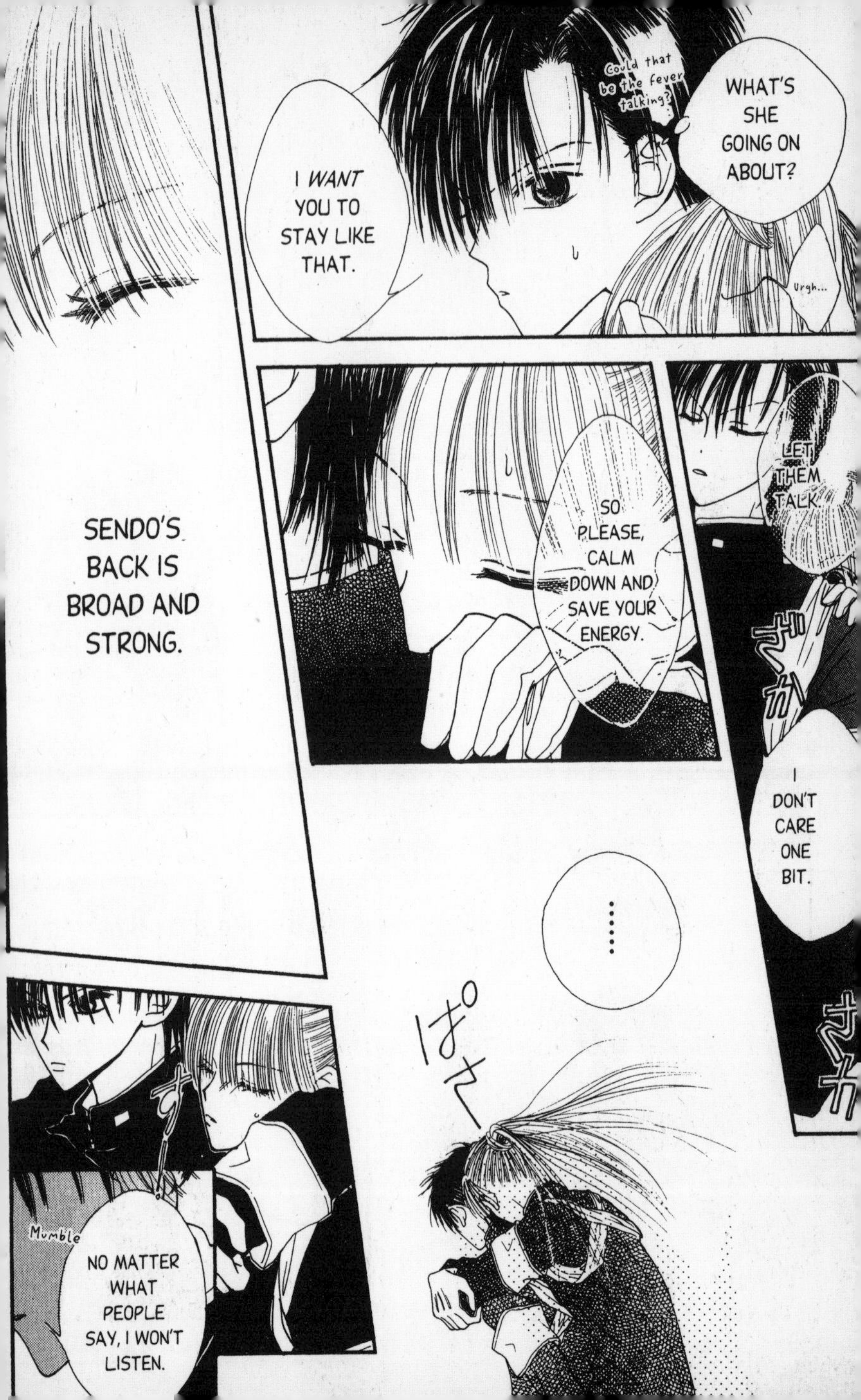
WHAT'S SHE GOING ON ABOUT?
Could that be the fever talking?
Urgh...
I *WANT* YOU TO STAY LIKE THAT.
LET THEM TALK.
ざわ
I DON'T CARE ONE BIT.
ざわ
SO PLEASE, CALM DOWN AND SAVE YOUR ENERGY.
......
ぱさ
SENDO'S BACK IS BROAD AND STRONG.
Mumble
NO MATTER WHAT PEOPLE SAY, I WON'T LISTEN.

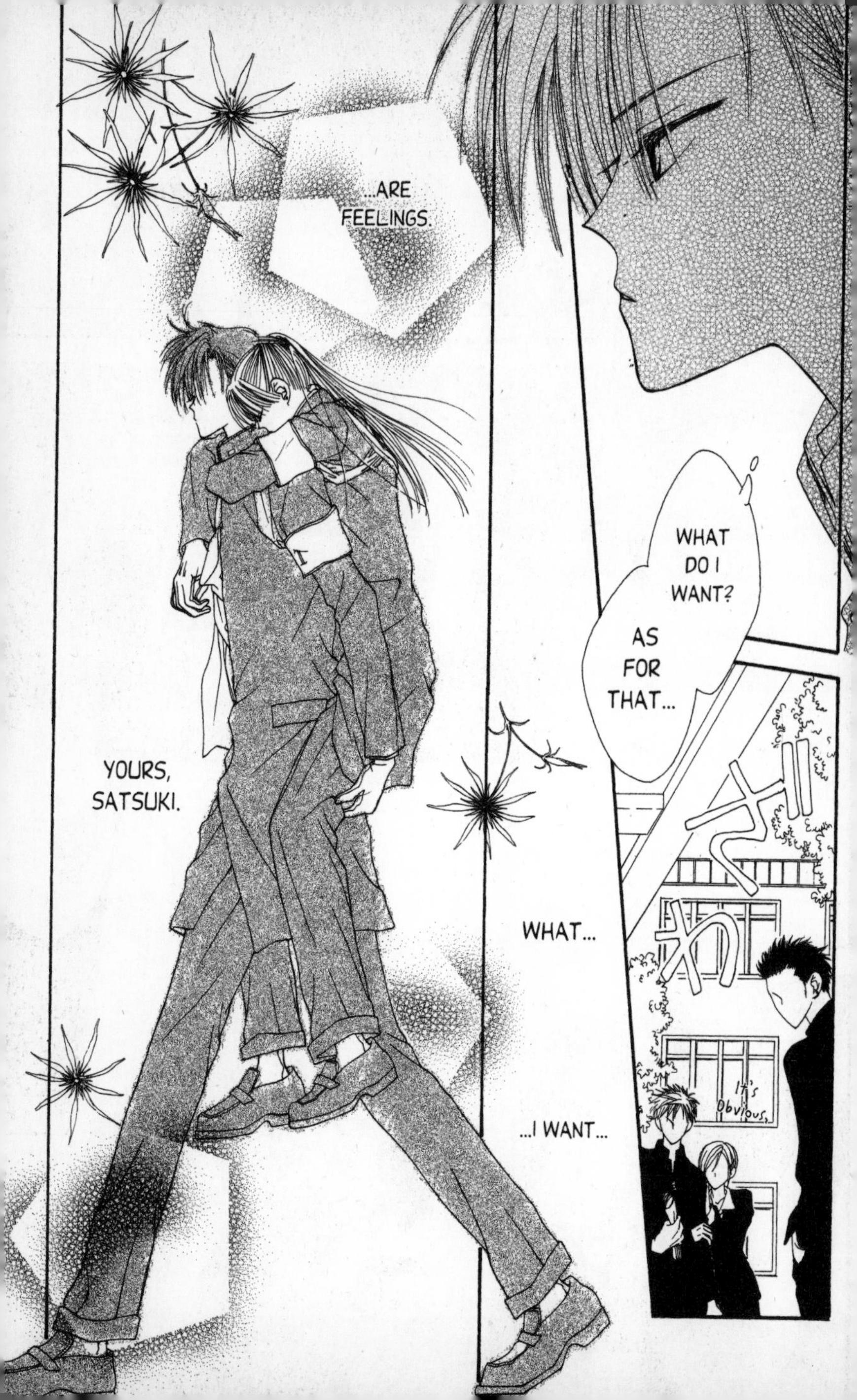
WHAT DO I WANT?
AS FOR THAT...
It's obvious.
WHAT...
...I WANT...
...ARE FEELINGS.
YOURS, SATSUKI.

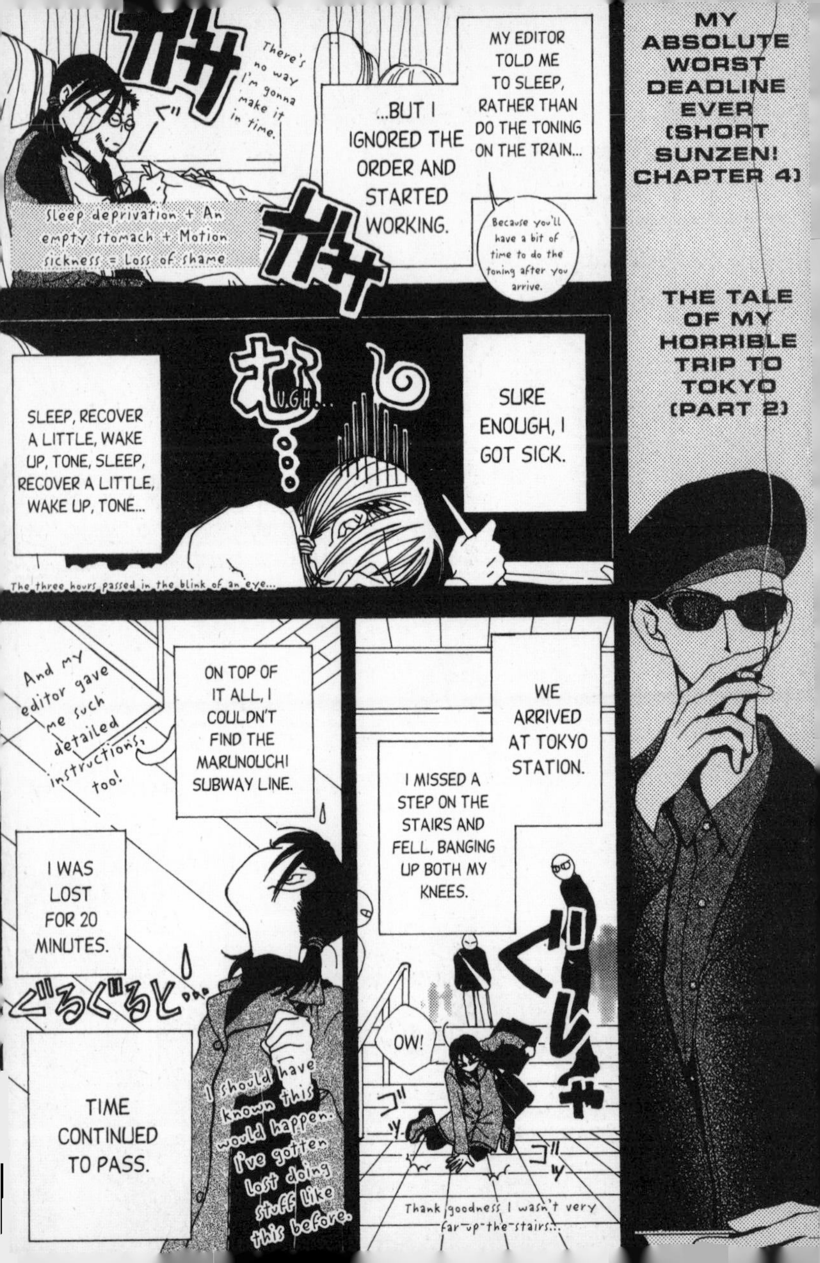
MY ABSOLUTE WORST DEADLINE EVER (SHORT SUNZEN! CHAPTER 4)
THE TALE OF MY HORRIBLE TRIP TO TOKYO (PART 2)
MY EDITOR TOLD ME TO SLEEP, RATHER THAN DO THE TONING ON THE TRAIN...
Because you'll have a bit of time to do the toning after you arrive.
...BUT I IGNORED THE ORDER AND STARTED WORKING.
There's no way I'm gonna make it in time.
Sleep deprivation + An empty stomach + Motion sickness = Loss of shame
SURE ENOUGH, I GOT SICK.
UGH...
SLEEP, RECOVER A LITTLE, WAKE UP, TONE, SLEEP, RECOVER A LITTLE, WAKE UP, TONE...
The three hours passed in the blink of an eye...
WE ARRIVED AT TOKYO STATION.
I MISSED A STEP ON THE STAIRS AND FELL, BANGING UP BOTH MY KNEES.
OW!
Thank goodness I wasn't very far up the stairs...
ON TOP OF IT ALL, I COULDN'T FIND THE MARUNOUCHI SUBWAY LINE.
And my editor gave me such detailed instructions, too!
I WAS LOST FOR 20 MINUTES.
TIME CONTINUED TO PASS.
I should have known this would happen. I've gotten lost doing stuff like this before.

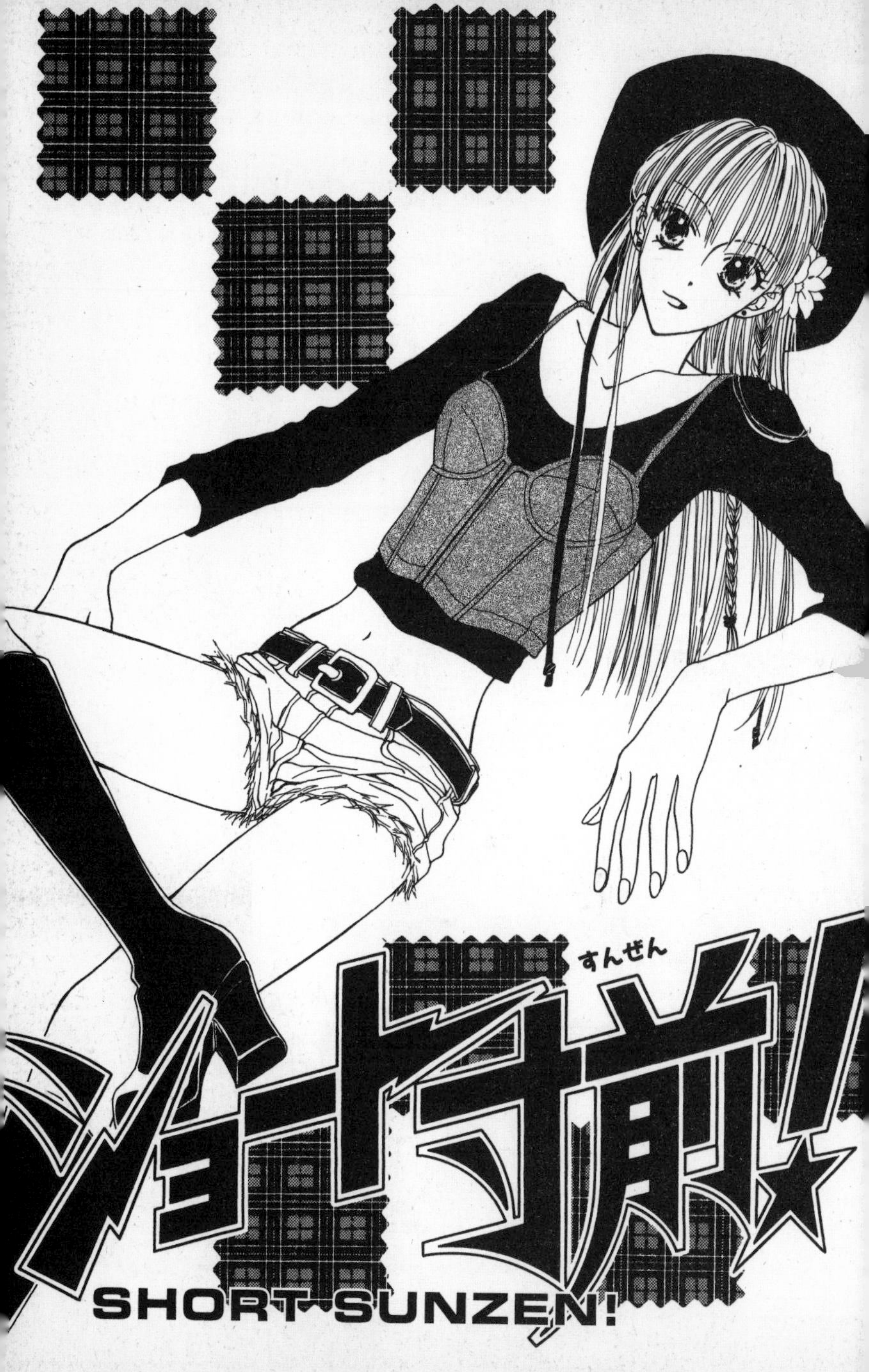
すんぜん
ショート寸前!!★
SHORT SUNZEN!

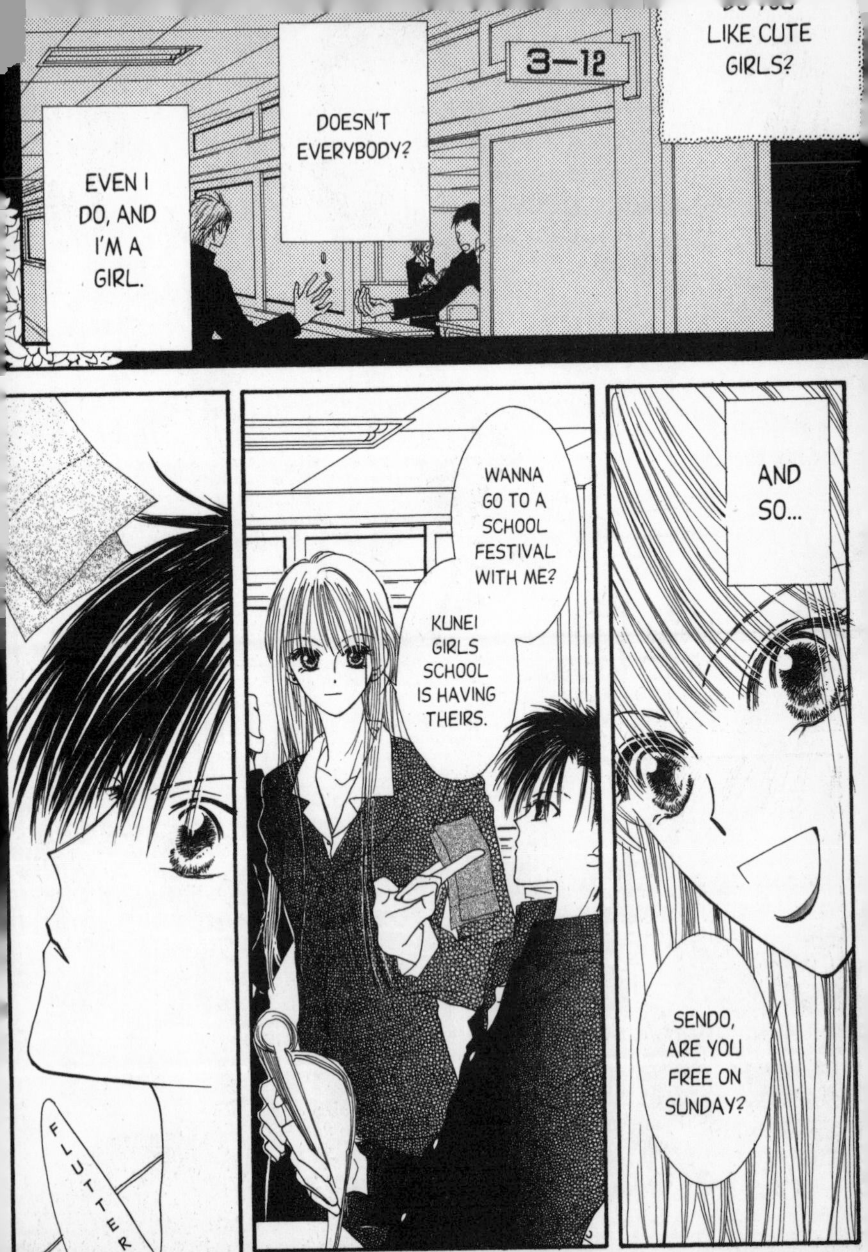

LIKE CUTE GIRLS?
3-12
DOESN'T EVERYBODY?
EVEN I DO, AND I'M A GIRL.
AND SO...
SENDO, ARE YOU FREE ON SUNDAY?
WANNA GO TO A SCHOOL FESTIVAL WITH ME?
KUNEI GIRLS SCHOOL IS HAVING THEIRS.
FLUTTER

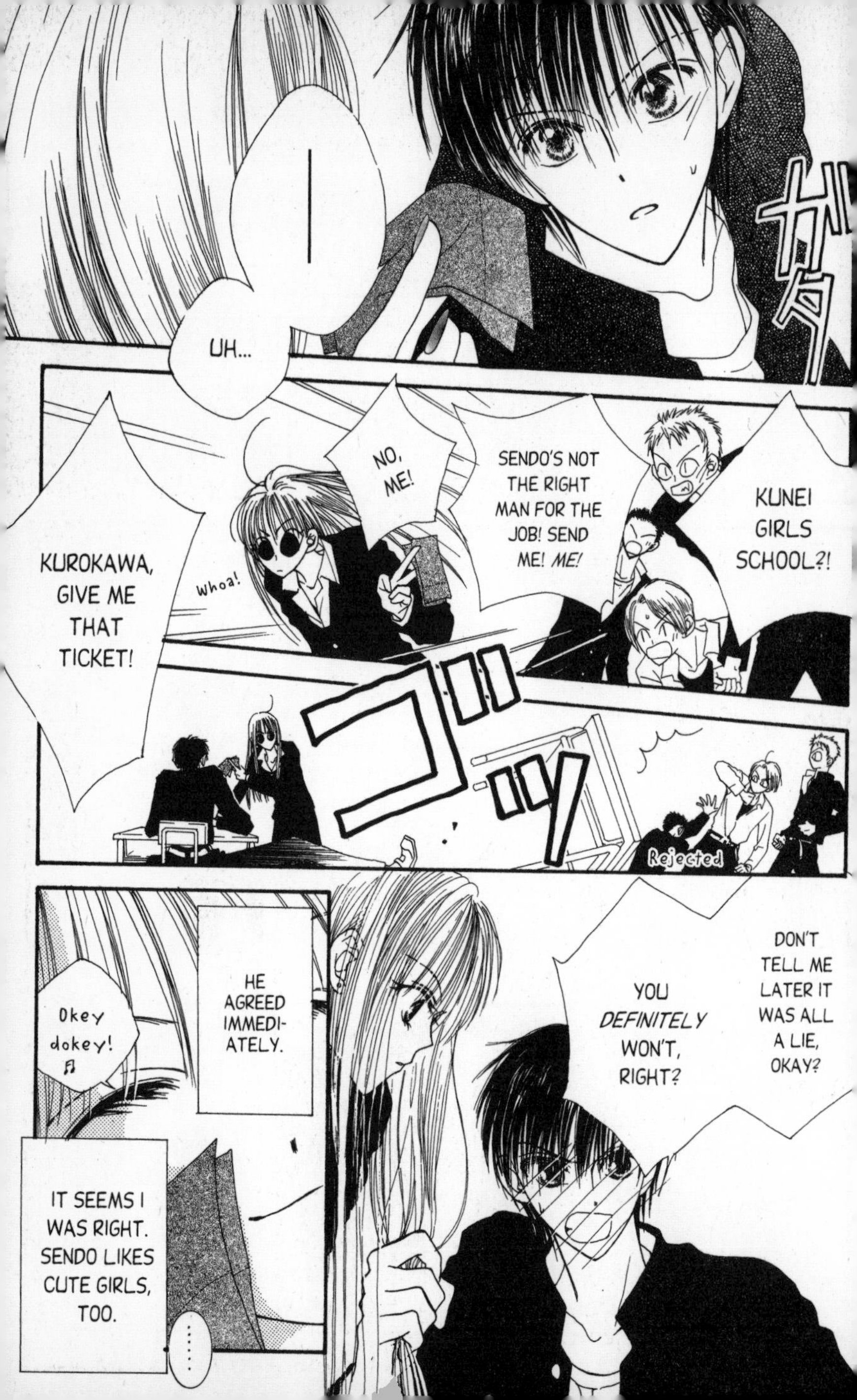
UH...
KUNEI GIRLS SCHOOL?!
SENDO'S NOT THE RIGHT MAN FOR THE JOB! SEND ME! *ME!*
NO, ME!
Whoa!
KUROKAWA, GIVE ME THAT TICKET!
Rejected
DON'T TELL ME LATER IT WAS ALL A LIE, OKAY?
YOU *DEFINITELY* WON'T, RIGHT?
HE AGREED IMMEDIATELY.
Okey dokey! ♫
IT SEEMS I WAS RIGHT. SENDO LIKES CUTE GIRLS, TOO.
......

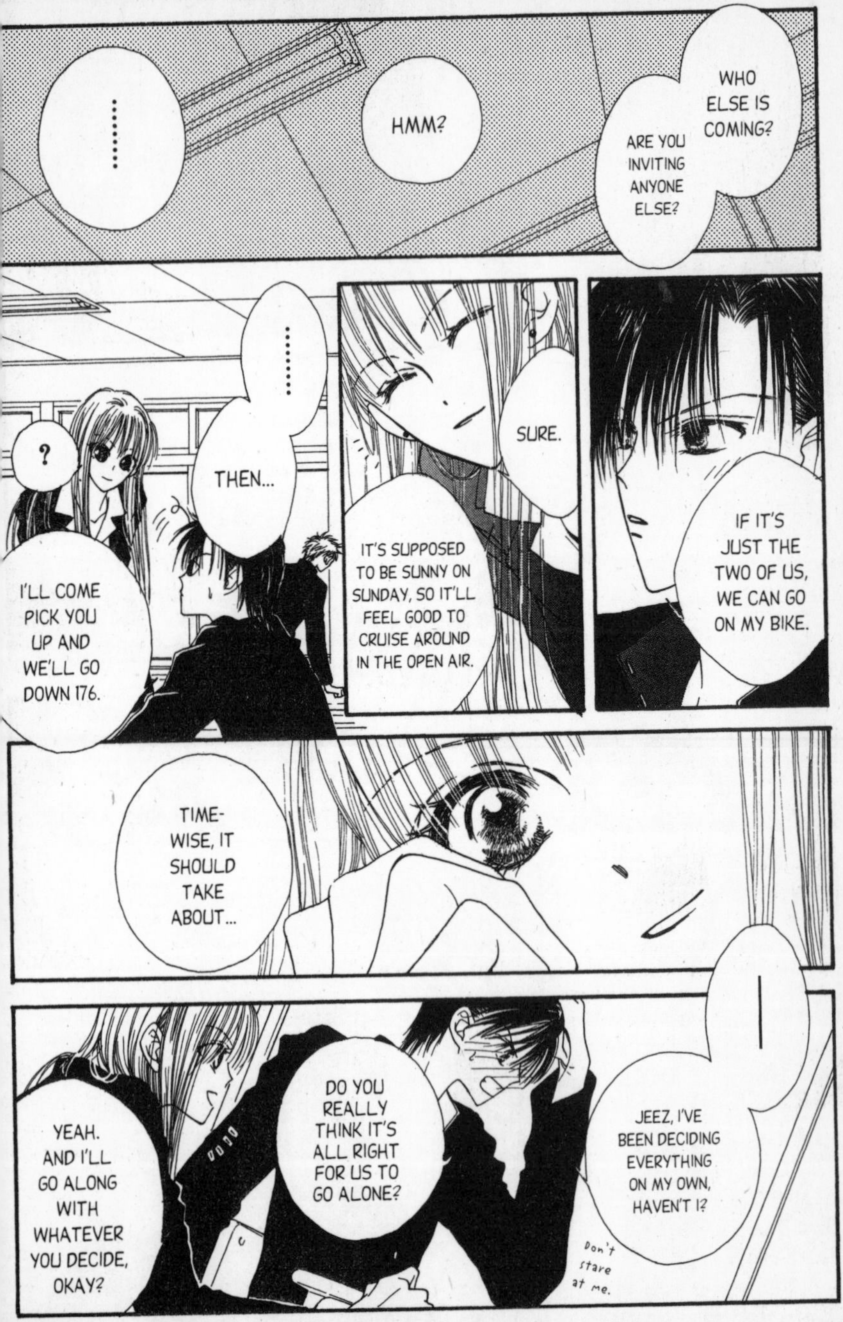
WHO ELSE IS COMING?
ARE YOU INVITING ANYONE ELSE?
HMM?
......
IF IT'S JUST THE TWO OF US, WE CAN GO ON MY BIKE.
SURE.
IT'S SUPPOSED TO BE SUNNY ON SUNDAY, SO IT'LL FEEL GOOD TO CRUISE AROUND IN THE OPEN AIR.
......
THEN...
?
I'LL COME PICK YOU UP AND WE'LL GO DOWN 176.
TIME-WISE, IT SHOULD TAKE ABOUT...
—
JEEZ, I'VE BEEN DECIDING EVERYTHING ON MY OWN, HAVEN'T I?
Don't stare at me.
DO YOU REALLY THINK IT'S ALL RIGHT FOR US TO GO ALONE?
YEAH. AND I'LL GO ALONG WITH WHATEVER YOU DECIDE, OKAY?

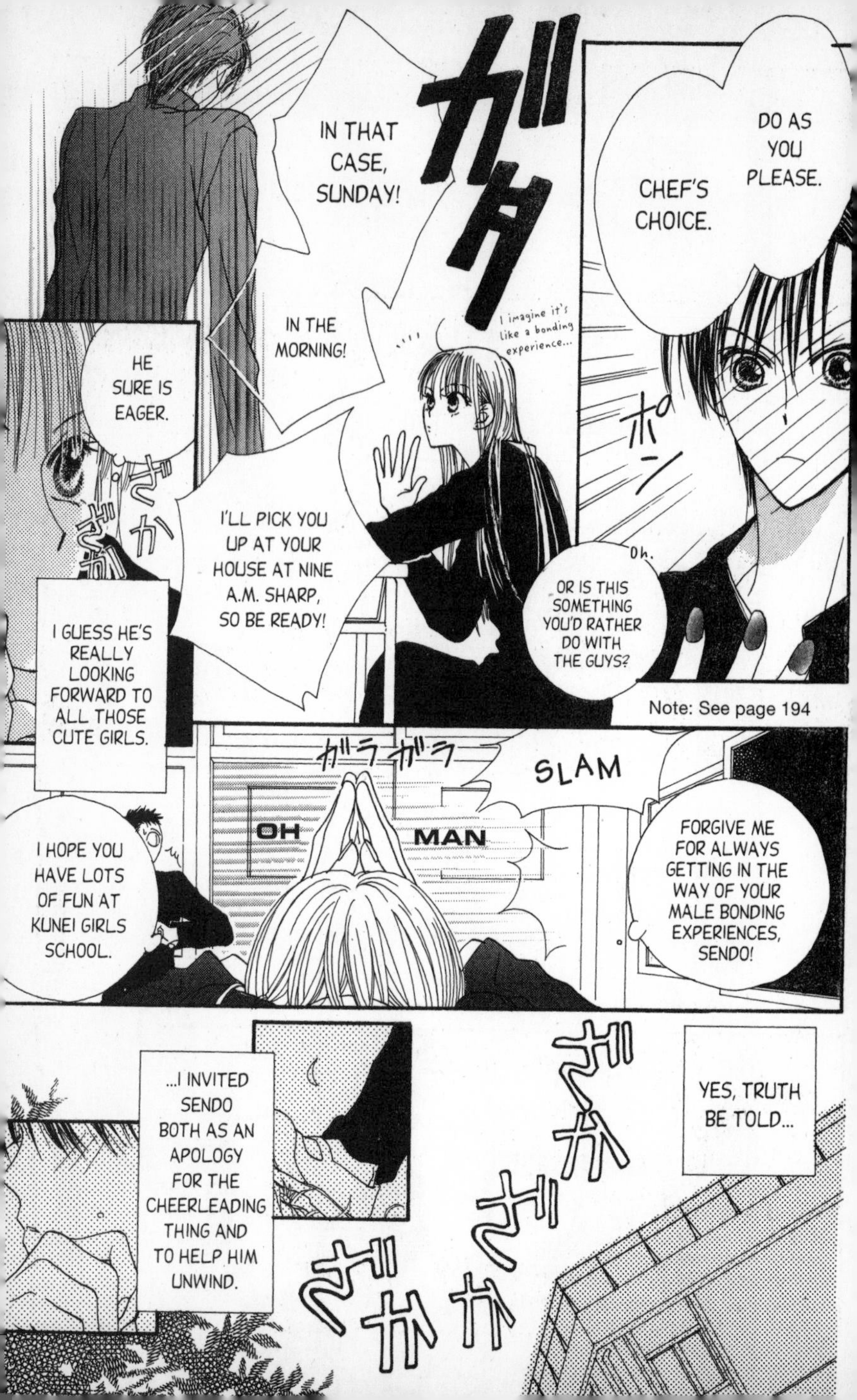

DO AS YOU PLEASE.
CHEF'S CHOICE.
ポーン
Oh.
OR IS THIS SOMETHING YOU'D RATHER DO WITH THE GUYS?
Note: See page 194
ガタ
IN THAT CASE, SUNDAY!
IN THE MORNING!
...
I imagine it's like a bonding experience...
I'LL PICK YOU UP AT YOUR HOUSE AT NINE A.M. SHARP, SO BE READY!
HE SURE IS EAGER.
ざわざわ
I GUESS HE'S REALLY LOOKING FORWARD TO ALL THOSE CUTE GIRLS.
FORGIVE ME FOR ALWAYS GETTING IN THE WAY OF YOUR MALE BONDING EXPERIENCES, SENDO!
SLAM
ガラガラ
OH MAN
I HOPE YOU HAVE LOTS OF FUN AT KUNEI GIRLS SCHOOL.
YES, TRUTH BE TOLD...
ざわざわ
...I INVITED SENDO BOTH AS AN APOLOGY FOR THE CHEERLEADING THING AND TO HELP HIM UNWIND.

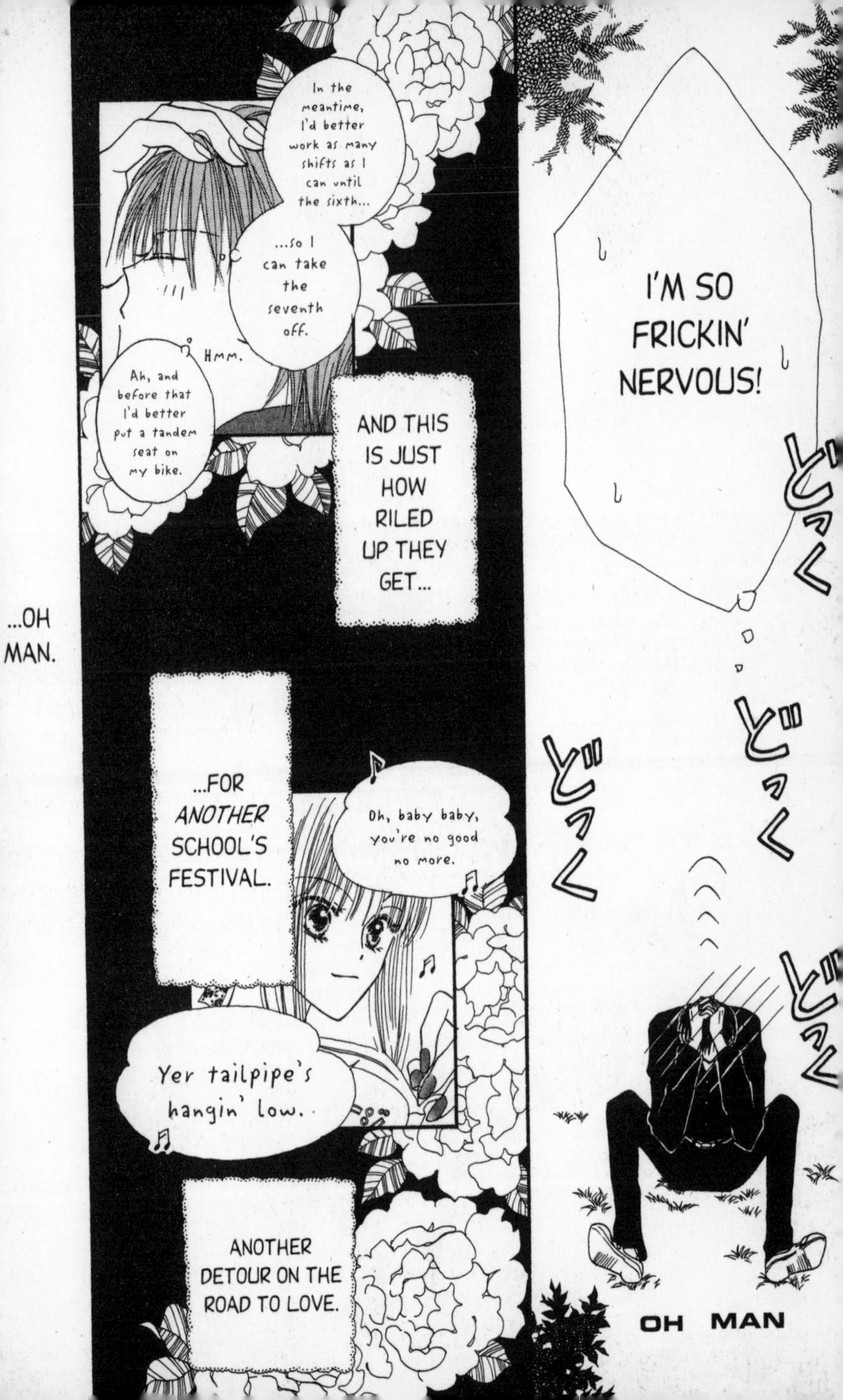
I'M SO FRICKIN' NERVOUS!
どっく
どっく
どっく
どっく
OH MAN
In the meantime, I'd better work as many shifts as I can until the sixth...
...so I can take the seventh off.
HMM.
Ah, and before that I'd better put a tandem seat on my bike.
AND THIS IS JUST HOW RILED UP THEY GET...
...FOR ANOTHER SCHOOL'S FESTIVAL.
Oh, baby baby, you're no good no more.
Yer tailpipe's hangin' low.
ANOTHER DETOUR ON THE ROAD TO LOVE.
...OH MAN.

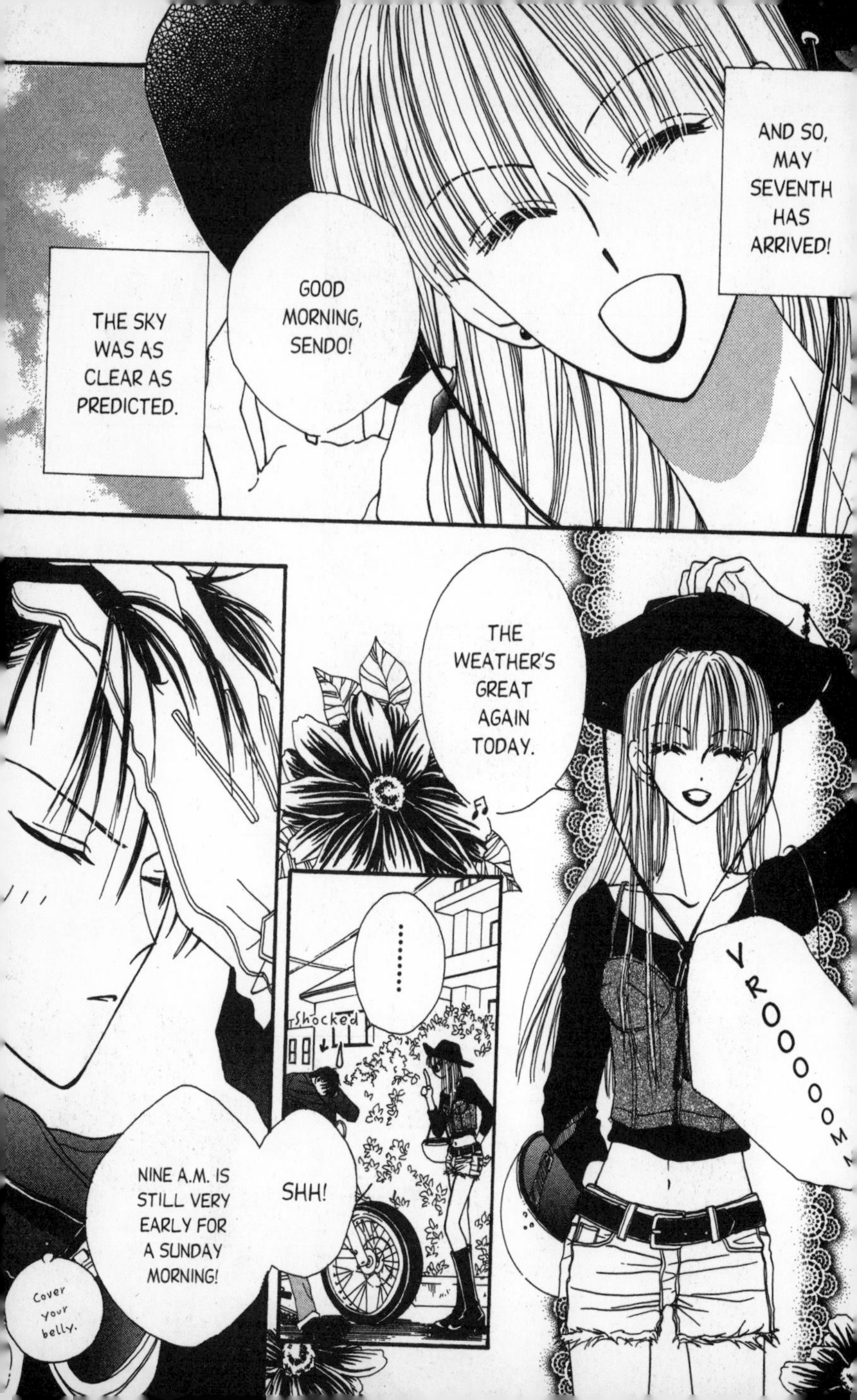
AND SO, MAY SEVENTH HAS ARRIVED!
GOOD MORNING, SENDO!
THE SKY WAS AS CLEAR AS PREDICTED.
THE WEATHER'S GREAT AGAIN TODAY.
VROOOOOOM
......
Shocked
SHH!
NINE A.M. IS STILL VERY EARLY FOR A SUNDAY MORNING!
Cover your belly.

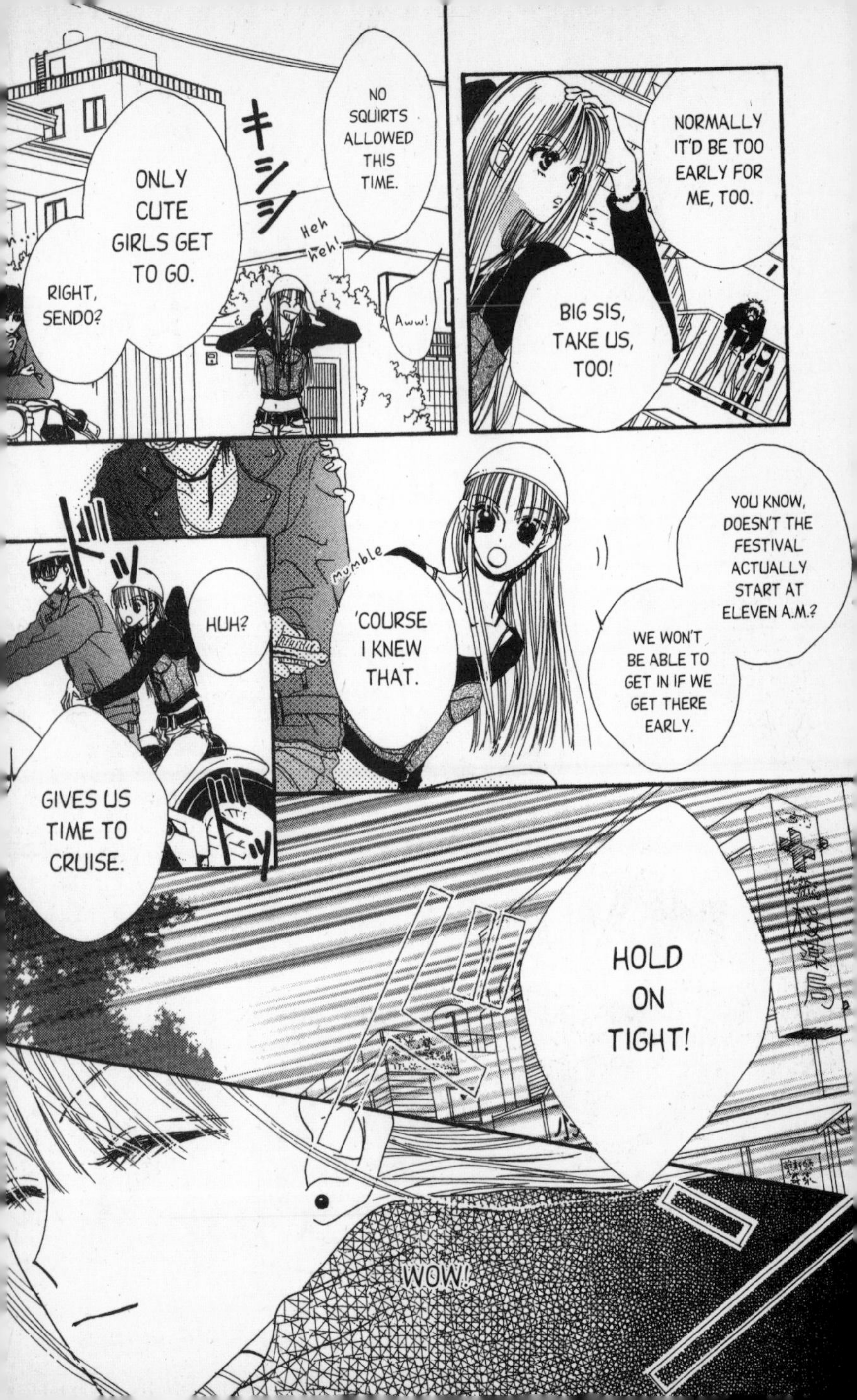
NORMALLY IT'D BE TOO EARLY FOR ME, TOO.
BIG SIS, TAKE US, TOO!
NO SQUIRTS ALLOWED THIS TIME.
キシシ
Heh heh!
Aww!
ONLY CUTE GIRLS GET TO GO.
RIGHT, SENDO?
YOU KNOW, DOESN'T THE FESTIVAL ACTUALLY START AT ELEVEN A.M.?
WE WON'T BE ABLE TO GET IN IF WE GET THERE EARLY.
mumble
'COURSE I KNEW THAT.
HUH?
GIVES US TIME TO CRUISE.
HOLD ON TIGHT!
WOW!

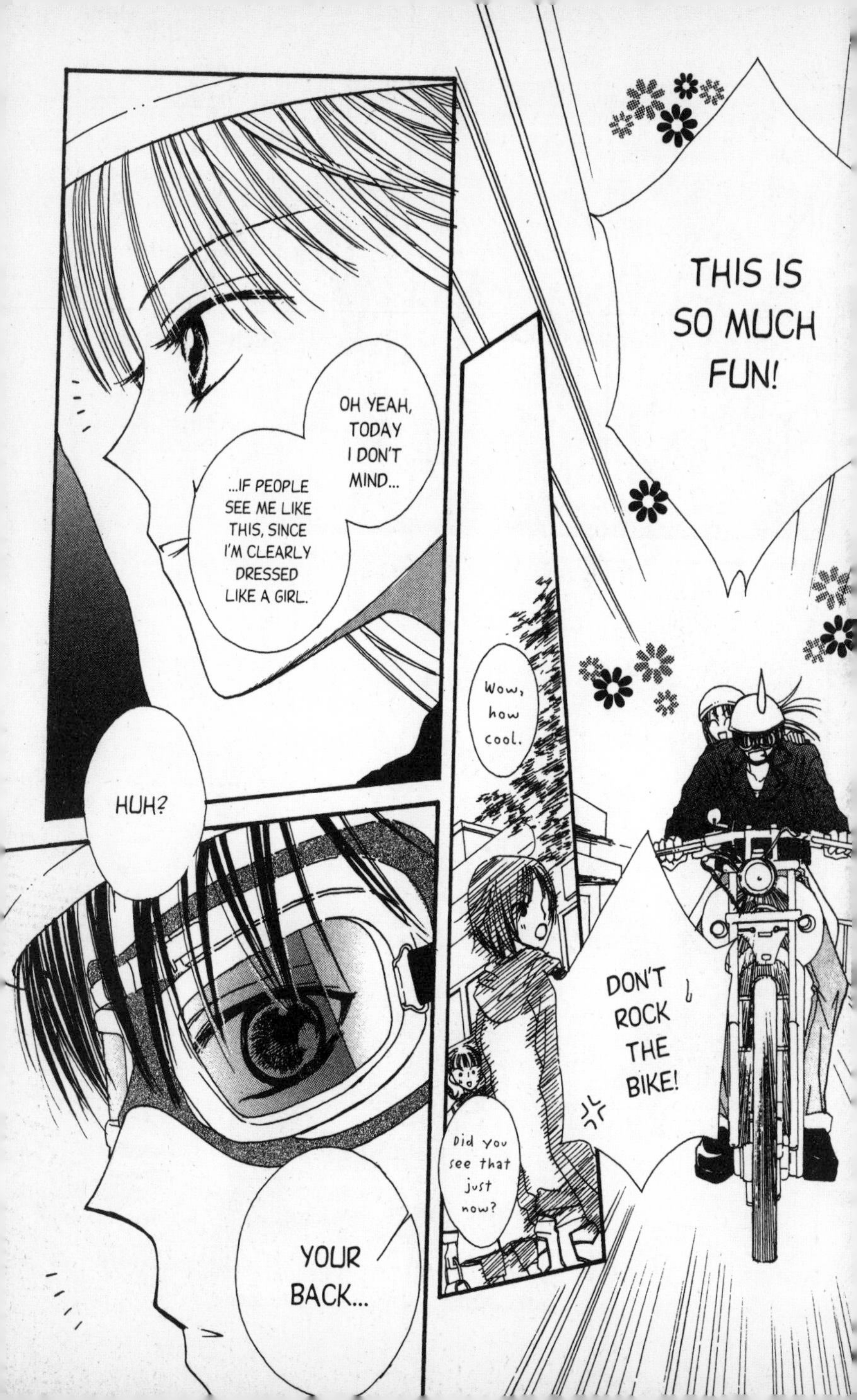
THIS IS SO MUCH FUN!
DON'T ROCK THE BIKE!
Wow, how cool.
Did you see that just now?
OH YEAH, TODAY I DON'T MIND...
...IF PEOPLE SEE ME LIKE THIS, SINCE I'M CLEARLY DRESSED LIKE A GIRL.
HUH?
YOUR BACK...

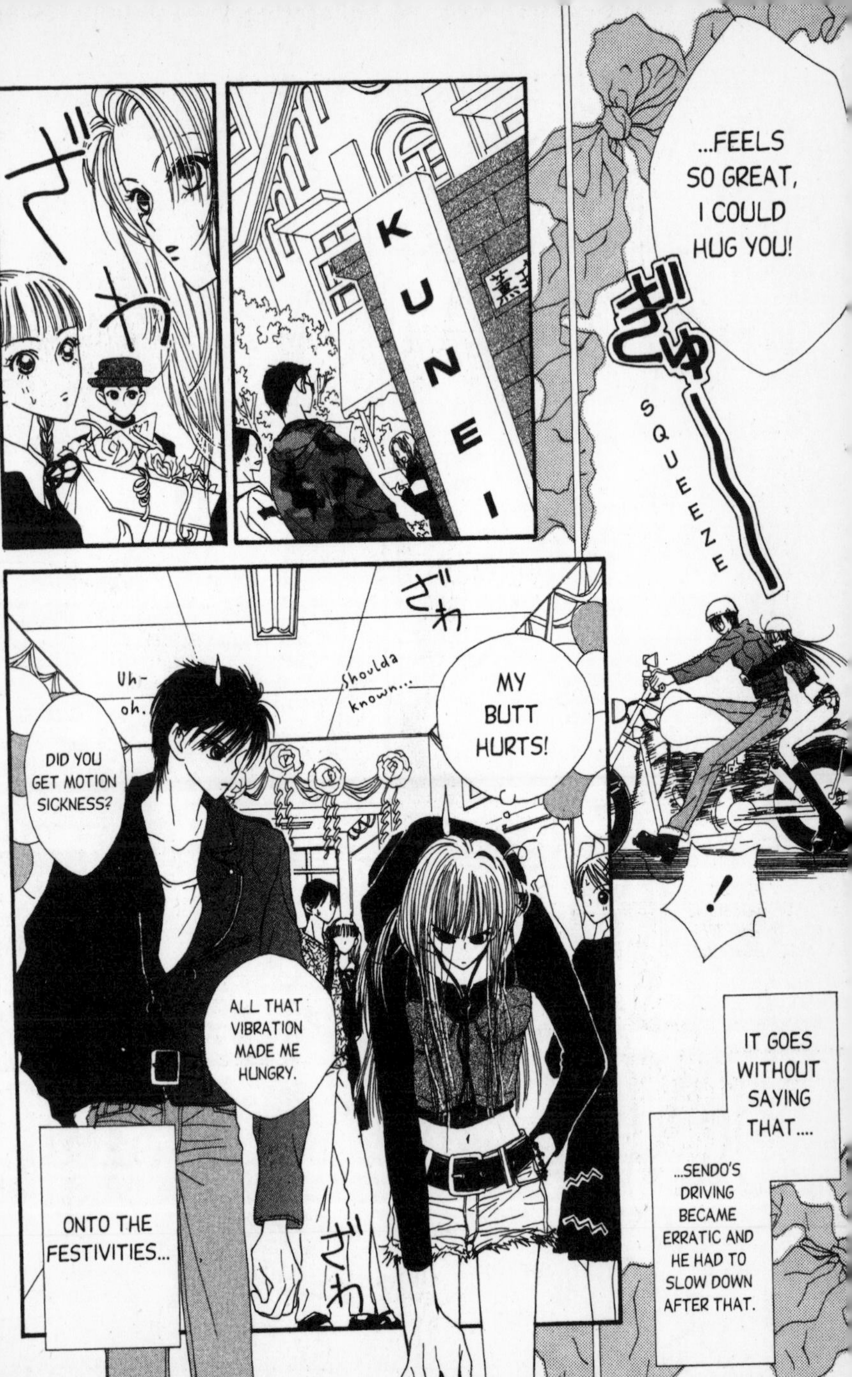

...FEELS SO GREAT, I COULD HUG YOU!
ぎゅー
SQUEEZE
!
IT GOES WITHOUT SAYING THAT....
...SENDO'S DRIVING BECAME ERRATIC AND HE HAD TO SLOW DOWN AFTER THAT.
KUNEI
ざわっ
ざわ
MY BUTT HURTS!
Shoulda known...
Uh-oh.
DID YOU GET MOTION SICKNESS?
ALL THAT VIBRATION MADE ME HUNGRY.
ざわ
ONTO THE FESTIVITIES...

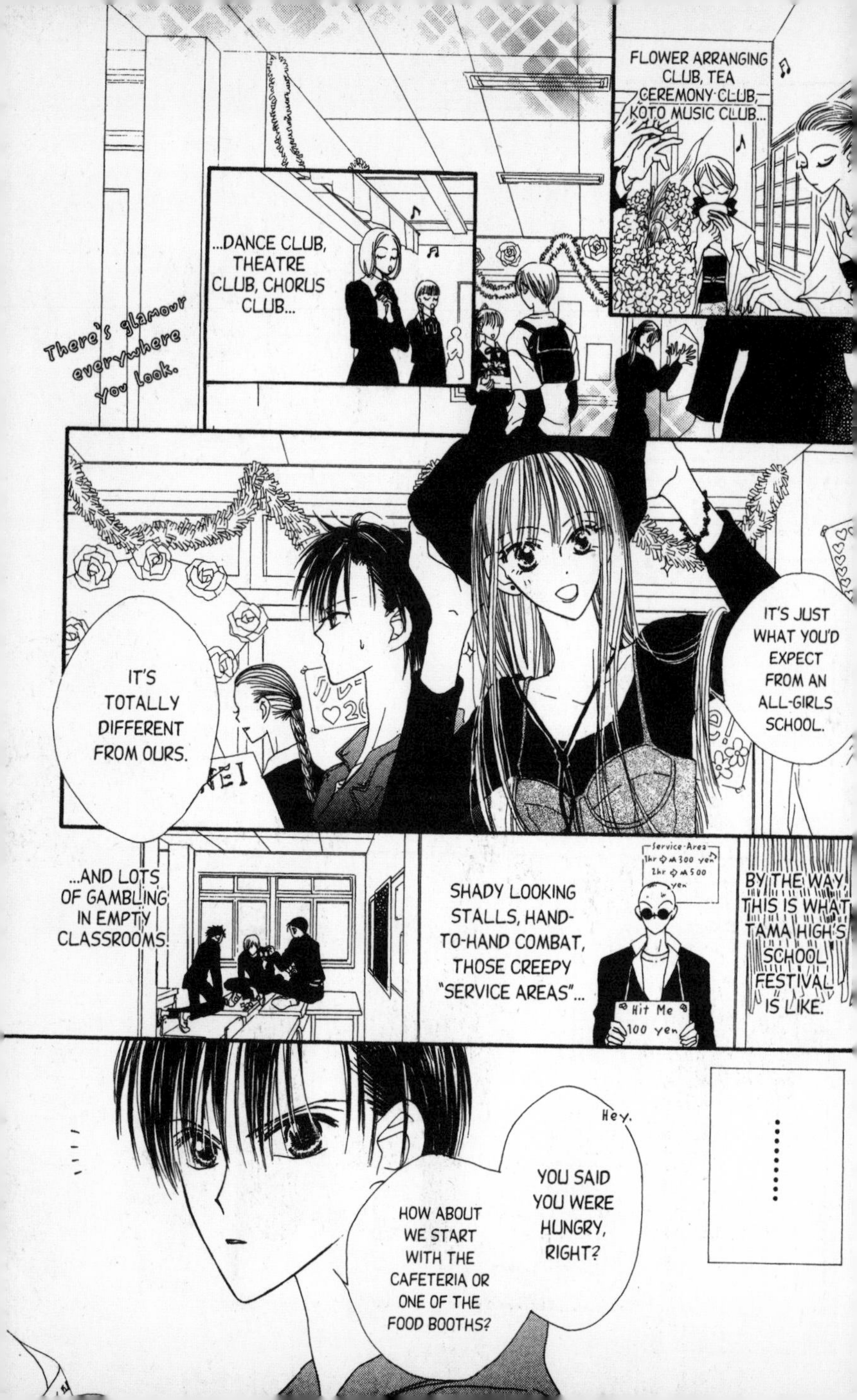
FLOWER ARRANGING CLUB, TEA CEREMONY CLUB, KOTO MUSIC CLUB...
...DANCE CLUB, THEATRE CLUB, CHORUS CLUB...
There's glamour everywhere you look.
IT'S JUST WHAT YOU'D EXPECT FROM AN ALL-GIRLS SCHOOL.
IT'S TOTALLY DIFFERENT FROM OURS.
BY THE WAY, THIS IS WHAT TAMA HIGH'S SCHOOL FESTIVAL IS LIKE.
Service Area
Hit Me 100 yen
SHADY LOOKING STALLS, HAND-TO-HAND COMBAT, THOSE CREEPY "SERVICE AREAS"...
...AND LOTS OF GAMBLING IN EMPTY CLASSROOMS!
....
Hey.
YOU SAID YOU WERE HUNGRY, RIGHT?
HOW ABOUT WE START WITH THE CAFETERIA OR ONE OF THE FOOD BOOTHS?
...

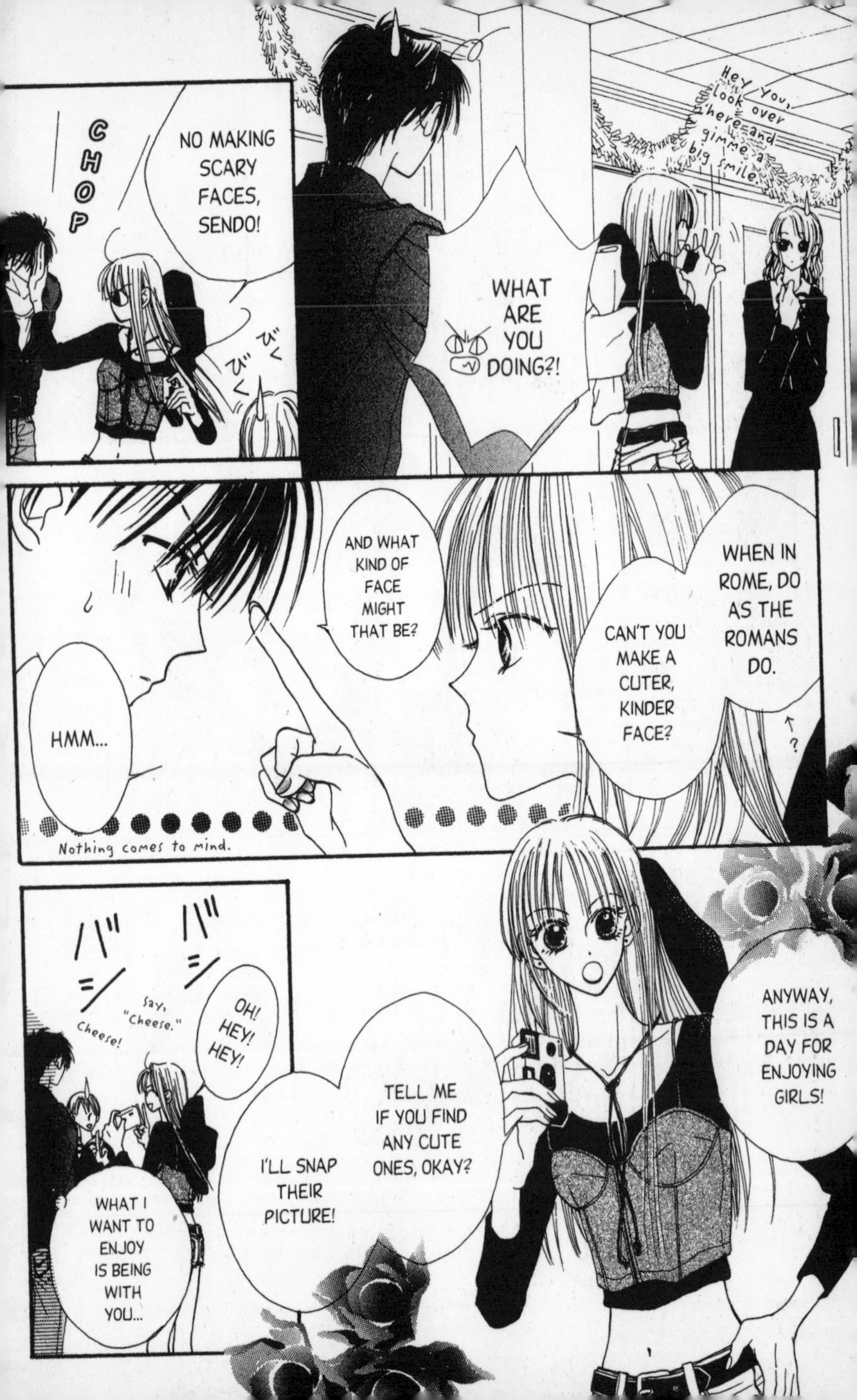
Hey you, look over here and gimme a big smile.
WHAT ARE YOU DOING?!
NO MAKING SCARY FACES, SENDO!
CHOP
びくびく
WHEN IN ROME, DO AS THE ROMANS DO.
?
CAN'T YOU MAKE A CUTER, KINDER FACE?
AND WHAT KIND OF FACE MIGHT THAT BE?
HMM...
Nothing comes to mind.
ANYWAY, THIS IS A DAY FOR ENJOYING GIRLS!
TELL ME IF YOU FIND ANY CUTE ONES, OKAY?
I'LL SNAP THEIR PICTURE!
バババ
OH! HEY! HEY!
Say, "Cheese."
Cheese!
WHAT I WANT TO ENJOY IS BEING WITH YOU...

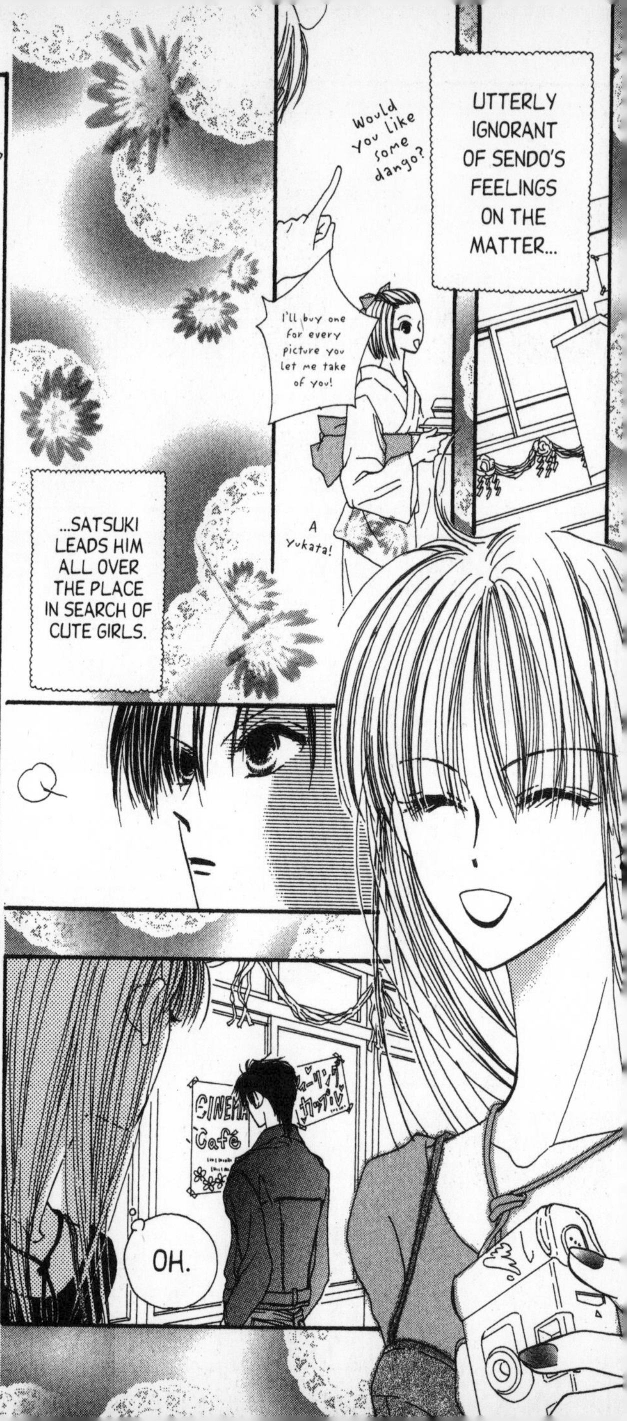
UTTERLY IGNORANT OF SENDO'S FEELINGS ON THE MATTER...
Would you like some dango?
I'll buy one for every picture you let me take of you!
A yukata!
...SATSUKI LEADS HIM ALL OVER THE PLACE IN SEARCH OF CUTE GIRLS.
CINEMA
Café
OH.

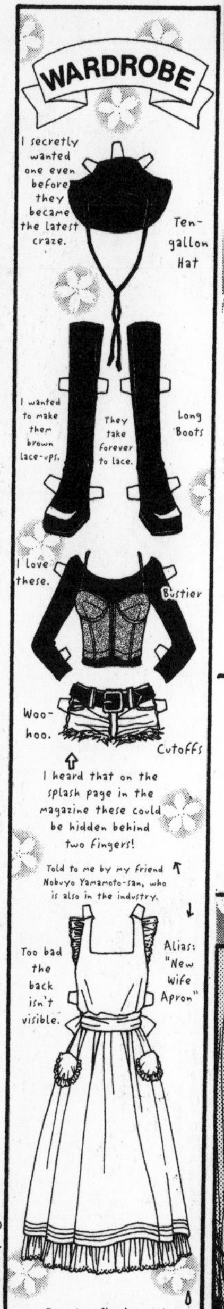
WARDROBE
I secretly wanted one even before they became the latest craze.
Ten-gallon Hat
I wanted to make them brown lace-ups.
They take forever to lace.
Long Boots
I love these.
Bustier
Woo-hoo.
Cutoffs
I heard that on the splash page in the magazine these could be hidden behind two fingers!
Told to me by my friend Nobuyo Yamamoto-san, who is also in the industry.
Too bad the back isn't visible.
Alias: "New Wife Apron"
Barely fit it all!

Oh! People who have made new clothes, please photocopy them and send them in to the publisher, okay? Please!

Note: See page 194

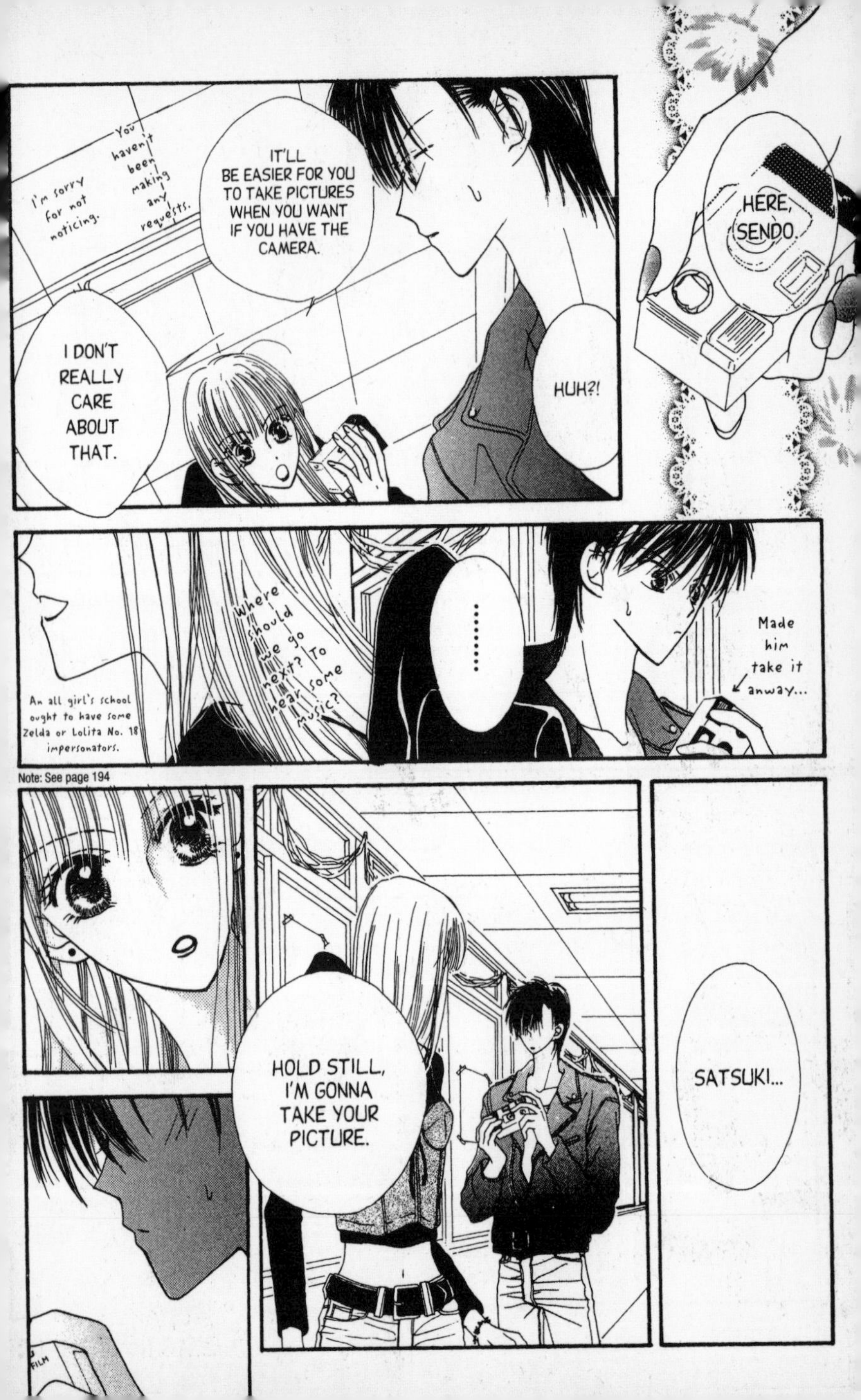
HERE, SENDO.
HUH?!
IT'LL BE EASIER FOR YOU TO TAKE PICTURES WHEN YOU WANT IF YOU HAVE THE CAMERA.
You haven't been making any requests.
I'm sorry for not noticing.
I DON'T REALLY CARE ABOUT THAT.
Made him take it anway...
......
Where should we go next? To hear some music?
An all girl's school ought to have some Zelda or Lolita No. 18 impersonators.
SATSUKI...
HOLD STILL, I'M GONNA TAKE YOUR PICTURE.
Note: See page 194

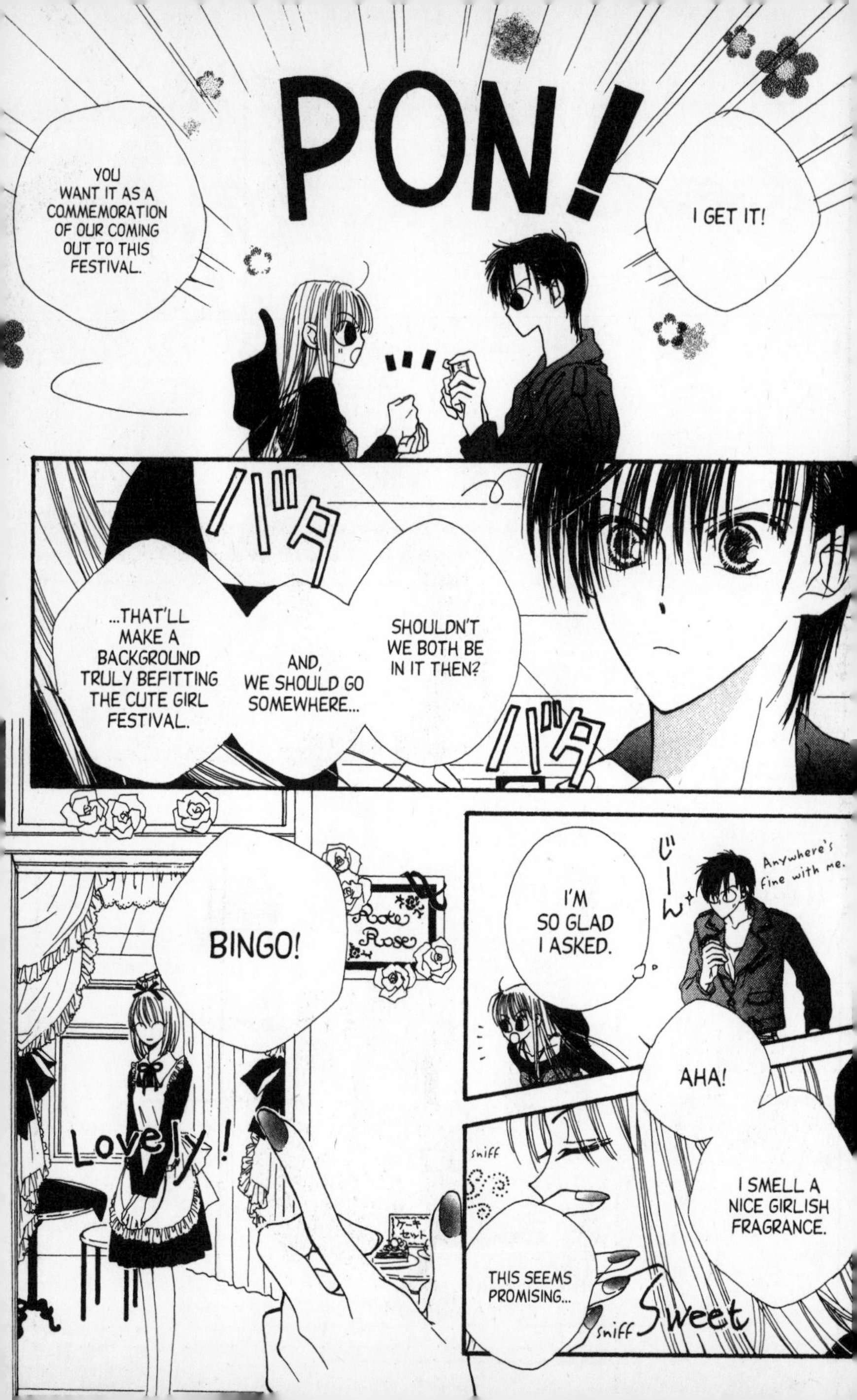
I GET IT!
PON!
YOU WANT IT AS A COMMEMORATION OF OUR COMING OUT TO THIS FESTIVAL.
バタ
SHOULDN'T WE BOTH BE IN IT THEN?
バタ
AND, WE SHOULD GO SOMEWHERE...
...THAT'LL MAKE A BACKGROUND TRULY BEFITTING THE CUTE GIRL FESTIVAL.
Anywhere's fine with me.
じーん
I'M SO GLAD I ASKED.
AHA!
I SMELL A NICE GIRLISH FRAGRANCE.
sniff
Sweet
sniff
THIS SEEMS PROMISING...
BINGO!
Rote Rose
Lovely!
ケーキセット

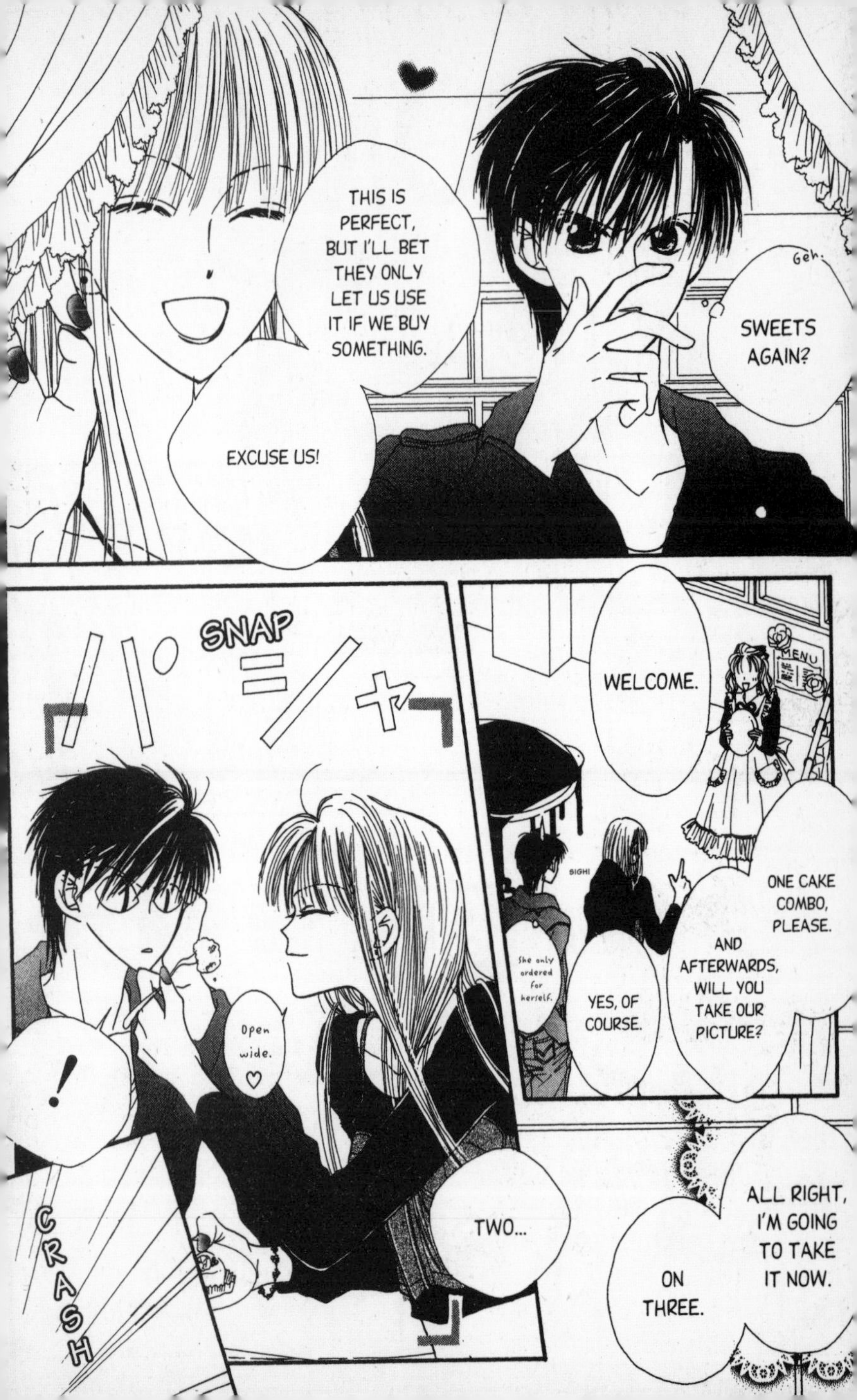
Geh.
SWEETS AGAIN?
THIS IS PERFECT, BUT I'LL BET THEY ONLY LET US USE IT IF WE BUY SOMETHING.
EXCUSE US!
WELCOME.
ONE CAKE COMBO, PLEASE.
AND AFTERWARDS, WILL YOU TAKE OUR PICTURE?
SIGH!
YES, OF COURSE.
She only ordered for herself.
ALL RIGHT, I'M GOING TO TAKE IT NOW.
ON THREE.
SNAP
TWO...
Open wide. ♡
!
CRASH

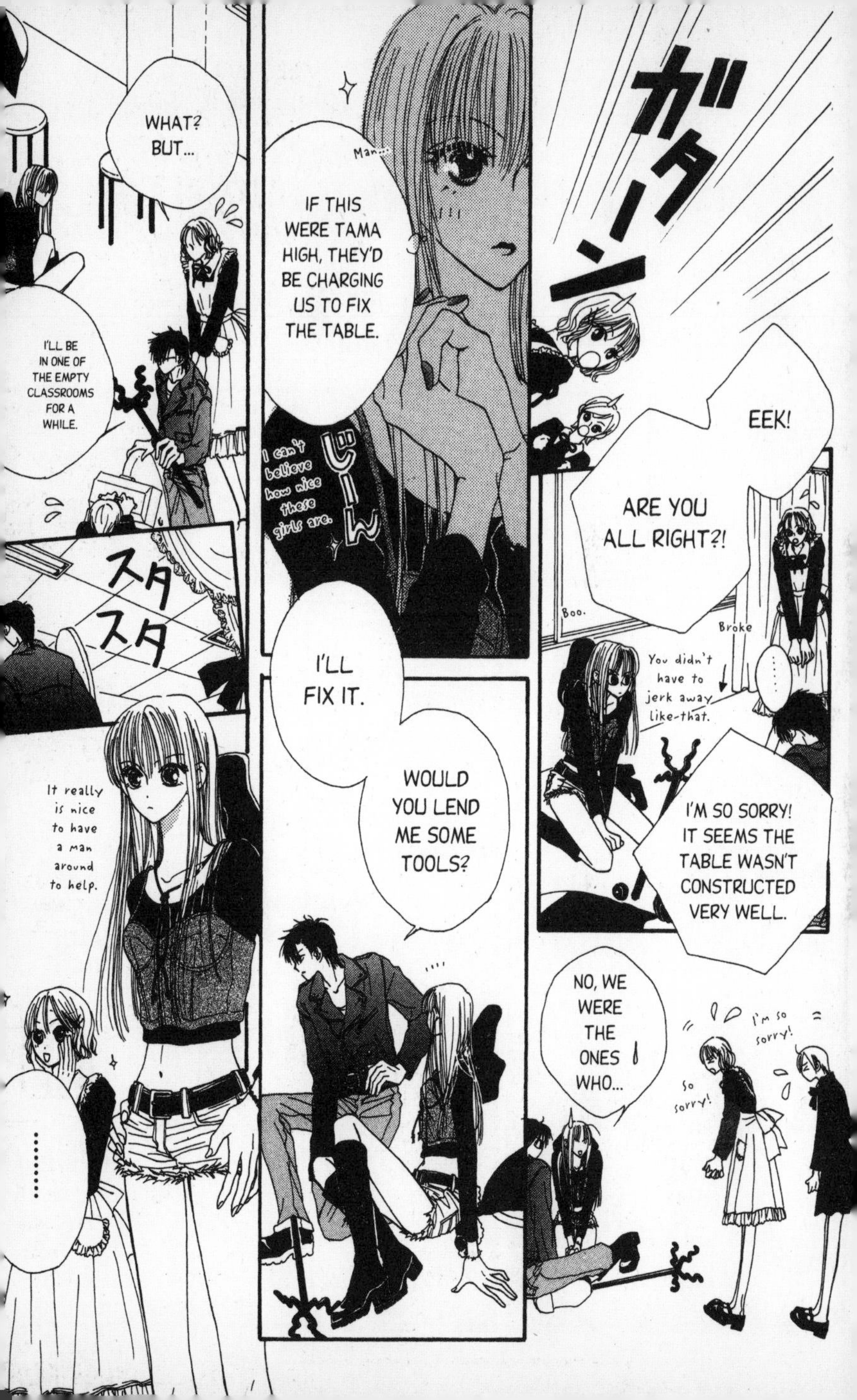
ガターン
EEK!
ARE YOU ALL RIGHT?!
Boo.
Broke
You didn't have to jerk away like-that.
......
I'M SO SORRY! IT SEEMS THE TABLE WASN'T CONSTRUCTED VERY WELL.
NO, WE WERE THE ONES WHO...
I'm so sorry!
So sorry!
Man...
IF THIS WERE TAMA HIGH, THEY'D BE CHARGING US TO FIX THE TABLE.
じーん
I can't believe how nice these girls are.
I'LL FIX IT.
WOULD YOU LEND ME SOME TOOLS?
....
WHAT? BUT...
I'LL BE IN ONE OF THE EMPTY CLASSROOMS FOR A WHILE.
スタスタ
It really is nice to have a man around to help.
....

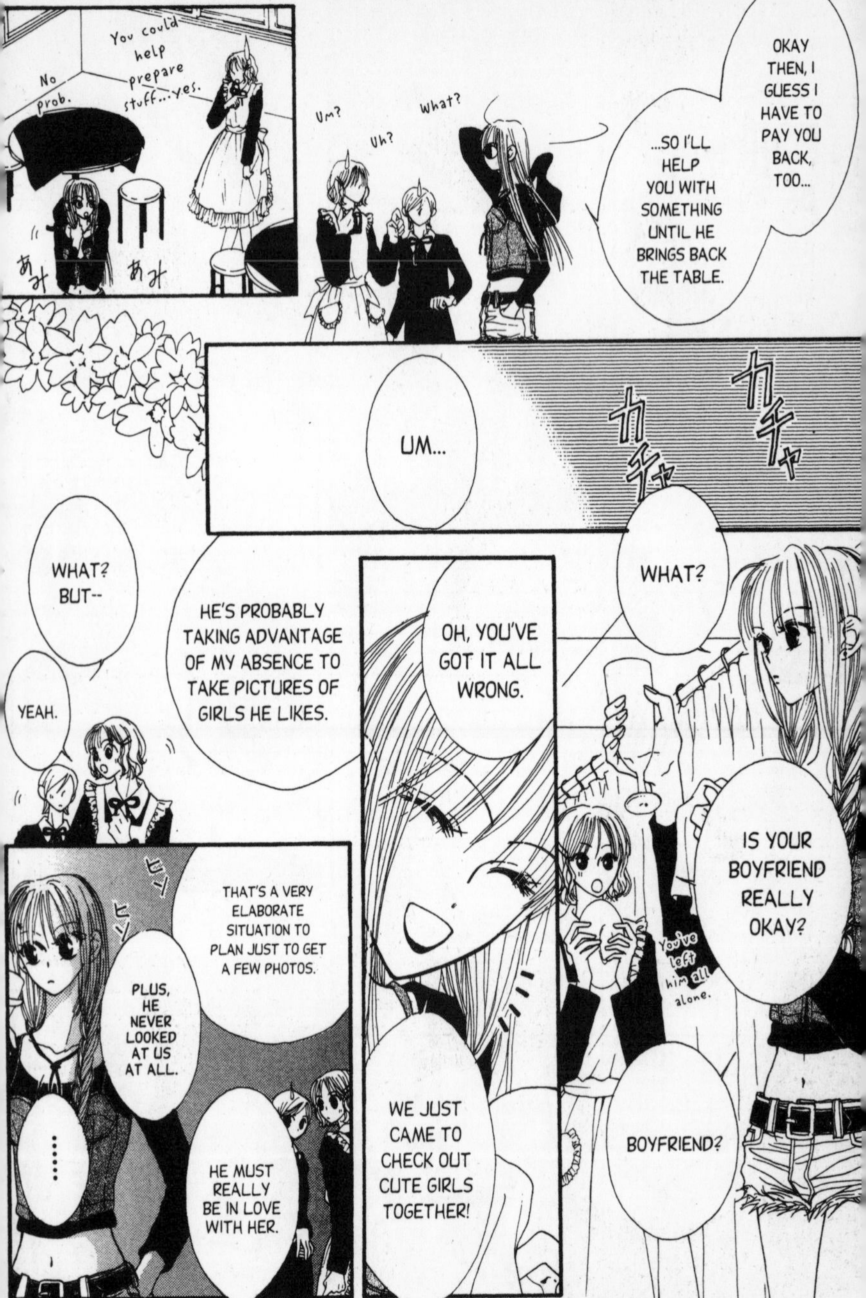
OKAY THEN, I GUESS I HAVE TO PAY YOU BACK, TOO...
...SO I'LL HELP YOU WITH SOMETHING UNTIL HE BRINGS BACK THE TABLE.
What?
Uh?
Um?
You could help prepare stuff...yes.
No prob.
あみ
あみ
カチャ
カチャ
UM...
WHAT?
IS YOUR BOYFRIEND REALLY OKAY?
You've left him all alone.
BOYFRIEND?
OH, YOU'VE GOT IT ALL WRONG.
WE JUST CAME TO CHECK OUT CUTE GIRLS TOGETHER!
HE'S PROBABLY TAKING ADVANTAGE OF MY ABSENCE TO TAKE PICTURES OF GIRLS HE LIKES.
WHAT? BUT--
YEAH.
THAT'S A VERY ELABORATE SITUATION TO PLAN JUST TO GET A FEW PHOTOS.
ヒソ
ヒソ
PLUS, HE NEVER LOOKED AT US AT ALL.
HE MUST REALLY BE IN LOVE WITH HER.
......

He's not my boyfriend, he's my friend.

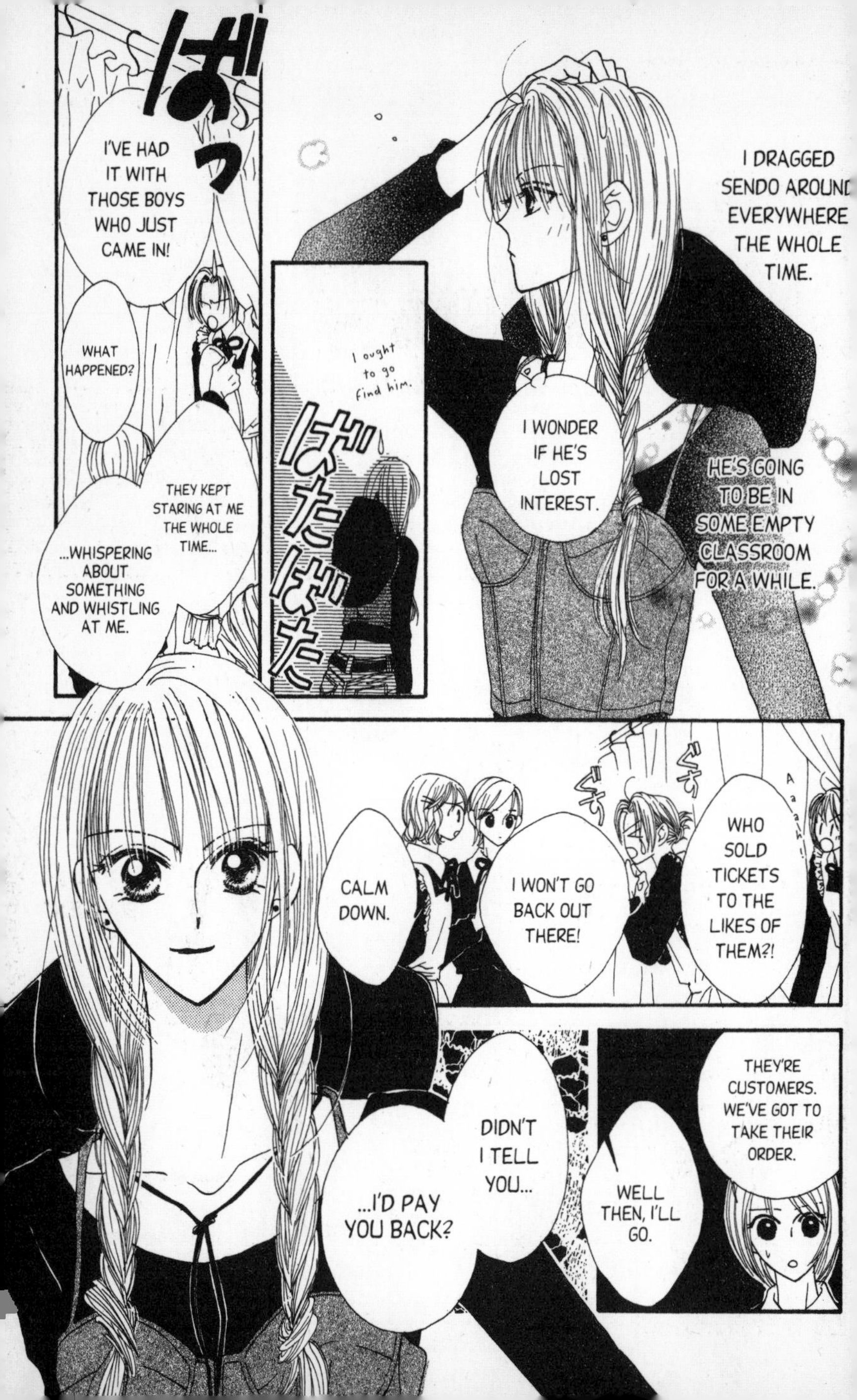
I DRAGGED SENDO AROUND EVERYWHERE THE WHOLE TIME.
I WONDER IF HE'S LOST INTEREST.
HE'S GOING TO BE IN SOME EMPTY CLASSROOM FOR A WHILE.
I ought to go find him.
はたはた
ぱっ
I'VE HAD IT WITH THOSE BOYS WHO JUST CAME IN!
WHAT HAPPENED?
THEY KEPT STARING AT ME THE WHOLE TIME...
...WHISPERING ABOUT SOMETHING AND WHISTLING AT ME.
Aaah!
ぐすっ ぐすっ
WHO SOLD TICKETS TO THE LIKES OF THEM?!
I WON'T GO BACK OUT THERE!
CALM DOWN.
THEY'RE CUSTOMERS. WE'VE GOT TO TAKE THEIR ORDER.
WELL THEN, I'LL GO.
DIDN'T I TELL YOU...
...I'D PAY YOU BACK?

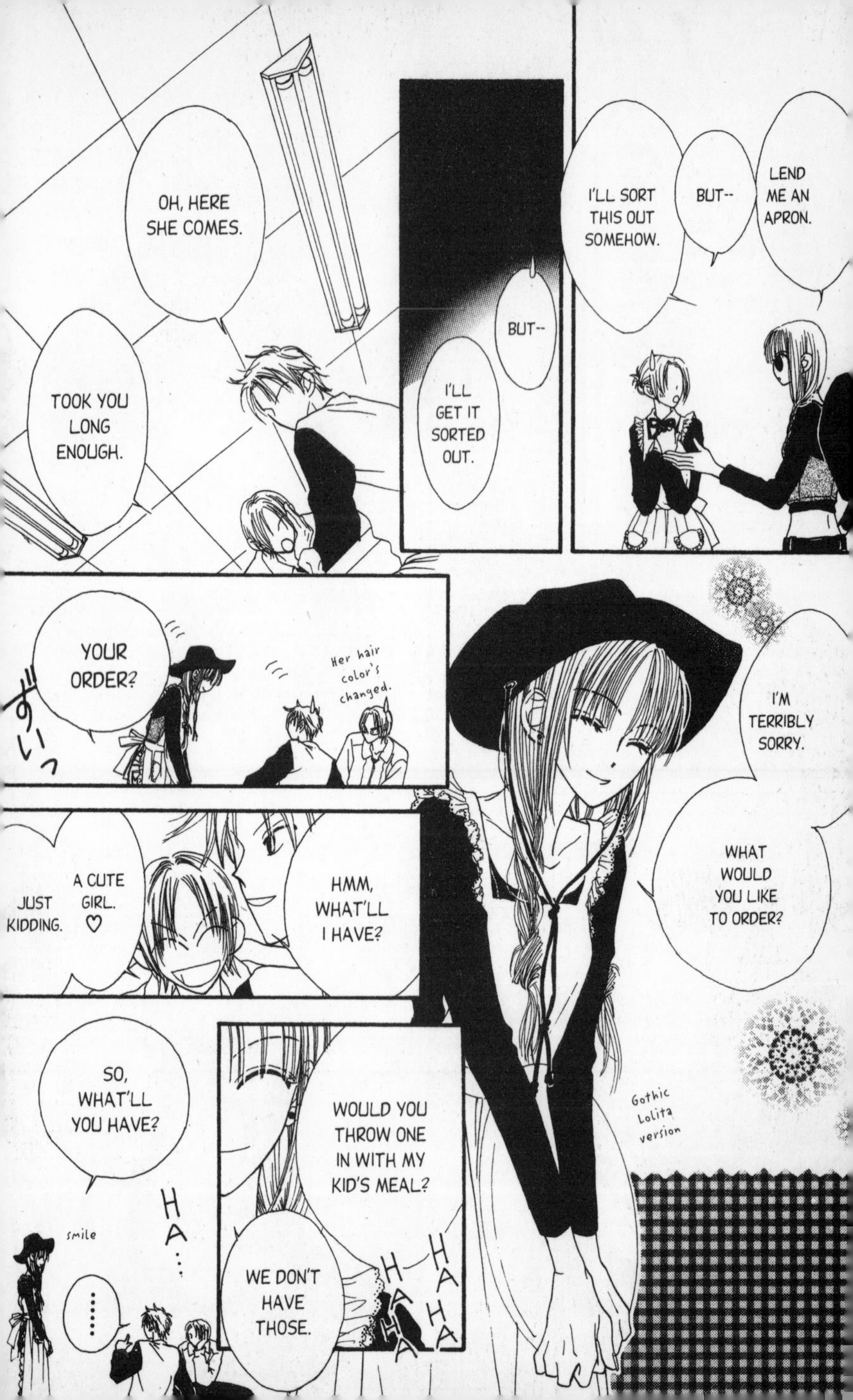
LEND ME AN APRON.
BUT--
I'LL SORT THIS OUT SOMEHOW.
BUT--
I'LL GET IT SORTED OUT.
OH, HERE SHE COMES.
TOOK YOU LONG ENOUGH.
I'M TERRIBLY SORRY.
WHAT WOULD YOU LIKE TO ORDER?
Gothic Lolita version
Her hair color's changed.
YOUR ORDER?
ずいっ
HMM, WHAT'LL I HAVE?
A CUTE GIRL. ♡
JUST KIDDING.
WOULD YOU THROW ONE IN WITH MY KID'S MEAL?
WE DON'T HAVE THOSE.
HAHA
HAHA
SO, WHAT'LL YOU HAVE?
HA...
smile
......

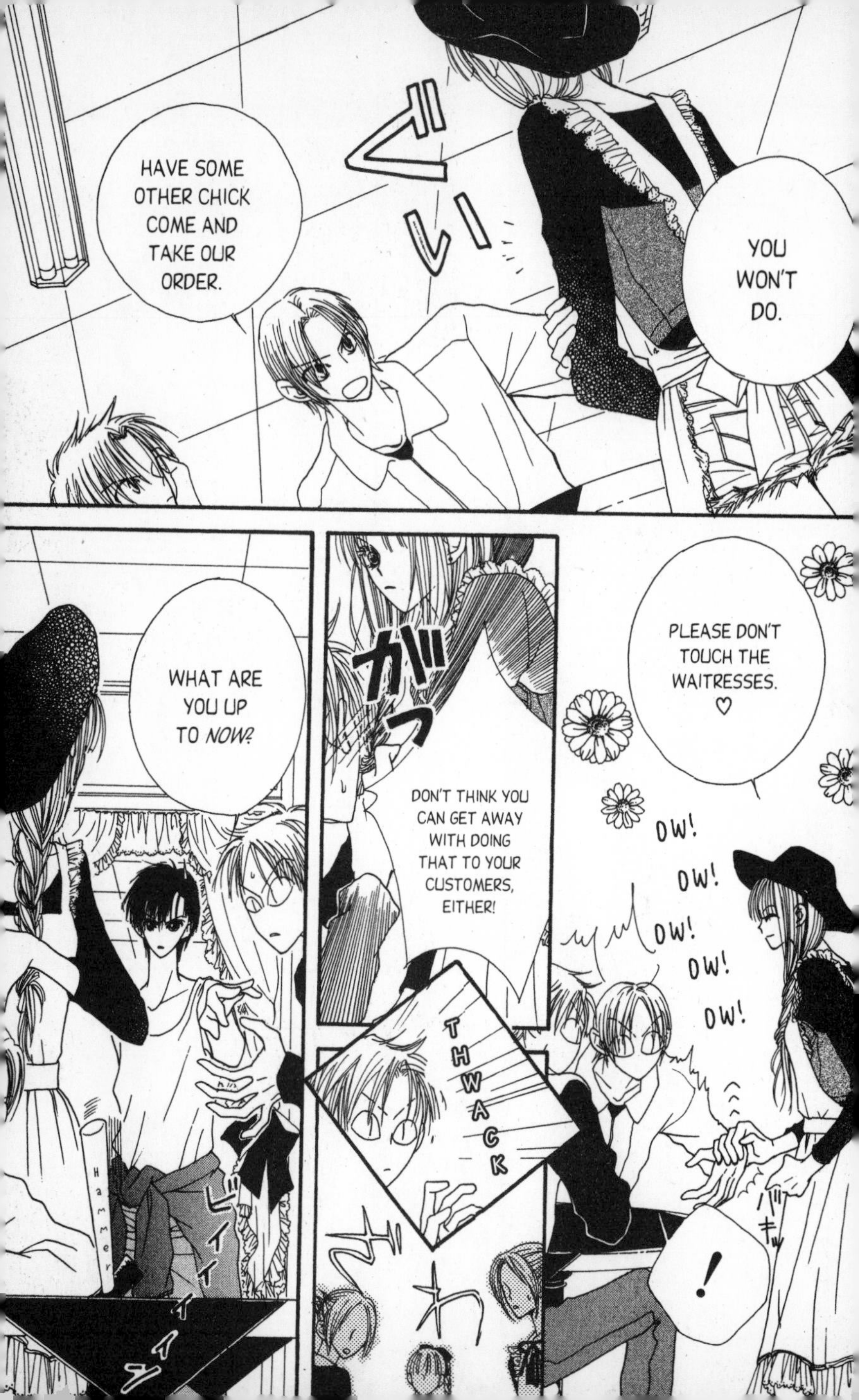
YOU WON'T DO.
HAVE SOME OTHER CHICK COME AND TAKE OUR ORDER.
PLEASE DON'T TOUCH THE WAITRESSES. ♡
OW! OW! OW! OW! OW!
!
DON'T THINK YOU CAN GET AWAY WITH DOING THAT TO YOUR CUSTOMERS, EITHER!
THWACK
WHAT ARE YOU UP TO *NOW?*
Hammer

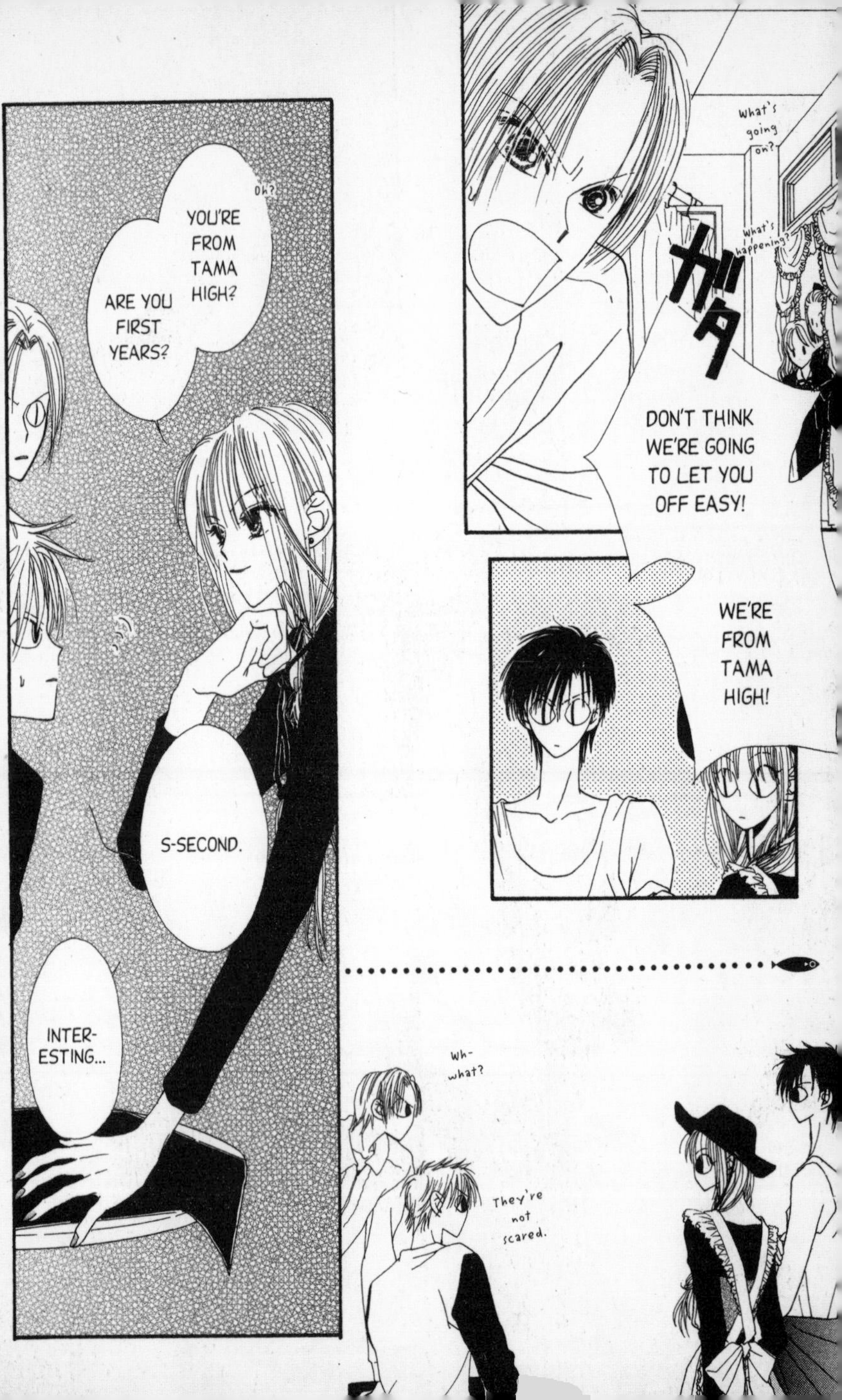
What's going on?
What's happening?
ガタ
DON'T THINK WE'RE GOING TO LET YOU OFF EASY!
WE'RE FROM TAMA HIGH!
Oh?
YOU'RE FROM TAMA HIGH?
ARE YOU FIRST YEARS?
S-SECOND.
INTER-ESTING...
Wh-what?
They're not scared.

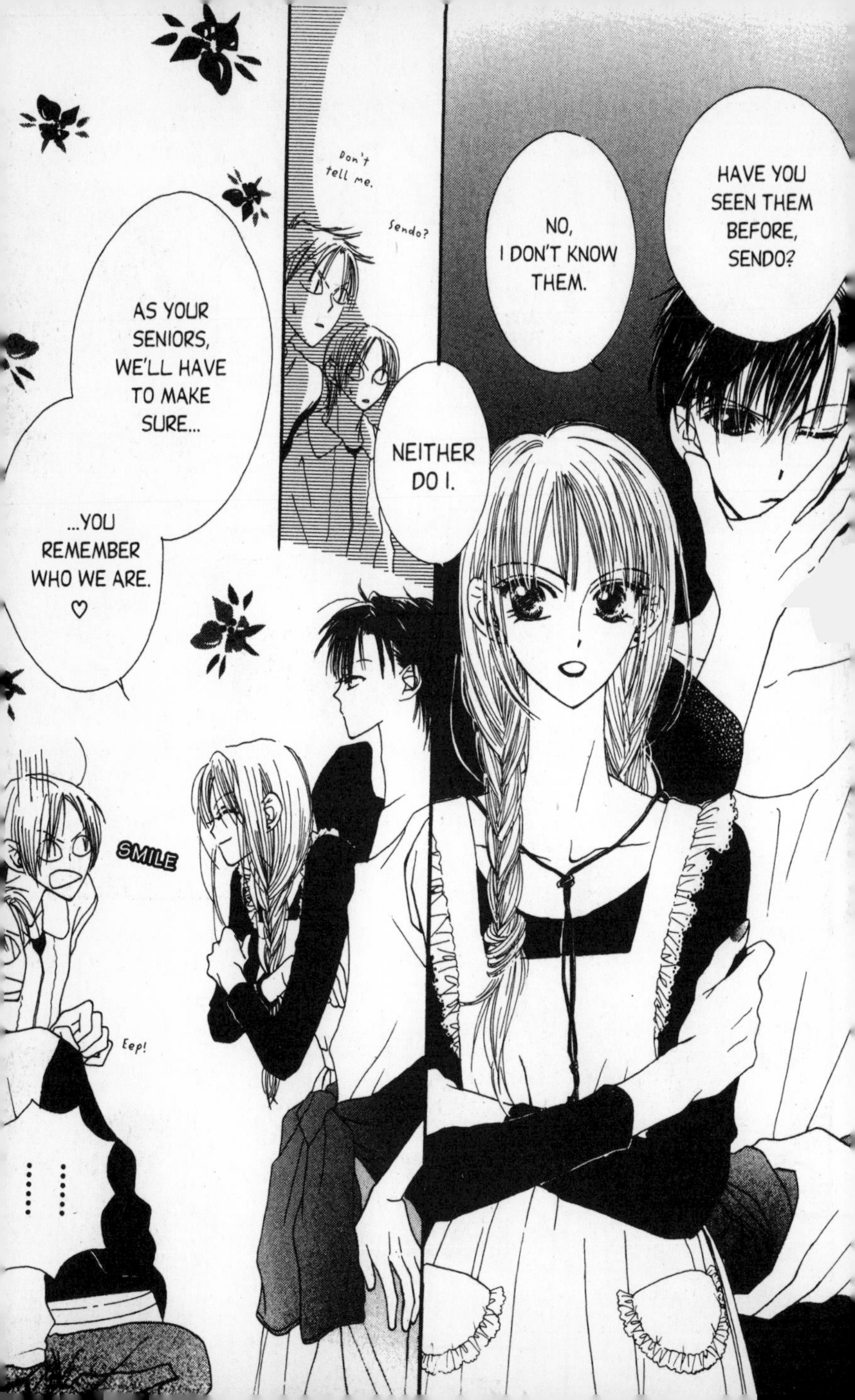
HAVE YOU SEEN THEM BEFORE, SENDO?
NO, I DON'T KNOW THEM.
NEITHER DO I.
Sendo?
Don't tell me.
AS YOUR SENIORS, WE'LL HAVE TO MAKE SURE...
...YOU REMEMBER WHO WE ARE. ♡
SMILE
Eep!
......
......

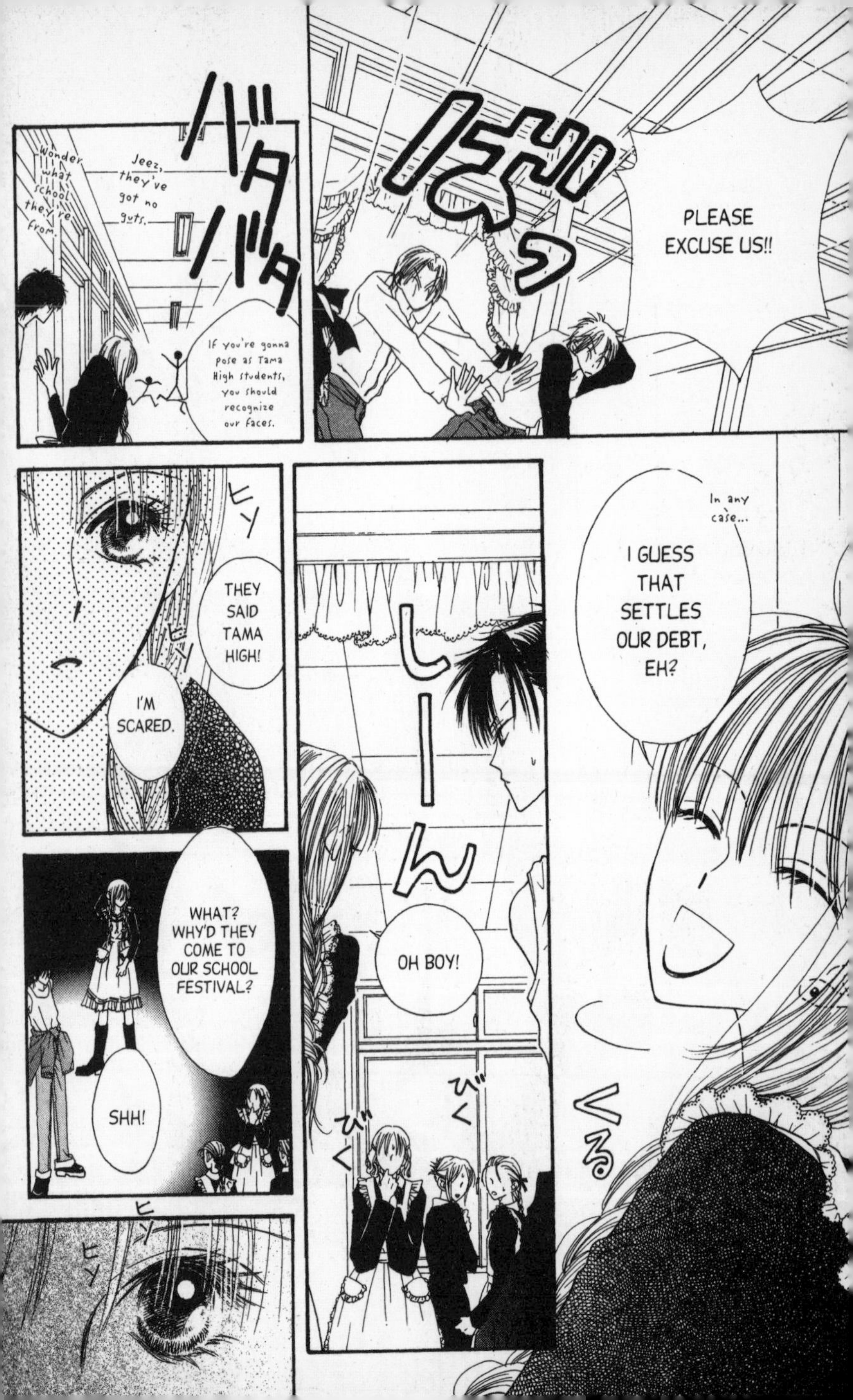
PLEASE EXCUSE US!!
バタバタ
Jeez, they've got no guts.
Wonder what school they're from.
If you're gonna pose as Tama High students, you should recognize our faces.
In any case...
I GUESS THAT SETTLES OUR DEBT, EH?
くる
しーん
OH BOY!
びくびく
ヒソ
THEY SAID TAMA HIGH!
I'M SCARED.
WHAT? WHY'D THEY COME TO OUR SCHOOL FESTIVAL?
SHH!
ヒソヒソ

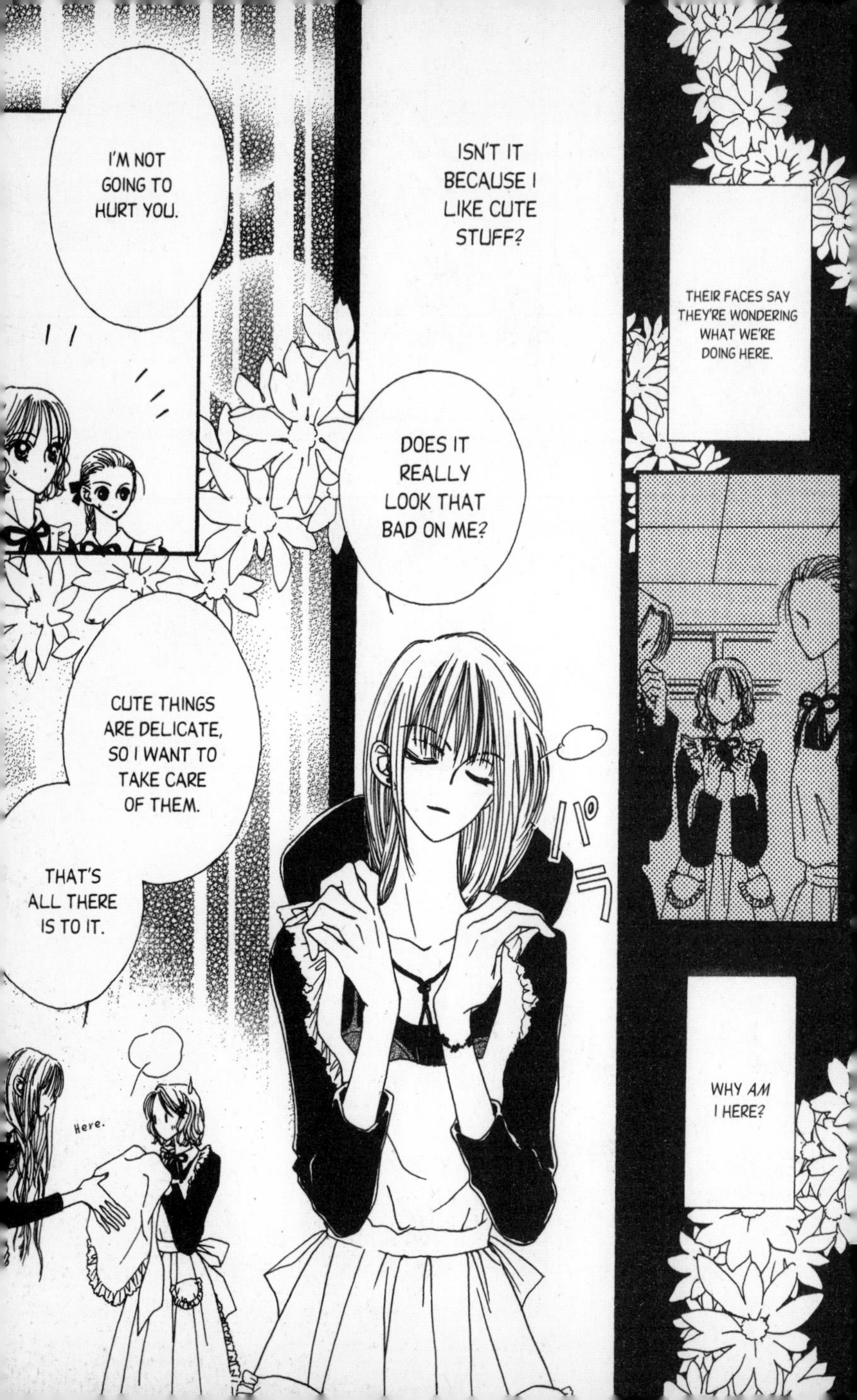
THEIR FACES SAY THEY'RE WONDERING WHAT WE'RE DOING HERE.
WHY *AM* I HERE?
ISN'T IT BECAUSE I LIKE CUTE STUFF?
DOES IT REALLY LOOK THAT BAD ON ME?
パラ
I'M NOT GOING TO HURT YOU.
CUTE THINGS ARE DELICATE, SO I WANT TO TAKE CARE OF THEM.
THAT'S ALL THERE IS TO IT.
Here.

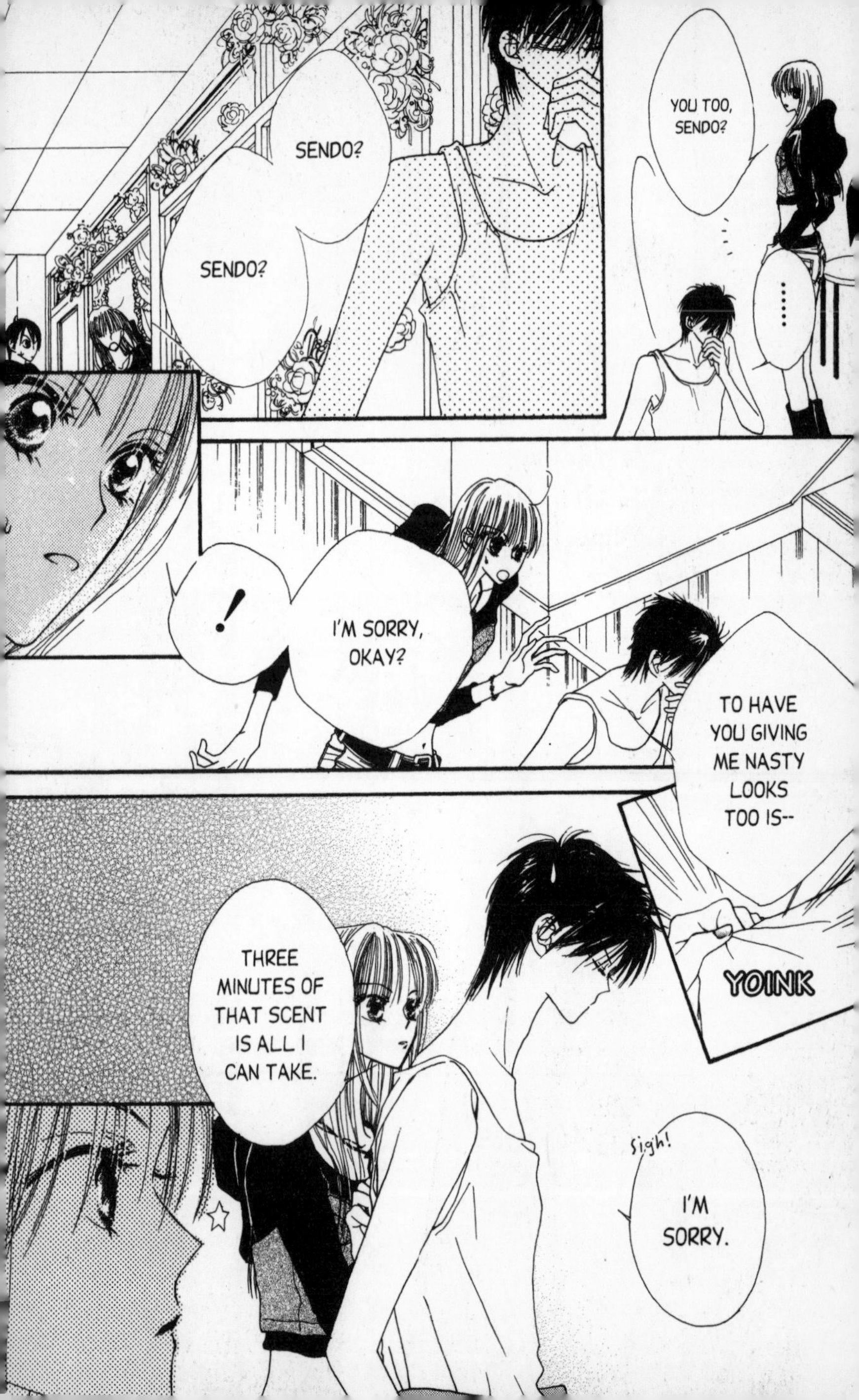
YOU TOO, SENDO?
......
SENDO?
SENDO?
TO HAVE YOU GIVING ME NASTY LOOKS TOO IS--
I'M SORRY, OKAY?
!
YOINK
Sigh!
I'M SORRY.
THREE MINUTES OF THAT SCENT IS ALL I CAN TAKE.

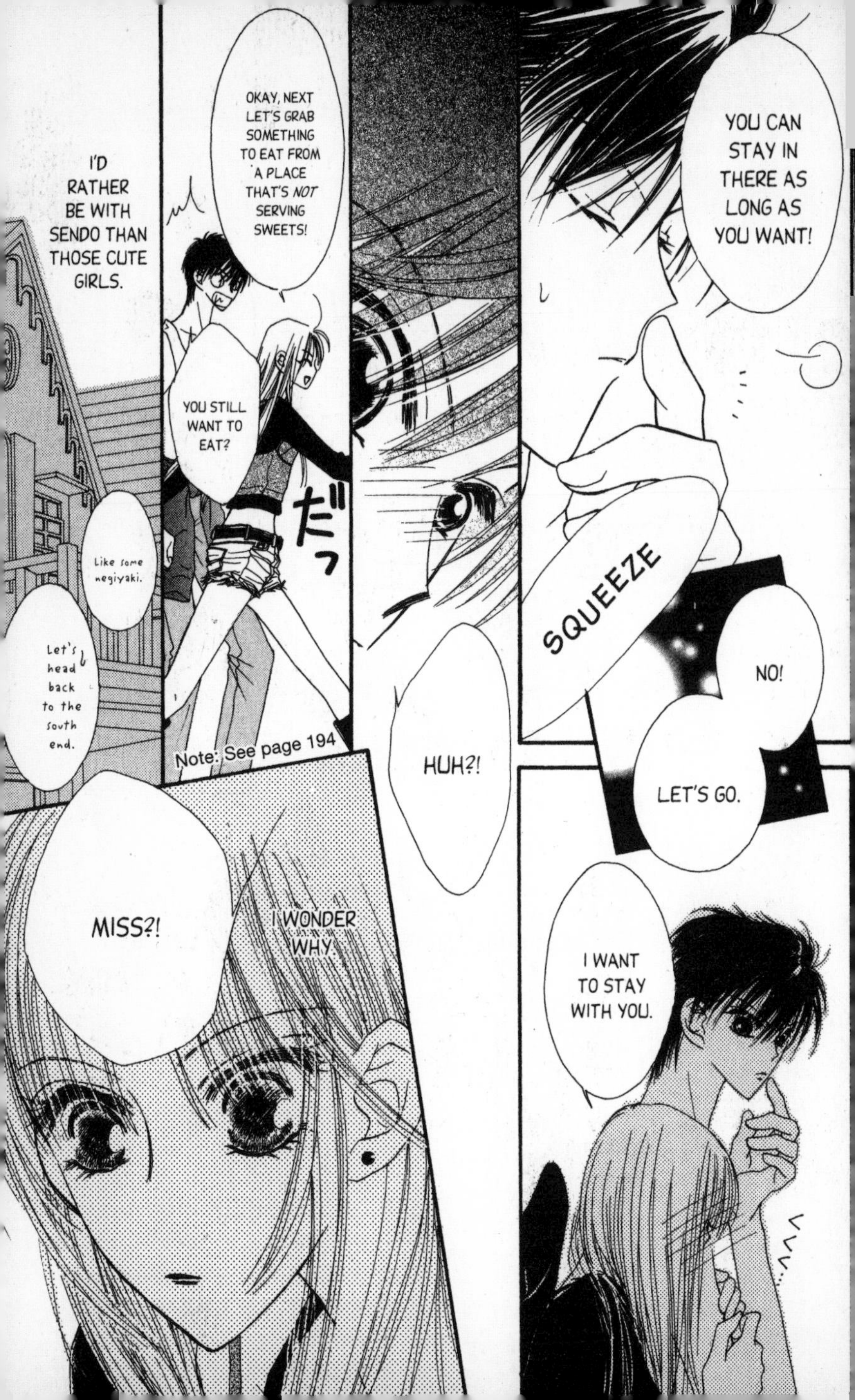
YOU CAN STAY IN THERE AS LONG AS YOU WANT!
SQUEEZE
NO!
LET'S GO.
HUH?!
OKAY, NEXT LET'S GRAB SOMETHING TO EAT FROM A PLACE THAT'S *NOT* SERVING SWEETS!
YOU STILL WANT TO EAT?
だっ
I'D RATHER BE WITH SENDO THAN THOSE CUTE GIRLS.
Like some negiyaki.
Let's head back to the south end.
Note: See page 194
I WANT TO STAY WITH YOU.
MISS?!
I WONDER WHY.

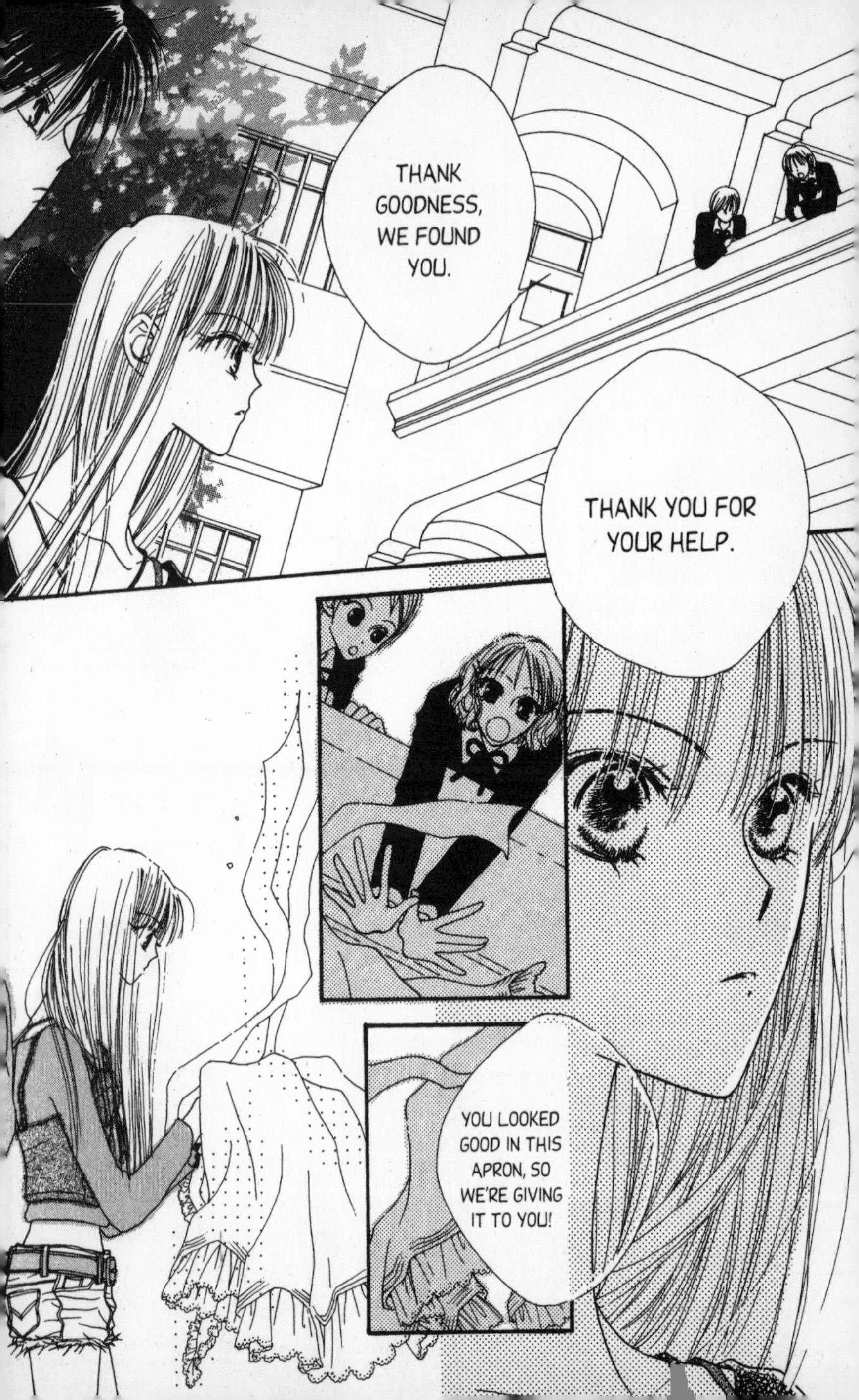
THANK GOODNESS, WE FOUND YOU.
THANK YOU FOR YOUR HELP.
YOU LOOKED GOOD IN THIS APRON, SO WE'RE GIVING IT TO YOU!

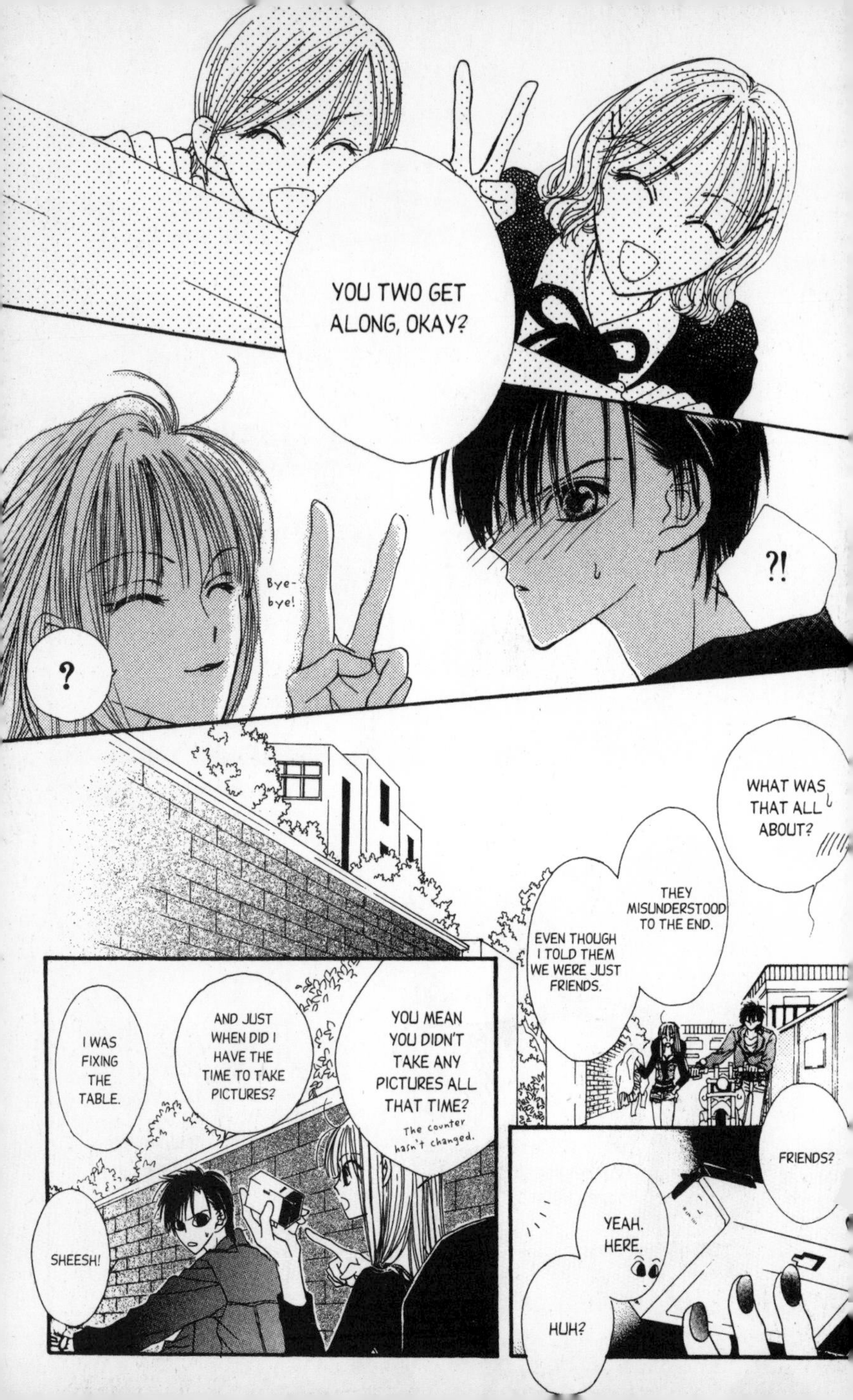
YOU TWO GET ALONG, OKAY?
?!
Bye-bye!
?
WHAT WAS THAT ALL ABOUT?
THEY MISUNDERSTOOD TO THE END.
EVEN THOUGH I TOLD THEM WE WERE JUST FRIENDS.
FRIENDS?
YEAH. HERE.
HUH?
YOU MEAN YOU DIDN'T TAKE ANY PICTURES ALL THAT TIME?
The counter hasn't changed.
AND JUST WHEN DID I HAVE THE TIME TO TAKE PICTURES?
I WAS FIXING THE TABLE.
SHEESH!

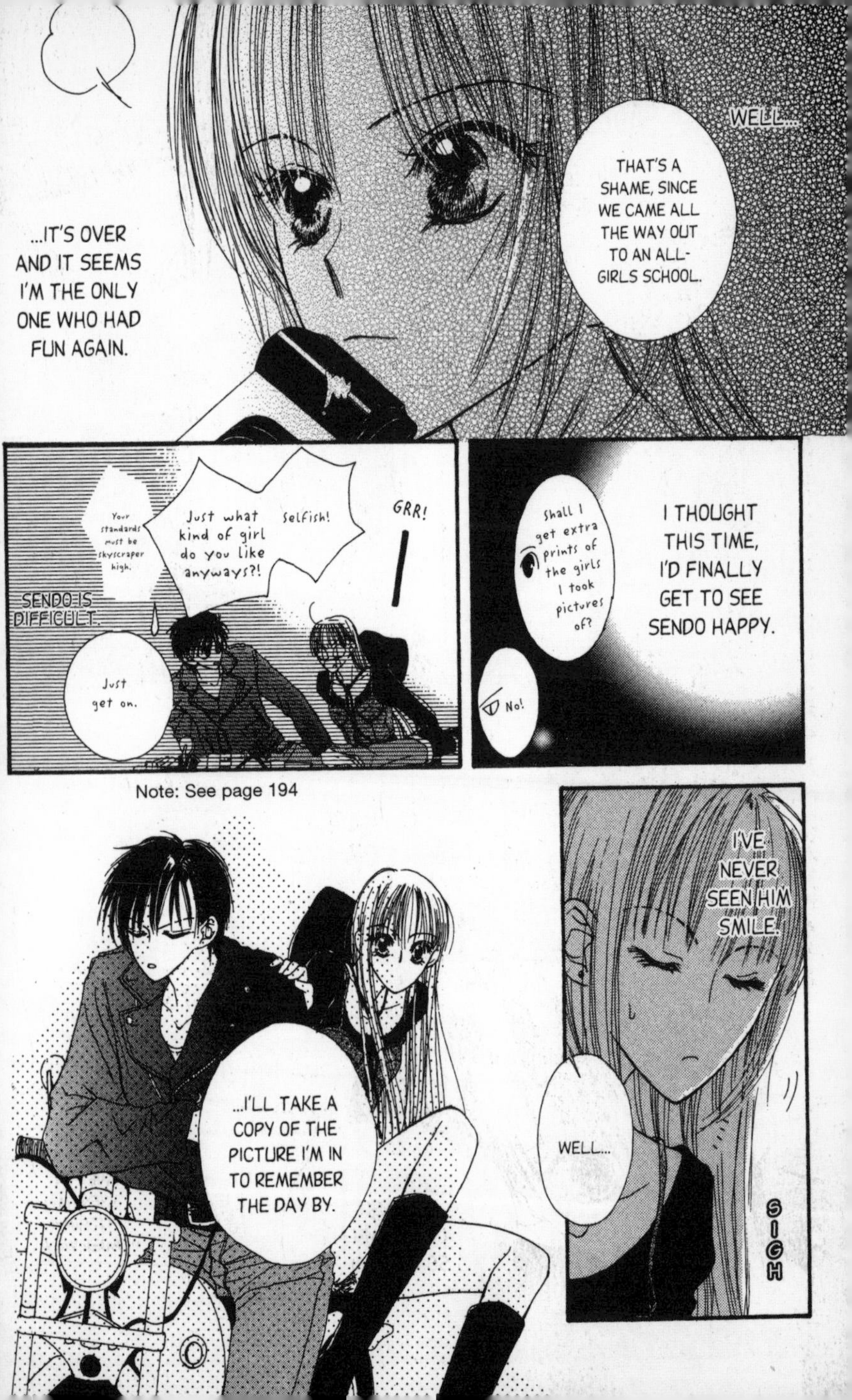
WELL...
THAT'S A SHAME, SINCE WE CAME ALL THE WAY OUT TO AN ALL-GIRLS SCHOOL.
...IT'S OVER AND IT SEEMS I'M THE ONLY ONE WHO HAD FUN AGAIN.
I THOUGHT THIS TIME, I'D FINALLY GET TO SEE SENDO HAPPY.
Shall I get extra prints of the girls I took pictures of?
No!
GRR!
Selfish!
Just what kind of girl do you like anyways?!
Your standards must be skyscraper high.
SENDO IS DIFFICULT.
Just get on.
I'VE NEVER SEEN HIM SMILE.
SIGH
WELL...
...I'LL TAKE A COPY OF THE PICTURE I'M IN TO REMEMBER THE DAY BY.
Note: See page 194

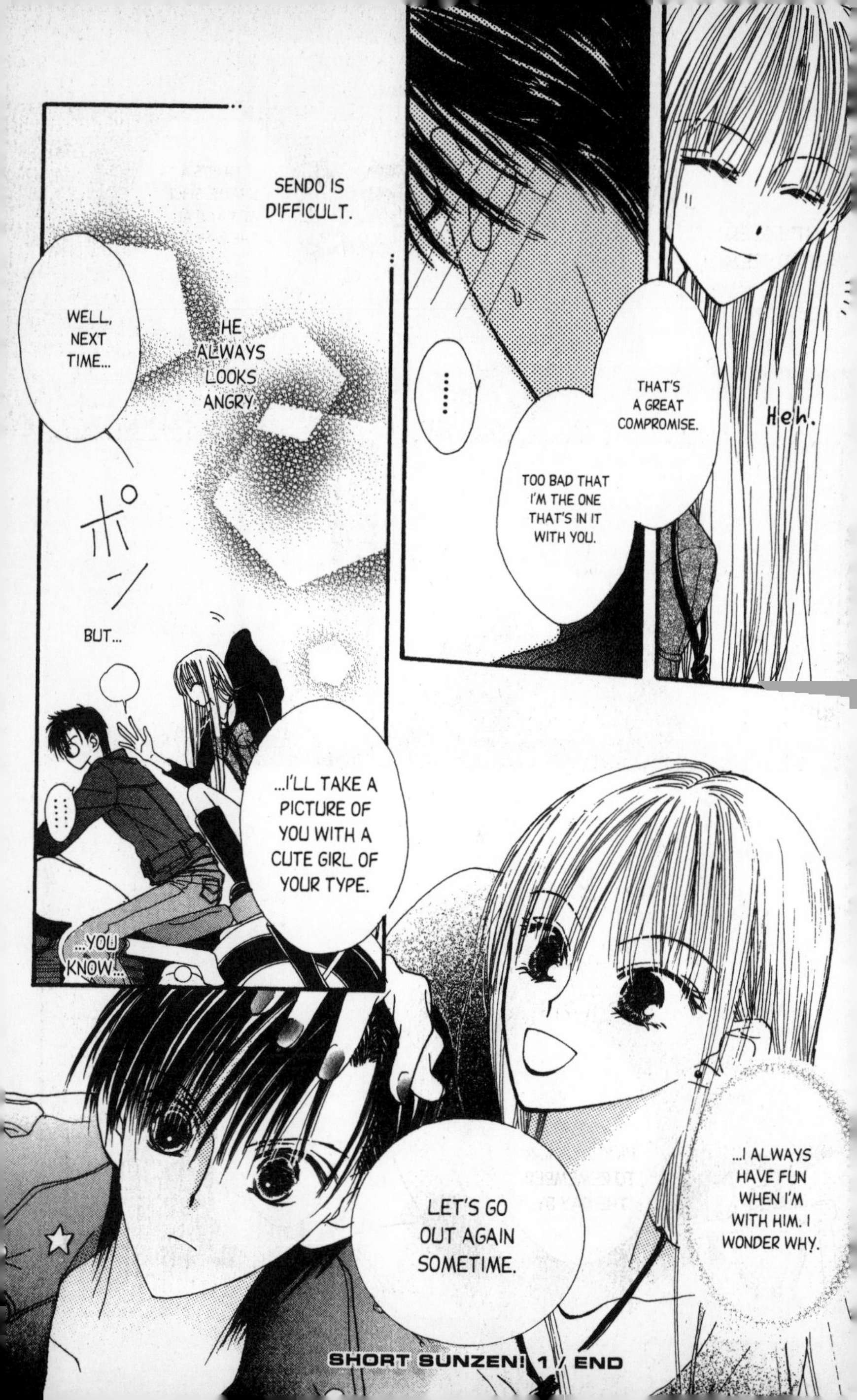
Heh.
THAT'S A GREAT COMPROMISE.
TOO BAD THAT I'M THE ONE THAT'S IN IT WITH YOU.
......
SENDO IS DIFFICULT.
HE ALWAYS LOOKS ANGRY.
WELL, NEXT TIME...
ポン
BUT...
...I'LL TAKE A PICTURE OF YOU WITH A CUTE GIRL OF YOUR TYPE.
......
...YOU KNOW...
...I ALWAYS HAVE FUN WHEN I'M WITH HIM. I WONDER WHY.
LET'S GO OUT AGAIN SOMETIME.
SHORT SUNZEN! 1 / END

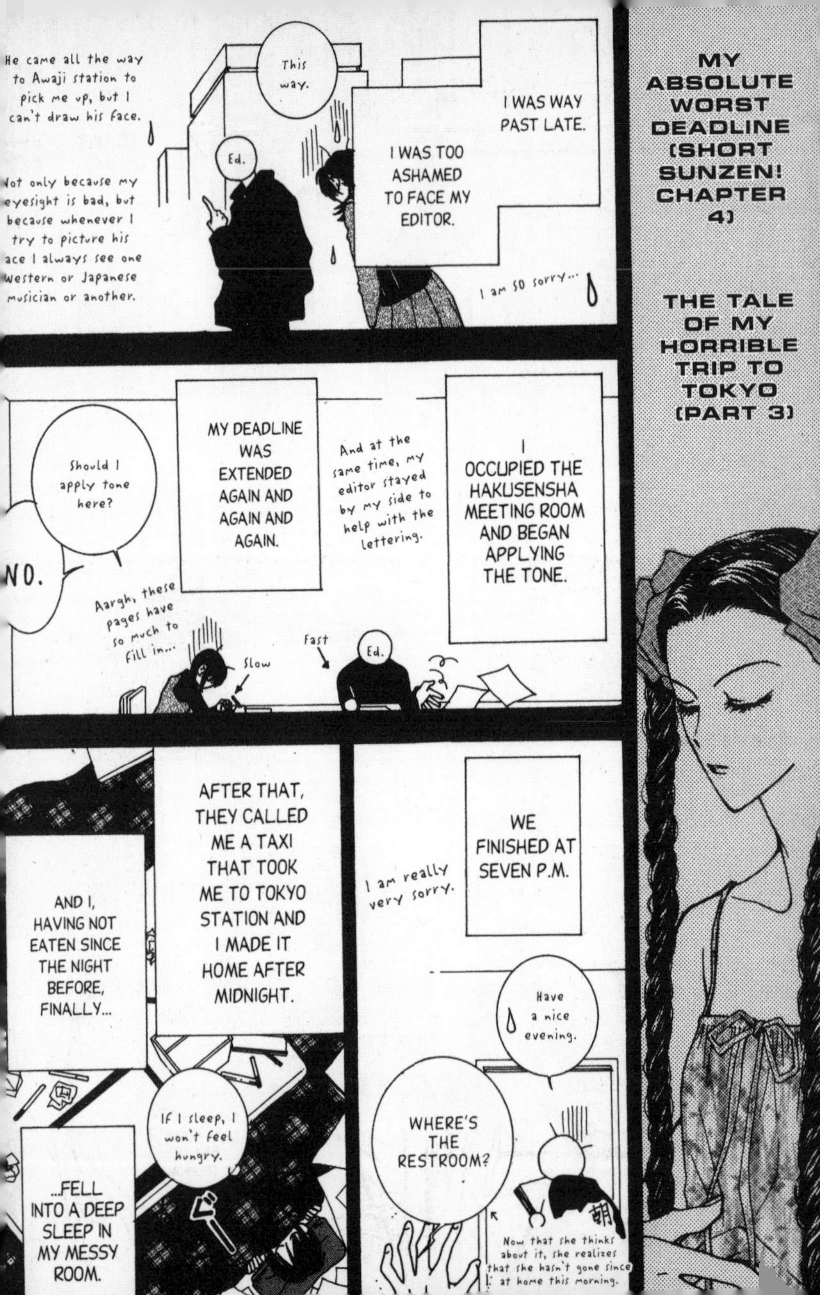
MY ABSOLUTE WORST DEADLINE (SHORT SUNZEN! CHAPTER 4)
THE TALE OF MY HORRIBLE TRIP TO TOKYO (PART 3)
I WAS WAY PAST LATE.
I WAS TOO ASHAMED TO FACE MY EDITOR.
This way.
Ed.
I am so sorry...
He came all the way to Awaji station to pick me up, but I can't draw his face.
Not only because my eyesight is bad, but because whenever I try to picture his ace I always see one western or Japanese musician or another.
I OCCUPIED THE HAKUSENSHA MEETING ROOM AND BEGAN APPLYING THE TONE.
And at the same time, my editor stayed by my side to help with the lettering.
MY DEADLINE WAS EXTENDED AGAIN AND AGAIN AND AGAIN.
Should I apply tone here?
NO.
Aargh, these pages have so much to fill in...
Fast
Ed.
Slow
WE FINISHED AT SEVEN P.M.
I am really very sorry.
Have a nice evening.
WHERE'S THE RESTROOM?
朝
Now that she thinks about it, she realizes that she hasn't gone since at home this morning.
AFTER THAT, THEY CALLED ME A TAXI THAT TOOK ME TO TOKYO STATION AND I MADE IT HOME AFTER MIDNIGHT.
AND I, HAVING NOT EATEN SINCE THE NIGHT BEFORE, FINALLY...
If I sleep, I won't feel hungry.
...FELL INTO A DEEP SLEEP IN MY MESSY ROOM.

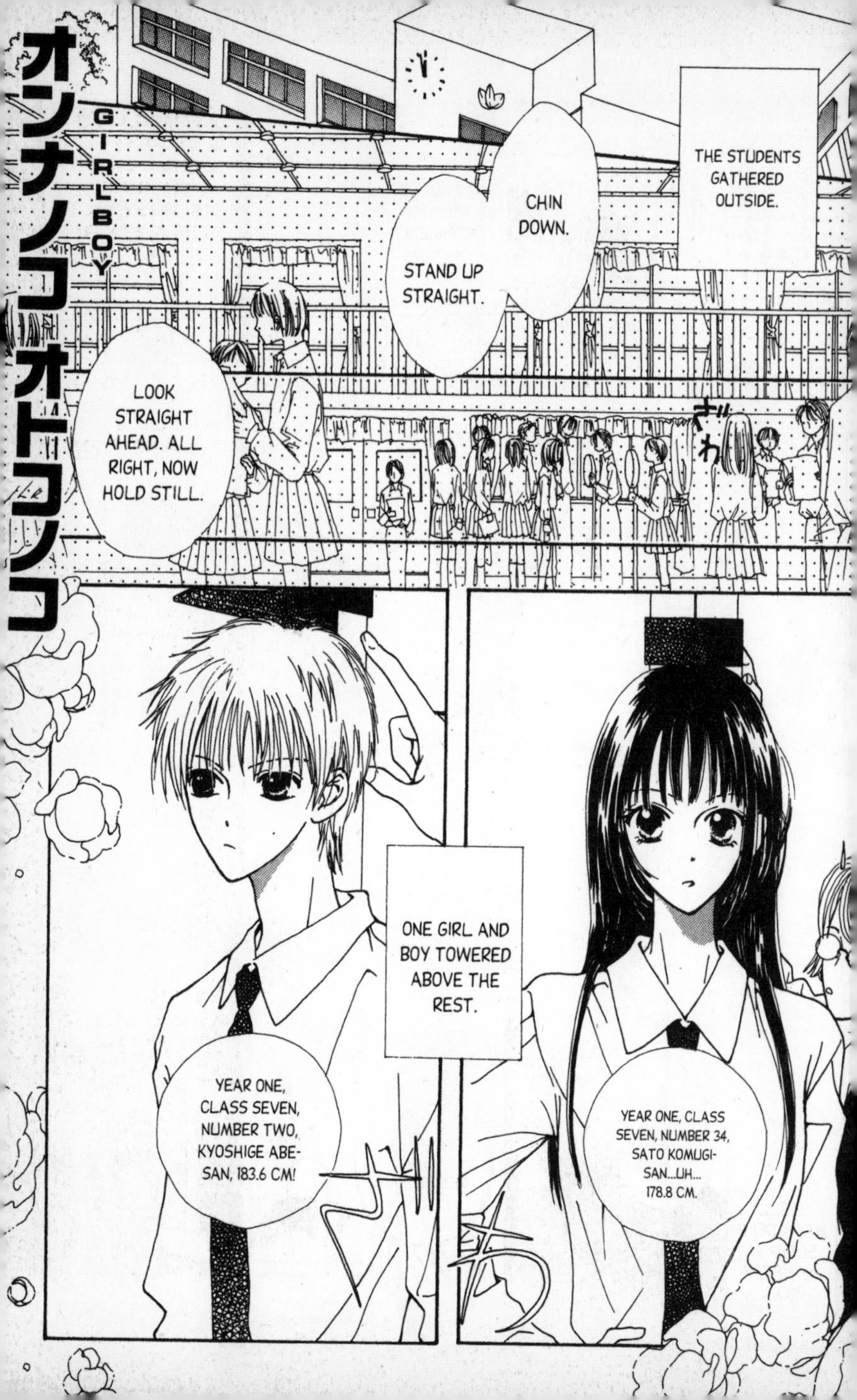
オンナノコオトコノコ
GIRL BOY
THE STUDENTS GATHERED OUTSIDE.
CHIN DOWN.
STAND UP STRAIGHT.
LOOK STRAIGHT AHEAD. ALL RIGHT, NOW HOLD STILL.
ざわ
ONE GIRL AND BOY TOWERED ABOVE THE REST.
YEAR ONE, CLASS SEVEN, NUMBER 34, SATO KOMUGI-SAN...UH... 178.8 CM.
YEAR ONE, CLASS SEVEN, NUMBER TWO, KYOSHIGE ABE-SAN, 183.6 CM!

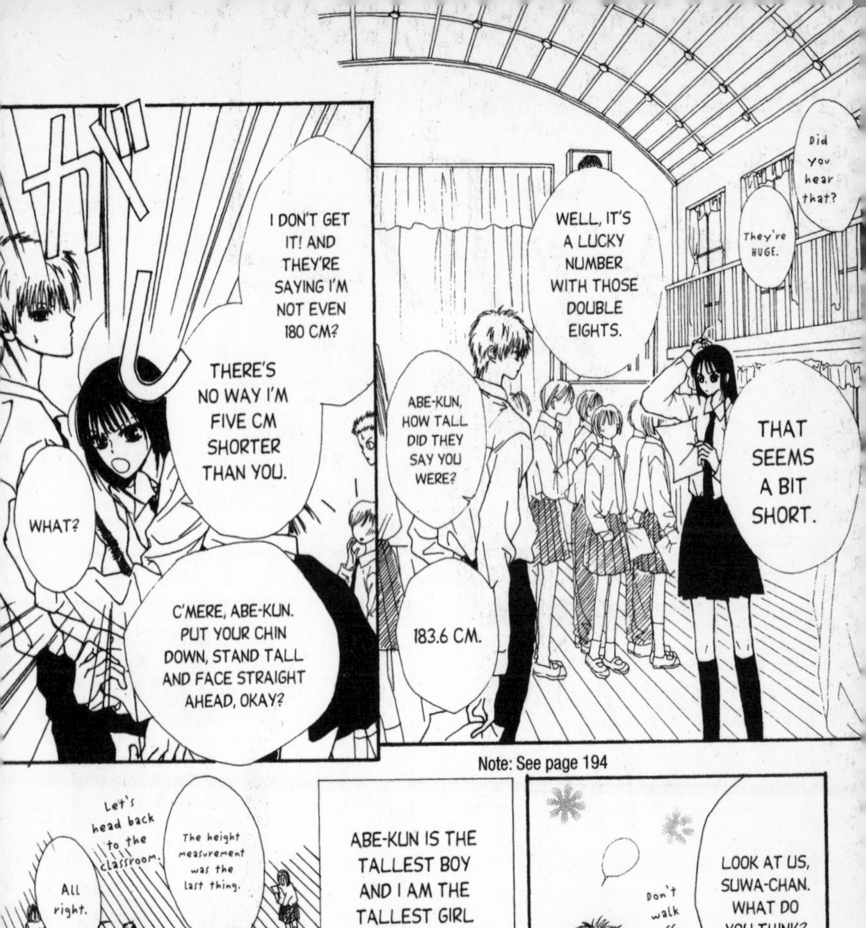
THAT SEEMS A BIT SHORT.
ABE-KUN, HOW TALL DID THEY SAY YOU WERE?
183.6 CM.
WELL, IT'S A LUCKY NUMBER WITH THOSE DOUBLE EIGHTS.
Did you hear that?
They're HUGE.
I DON'T GET IT! AND THEY'RE SAYING I'M NOT EVEN 180 CM?
THERE'S NO WAY I'M FIVE CM SHORTER THAN YOU.
WHAT?
C'MERE, ABE-KUN. PUT YOUR CHIN DOWN, STAND TALL AND FACE STRAIGHT AHEAD, OKAY?

Note: See page 194

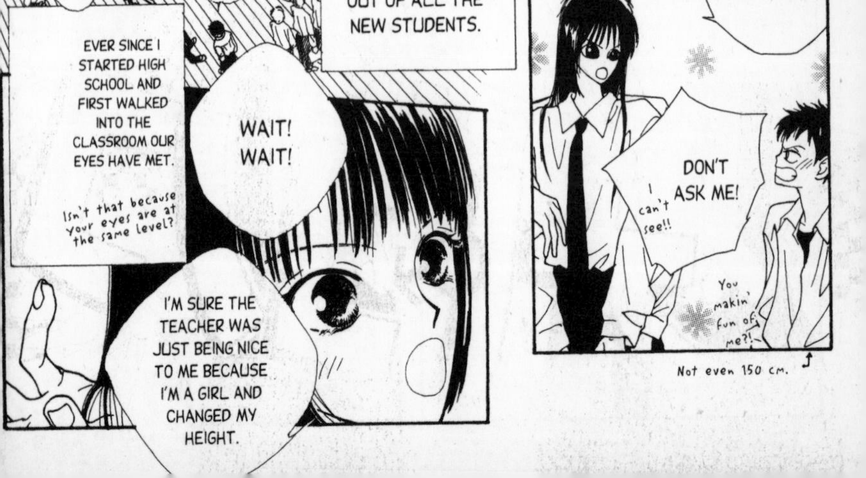
LOOK AT US, SUWA-CHAN. WHAT DO YOU THINK?
Don't walk off.
DON'T ASK ME!
I can't see!!
You makin' fun of me?!
Not even 150 cm.
ABE-KUN IS THE TALLEST BOY AND I AM THE TALLEST GIRL OUT OF ALL THE NEW STUDENTS.
Let's head back to the classroom.
The height measurement was the last thing.
All right.
EVER SINCE I STARTED HIGH SCHOOL AND FIRST WALKED INTO THE CLASSROOM OUR EYES HAVE MET.
Isn't that because your eyes are at the same level?
WAIT! WAIT!
I'M SURE THE TEACHER WAS JUST BEING NICE TO ME BECAUSE I'M A GIRL AND CHANGED MY HEIGHT.

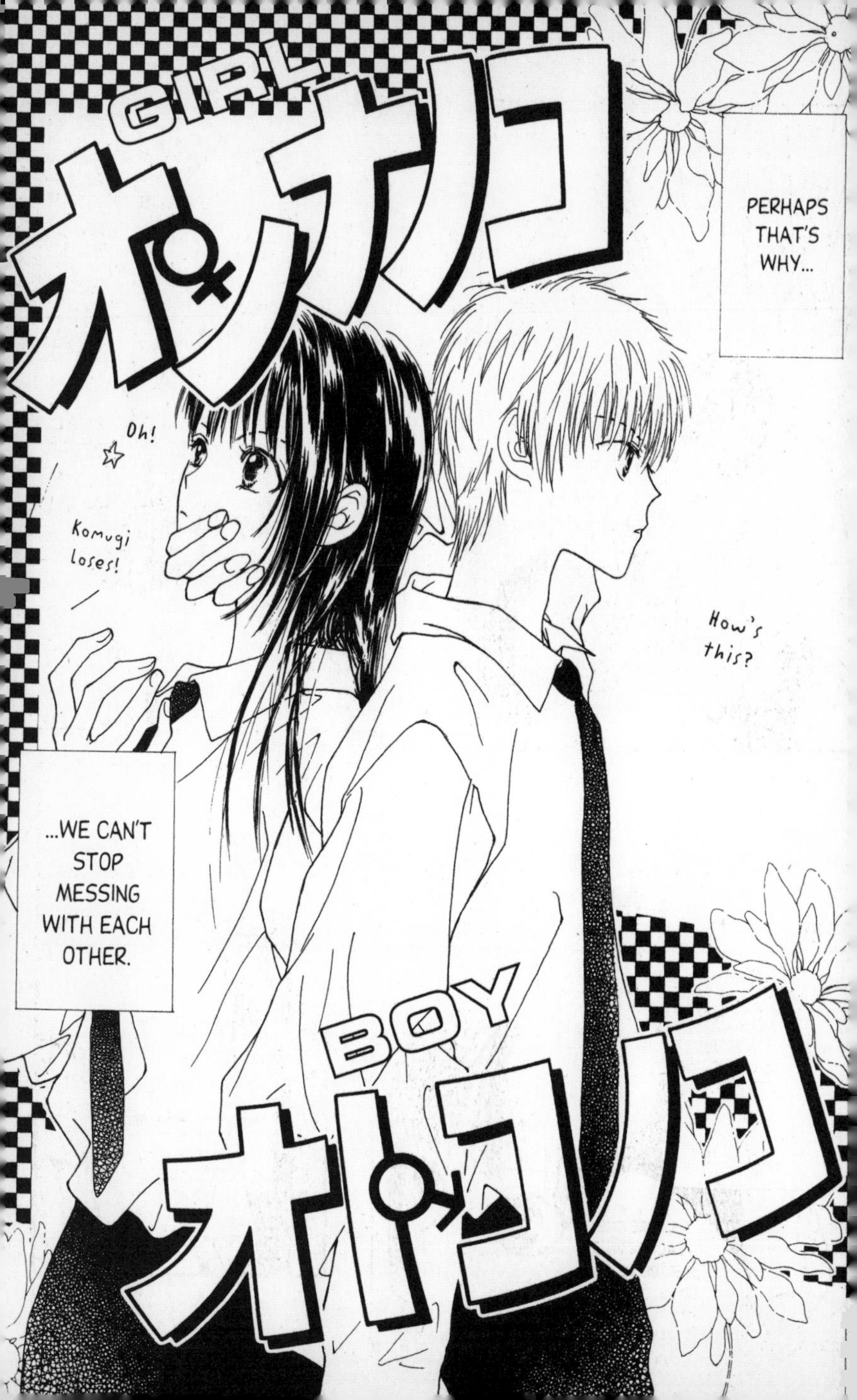
PERHAPS THAT'S WHY...
How's this?
GIRL
Oh!
Komugi loses!
...WE CAN'T STOP MESSING WITH EACH OTHER.
BOY

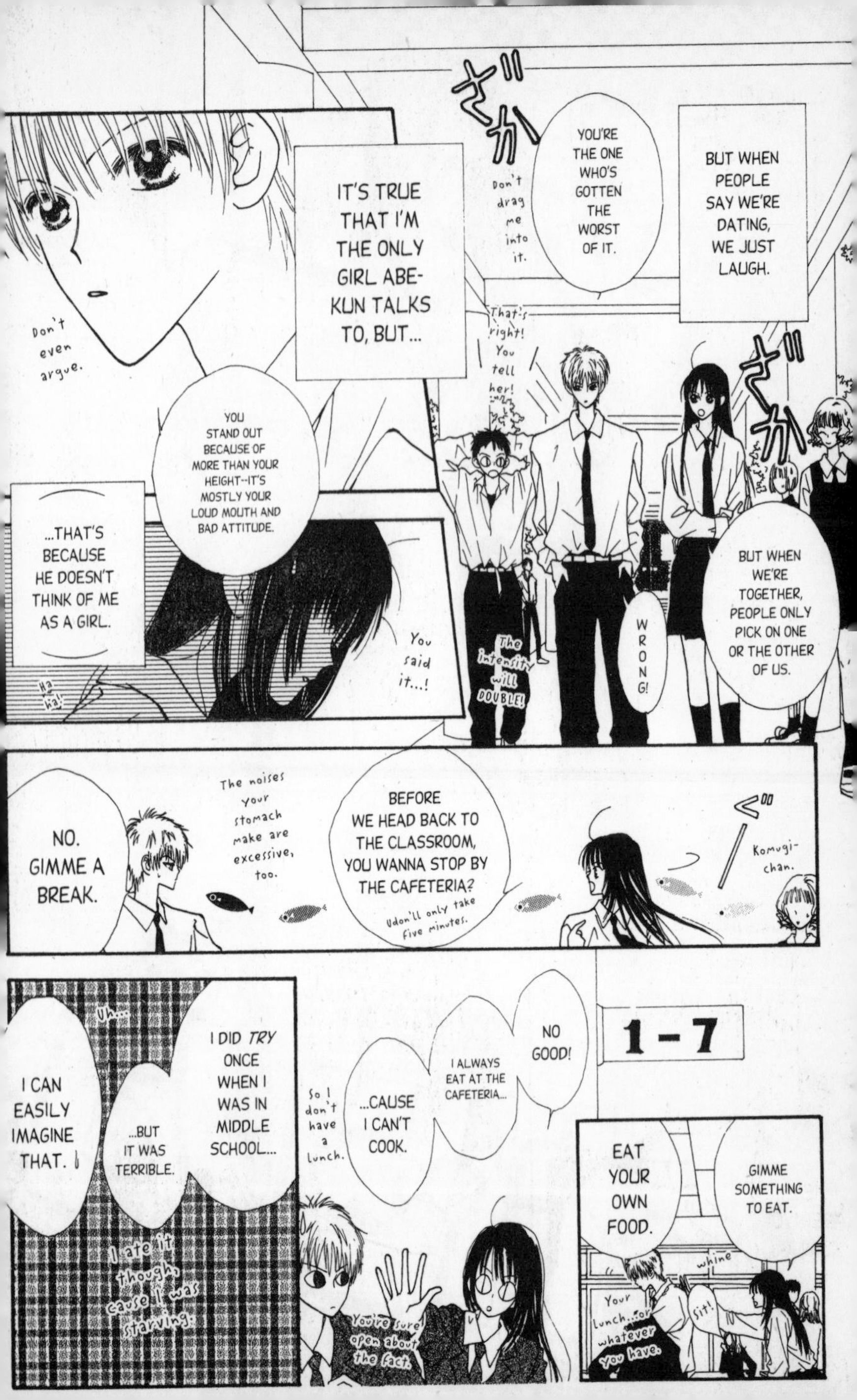
BUT WHEN PEOPLE SAY WE'RE DATING, WE JUST LAUGH.
YOU'RE THE ONE WHO'S GOTTEN THE WORST OF IT.
Don't drag me into it.
That's right! You tell her!
BUT WHEN WE'RE TOGETHER, PEOPLE ONLY PICK ON ONE OR THE OTHER OF US.
WRONG!
The intensity will DOUBLE!
IT'S TRUE THAT I'M THE ONLY GIRL ABE-KUN TALKS TO, BUT...
Don't even argue.
YOU STAND OUT BECAUSE OF MORE THAN YOUR HEIGHT--IT'S MOSTLY YOUR LOUD MOUTH AND BAD ATTITUDE.
...THAT'S BECAUSE HE DOESN'T THINK OF ME AS A GIRL.
You said it...!
Ha ha!
Komugi-chan.
BEFORE WE HEAD BACK TO THE CLASSROOM, YOU WANNA STOP BY THE CAFETERIA?
Udon'll only take five minutes.
The noises your stomach make are excessive, too.
NO. GIMME A BREAK.
1 - 7
GIMME SOMETHING TO EAT.
EAT YOUR OWN FOOD.
whine
Sit!
Your lunch...or whatever you have.
NO GOOD!
I ALWAYS EAT AT THE CAFETERIA...
...CAUSE I CAN'T COOK.
So I don't have a lunch.
I DID TRY ONCE WHEN I WAS IN MIDDLE SCHOOL...
...BUT IT WAS TERRIBLE.
I CAN EASILY IMAGINE THAT.
Uh...
I ate it though, cause I was starving.
You're sure open about the fact.

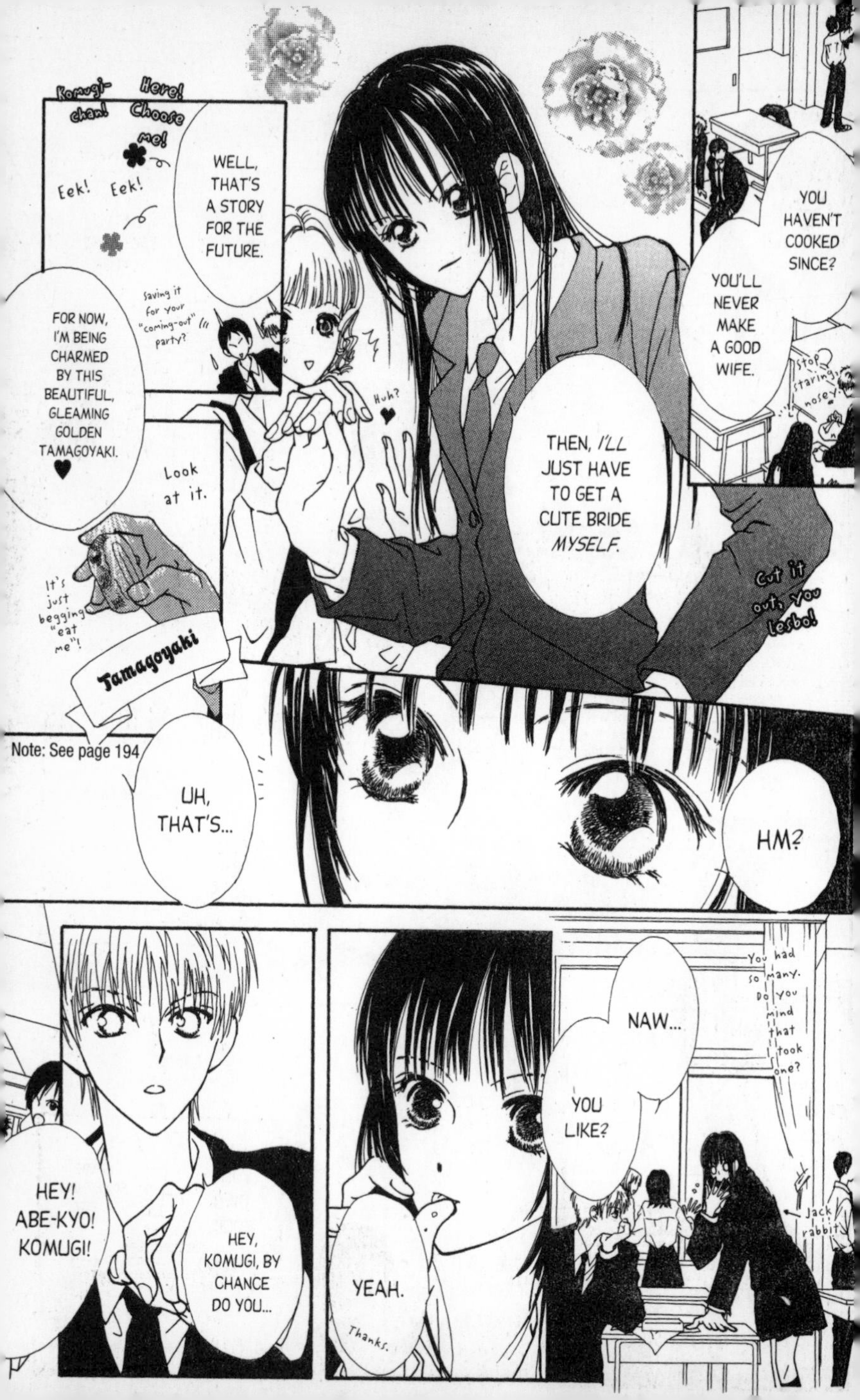
YOU HAVEN'T COOKED SINCE?
YOU'LL NEVER MAKE A GOOD WIFE.
Stop staring, nosey.
THEN, I'LL JUST HAVE TO GET A CUTE BRIDE *MYSELF*.
Cut it out, you lesbo!
Komugi-chan!
Here! Choose me!
Eek! Eek!
WELL, THAT'S A STORY FOR THE FUTURE.
Saving it for your "coming-out" party?
Huh?
FOR NOW, I'M BEING CHARMED BY THIS BEAUTIFUL, GLEAMING GOLDEN TAMAGOYAKI. ♥
Look at it.
It's just begging "eat me"!
Tamagoyaki
HM?
UH, THAT'S...
NAW...
You had so many. Do you mind that I took one?
YOU LIKE?
Jack rabbit
YEAH.
Thanks.
HEY, KOMUGI, BY CHANCE DO YOU...
HEY! ABE-KYO! KOMUGI!
Note: See page 194

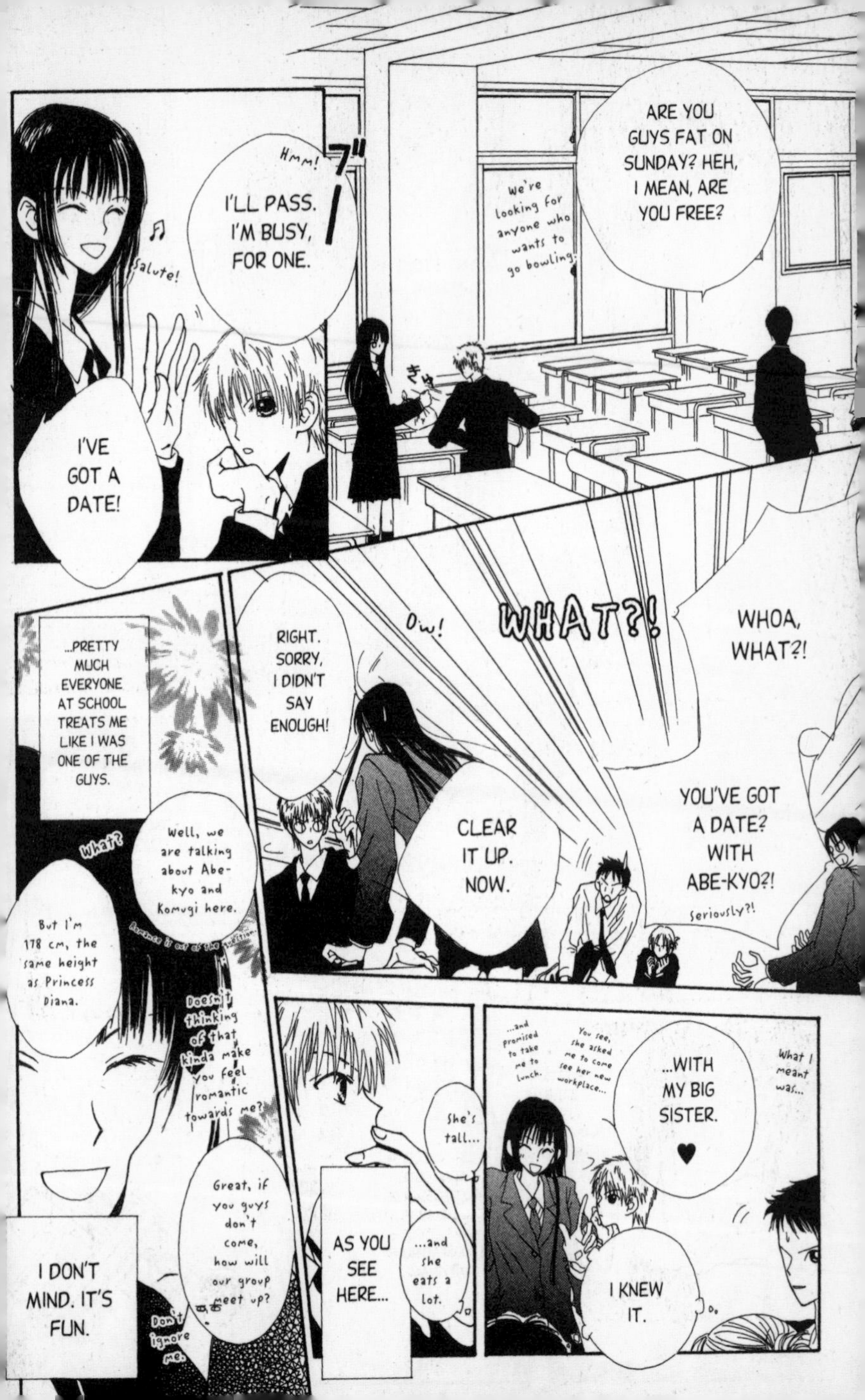

we're looking for anyone who wants to go bowling.
ARE YOU GUYS FAT ON SUNDAY? HEH, I MEAN, ARE YOU FREE?
Hmm!
I'LL PASS. I'M BUSY, FOR ONE.
Salute!
I'VE GOT A DATE!
WHAT?!
WHOA, WHAT?!
YOU'VE GOT A DATE? WITH ABE-KYO?!
seriously?!
CLEAR IT UP. NOW.
Ow!
RIGHT. SORRY, I DIDN'T SAY ENOUGH!
...PRETTY MUCH EVERYONE AT SCHOOL TREATS ME LIKE I WAS ONE OF THE GUYS.
What?
Well, we are talking about Abe-kyo and Komugi here.
But I'm 178 cm, the same height as Princess Diana.
Doesn't thinking of that kinda make you feel romantic towards me?
What I meant was...
You see, she asked me to come see her new workplace...
...and promised to take me to lunch.
...WITH MY BIG SISTER.
I KNEW IT.
She's tall...
...and she eats a lot.
AS YOU SEE HERE...
Great, if you guys don't come, how will our group meet up?
Don't ignore me.
I DON'T MIND. IT'S FUN.

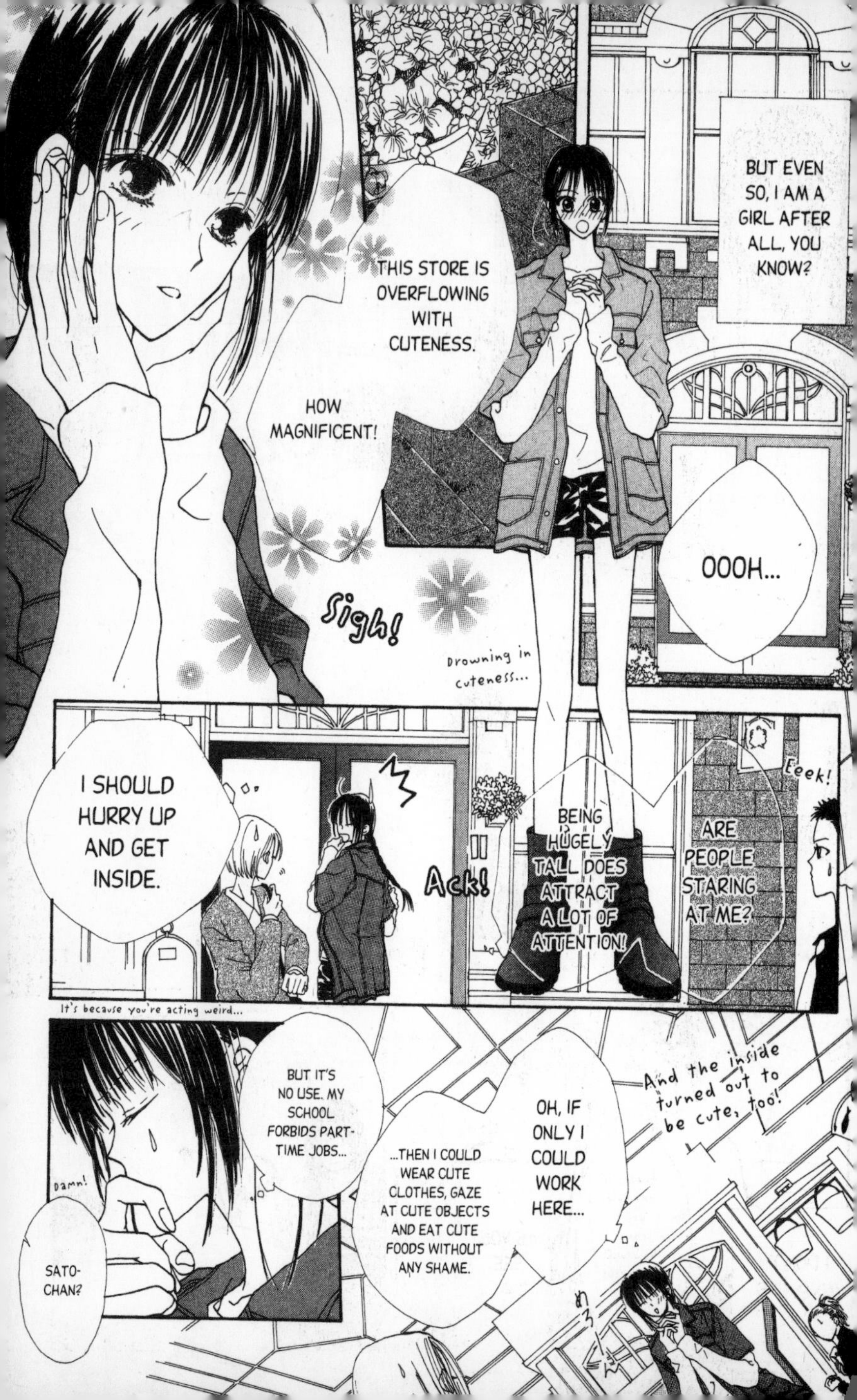
BUT EVEN SO, I AM A GIRL AFTER ALL, YOU KNOW?
OOOH...
THIS STORE IS OVERFLOWING WITH CUTENESS.
HOW MAGNIFICENT!
Sigh!
Drowning in cuteness...
Eeek!
ARE PEOPLE STARING AT ME?
BEING HUGELY TALL DOES ATTRACT A LOT OF ATTENTION!
Ack!
I SHOULD HURRY UP AND GET INSIDE.
It's because you're acting weird...
And the inside turned out to be cute, too!
OH, IF ONLY I COULD WORK HERE...
...THEN I COULD WEAR CUTE CLOTHES, GAZE AT CUTE OBJECTS AND EAT CUTE FOODS WITHOUT ANY SHAME.
BUT IT'S NO USE. MY SCHOOL FORBIDS PART-TIME JOBS...
Damn!
SATO-CHAN?

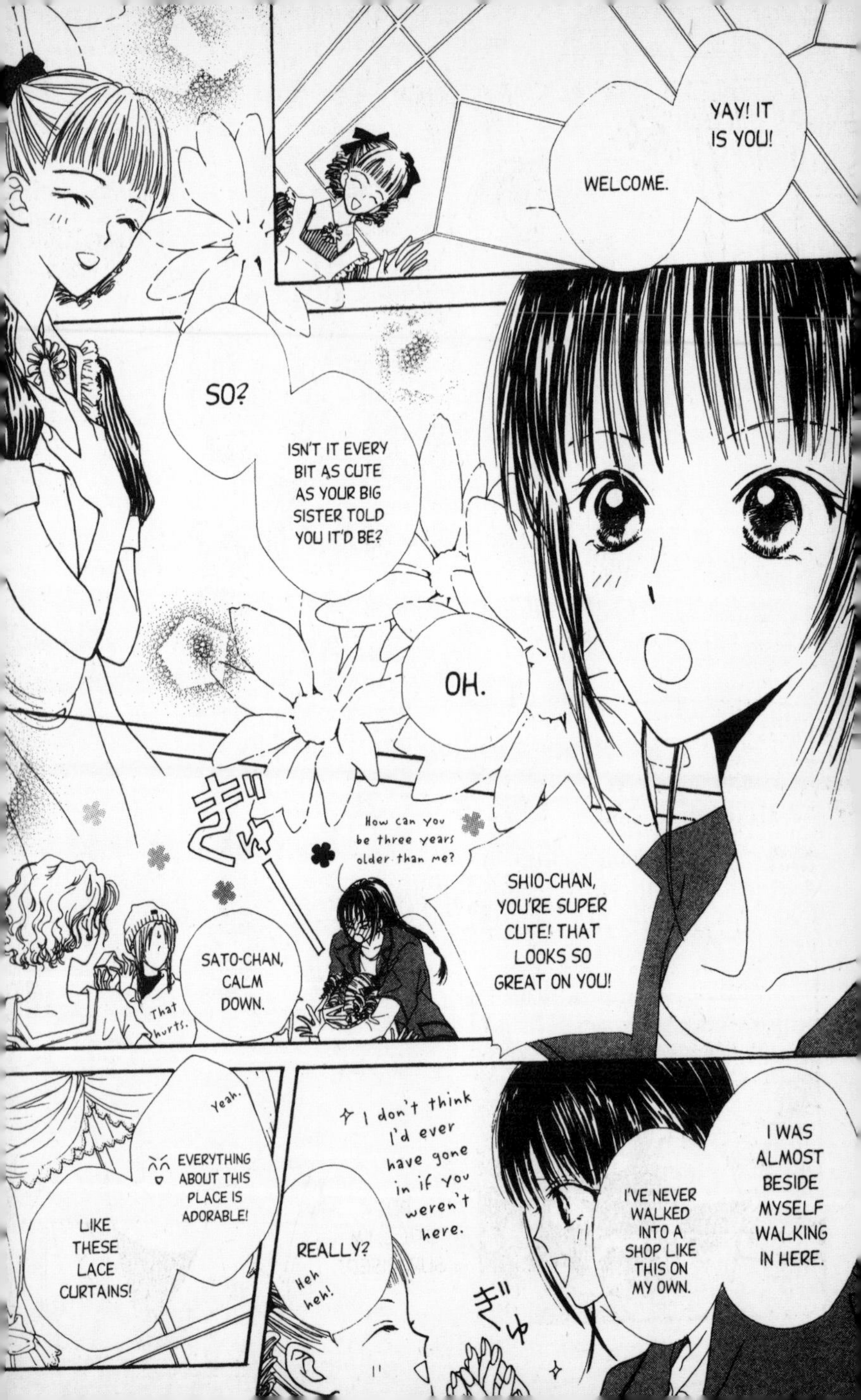
YAY! IT IS YOU!
WELCOME.
SO?
ISN'T IT EVERY BIT AS CUTE AS YOUR BIG SISTER TOLD YOU IT'D BE?
OH.
SHIO-CHAN, YOU'RE SUPER CUTE! THAT LOOKS SO GREAT ON YOU!
How can you be three years older than me?
ぎゅー
SATO-CHAN, CALM DOWN.
That hurts.
I WAS ALMOST BESIDE MYSELF WALKING IN HERE.
I'VE NEVER WALKED INTO A SHOP LIKE THIS ON MY OWN.
ぎゅ
I don't think I'd ever have gone in if you weren't here.
REALLY?
Heh heh!
Yeah.
EVERYTHING ABOUT THIS PLACE IS ADORABLE!
LIKE THESE LACE CURTAINS!

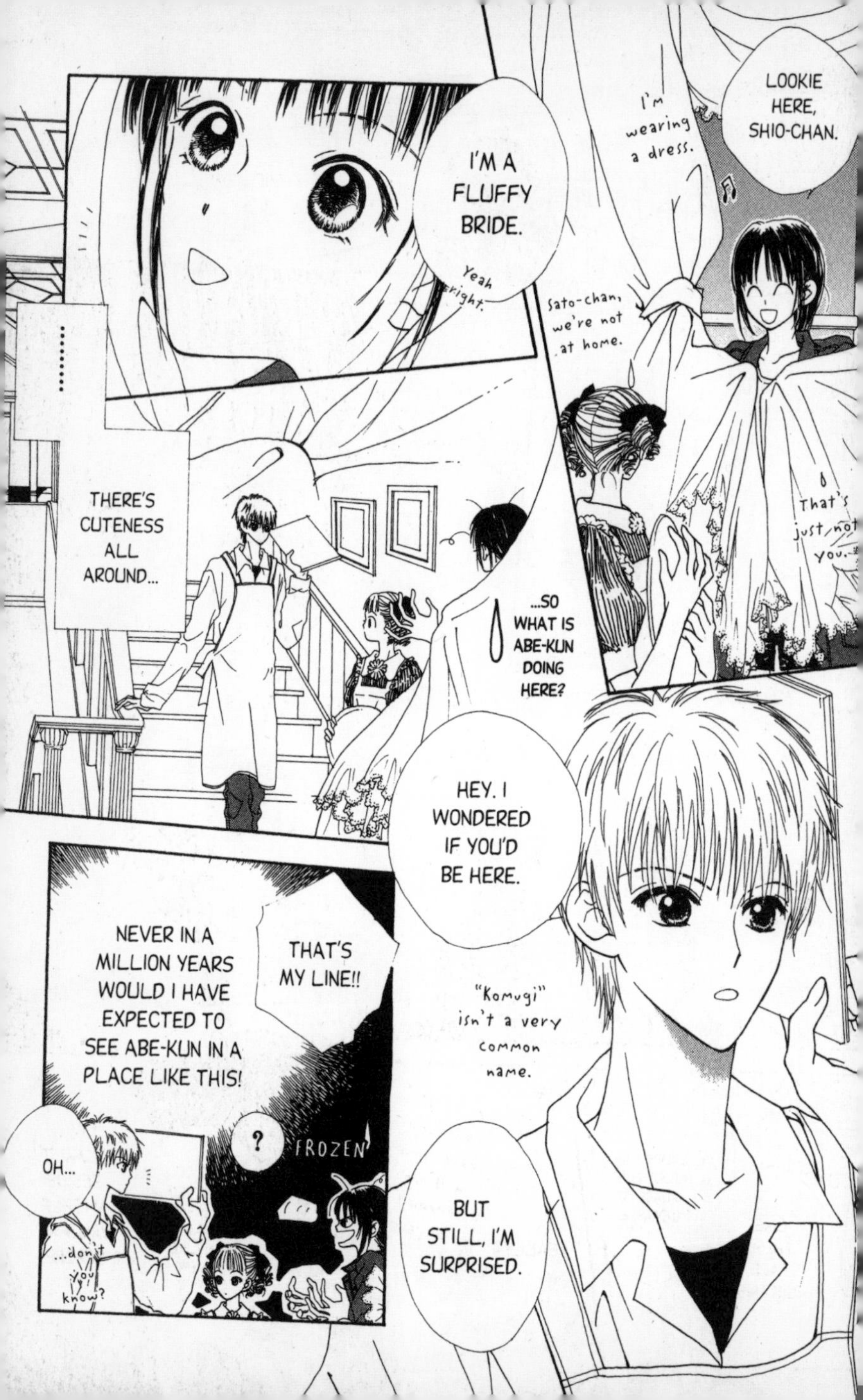
LOOKIE HERE, SHIO-CHAN.
I'm wearing a dress.
Sato-chan, we're not at home.
That's just not you.
I'M A FLUFFY BRIDE.
Yeah right.
......
THERE'S CUTENESS ALL AROUND...
...SO WHAT IS ABE-KUN DOING HERE?
HEY. I WONDERED IF YOU'D BE HERE.
"Komugi" isn't a very common name.
BUT STILL, I'M SURPRISED.
NEVER IN A MILLION YEARS WOULD I HAVE EXPECTED TO SEE ABE-KUN IN A PLACE LIKE THIS!
THAT'S MY LINE!!
?
FROZEN
OH...
...don't you know?

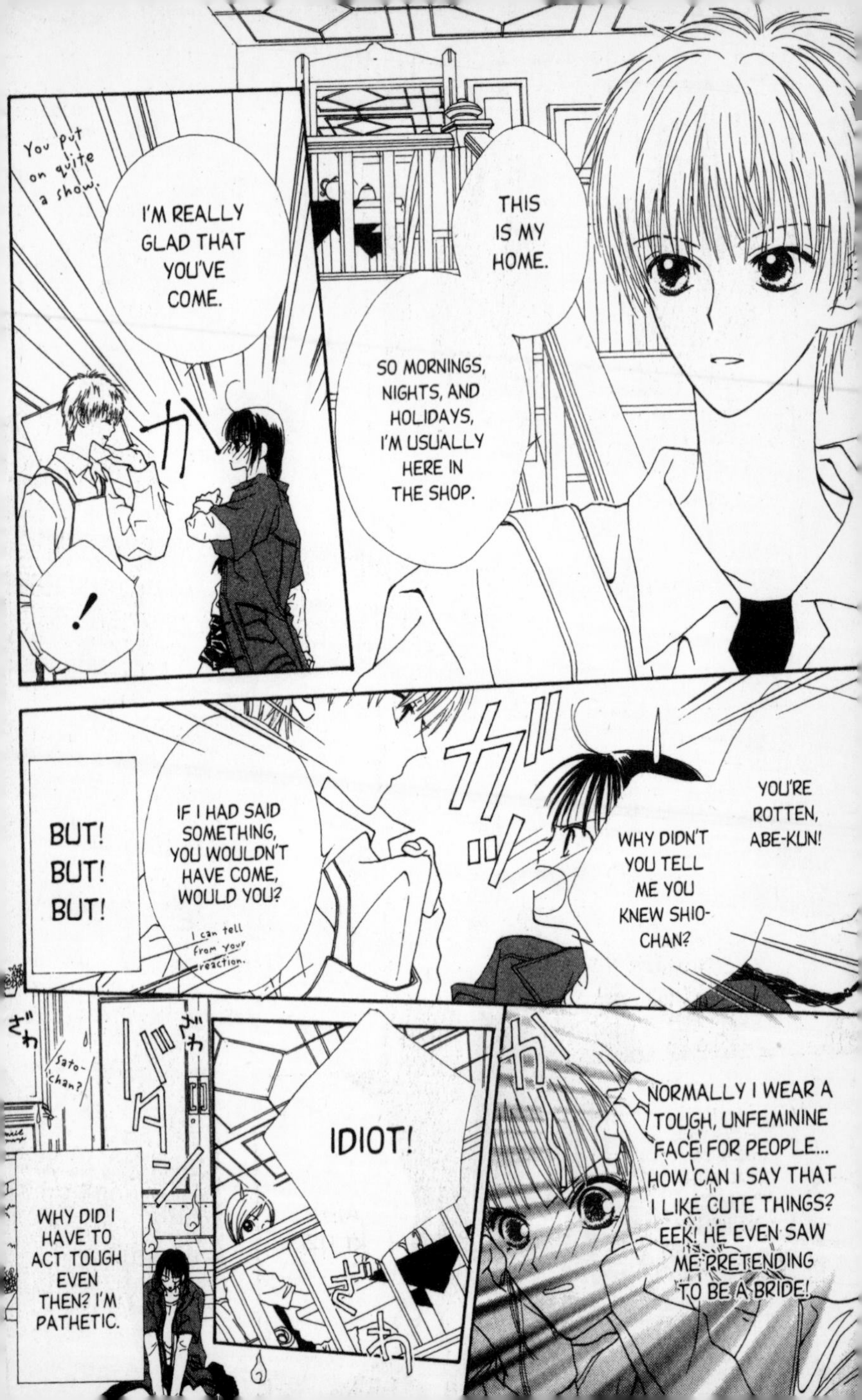
THIS IS MY HOME.
SO MORNINGS, NIGHTS, AND HOLIDAYS, I'M USUALLY HERE IN THE SHOP.
I'M REALLY GLAD THAT YOU'VE COME.
You put on quite a show.
!
YOU'RE ROTTEN, ABE-KUN!
WHY DIDN'T YOU TELL ME YOU KNEW SHIO-CHAN?
IF I HAD SAID SOMETHING, YOU WOULDN'T HAVE COME, WOULD YOU?
I can tell from your reaction.
BUT! BUT! BUT!
NORMALLY I WEAR A TOUGH, UNFEMININE FACE FOR PEOPLE... HOW CAN I SAY THAT I LIKE CUTE THINGS? EEK! HE EVEN SAW ME PRETENDING TO BE A BRIDE!
IDIOT!
Sato-chan?
WHY DID I HAVE TO ACT TOUGH EVEN THEN? I'M PATHETIC.

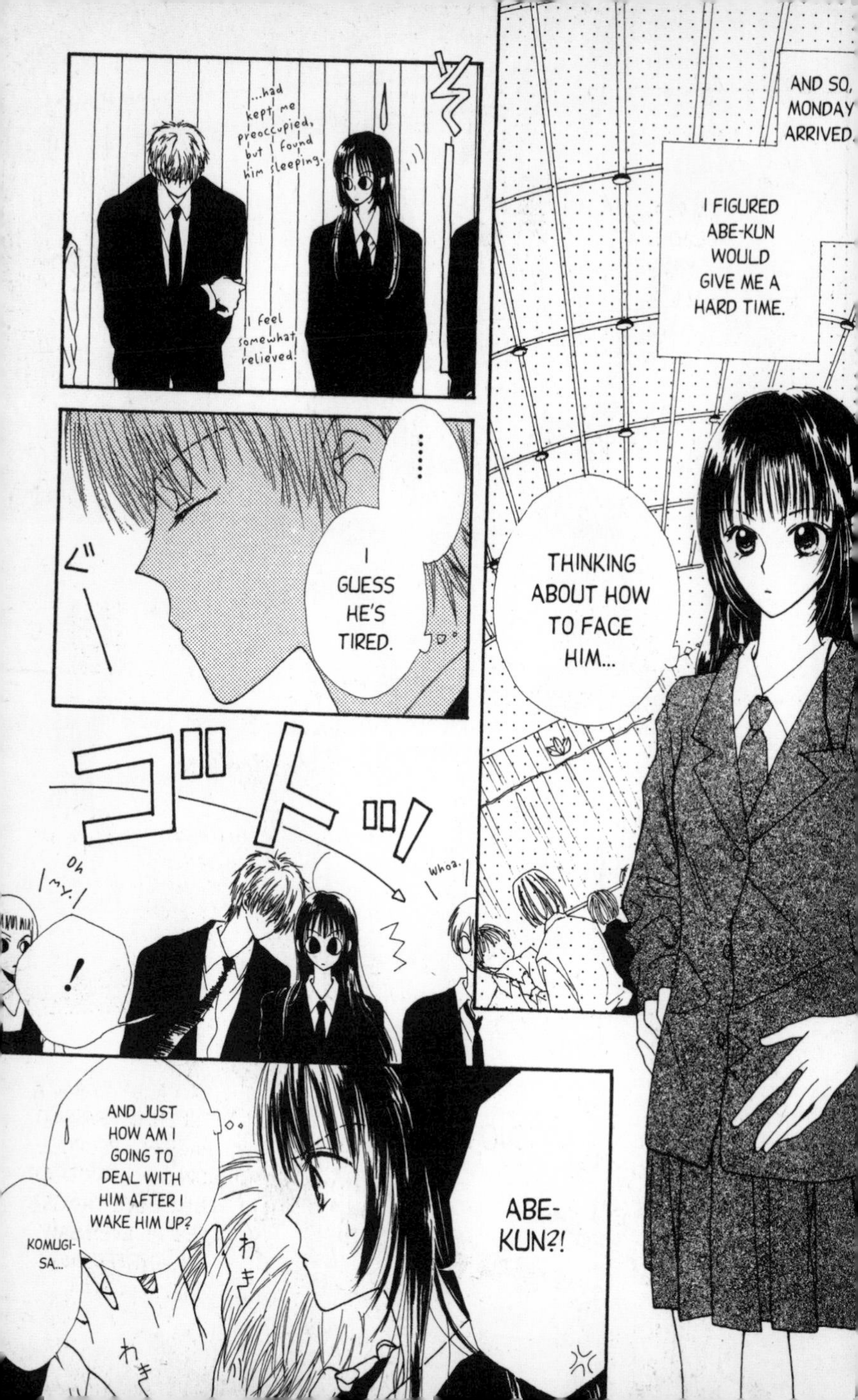
AND SO, MONDAY ARRIVED.
I FIGURED ABE-KUN WOULD GIVE ME A HARD TIME.
THINKING ABOUT HOW TO FACE HIM...
...had kept me preoccupied, but I found him sleeping.
I feel somewhat relieved!
......
I GUESS HE'S TIRED.
ゴトッ
Whoa.
!
Oh my.
ABE-KUN?!
AND JUST HOW AM I GOING TO DEAL WITH HIM AFTER I WAKE HIM UP?
KOMUGI-SA...
わき
わき

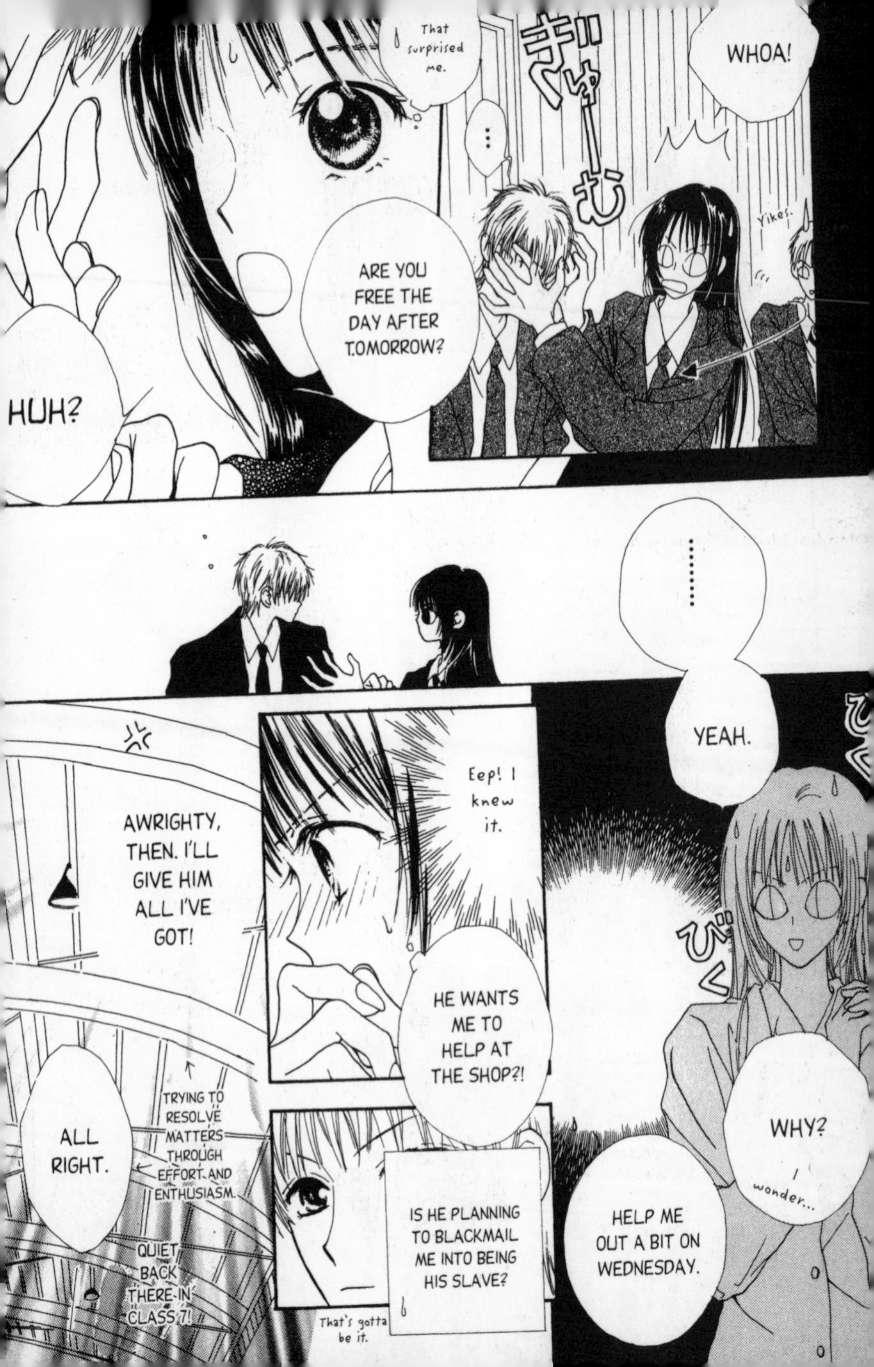

WHOA!
ぎゅーむ
Yikes.
...
That surprised me.
ARE YOU FREE THE DAY AFTER TOMORROW?
HUH?
......
YEAH.
びく
WHY?
I wonder...
HELP ME OUT A BIT ON WEDNESDAY.
Eep! I knew it.
HE WANTS ME TO HELP AT THE SHOP?!
IS HE PLANNING TO BLACKMAIL ME INTO BEING HIS SLAVE?
That's gotta be it.
AWRIGHTY, THEN. I'LL GIVE HIM ALL I'VE GOT!
TRYING TO RESOLVE MATTERS THROUGH EFFORT AND ENTHUSIASM.
ALL RIGHT.
QUIET BACK THERE IN CLASS 7!

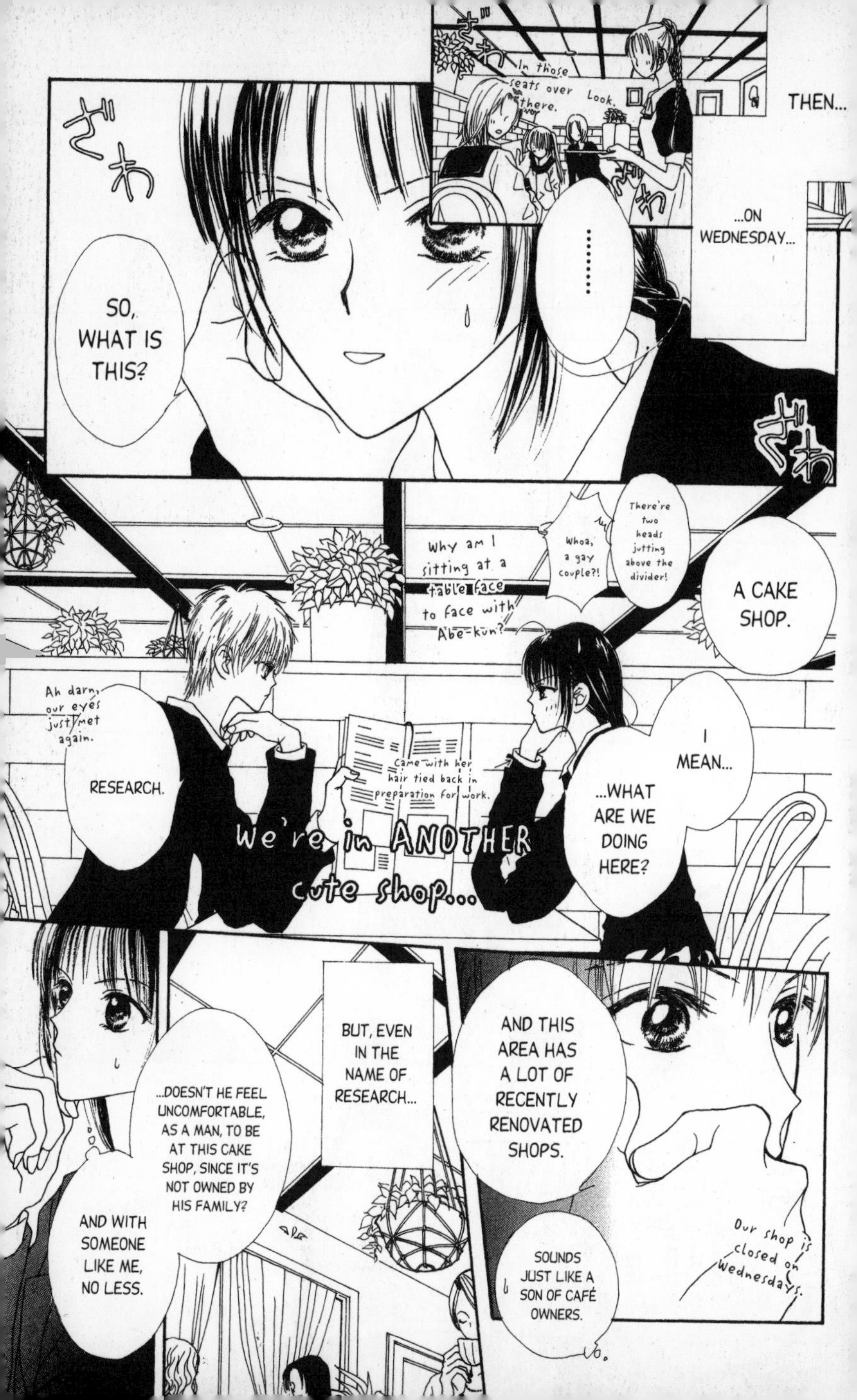
THEN...
ざわ
In those seats over there.
Look.
ざわ
...ON WEDNESDAY...
......
SO, WHAT IS THIS?
ざわ
ざわ
A CAKE SHOP.
There're two heads jutting above the divider!
Whoa, a gay couple?!
Why am I sitting at a table face to face with Abe-kun?
I MEAN...
...WHAT ARE WE DOING HERE?
Came with her hair tied back in preparation for work.
RESEARCH.
Ah darn, our eyes just met again.
We're in ANOTHER cute shop...
AND THIS AREA HAS A LOT OF RECENTLY RENOVATED SHOPS.
Our shop is closed on Wednesdays.
SOUNDS JUST LIKE A SON OF CAFÉ OWNERS.
BUT, EVEN IN THE NAME OF RESEARCH...
...DOESN'T HE FEEL UNCOMFORTABLE, AS A MAN, TO BE AT THIS CAKE SHOP, SINCE IT'S NOT OWNED BY HIS FAMILY?
AND WITH SOMEONE LIKE ME, NO LESS.

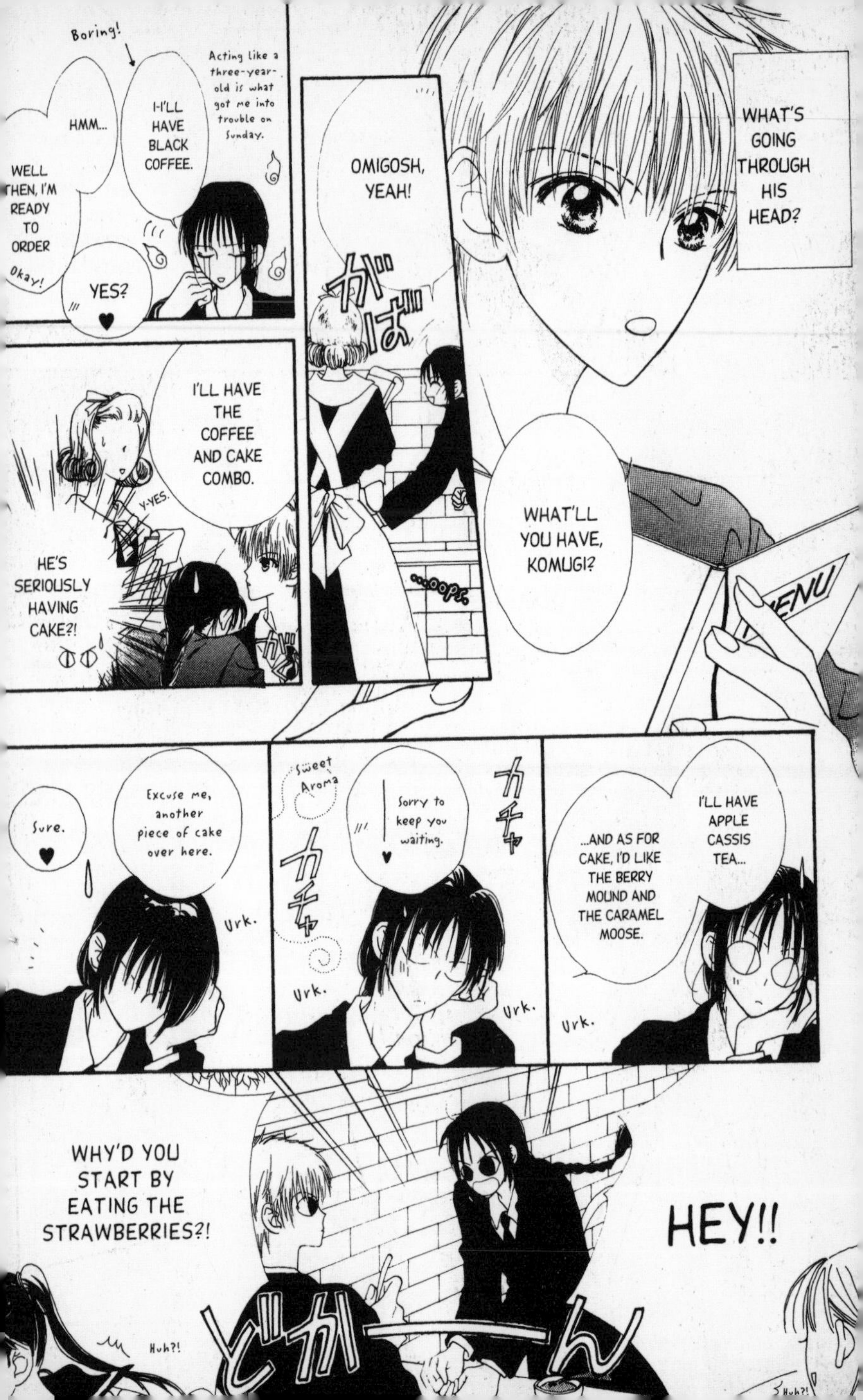
WHAT'S GOING THROUGH HIS HEAD?
WHAT'LL YOU HAVE, KOMUGI?
MENU
OMIGOSH, YEAH!
...oops.
Acting like a three-year-old is what got me into trouble on Sunday.
Boring!
I-I'LL HAVE BLACK COFFEE.
HMM...
WELL THEN, I'M READY TO ORDER
YES?
Okay!
I'LL HAVE THE COFFEE AND CAKE COMBO.
Y-YES.
HE'S SERIOUSLY HAVING CAKE?!
I'LL HAVE APPLE CASSIS TEA...
...AND AS FOR CAKE, I'D LIKE THE BERRY MOUND AND THE CARAMEL MOOSE.
Urk.
Urk.
Sweet Aroma
Sorry to keep you waiting.
Urk.
Excuse me, another piece of cake over here.
Sure.
Urk.
HEY!!
WHY'D YOU START BY EATING THE STRAWBERRIES?!
Huh?!
Huh?!

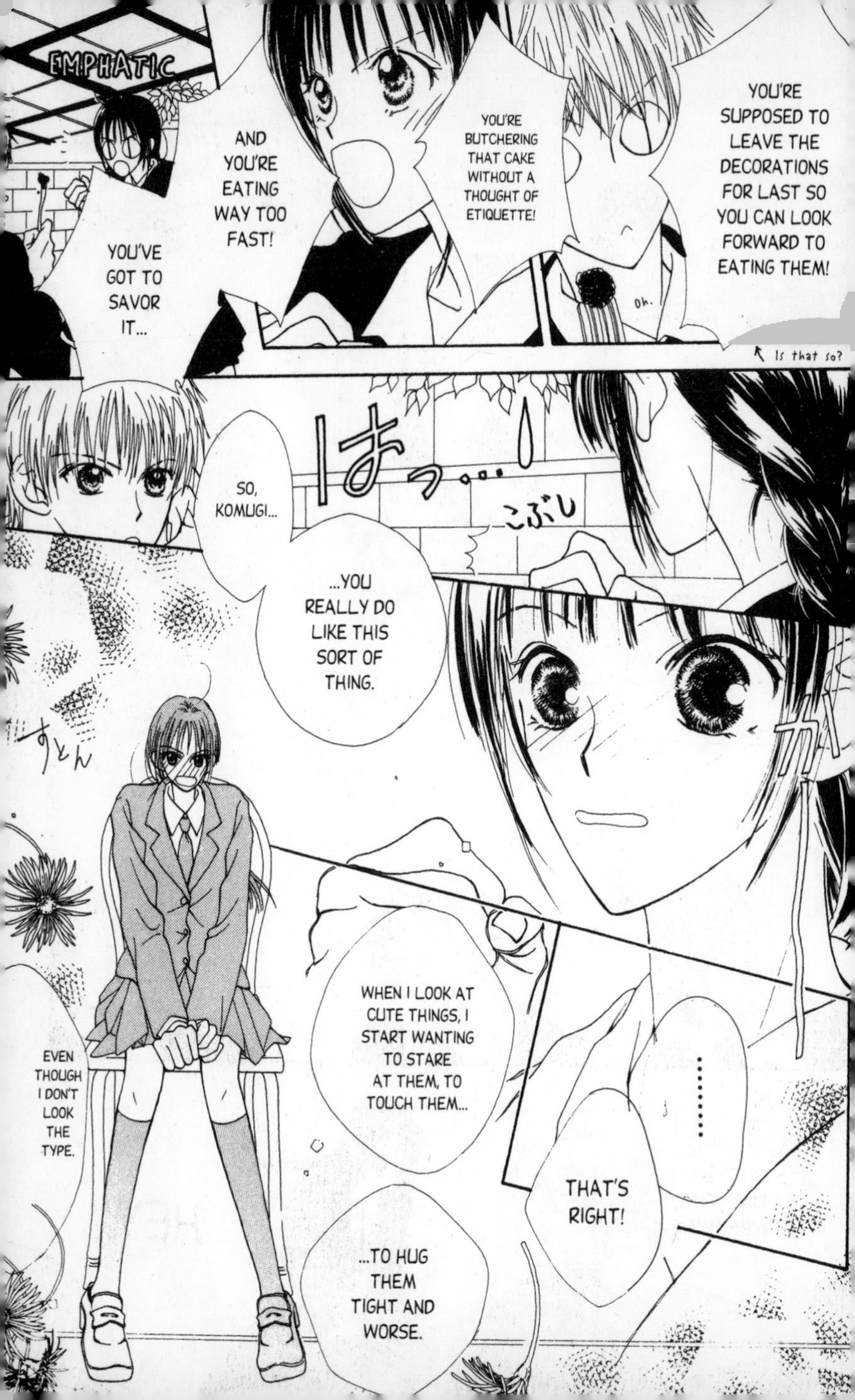
YOU'RE SUPPOSED TO LEAVE THE DECORATIONS FOR LAST SO YOU CAN LOOK FORWARD TO EATING THEM!
Oh.
Is that so?
YOU'RE BUTCHERING THAT CAKE WITHOUT A THOUGHT OF ETIQUETTE!
AND YOU'RE EATING WAY TOO FAST!
EMPHATIC
YOU'VE GOT TO SAVOR IT...
はっ...
こぶし
SO, KOMUGI...
...YOU REALLY DO LIKE THIS SORT OF THING.
....
THAT'S RIGHT!
WHEN I LOOK AT CUTE THINGS, I START WANTING TO STARE AT THEM, TO TOUCH THEM...
...TO HUG THEM TIGHT AND WORSE.
すとん
EVEN THOUGH I DON'T LOOK THE TYPE.

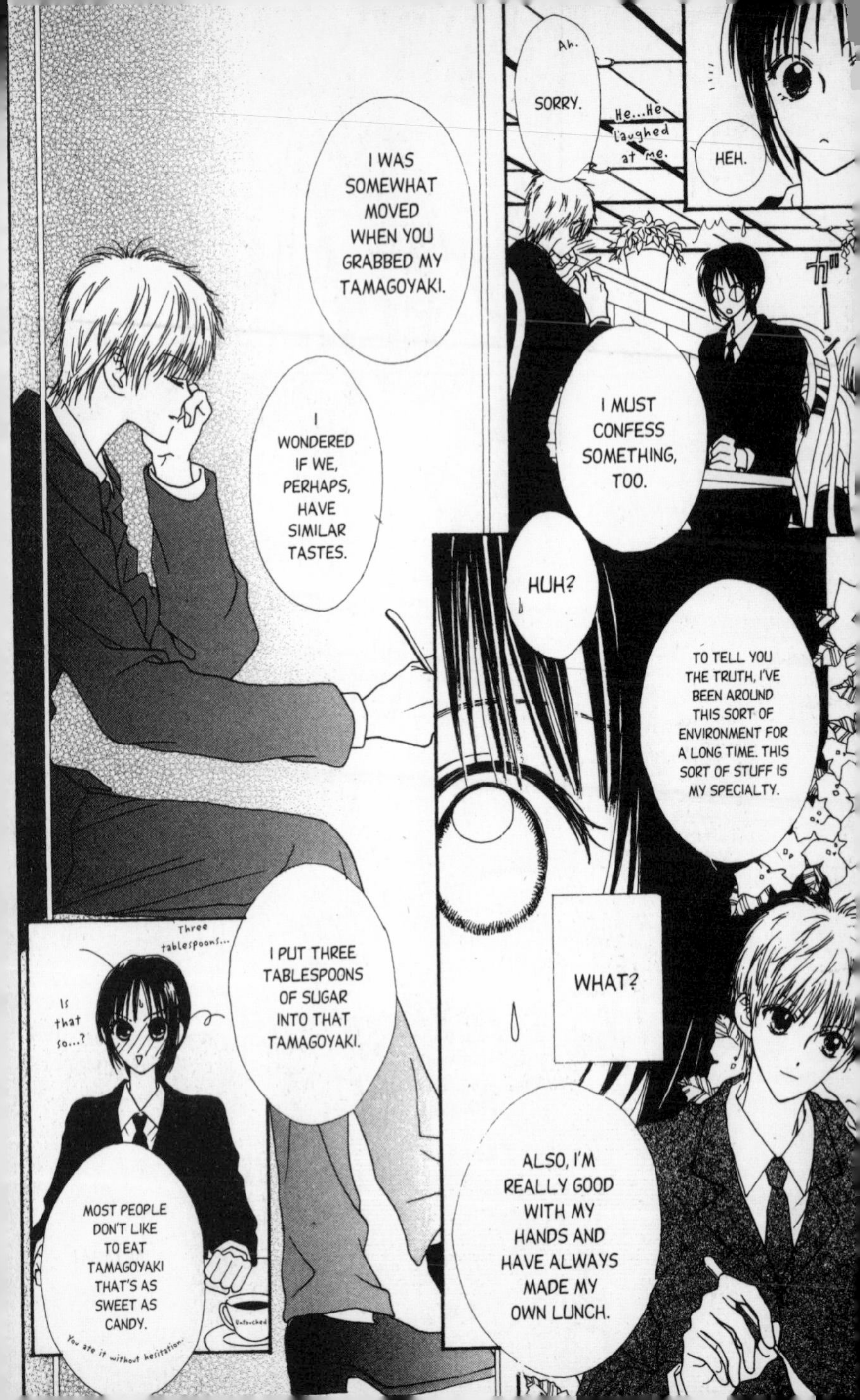
HEH.
He...He laughed at me.
Ah.
SORRY.
I MUST CONFESS SOMETHING, TOO.
HUH?
TO TELL YOU THE TRUTH, I'VE BEEN AROUND THIS SORT OF ENVIRONMENT FOR A LONG TIME. THIS SORT OF STUFF IS MY SPECIALTY.
WHAT?
ALSO, I'M REALLY GOOD WITH MY HANDS AND HAVE ALWAYS MADE MY OWN LUNCH.
I WAS SOMEWHAT MOVED WHEN YOU GRABBED MY TAMAGOYAKI.
I WONDERED IF WE, PERHAPS, HAVE SIMILAR TASTES.
I PUT THREE TABLESPOONS OF SUGAR INTO THAT TAMAGOYAKI.
Three tablespoons...
Is that so...?
MOST PEOPLE DON'T LIKE TO EAT TAMAGOYAKI THAT'S AS SWEET AS CANDY.
Untouched
You ate it without hesitation.

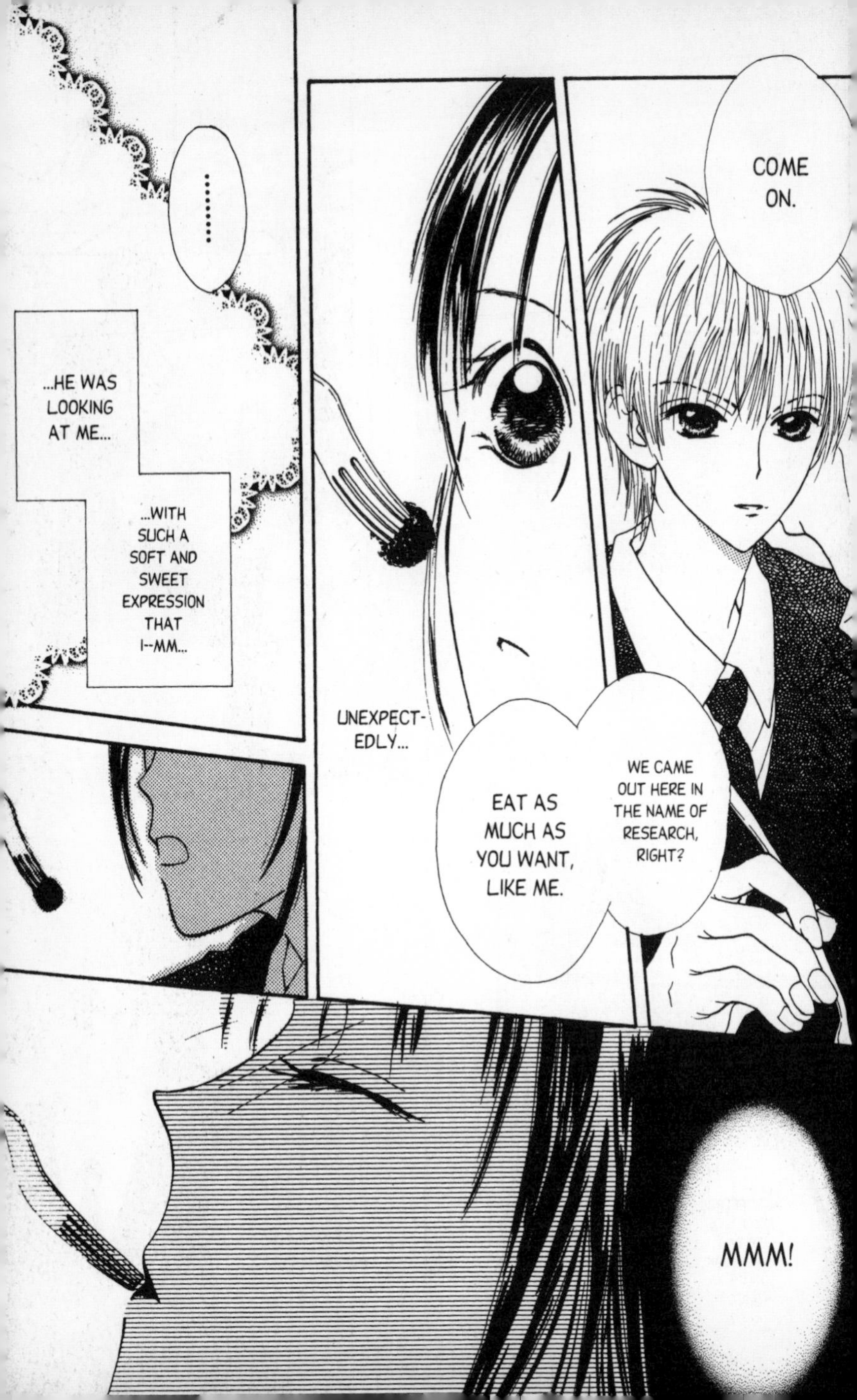
COME ON.
WE CAME OUT HERE IN THE NAME OF RESEARCH, RIGHT?
EAT AS MUCH AS YOU WANT, LIKE ME.
UNEXPECT-EDLY...
......
...HE WAS LOOKING AT ME...
...WITH SUCH A SOFT AND SWEET EXPRESSION THAT I--MM...
MMM!

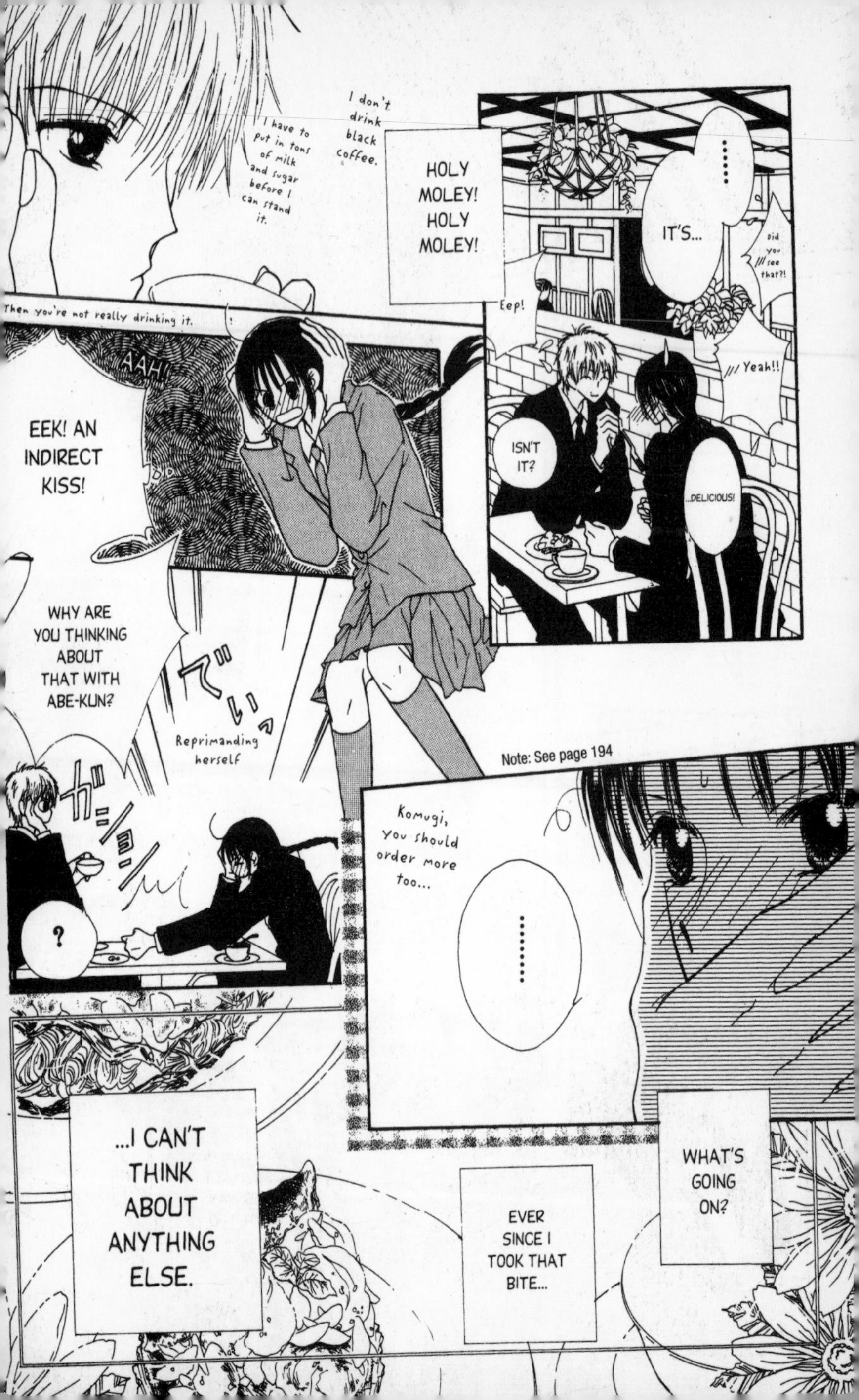

......
IT'S...
Did you see that?!
Yeah!!
Eep!
HOLY MOLEY! HOLY MOLEY!
ISN'T IT?
...DELICIOUS!
I don't drink black coffee.
I have to put in tons of milk and sugar before I can stand it.
Then you're not really drinking it.
AAH!
EEK! AN INDIRECT KISS!
WHY ARE YOU THINKING ABOUT THAT WITH ABE-KUN?
Reprimanding herself
Note: See page 194
Komugi, you should order more too...
......
?
WHAT'S GOING ON?
EVER SINCE I TOOK THAT BITE...
...I CAN'T THINK ABOUT ANYTHING ELSE.

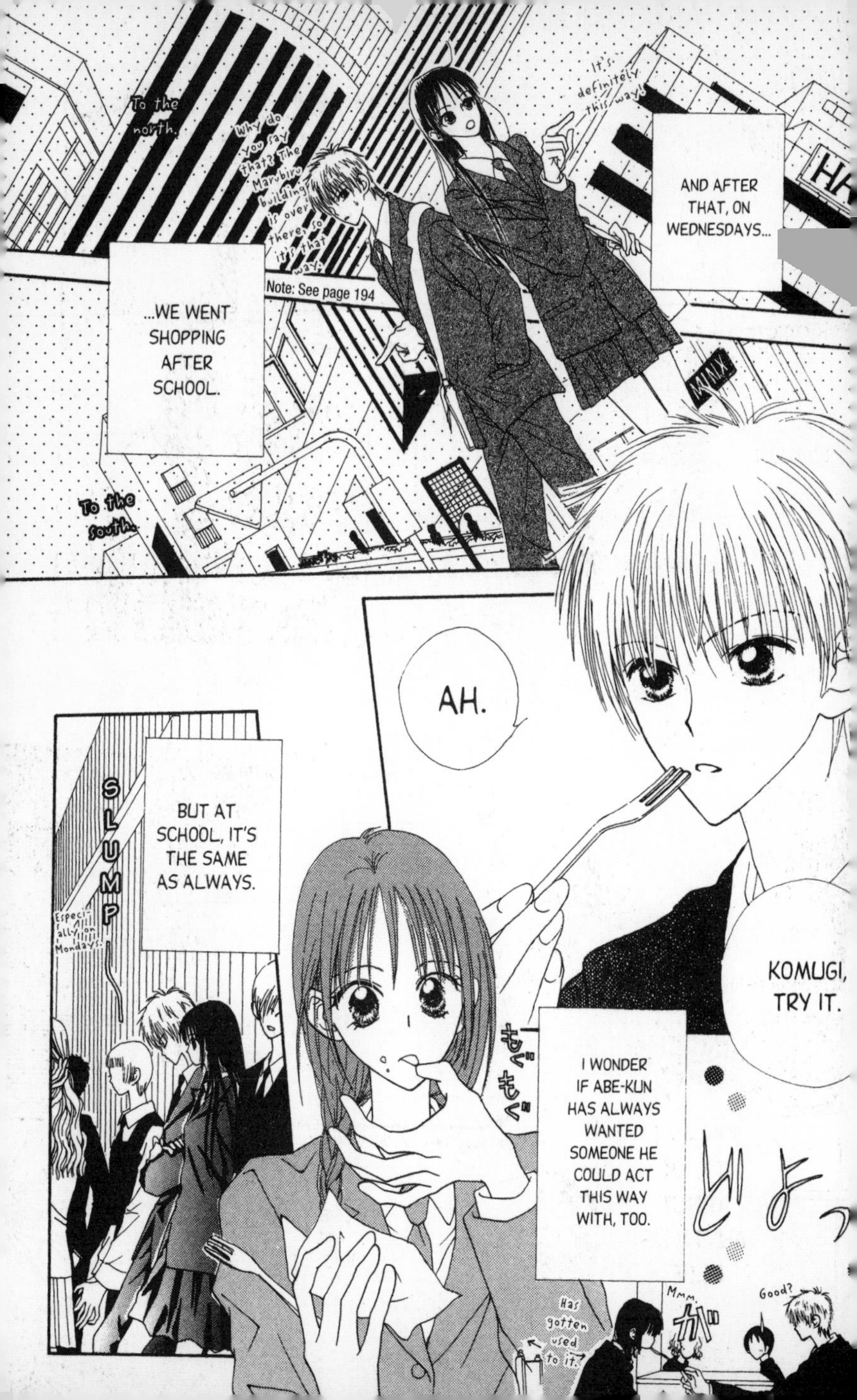
It's definitely this way!
AND AFTER THAT, ON WEDNESDAYS...
Why do you say that? The Marubiru building is over there, so it's that way.
To the north.
...WE WENT SHOPPING AFTER SCHOOL.
Note: See page 194
To the south.
AH.
KOMUGI, TRY IT.
I WONDER IF ABE-KUN HAS ALWAYS WANTED SOMEONE HE COULD ACT THIS WAY WITH, TOO.
もぐもぐ
Good?
Mmm.
Has gotten used to it.
BUT AT SCHOOL, IT'S THE SAME AS ALWAYS.
SLUMP
Especially on Mondays.

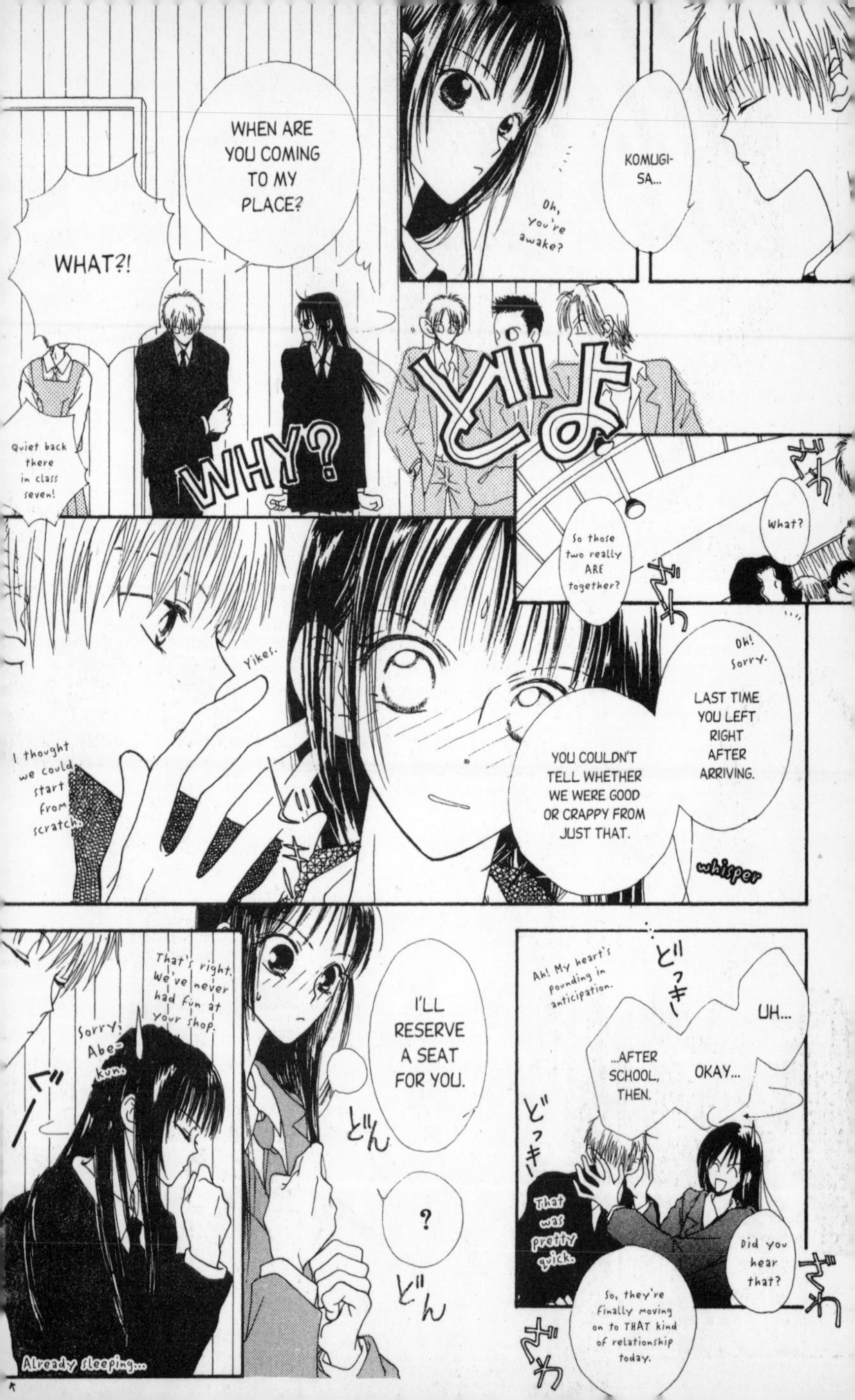
KOMUGI-SA...
Oh, you're awake?
WHEN ARE YOU COMING TO MY PLACE?
WHAT?!
WHY?
どよ
Quiet back there in class seven!
ざわ
What?
So those two really ARE together?
ざわ
Oh! Sorry.
LAST TIME YOU LEFT RIGHT AFTER ARRIVING.
YOU COULDN'T TELL WHETHER WE WERE GOOD OR CRAPPY FROM JUST THAT.
whisper
Yikes.
I thought we could start from scratch.
Ah! My heart's pounding in anticipation.
どっき
UH...
OKAY...
...AFTER SCHOOL, THEN.
どっき
That was pretty quick.
Did you hear that?
ざわ
So, they're finally moving on to THAT kind of relationship today.
ざわ
I'LL RESERVE A SEAT FOR YOU.
どん
?
どん
That's right. We've never had fun at your shop.
Sorry, Abe-kun.
ぐー
Already sleeping...

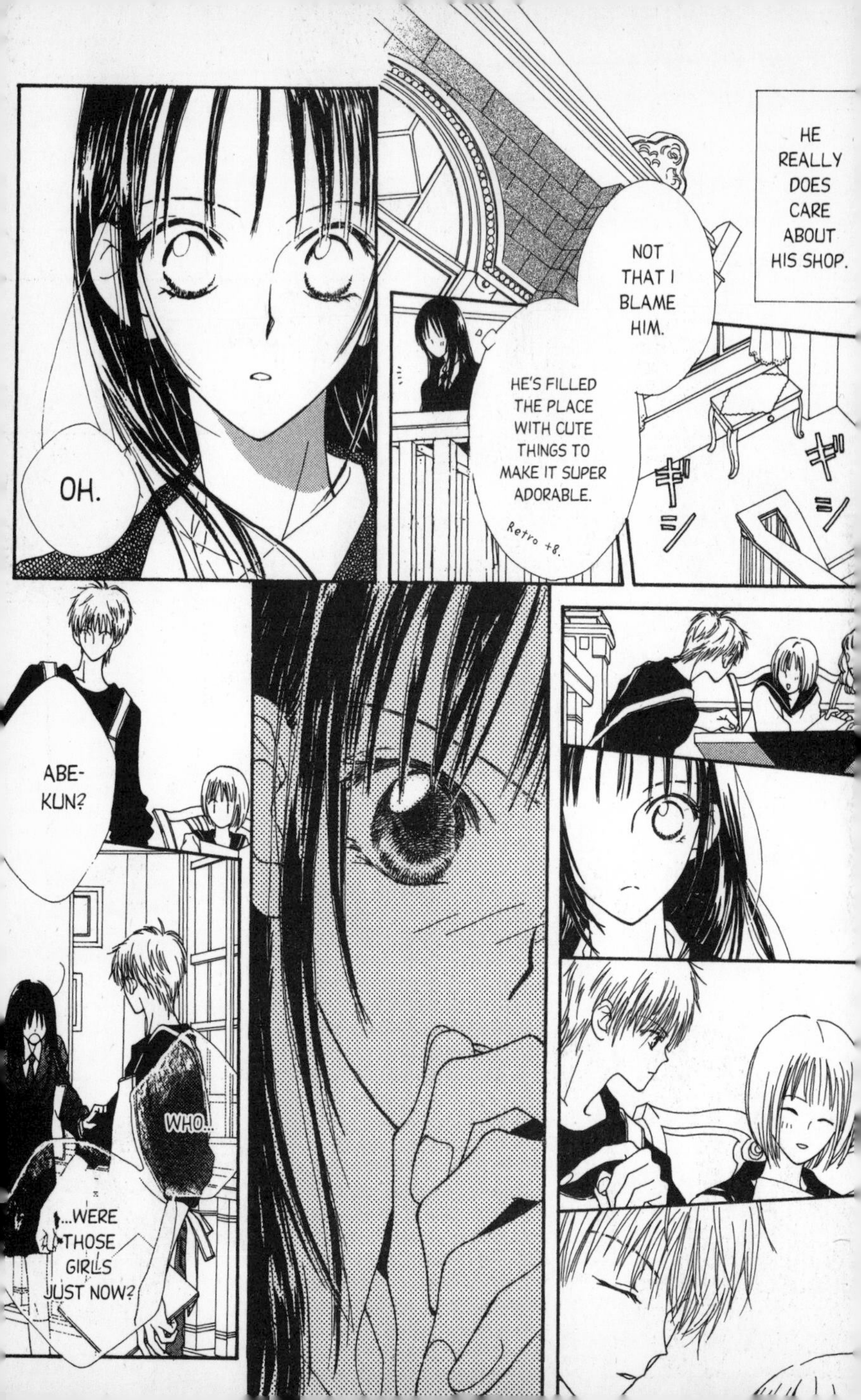
HE REALLY DOES CARE ABOUT HIS SHOP.
ギシ
ギシ
NOT THAT I BLAME HIM.
HE'S FILLED THE PLACE WITH CUTE THINGS TO MAKE IT SUPER ADORABLE.
Retro +8.
OH.
ABE-KUN?
WHO...
...WERE THOSE GIRLS JUST NOW?

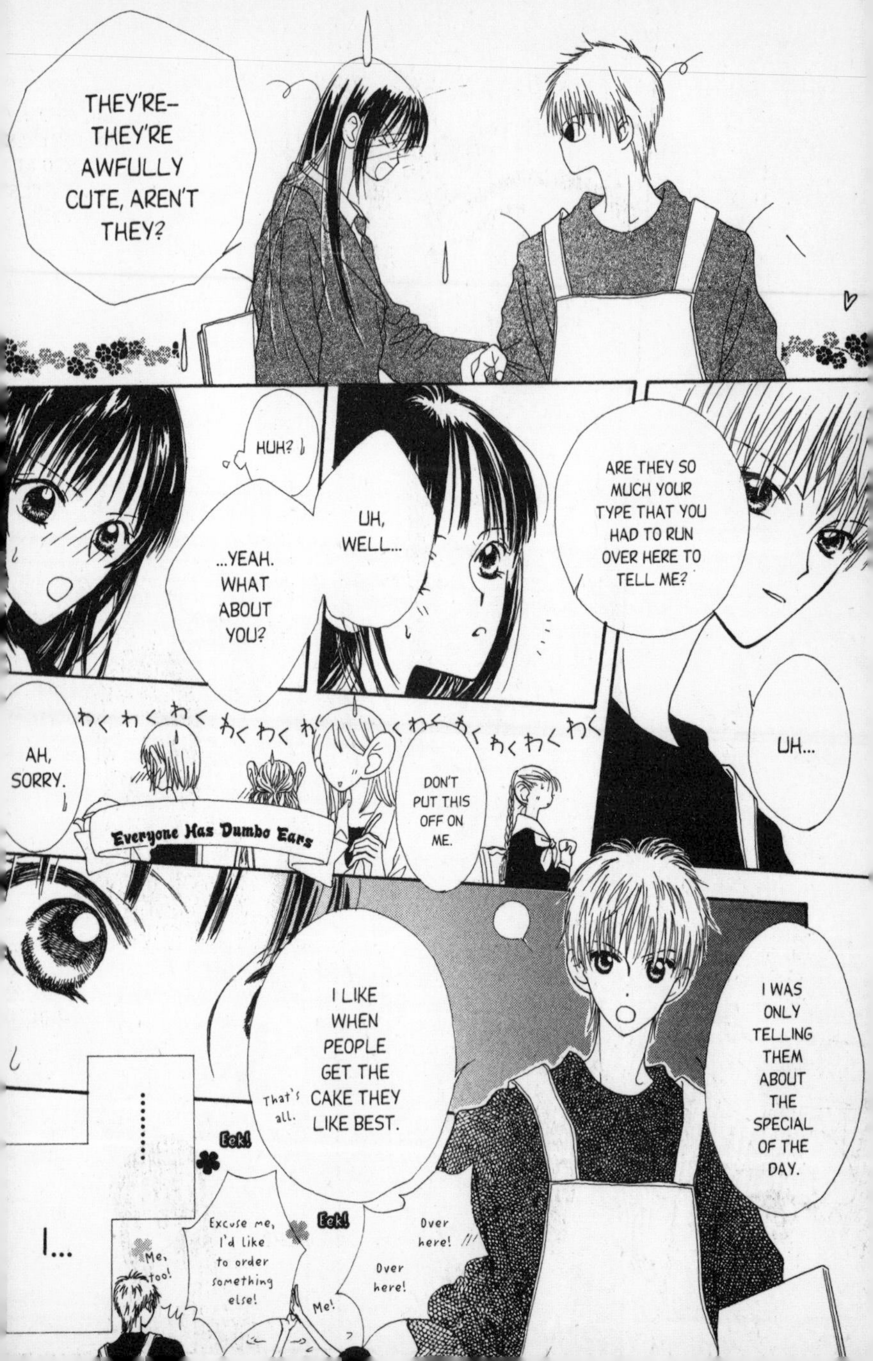
THEY'RE-- THEY'RE AWFULLY CUTE, AREN'T THEY?
ARE THEY SO MUCH YOUR TYPE THAT YOU HAD TO RUN OVER HERE TO TELL ME?
UH...
UH, WELL...
HUH?
...YEAH. WHAT ABOUT YOU?
わくわくわくわくわくわくわくわくわくわくわく
DON'T PUT THIS OFF ON ME.
AH, SORRY.
Everyone Has Dumbo Ears
I WAS ONLY TELLING THEM ABOUT THE SPECIAL OF THE DAY.
I LIKE WHEN PEOPLE GET THE CAKE THEY LIKE BEST.
That's all.
Over here!
Eek!
Over here!
Me!
Excuse me, I'd like to order something else!
Me, too!
Eek!
......
I...

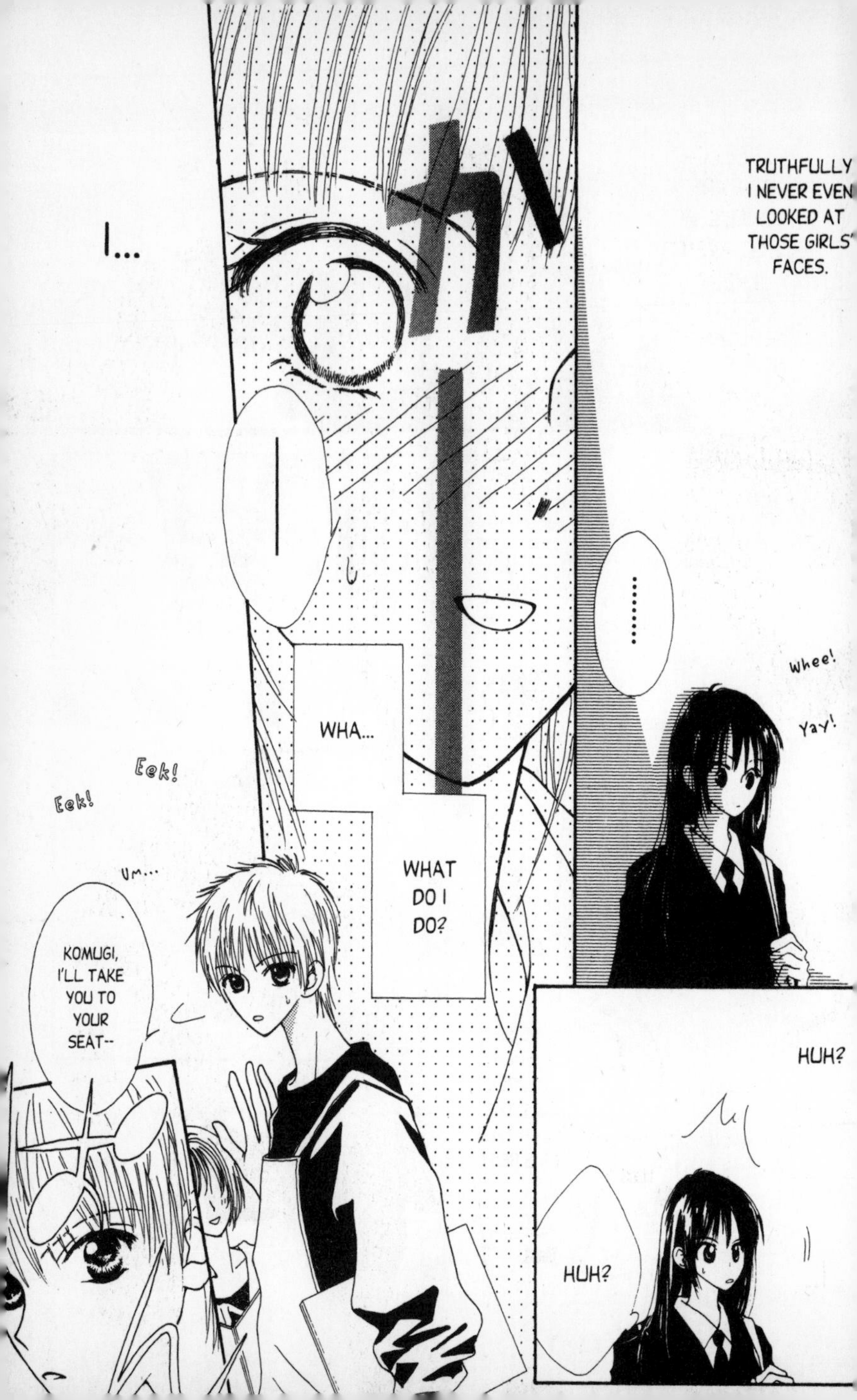
TRUTHFULLY I NEVER EVEN LOOKED AT THOSE GIRLS' FACES.
......
Whee!
Yay!
WHA...
WHAT DO I DO?
I...
HUH?
HUH?
Eek!
Eek!
Um...
KOMUGI, I'LL TAKE YOU TO YOUR SEAT--

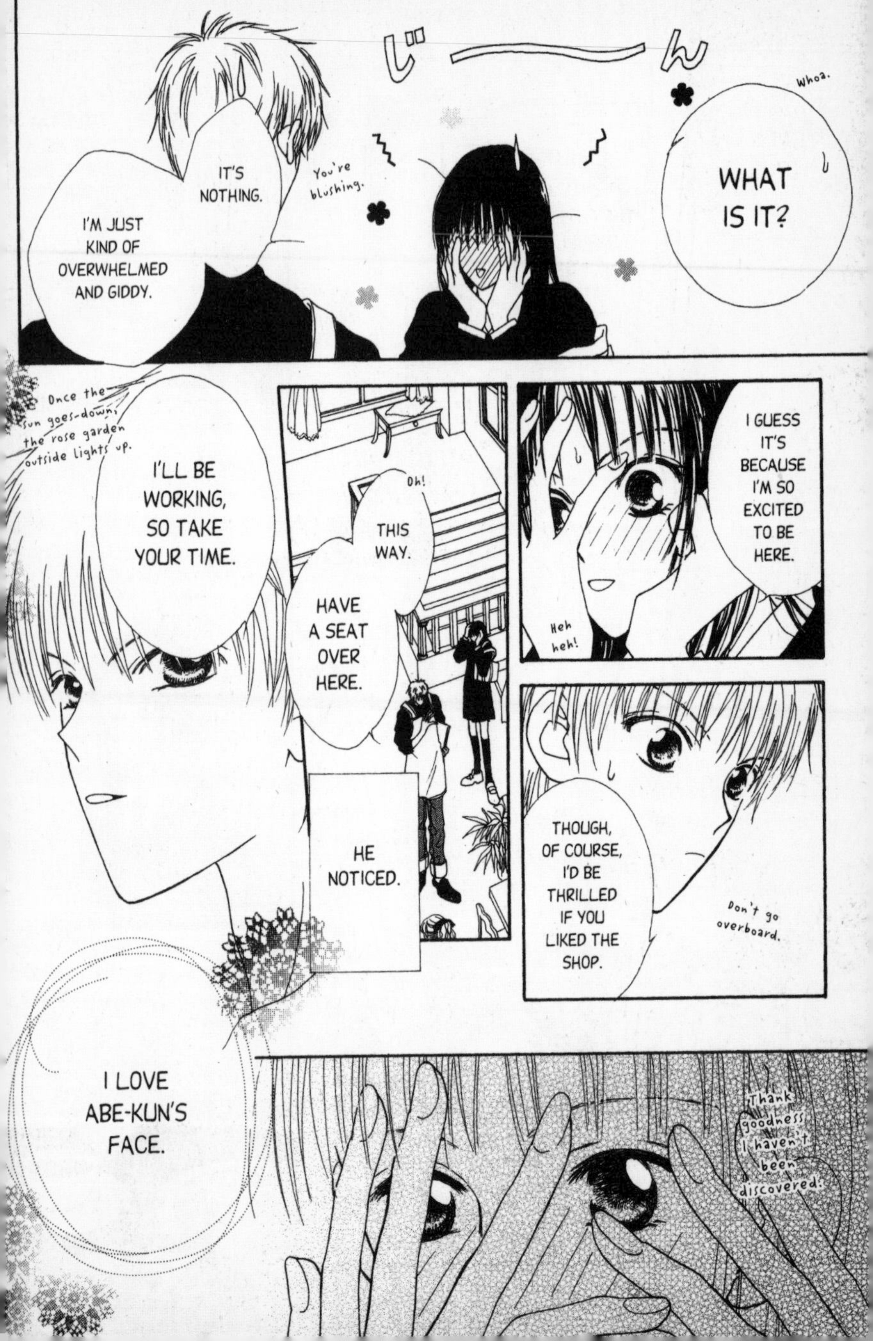
じーーーん
Whoa.
WHAT IS IT?
You're blushing.
IT'S NOTHING.
I'M JUST KIND OF OVERWHELMED AND GIDDY.
I GUESS IT'S BECAUSE I'M SO EXCITED TO BE HERE.
Heh heh!
THOUGH, OF COURSE, I'D BE THRILLED IF YOU LIKED THE SHOP.
Don't go overboard.
Oh!
THIS WAY.
HAVE A SEAT OVER HERE.
HE NOTICED.
I'LL BE WORKING, SO TAKE YOUR TIME.
Once the sun goes-down, the rose garden outside lights up.
Thank goodness I haven't been discovered.
I LOVE ABE-KUN'S FACE.

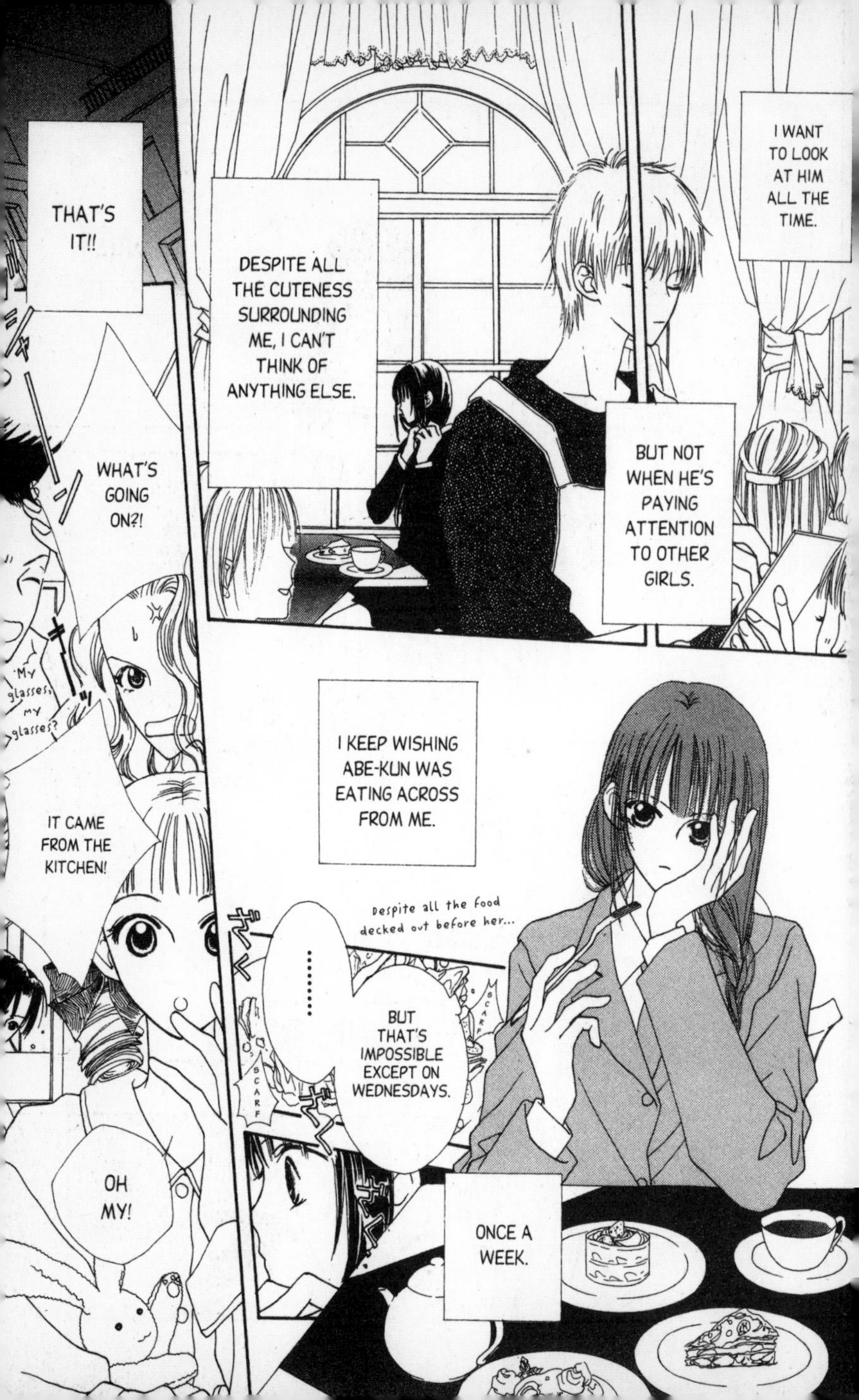

I WANT TO LOOK AT HIM ALL THE TIME.
BUT NOT WHEN HE'S PAYING ATTENTION TO OTHER GIRLS.
DESPITE ALL THE CUTENESS SURROUNDING ME, I CAN'T THINK OF ANYTHING ELSE.
I KEEP WISHING ABE-KUN WAS EATING ACROSS FROM ME.
Despite all the food decked out before her...
SCARF
......
BUT THAT'S IMPOSSIBLE EXCEPT ON WEDNESDAYS.
SCARF
ONCE A WEEK.
THAT'S IT!!
WHAT'S GOING ON?!
My glasses, my glasses?
IT CAME FROM THE KITCHEN!
OH MY!

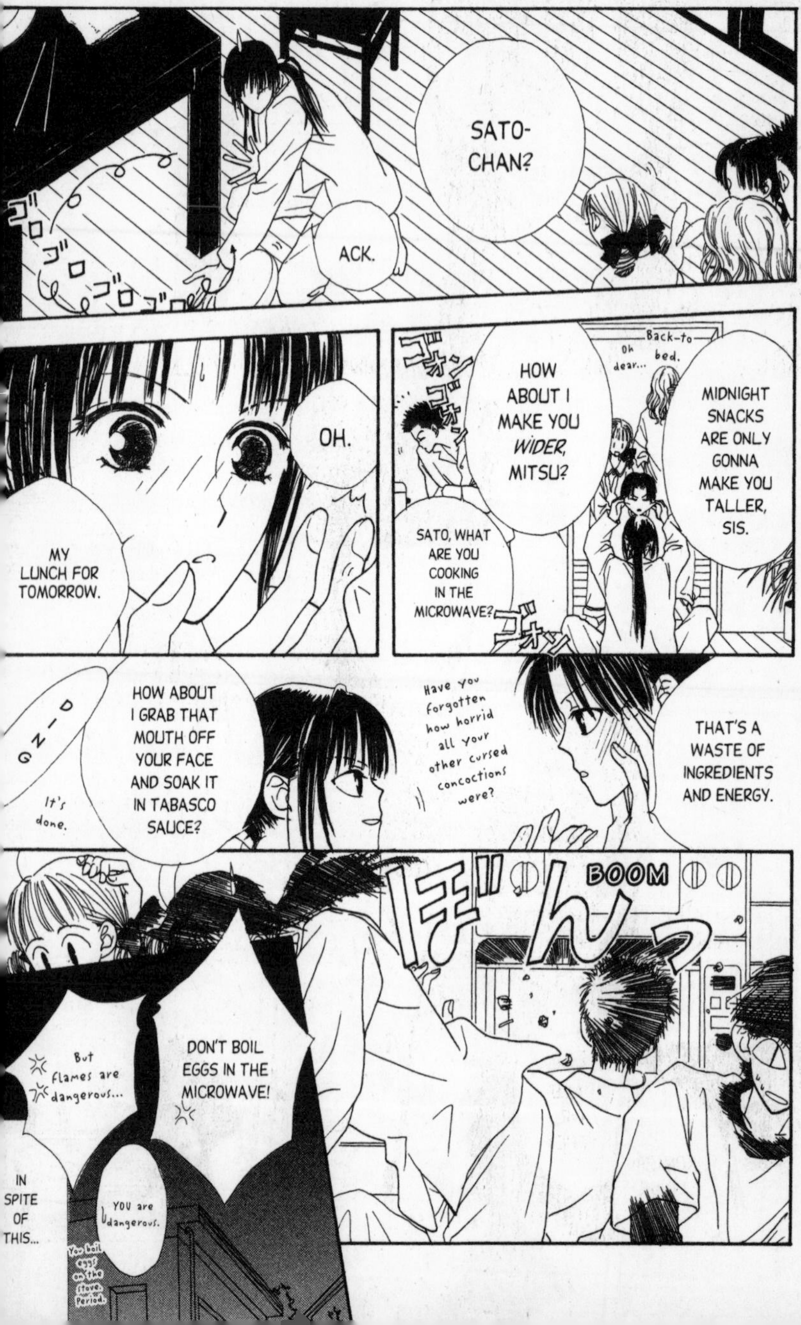
SATO-CHAN?
ACK.
ゴロゴロゴロゴロ
Back-to bed.
Oh dear...
MIDNIGHT SNACKS ARE ONLY GONNA MAKE YOU TALLER, SIS.
HOW ABOUT I MAKE YOU *WIDER*, MITSU?
SATO, WHAT ARE YOU COOKING IN THE MICROWAVE?
ゴォンゴォン
ゴォン
OH.
MY LUNCH FOR TOMORROW.
THAT'S A WASTE OF INGREDIENTS AND ENERGY.
Have you forgotten how horrid all your other cursed concoctions were?
HOW ABOUT I GRAB THAT MOUTH OFF YOUR FACE AND SOAK IT IN TABASCO SAUCE?
DING
It's done.
ぼんっ
BOOM
DON'T BOIL EGGS IN THE MICROWAVE!
But flames are dangerous...
YOU are dangerous.
You boil eggs on the stove. Period.
IN SPITE OF THIS...

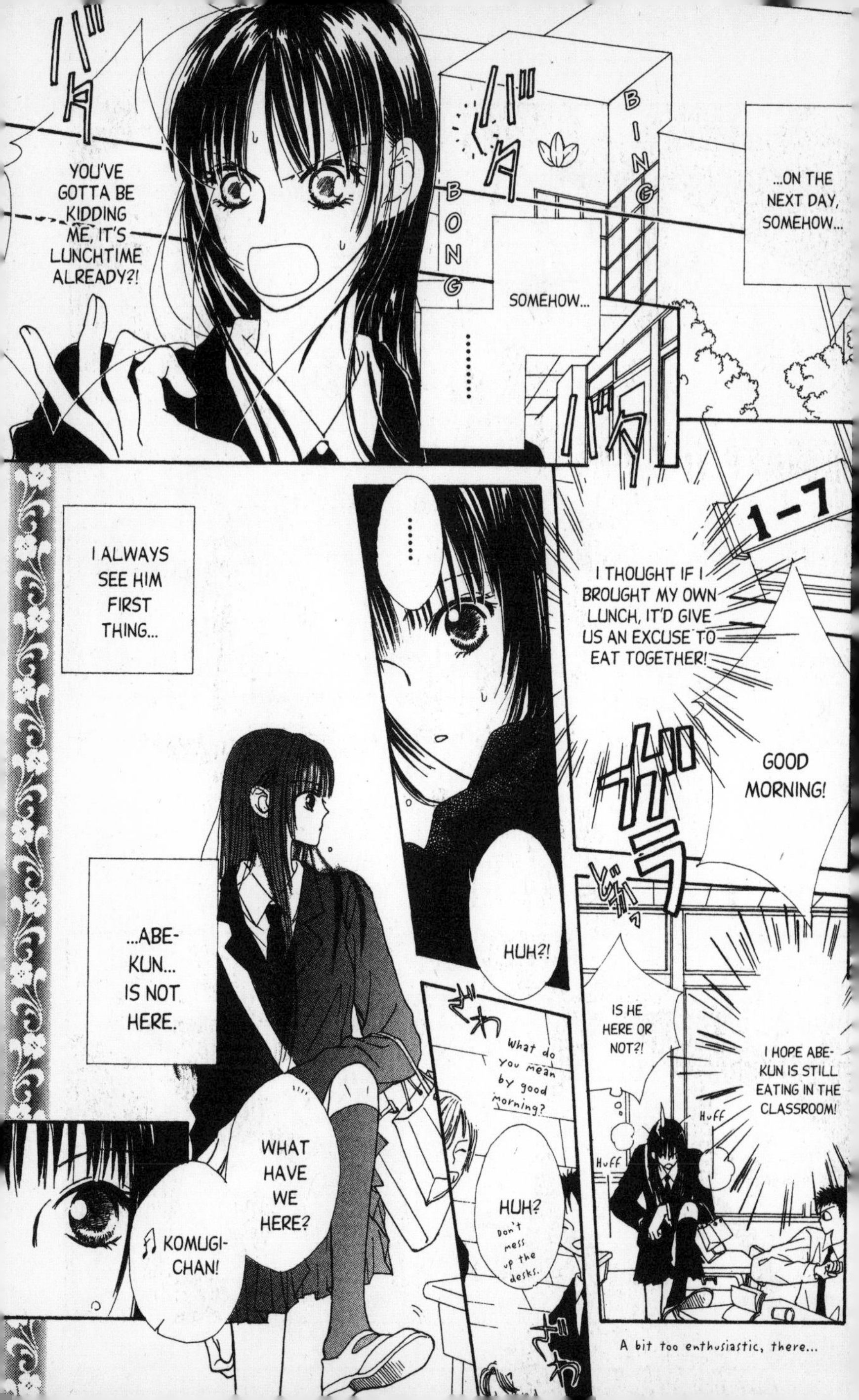
...ON THE NEXT DAY, SOMEHOW...
BING
BONG
バタ
SOMEHOW...
......
バタ
YOU'VE GOTTA BE KIDDING ME, IT'S LUNCHTIME ALREADY?!
1-7
I THOUGHT IF I BROUGHT MY OWN LUNCH, IT'D GIVE US AN EXCUSE TO EAT TOGETHER!
GOOD MORNING!
ガラ
I HOPE ABE-KUN IS STILL EATING IN THE CLASSROOM!
IS HE HERE OR NOT?!
Huff
Huff
A bit too enthusiastic, there...
......
HUH?!
What do you mean by good morning?
HUH?
Don't mess up the desks.
I ALWAYS SEE HIM FIRST THING...
...ABE-KUN... IS NOT HERE.
WHAT HAVE WE HERE?
KOMUGI-CHAN!

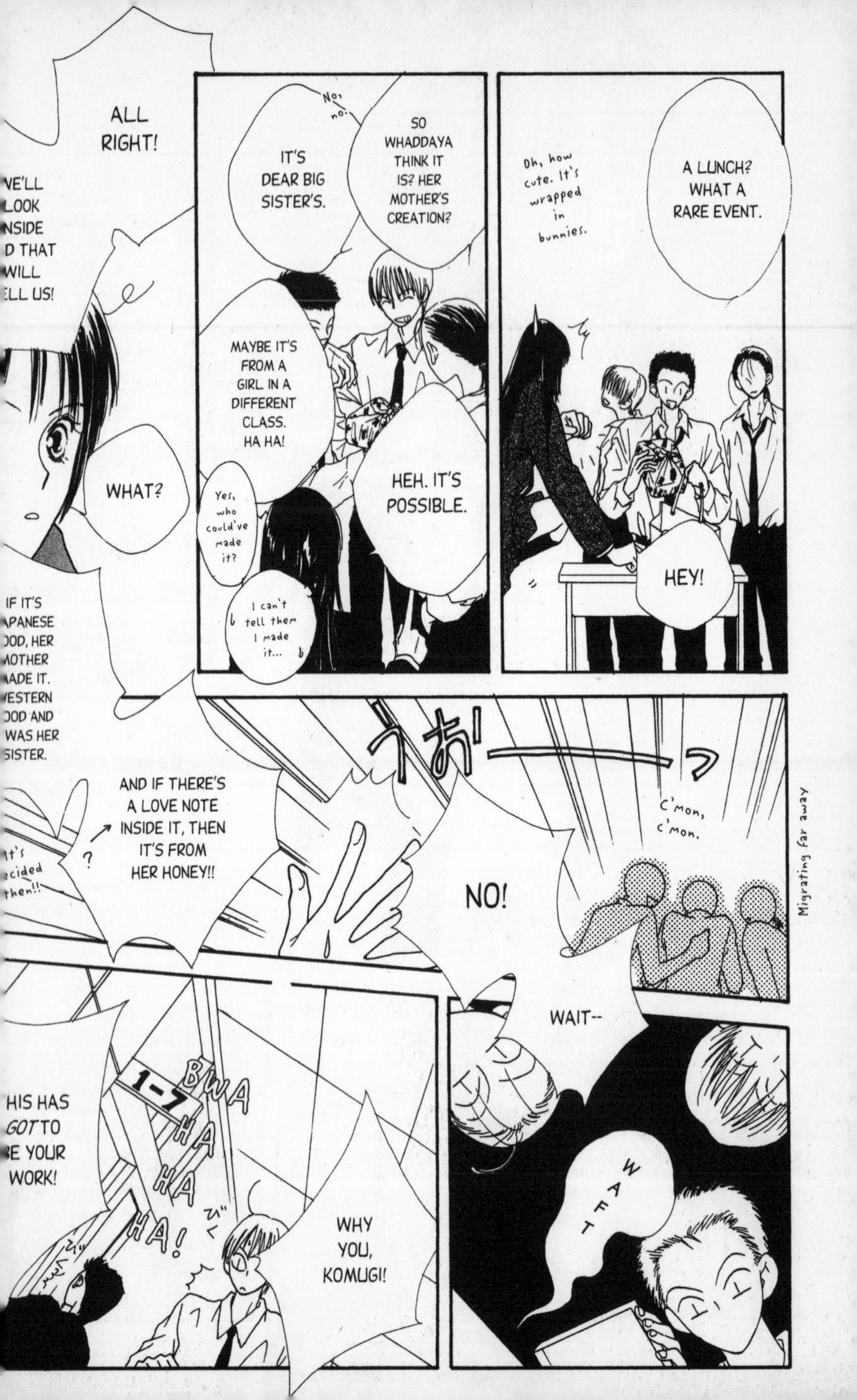

A LUNCH? WHAT A RARE EVENT.
Oh, how cute. It's wrapped in bunnies.
HEY!
SO WHADDAYA THINK IT IS? HER MOTHER'S CREATION?
No, no.
IT'S DEAR BIG SISTER'S.
MAYBE IT'S FROM A GIRL IN A DIFFERENT CLASS. HA HA!
HEH. IT'S POSSIBLE.
Yes, who could've made it?
I can't tell them I made it...
ALL RIGHT!
VE'LL LOOK NSIDE D THAT WILL ELL US!
WHAT?
IF IT'S APANESE OOD, HER MOTHER ADE IT. VESTERN OOD AND WAS HER SISTER.
AND IF THERE'S A LOVE NOTE INSIDE IT, THEN IT'S FROM HER HONEY!!
?
t's ecided then!!
うお!
C'mon, c'mon.
NO!
Migrating far away
WAIT--
WAFT
1-7
BWA HA HA HA!
HIS HAS GOT TO E YOUR WORK!
WHY YOU, KOMUGI!

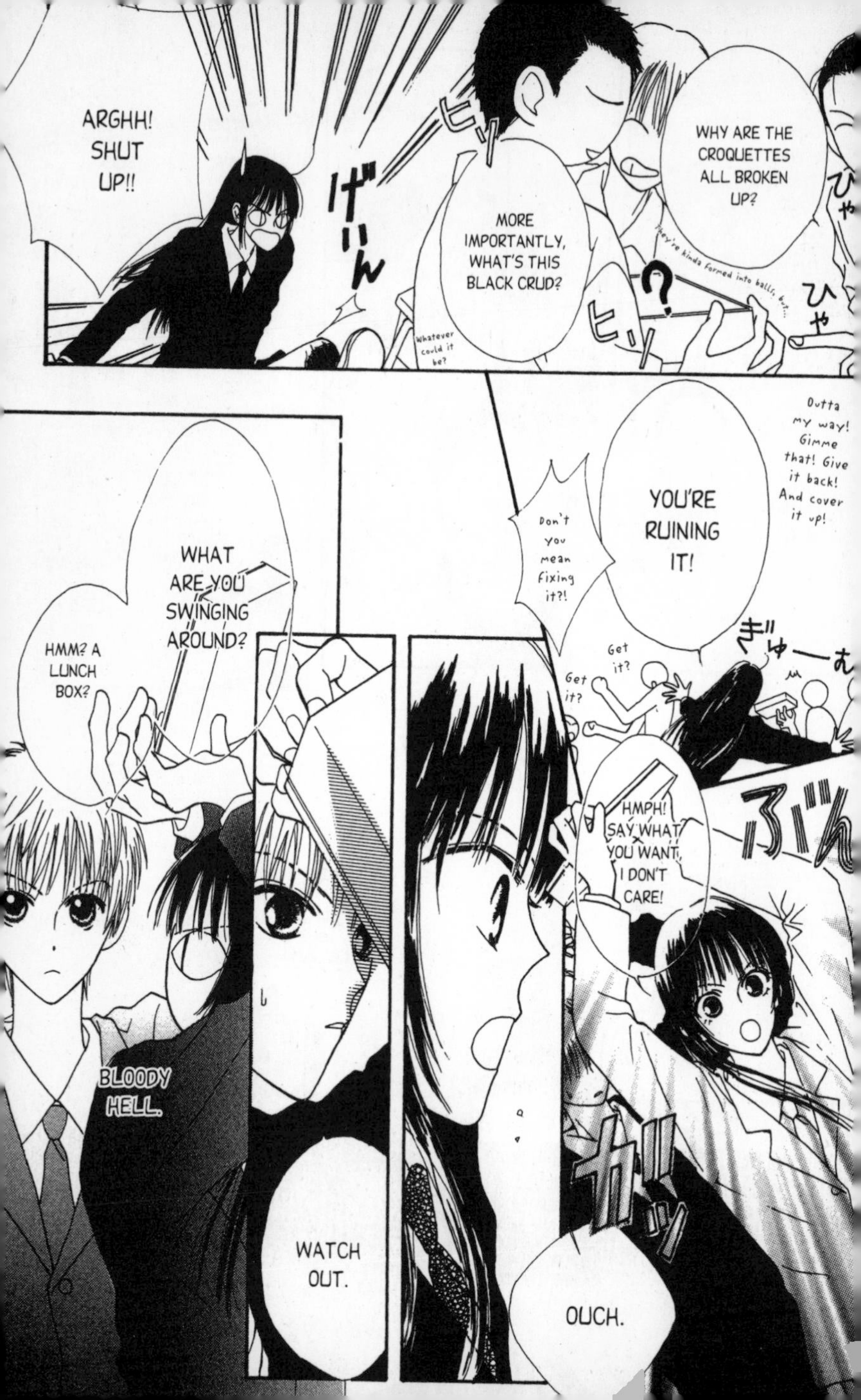
WHY ARE THE CROQUETTES ALL BROKEN UP?
They're kinda formed into balls, but...
ひゃ
ひゃ
?
ヒッ
MORE IMPORTANTLY, WHAT'S THIS BLACK CRUD?
Whatever could it be?
ヒッ
ARGHH! SHUT UP!!
Outta my way! Gimme that! Give it back! And cover it up!
YOU'RE RUINING IT!
Don't you mean fixing it?!
ぎゅーむ
Get it?
Get it?
HMPH! SAY WHAT YOU WANT, I DON'T CARE!
OUCH.
WATCH OUT.
WHAT ARE YOU SWINGING AROUND?
HMM? A LUNCH BOX?
BLOODY HELL.

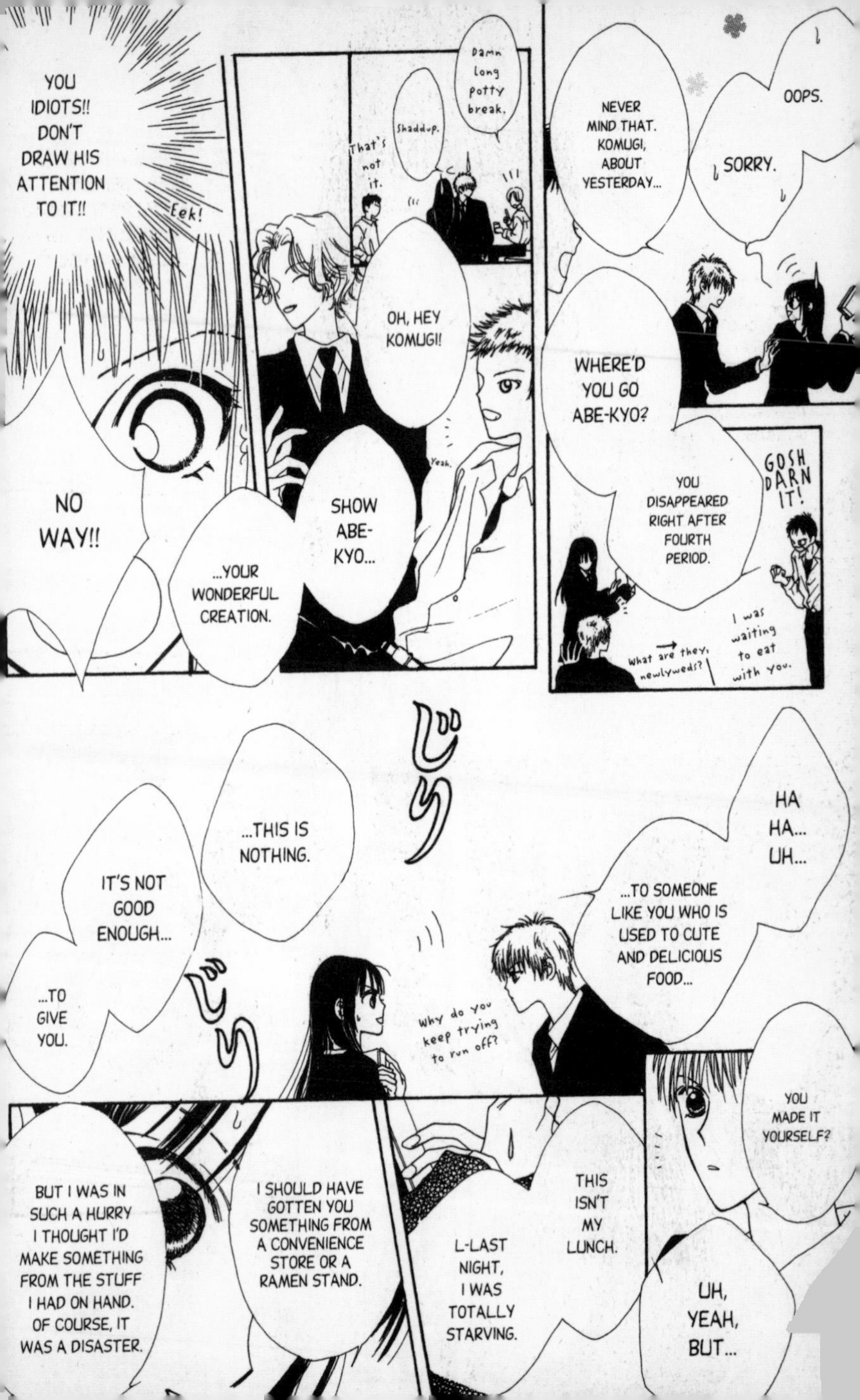
OOPS.
SORRY.
NEVER MIND THAT. KOMUGI, ABOUT YESTERDAY...
WHERE'D YOU GO ABE-KYO?
GOSH DARN IT!
YOU DISAPPEARED RIGHT AFTER FOURTH PERIOD.
I was waiting to eat with you.
What are they, newlyweds?
Damn long potty break.
Shaddup.
That's not it.
OH, HEY KOMUGI!
Yeah.
SHOW ABE-KYO...
...YOUR WONDERFUL CREATION.
YOU IDIOTS!! DON'T DRAW HIS ATTENTION TO IT!!
Eek!
NO WAY!!
HA HA... UH...
...TO SOMEONE LIKE YOU WHO IS USED TO CUTE AND DELICIOUS FOOD...
Why do you keep trying to run off?
...THIS IS NOTHING.
IT'S NOT GOOD ENOUGH...
...TO GIVE YOU.
YOU MADE IT YOURSELF?
UH, YEAH, BUT...
THIS ISN'T MY LUNCH.
L-LAST NIGHT, I WAS TOTALLY STARVING.
I SHOULD HAVE GOTTEN YOU SOMETHING FROM A CONVENIENCE STORE OR A RAMEN STAND.
BUT I WAS IN SUCH A HURRY I THOUGHT I'D MAKE SOMETHING FROM THE STUFF I HAD ON HAND. OF COURSE, IT WAS A DISASTER.

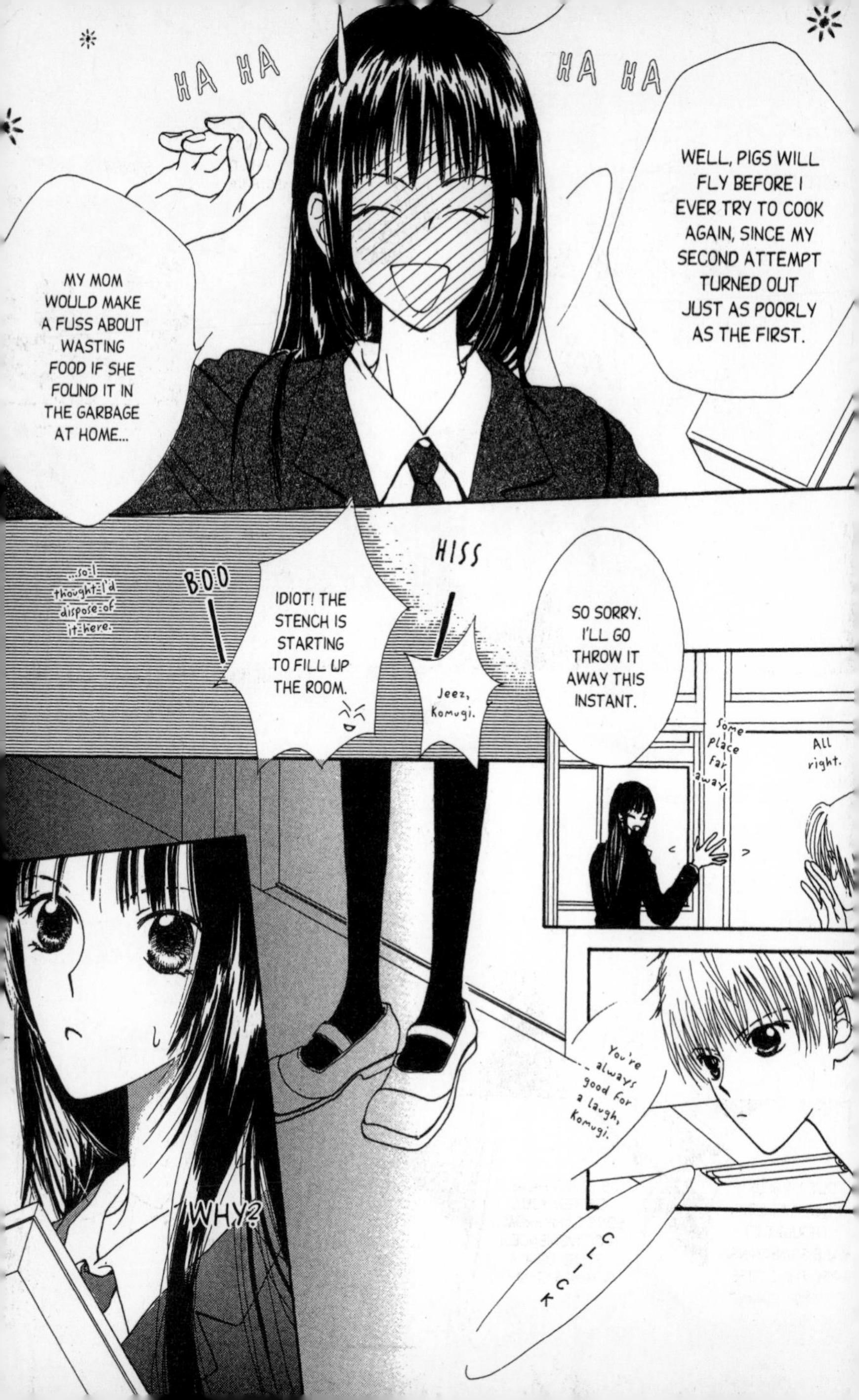
HA HA
HA HA
WELL, PIGS WILL FLY BEFORE I EVER TRY TO COOK AGAIN, SINCE MY SECOND ATTEMPT TURNED OUT JUST AS POORLY AS THE FIRST.
MY MOM WOULD MAKE A FUSS ABOUT WASTING FOOD IF SHE FOUND IT IN THE GARBAGE AT HOME...
SO SORRY. I'LL GO THROW IT AWAY THIS INSTANT.
Jeez, Komugi.
HISS
IDIOT! THE STENCH IS STARTING TO FILL UP THE ROOM.
BOO
...so I thought I'd dispose of it here.
All right.
Some place far away.
You're always good for a laugh, Komugi.
CLICK
WHY?

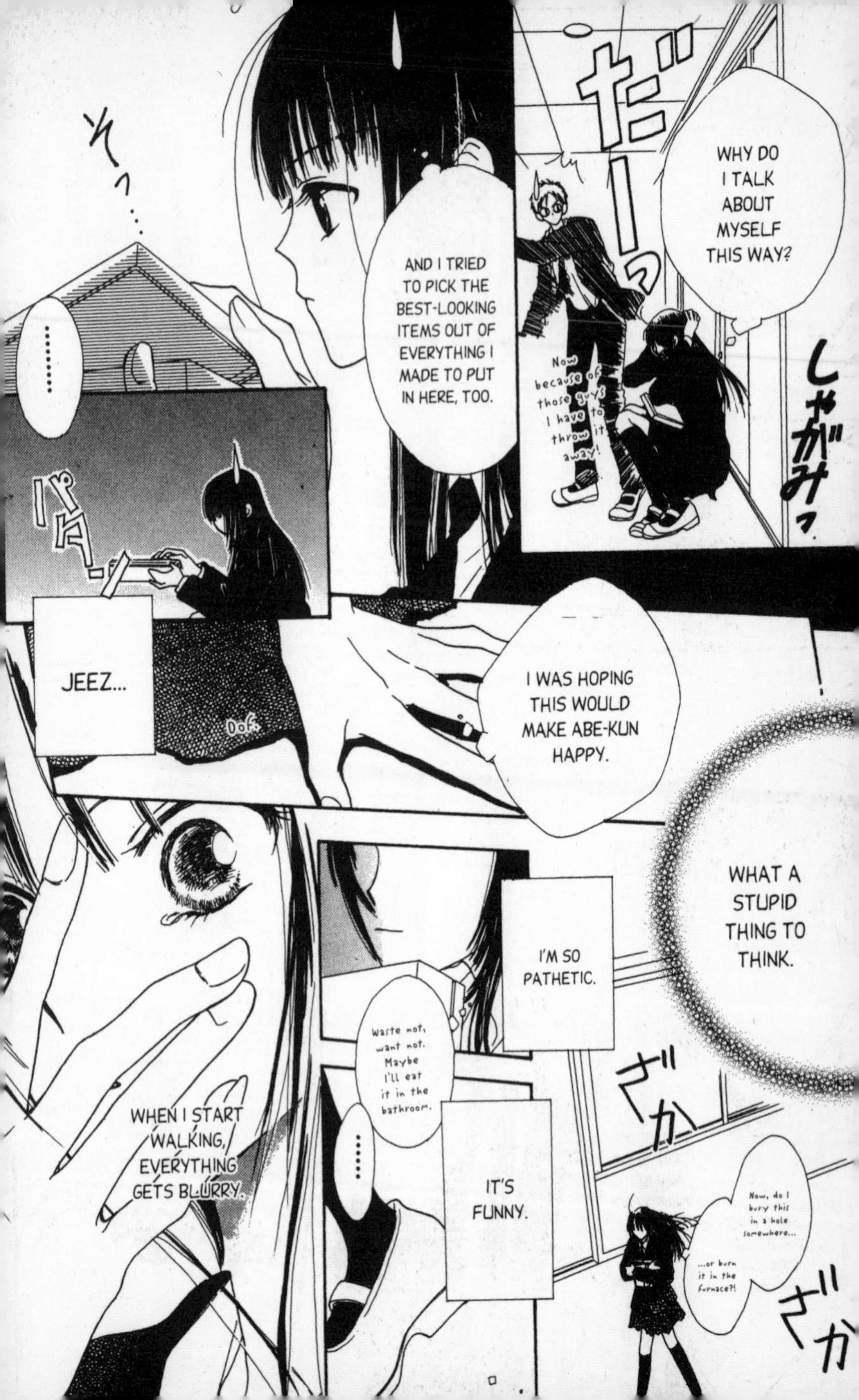
だーっ
WHY DO I TALK ABOUT MYSELF THIS WAY?
しゃがみっ
Now because of those guys I have to throw it away!
AND I TRIED TO PICK THE BEST-LOOKING ITEMS OUT OF EVERYTHING I MADE TO PUT IN HERE, TOO.
そっ…
……
パカ…
JEEZ...
Dof.
I WAS HOPING THIS WOULD MAKE ABE-KUN HAPPY.
WHAT A STUPID THING TO THINK.
ざか
Now, do I bury this in a hole somewhere...
...or burn it in the furnace?!
ざか
I'M SO PATHETIC.
Waste not, want not. Maybe I'll eat it in the bathroom.
......
IT'S FUNNY.
WHEN I START WALKING, EVERYTHING GETS BLURRY.

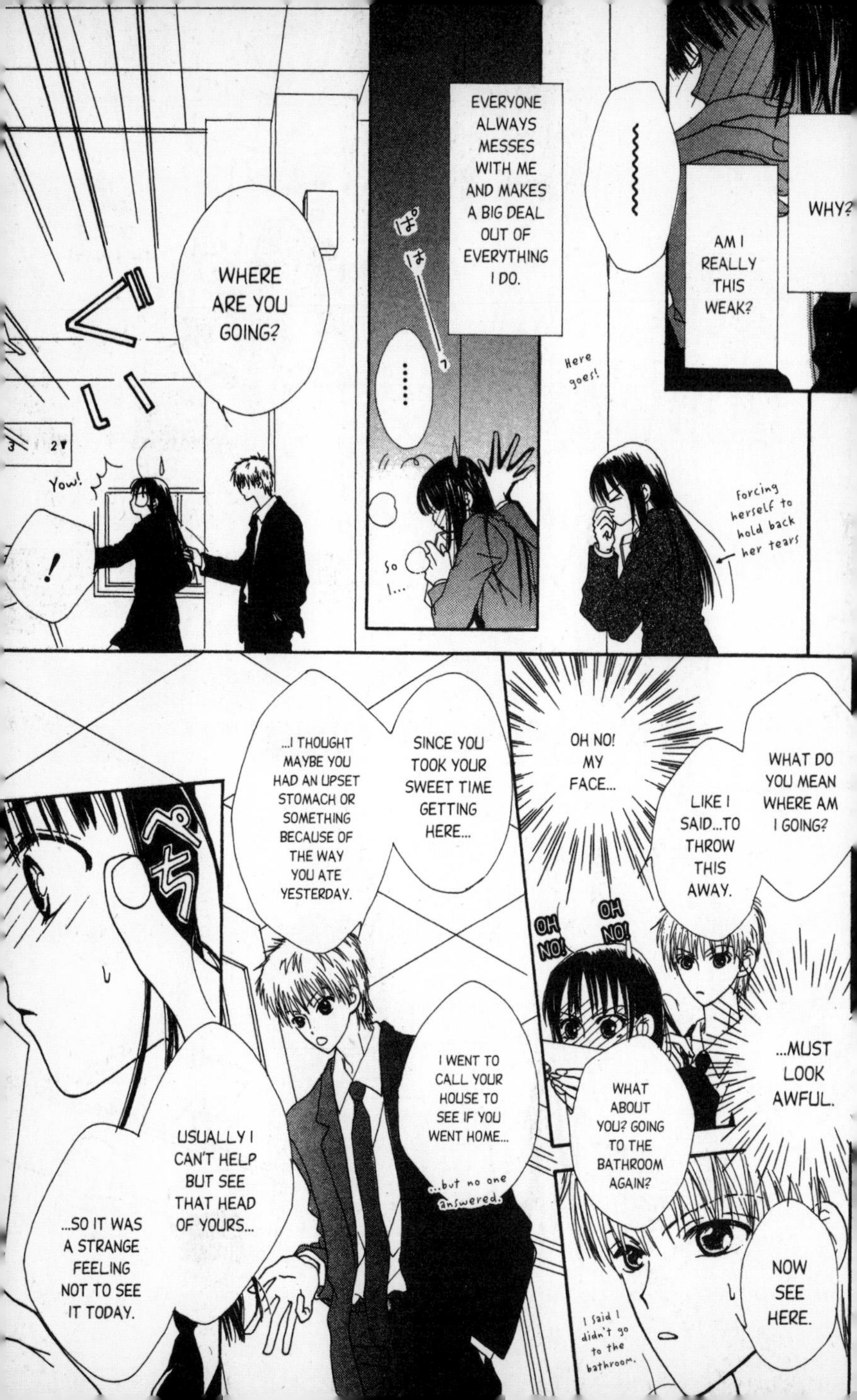
WHY?
AM I REALLY THIS WEAK?
......
Here goes!
Forcing herself to hold back her tears
EVERYONE ALWAYS MESSES WITH ME AND MAKES A BIG DEAL OUT OF EVERYTHING I DO.
ぱ は
......
So I...
WHERE ARE YOU GOING?
Yow!
!
3 2▼
WHAT DO YOU MEAN WHERE AM I GOING?
LIKE I SAID...TO THROW THIS AWAY.
OH NO! MY FACE...
OH NO! OH NO!
...MUST LOOK AWFUL.
WHAT ABOUT YOU? GOING TO THE BATHROOM AGAIN?
NOW SEE HERE.
I said I didn't go to the bathroom.
SINCE YOU TOOK YOUR SWEET TIME GETTING HERE...
...I THOUGHT MAYBE YOU HAD AN UPSET STOMACH OR SOMETHING BECAUSE OF THE WAY YOU ATE YESTERDAY.
I WENT TO CALL YOUR HOUSE TO SEE IF YOU WENT HOME...
...but no one answered.
ぺち
USUALLY I CAN'T HELP BUT SEE THAT HEAD OF YOURS...
...SO IT WAS A STRANGE FEELING NOT TO SEE IT TODAY.

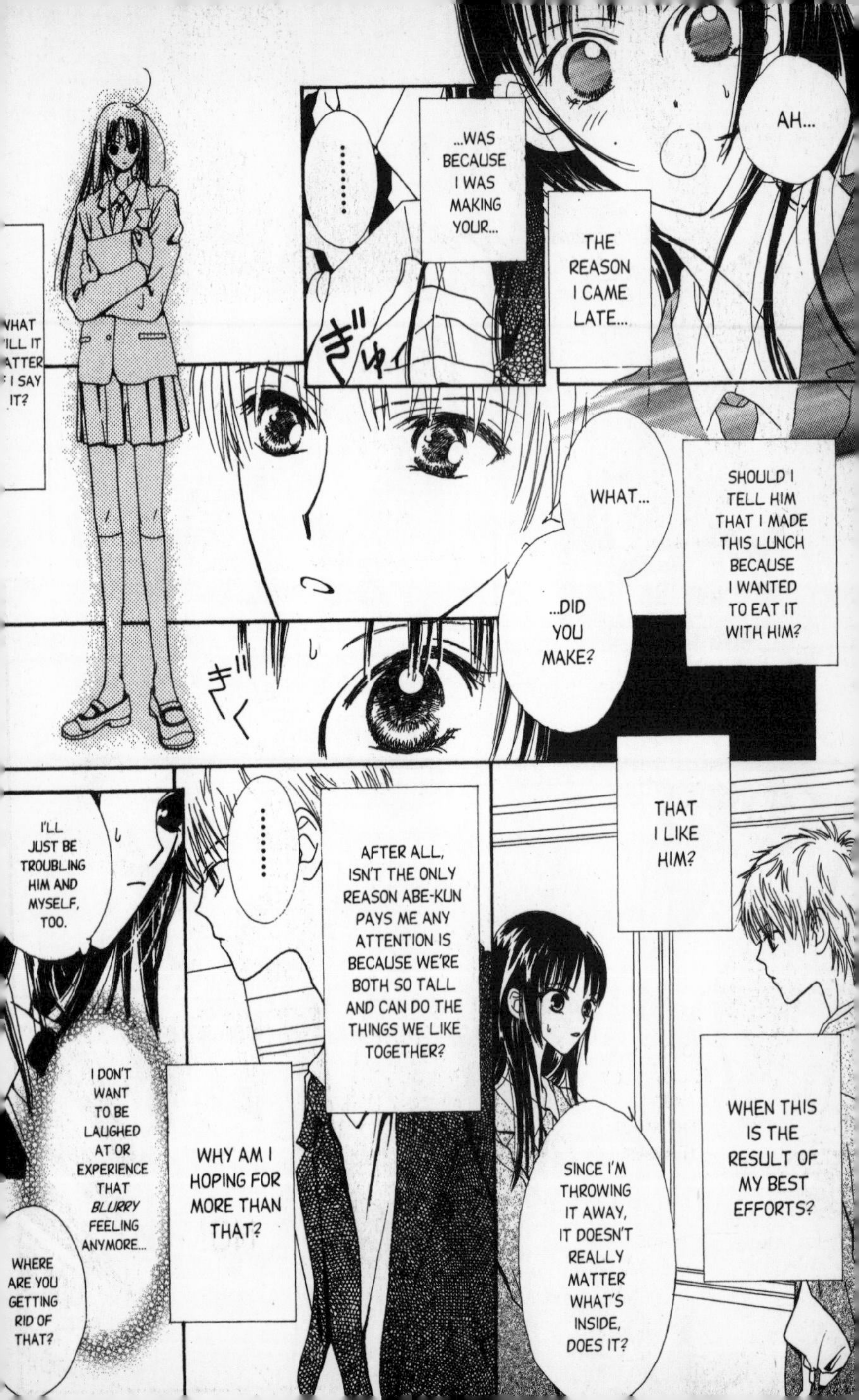
AH...
THE REASON I CAME LATE...
...WAS BECAUSE I WAS MAKING YOUR...
......
ぎゅ
SHOULD I TELL HIM THAT I MADE THIS LUNCH BECAUSE I WANTED TO EAT IT WITH HIM?
WHAT...
...DID YOU MAKE?
ぎく
WHAT ILL IT ATTER I SAY IT?
THAT I LIKE HIM?
WHEN THIS IS THE RESULT OF MY BEST EFFORTS?
SINCE I'M THROWING IT AWAY, IT DOESN'T REALLY MATTER WHAT'S INSIDE, DOES IT?
AFTER ALL, ISN'T THE ONLY REASON ABE-KUN PAYS ME ANY ATTENTION IS BECAUSE WE'RE BOTH SO TALL AND CAN DO THE THINGS WE LIKE TOGETHER?
......
WHY AM I HOPING FOR MORE THAN THAT?
I'LL JUST BE TROUBLING HIM AND MYSELF, TOO.
I DON'T WANT TO BE LAUGHED AT OR EXPERIENCE THAT *BLURRY* FEELING ANYMORE...
WHERE ARE YOU GETTING RID OF THAT?

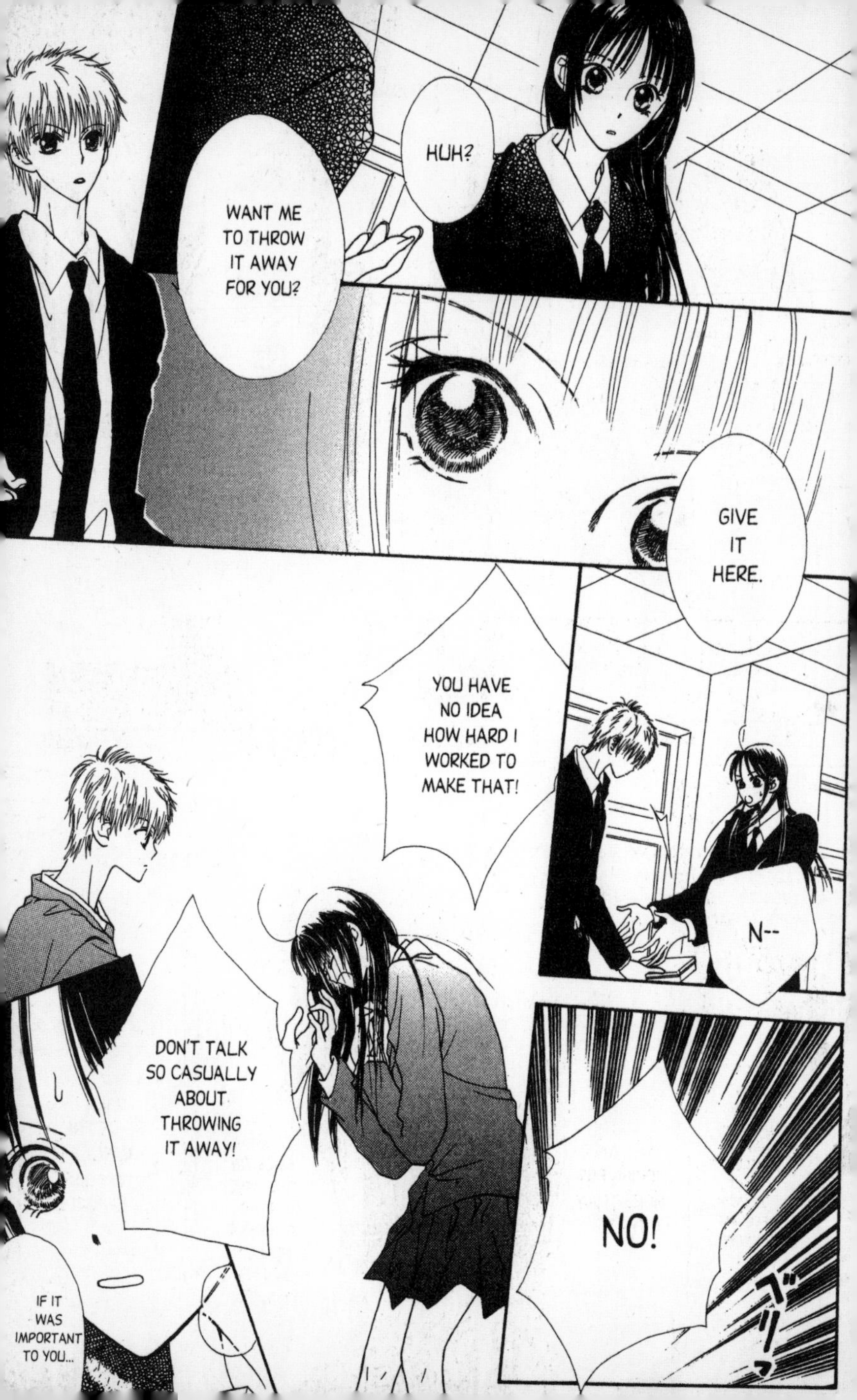
HUH?
GIVE IT HERE.
WANT ME TO THROW IT AWAY FOR YOU?
N--
NO!
YOU HAVE NO IDEA HOW HARD I WORKED TO MAKE THAT!
DON'T TALK SO CASUALLY ABOUT THROWING IT AWAY!
IF IT WAS IMPORTANT TO YOU...

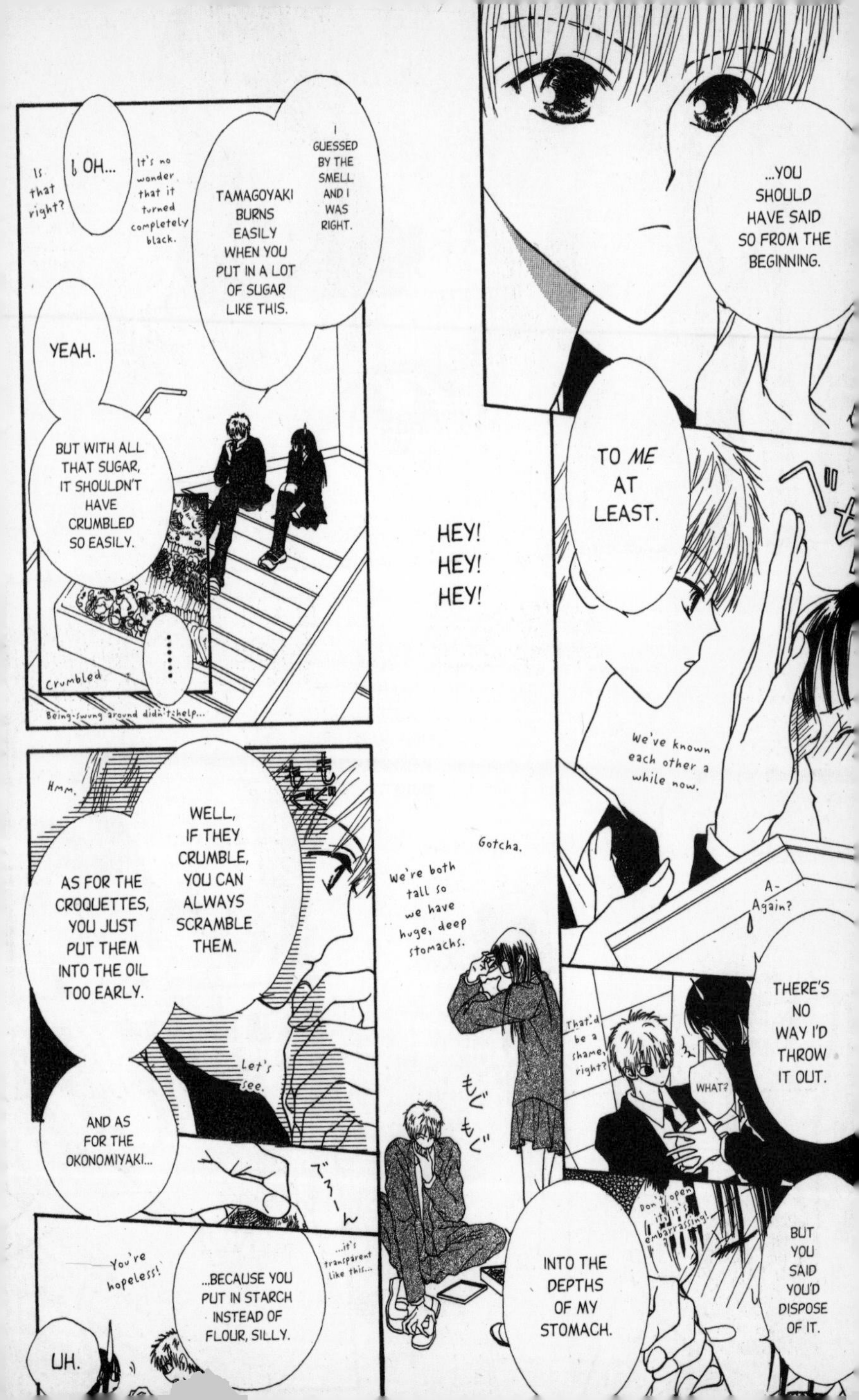
...YOU SHOULD HAVE SAID SO FROM THE BEGINNING.
TO *ME* AT LEAST.
We've known each other a while now.
A- Again?
THERE'S NO WAY I'D THROW IT OUT.
WHAT?
That'd be a shame, right?
BUT YOU SAID YOU'D DISPOSE OF IT.
Don't open it, it's embarrassing!
INTO THE DEPTHS OF MY STOMACH.
HEY! HEY! HEY!
Gotcha.
We're both tall so we have huge, deep stomachs.
もぐもぐ
I GUESSED BY THE SMELL AND I WAS RIGHT.
TAMAGOYAKI BURNS EASILY WHEN YOU PUT IN A LOT OF SUGAR LIKE THIS.
It's no wonder that it turned completely black.
OH...
Is that right?
YEAH.
BUT WITH ALL THAT SUGAR, IT SHOULDN'T HAVE CRUMBLED SO EASILY.
......
Crumbled
Being swung around didn't help...
もぐもぐ
WELL, IF THEY CRUMBLE, YOU CAN ALWAYS SCRAMBLE THEM.
Hmm.
AS FOR THE CROQUETTES, YOU JUST PUT THEM INTO THE OIL TOO EARLY.
Let's see.
AND AS FOR THE OKONOMIYAKI...
でろーん
...it's transparent like this...
...BECAUSE YOU PUT IN STARCH INSTEAD OF FLOUR, SILLY.
You're hopeless!
UH.

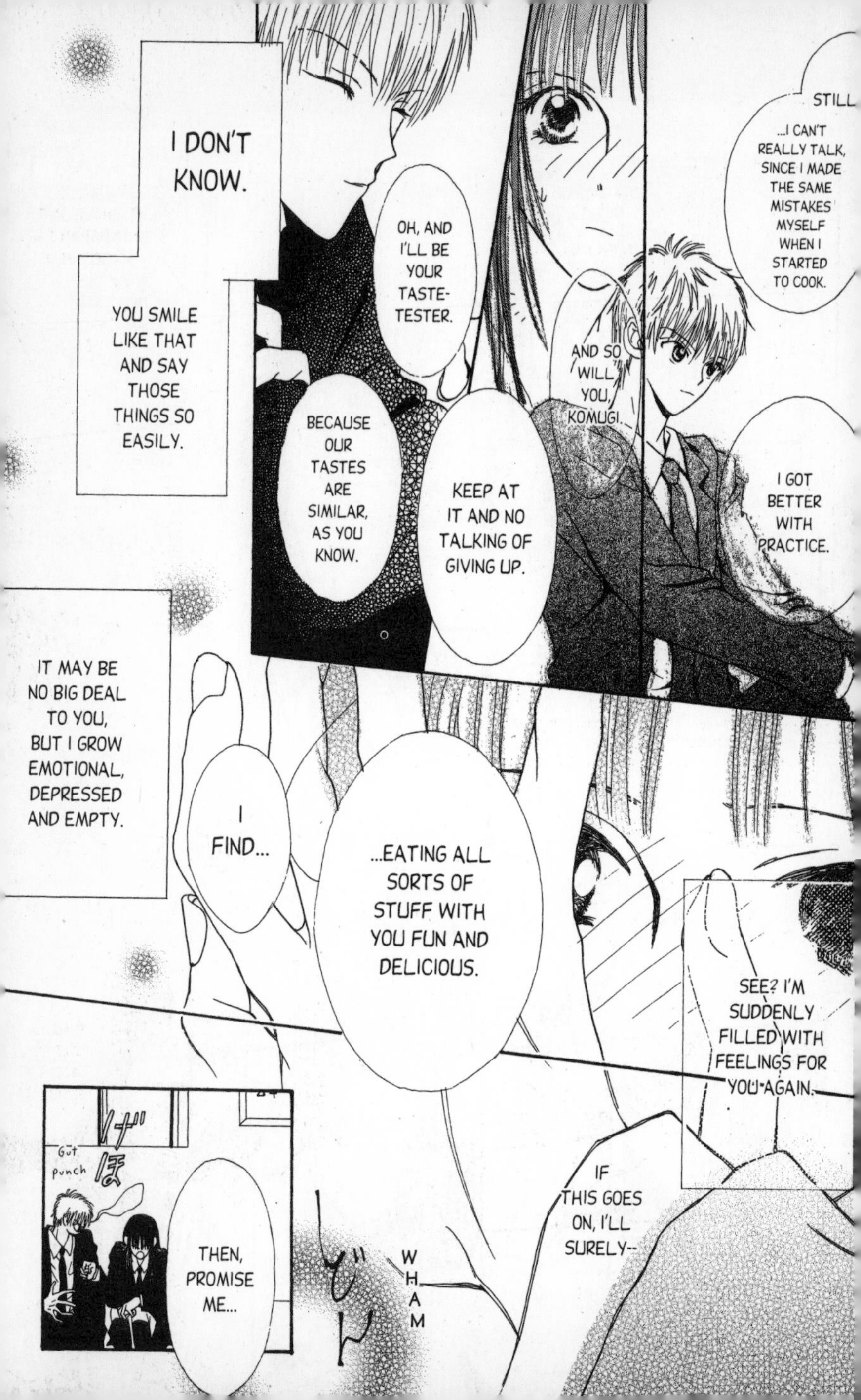
STILL
...I CAN'T REALLY TALK, SINCE I MADE THE SAME MISTAKES MYSELF WHEN I STARTED TO COOK.
I GOT BETTER WITH PRACTICE.
AND SO WILL YOU, KOMUGI.
KEEP AT IT AND NO TALKING OF GIVING UP.
OH, AND I'LL BE YOUR TASTE-TESTER.
BECAUSE OUR TASTES ARE SIMILAR, AS YOU KNOW.
I DON'T KNOW.
YOU SMILE LIKE THAT AND SAY THOSE THINGS SO EASILY.
I FIND...
...EATING ALL SORTS OF STUFF WITH YOU FUN AND DELICIOUS.
IT MAY BE NO BIG DEAL TO YOU, BUT I GROW EMOTIONAL, DEPRESSED AND EMPTY.
SEE? I'M SUDDENLY FILLED WITH FEELINGS FOR YOU AGAIN.
IF THIS GOES ON, I'LL SURELY--
THEN, PROMISE ME...
WHAM
Gut punch

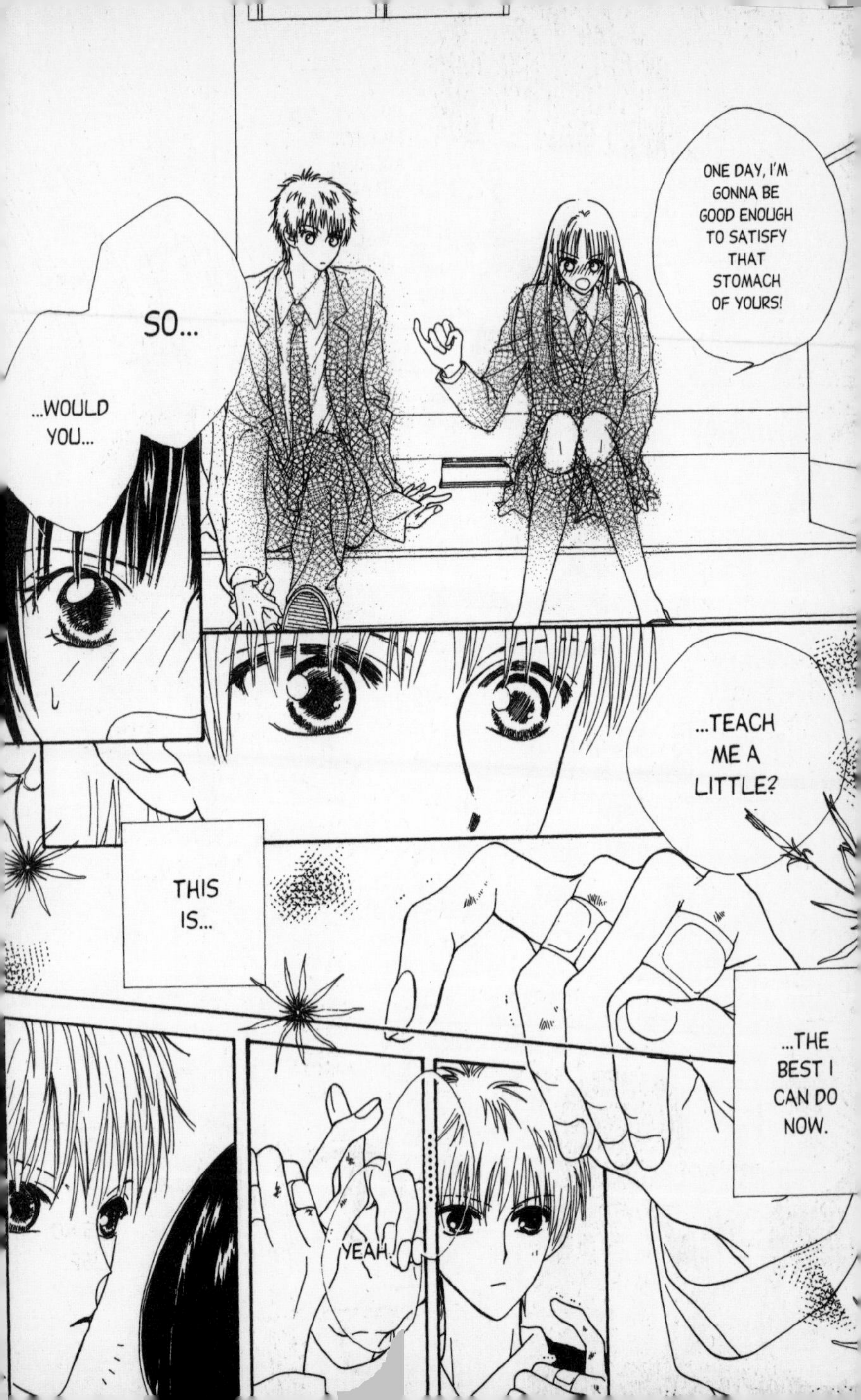
ONE DAY, I'M GONNA BE GOOD ENOUGH TO SATISFY THAT STOMACH OF YOURS!
SO...
...WOULD YOU...
...TEACH ME A LITTLE?
THIS IS...
...THE BEST I CAN DO NOW.
YEAH.

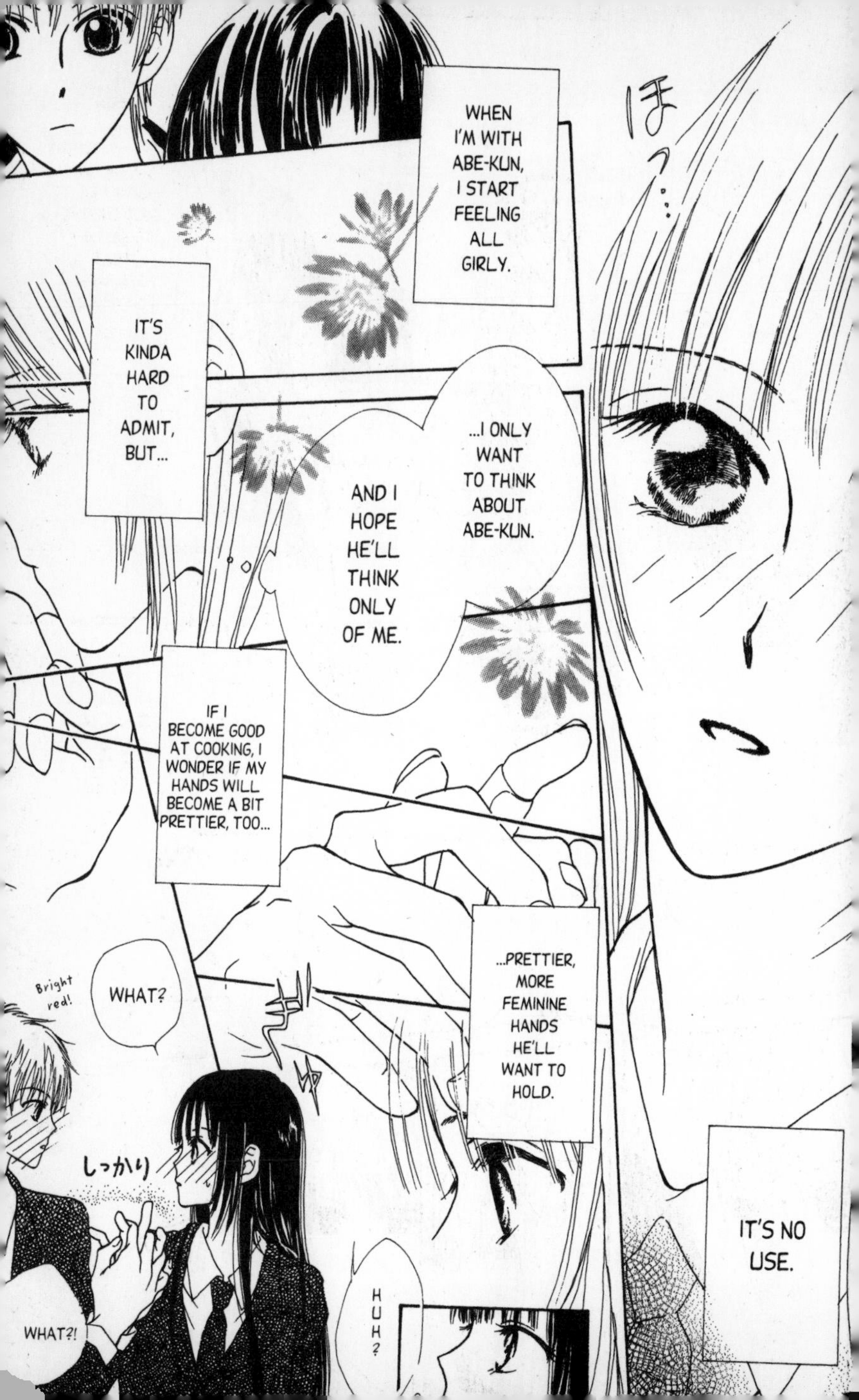
ほっ…
WHEN I'M WITH ABE-KUN, I START FEELING ALL GIRLY.
IT'S KINDA HARD TO ADMIT, BUT...
...I ONLY WANT TO THINK ABOUT ABE-KUN.
AND I HOPE HE'LL THINK ONLY OF ME.
IF I BECOME GOOD AT COOKING, I WONDER IF MY HANDS WILL BECOME A BIT PRETTIER, TOO...
...PRETTIER, MORE FEMININE HANDS HE'LL WANT TO HOLD.
IT'S NO USE.
HUH?
WHAT?
Bright red!
しっかり
WHAT?!

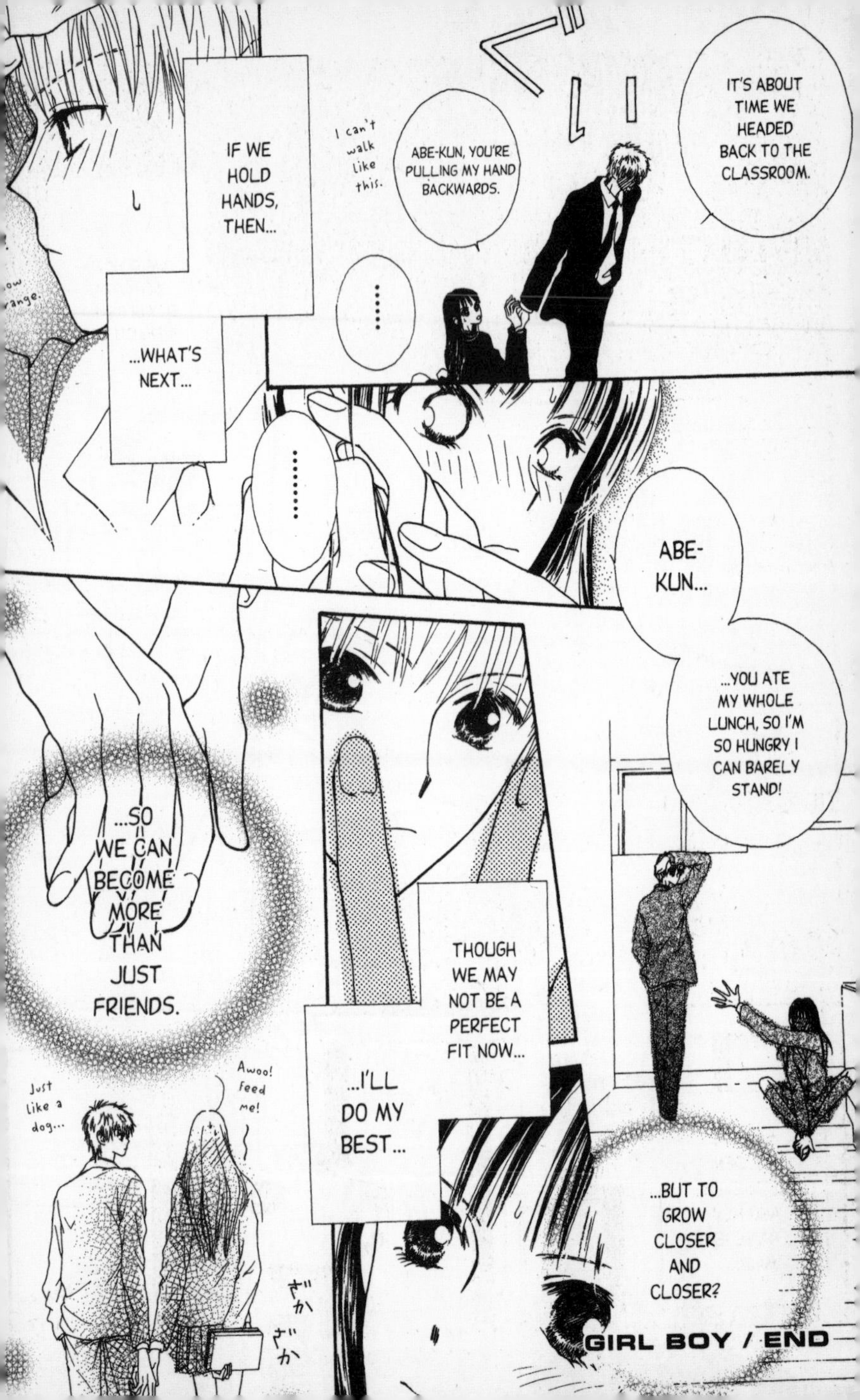
IT'S ABOUT TIME WE HEADED BACK TO THE CLASSROOM.
ABE-KUN, YOU'RE PULLING MY HAND BACKWARDS.
I can't walk like this.
......
IF WE HOLD HANDS, THEN...
...WHAT'S NEXT...
....
ABE-KUN...
...YOU ATE MY WHOLE LUNCH, SO I'M SO HUNGRY I CAN BARELY STAND!
...BUT TO GROW CLOSER AND CLOSER?
THOUGH WE MAY NOT BE A PERFECT FIT NOW...
...I'LL DO MY BEST...
...SO WE CAN BECOME MORE THAN JUST FRIENDS.
Awoo! Feed me!
Just like a dog...
ざか
ざか
GIRL BOY / END

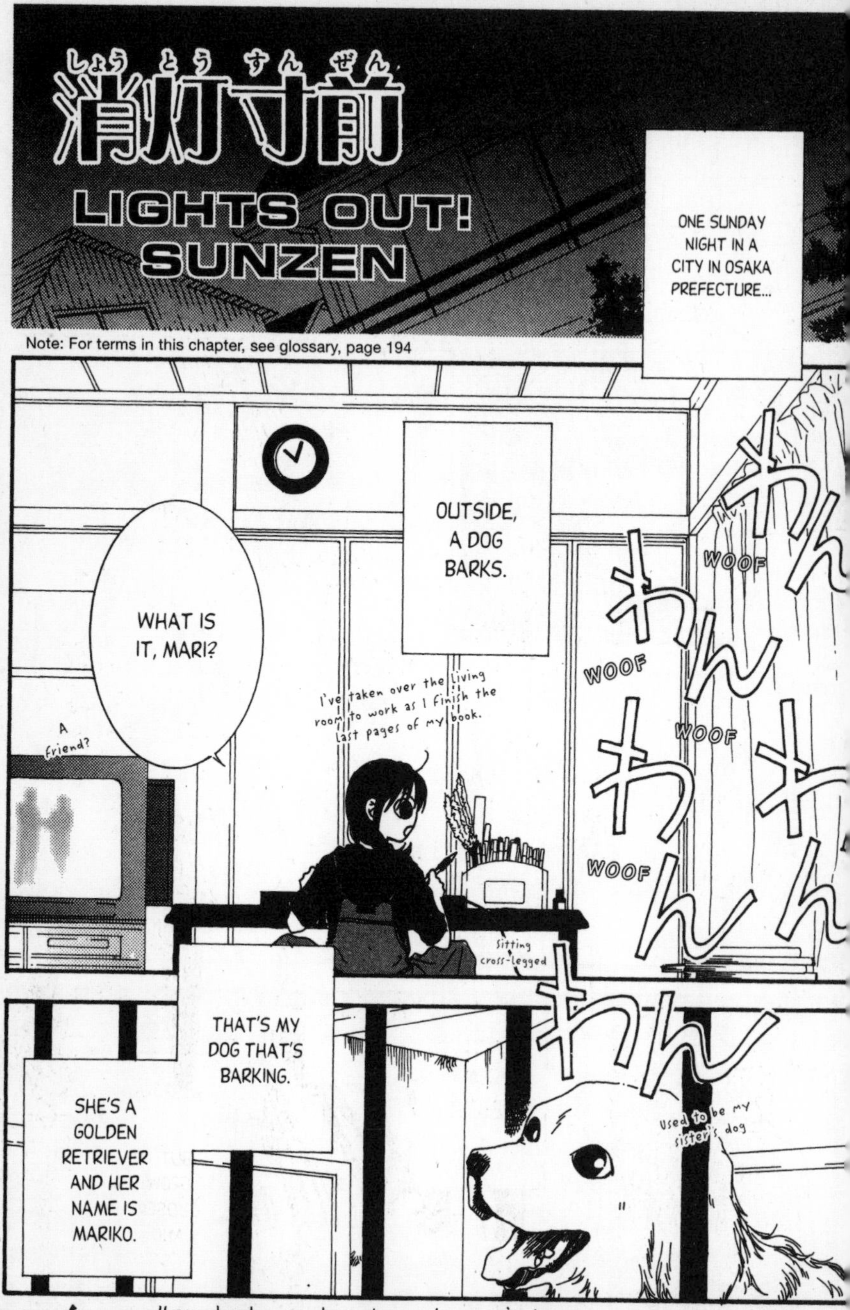
しょう とう すん ぜん
消灯寸前
LIGHTS OUT! SUNZEN
Note: For terms in this chapter, see glossary, page 194
ONE SUNDAY NIGHT IN A CITY IN OSAKA PREFECTURE...
わんわんわんわん
WOOF
WOOF
WOOF
WOOF
OUTSIDE, A DOG BARKS.
I've taken over the living room to work as I finish the last pages of my book.
WHAT IS IT, MARI?
A friend?
Sitting cross-legged
わん
Used to be my sister's dog
THAT'S MY DOG THAT'S BARKING.
SHE'S A GOLDEN RETRIEVER AND HER NAME IS MARIKO.
Her doghouse has two glass windows.

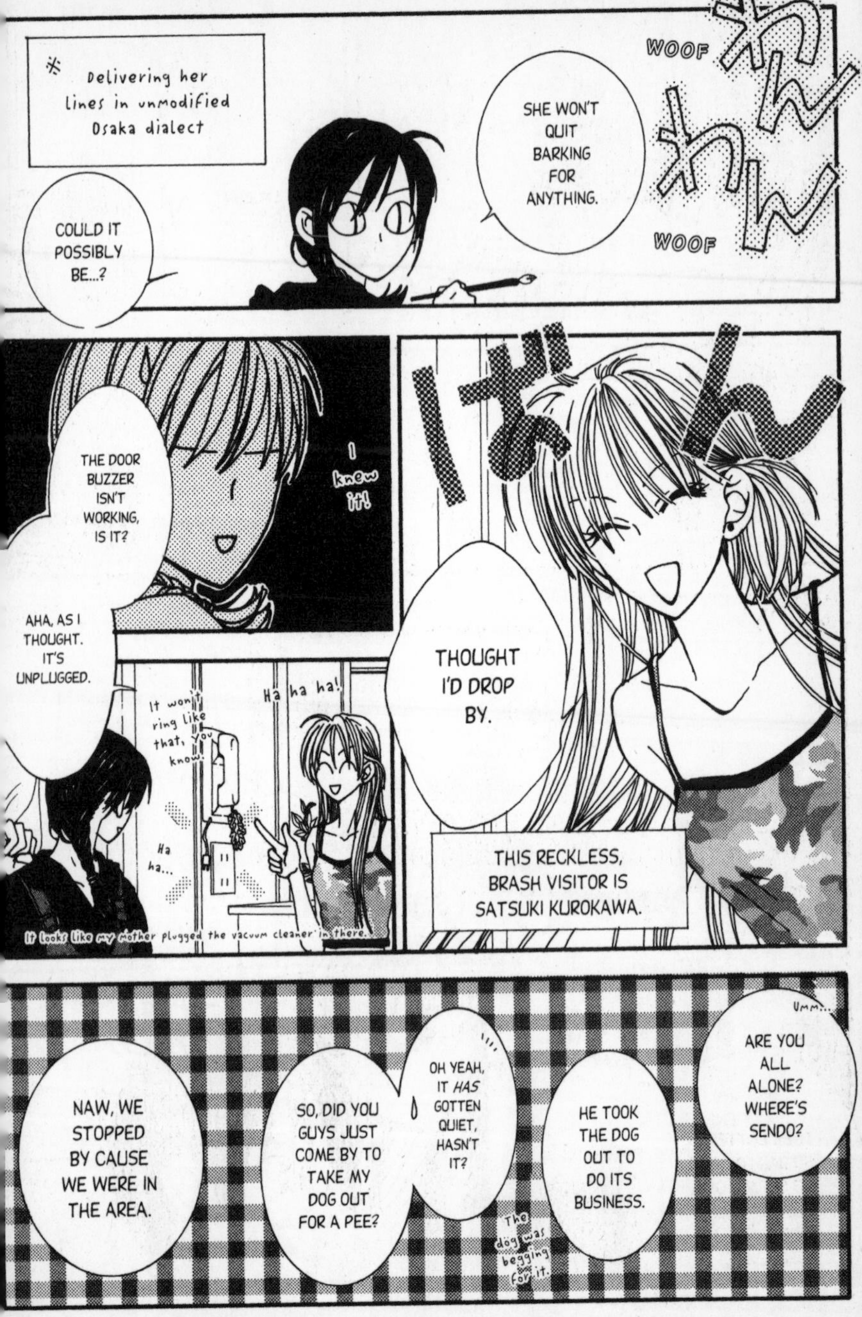

WOOF
WOOF
SHE WON'T QUIT BARKING FOR ANYTHING.
※ Delivering her lines in unmodified Osaka dialect
COULD IT POSSIBLY BE...?
THOUGHT I'D DROP BY.
THIS RECKLESS, BRASH VISITOR IS SATSUKI KUROKAWA.
I knew it!
THE DOOR BUZZER ISN'T WORKING, IS IT?
Ha ha ha!
It won't ring like that, you know.
AHA, AS I THOUGHT. IT'S UNPLUGGED.
Ha ha...
It looks like my mother plugged the vacuum cleaner in there.
Umm...
ARE YOU ALL ALONE? WHERE'S SENDO?
HE TOOK THE DOG OUT TO DO ITS BUSINESS.
The dog was begging for it.
OH YEAH, IT *HAS* GOTTEN QUIET, HASN'T IT?
SO, DID YOU GUYS JUST COME BY TO TAKE MY DOG OUT FOR A PEE?
NAW, WE STOPPED BY CAUSE WE WERE IN THE AREA.

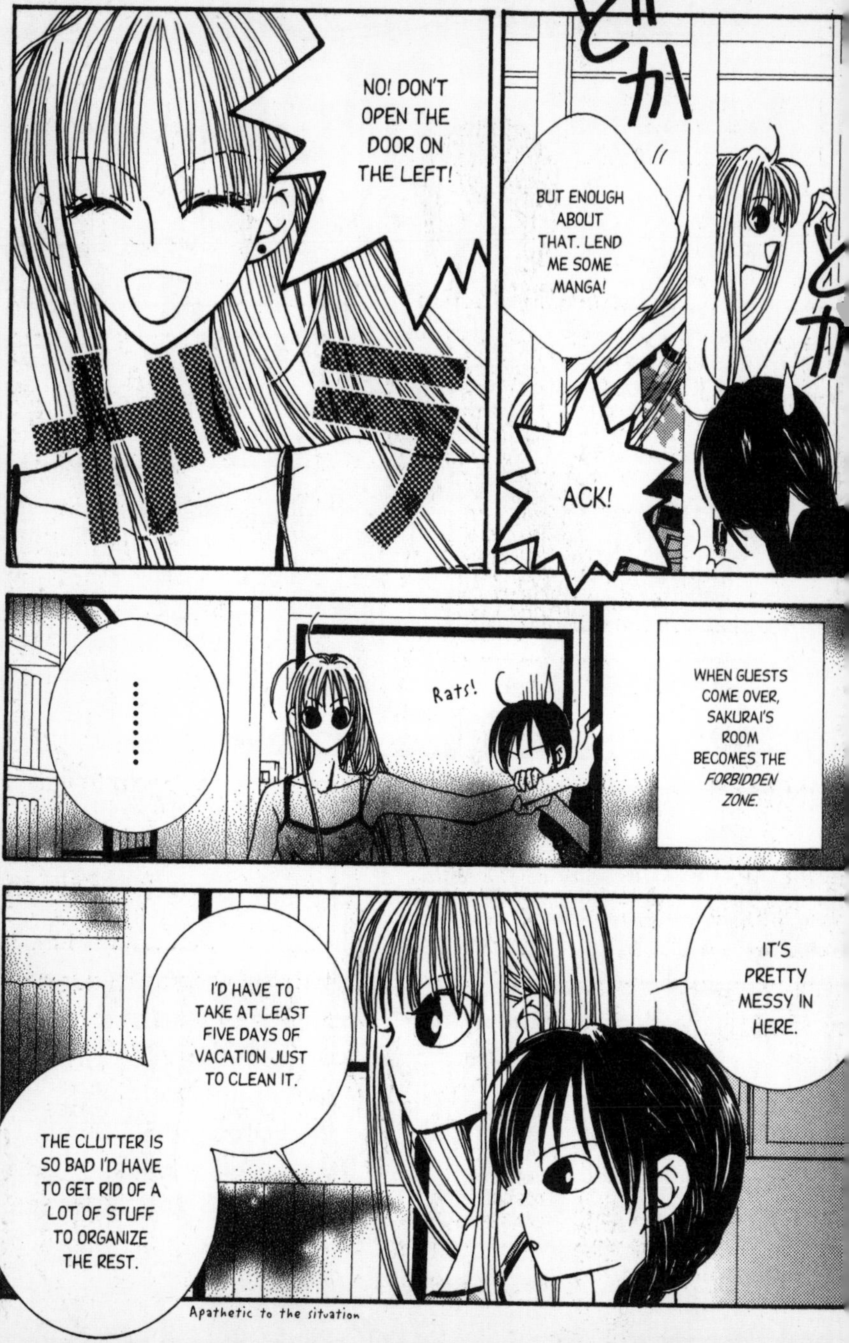
どか
BUT ENOUGH ABOUT THAT. LEND ME SOME MANGA!
ACK!
NO! DON'T OPEN THE DOOR ON THE LEFT!
ガラ
WHEN GUESTS COME OVER, SAKURAI'S ROOM BECOMES THE *FORBIDDEN ZONE.*
Rats!
……
IT'S PRETTY MESSY IN HERE.
I'D HAVE TO TAKE AT LEAST FIVE DAYS OF VACATION JUST TO CLEAN IT.
THE CLUTTER IS SO BAD I'D HAVE TO GET RID OF A LOT OF STUFF TO ORGANIZE THE REST.
Apathetic to the situation

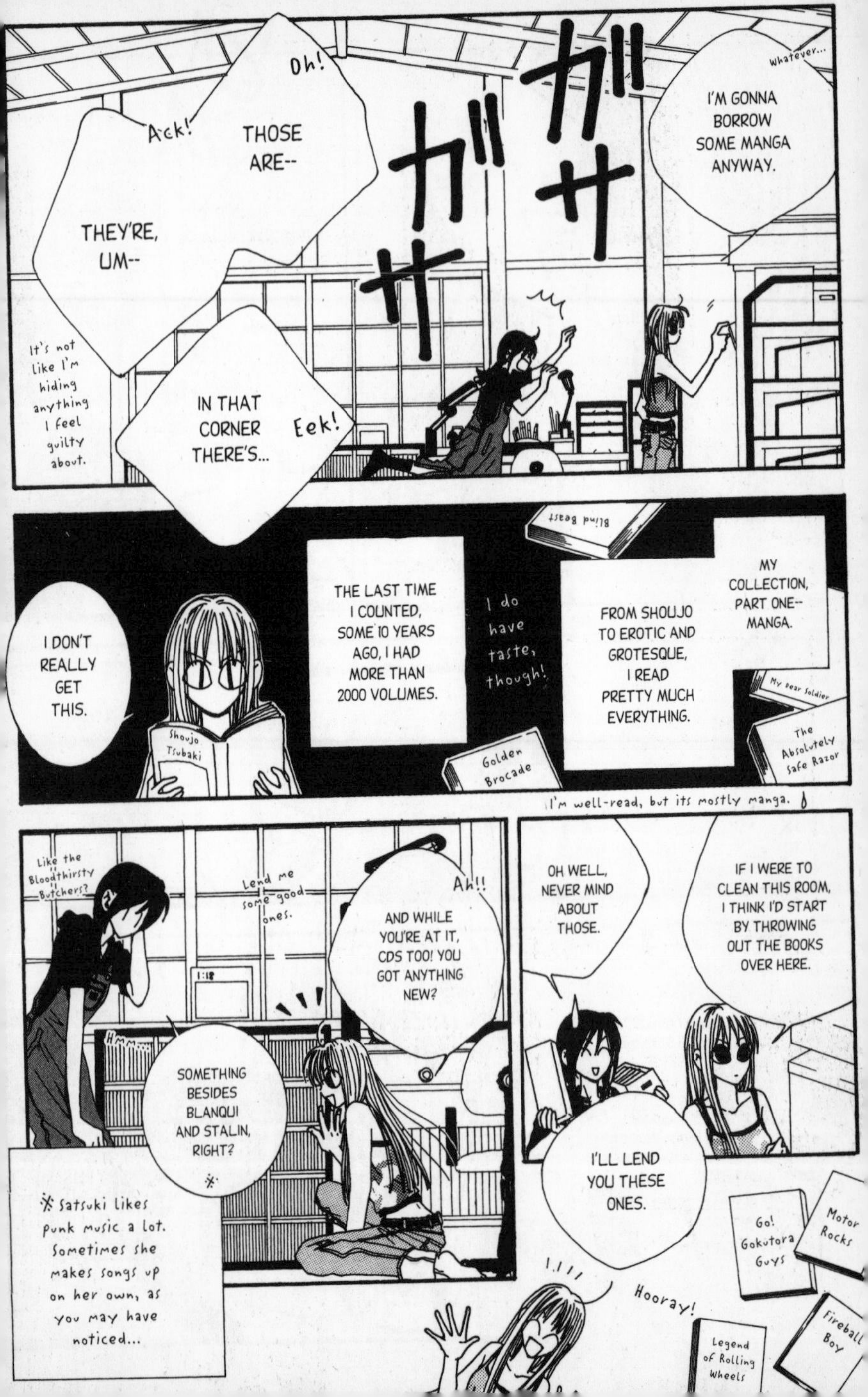
Whatever...
I'M GONNA BORROW SOME MANGA ANYWAY.
ガサガサ
Oh!
THOSE ARE--
Ack!
THEY'RE, UM--
IN THAT CORNER THERE'S...
Eek!
It's not like I'm hiding anything I feel guilty about.
Blind Beast
MY COLLECTION, PART ONE--MANGA.
FROM SHOUJO TO EROTIC AND GROTESQUE, I READ PRETTY MUCH EVERYTHING.
My Dear Soldier
The Absolutely Safe Razor
I do have taste, though!
THE LAST TIME I COUNTED, SOME 10 YEARS AGO, I HAD MORE THAN 2000 VOLUMES.
Golden Brocade
I DON'T REALLY GET THIS.
Shoujo Tsubaki
I'm well-read, but its mostly manga.
IF I WERE TO CLEAN THIS ROOM, I THINK I'D START BY THROWING OUT THE BOOKS OVER HERE.
OH WELL, NEVER MIND ABOUT THOSE.
I'LL LEND YOU THESE ONES.
Motor Rocks
Go! Gokutora Guys
Fireball Boy
Legend of Rolling Wheels
Hooray!
Ah!!
AND WHILE YOU'RE AT IT, CDS TOO! YOU GOT ANYTHING NEW?
Lend me some good ones.
Like the Bloodthirsty Butchers?
1:18
Hmm...
SOMETHING BESIDES BLANQUI AND STALIN, RIGHT? ※
※ Satsuki likes punk music a lot. Sometimes she makes songs up on her own, as you may have noticed...

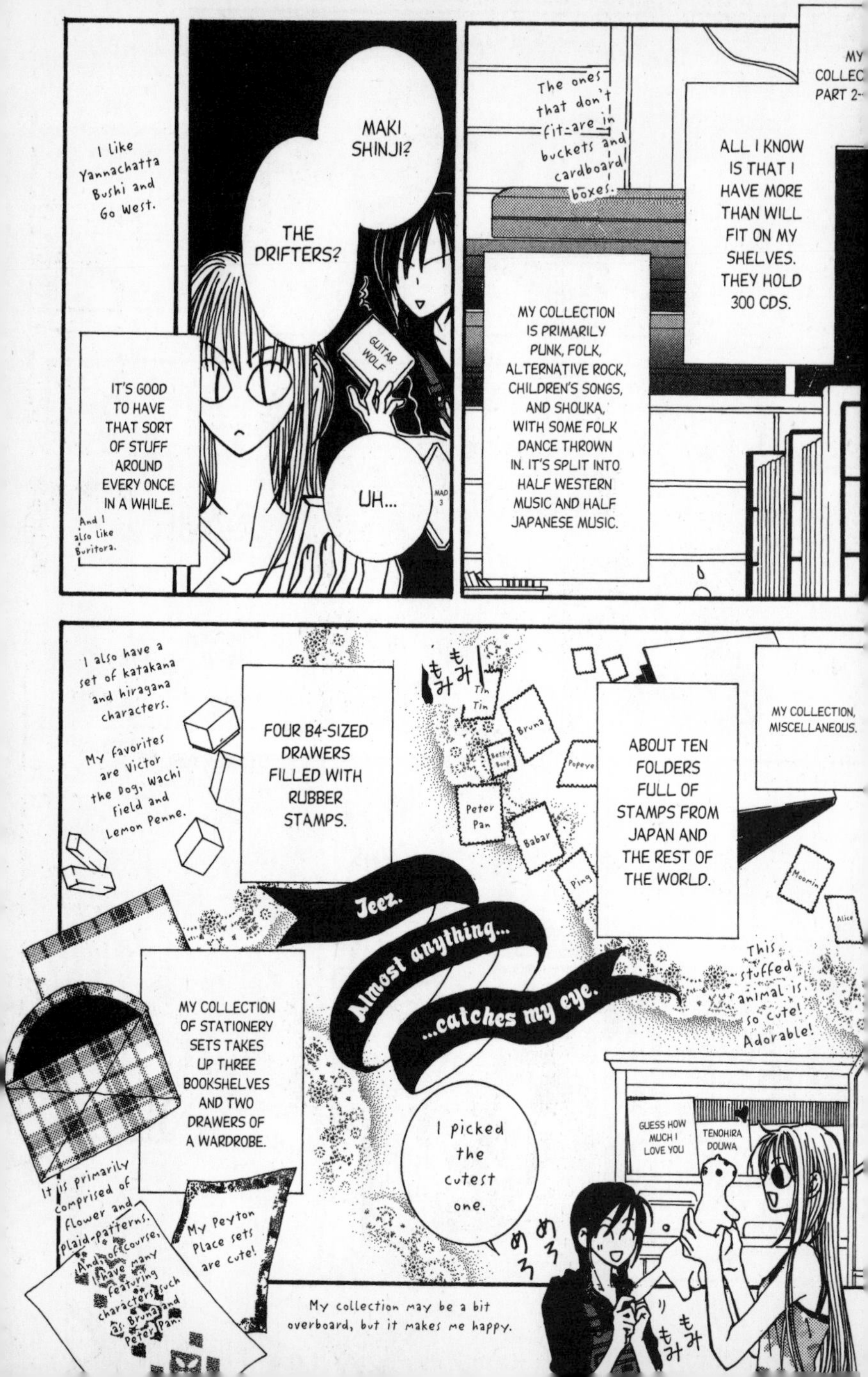
MY COLLEC PART 2--
ALL I KNOW IS THAT I HAVE MORE THAN WILL FIT ON MY SHELVES. THEY HOLD 300 CDS.
The ones that don't fit are in buckets and cardboard boxes.
MY COLLECTION IS PRIMARILY PUNK, FOLK, ALTERNATIVE ROCK, CHILDREN'S SONGS, AND SHOUKA, WITH SOME FOLK DANCE THROWN IN. IT'S SPLIT INTO HALF WESTERN MUSIC AND HALF JAPANESE MUSIC.
MAKI SHINJI?
THE DRIFTERS?
GUITAR WOLF
UH...
MAD 3
I like Yannachatta Bushi and Go West.
IT'S GOOD TO HAVE THAT SORT OF STUFF AROUND EVERY ONCE IN A WHILE.
And I also like Buritora.
MY COLLECTION, MISCELLANEOUS.
ABOUT TEN FOLDERS FULL OF STAMPS FROM JAPAN AND THE REST OF THE WORLD.
Moomin
Alice
もみもみ
Tin Tin
Bruna
Betty Boop
Popeye
Peter Pan
Babar
Ping
FOUR B4-SIZED DRAWERS FILLED WITH RUBBER STAMPS.
I also have a set of katakana and hiragana characters.
My favorites are Victor the Dog, Wachi Field and Lemon Penne.
Jeez.
Almost anything...
...catches my eye.
This stuffed animal is so cute! Adorable!
GUESS HOW MUCH I LOVE YOU
TENOHIRA DOUWA
めろめろ
もみもみ
I picked the cutest one.
MY COLLECTION OF STATIONERY SETS TAKES UP THREE BOOKSHELVES AND TWO DRAWERS OF A WARDROBE.
It is primarily comprised of flower and plaid-patterns.
And of course, I have many featuring characters such as Bruna and Peter Pan.
My Peyton Place sets are cute!
My collection may be a bit overboard, but it makes me happy.

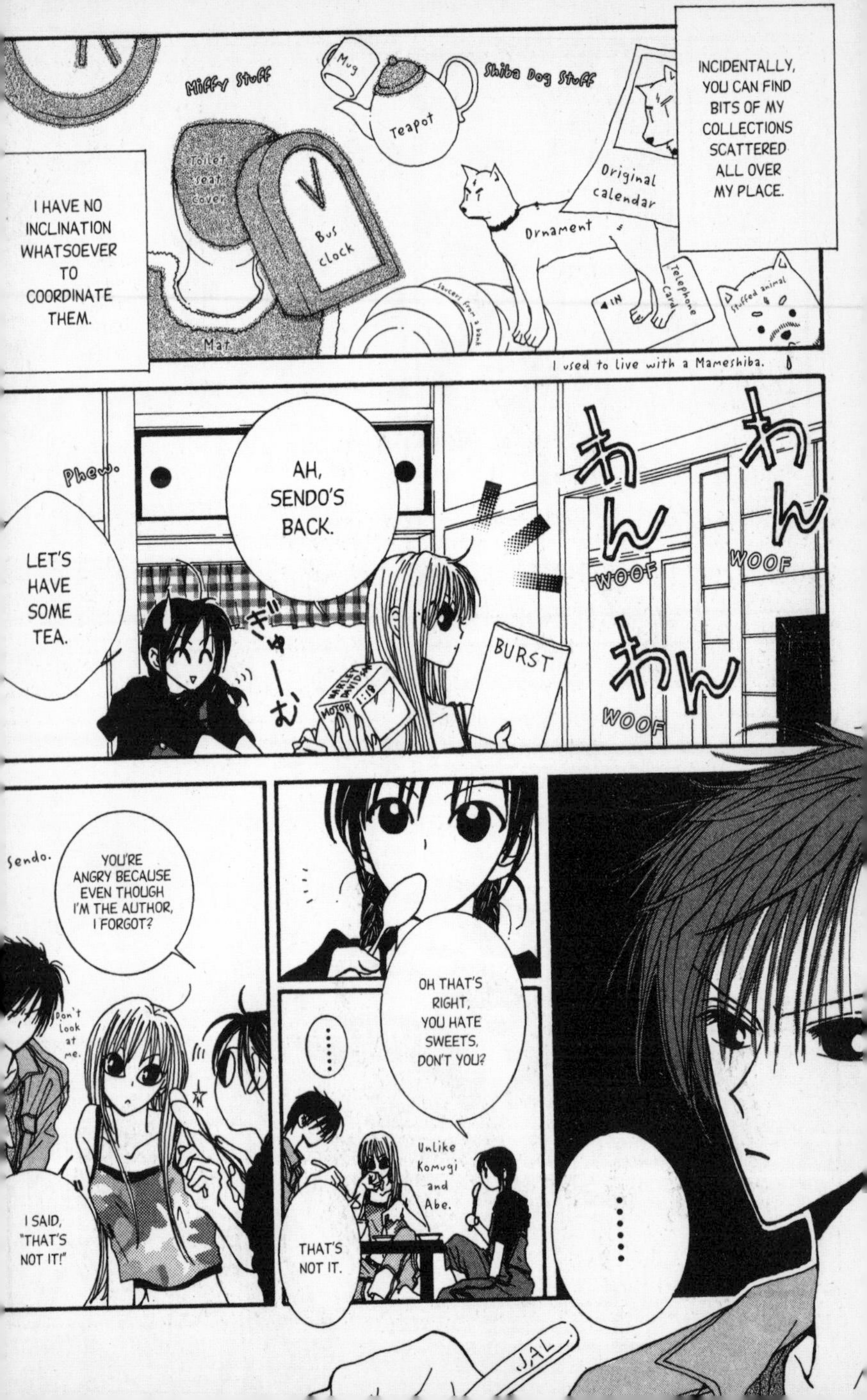
INCIDENTALLY, YOU CAN FIND BITS OF MY COLLECTIONS SCATTERED ALL OVER MY PLACE.
Shiba Dog Stuff
Original calendar
Ornament
Telephone Card
Stuffed animal
Miffy Stuff
Mug
Teapot
Toilet seat cover
Bus clock
Saucers from a bank
Mat
I HAVE NO INCLINATION WHATSOEVER TO COORDINATE THEM.
I used to live with a Mameshiba.
わんわん
WOOF
わん
WOOF
わん
WOOF
AH, SENDO'S BACK.
BURST
HARLEY DAVIDSON MOTOR 1:18
ぎゅーむ
Phew.
LET'S HAVE SOME TEA.
......
JAL
OH THAT'S RIGHT, YOU HATE SWEETS, DON'T YOU?
......
Unlike Komugi and Abe.
THAT'S NOT IT.
Sendo.
YOU'RE ANGRY BECAUSE EVEN THOUGH I'M THE AUTHOR, I FORGOT?
Don't look at me.
I SAID, "THAT'S NOT IT!"

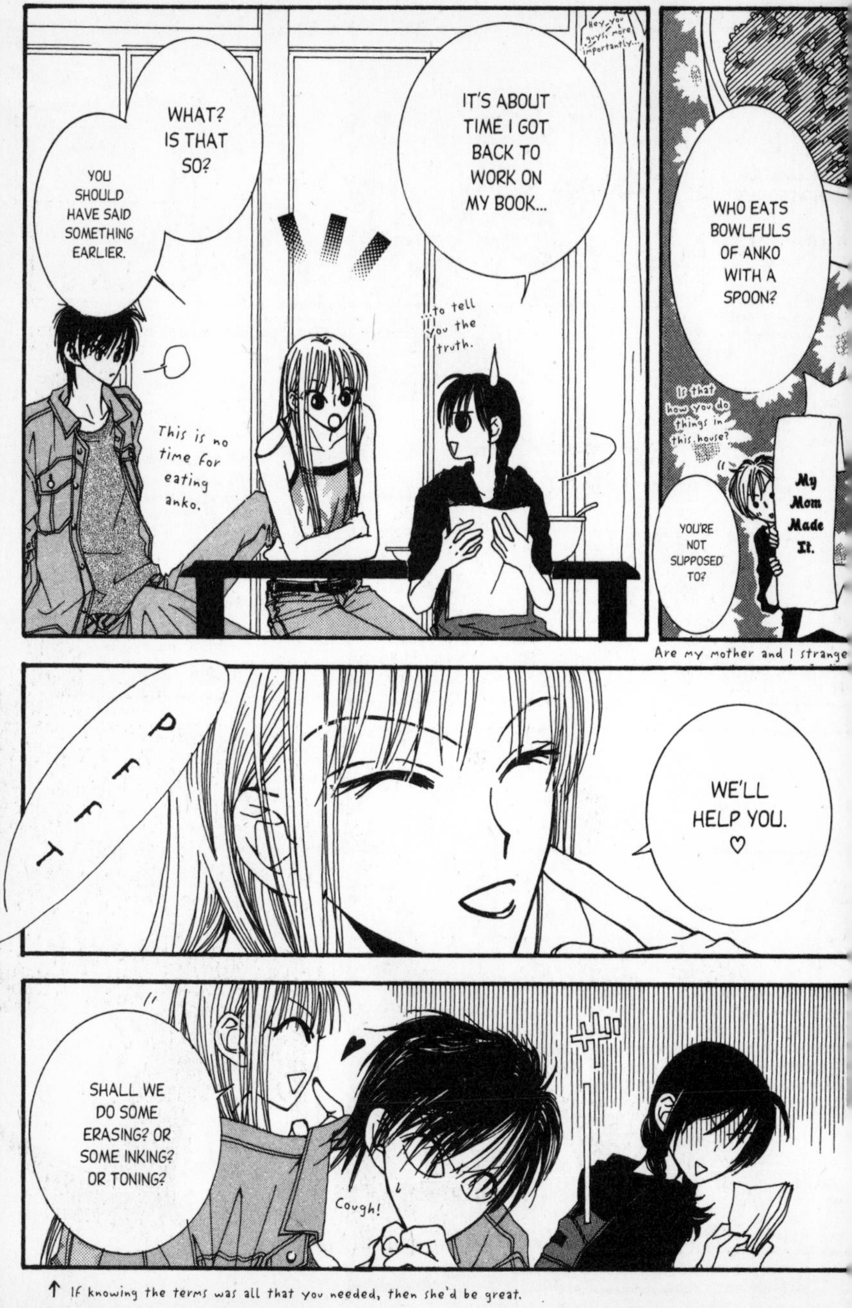
WHO EATS BOWLFULS OF ANKO WITH A SPOON?
Is that how you do things in this house?
My Mom Made It.
YOU'RE NOT SUPPOSED TO?
Hey, you guys, more importantly...
IT'S ABOUT TIME I GOT BACK TO WORK ON MY BOOK...
...to tell you the truth.
WHAT? IS THAT SO?
YOU SHOULD HAVE SAID SOMETHING EARLIER.
This is no time for eating anko.
Are my mother and I strange
WE'LL HELP YOU. ♡
PFFT
SHALL WE DO SOME ERASING? OR SOME INKING? OR TONING?
Cough!

↑ If knowing the terms was all that you needed, then she'd be great.

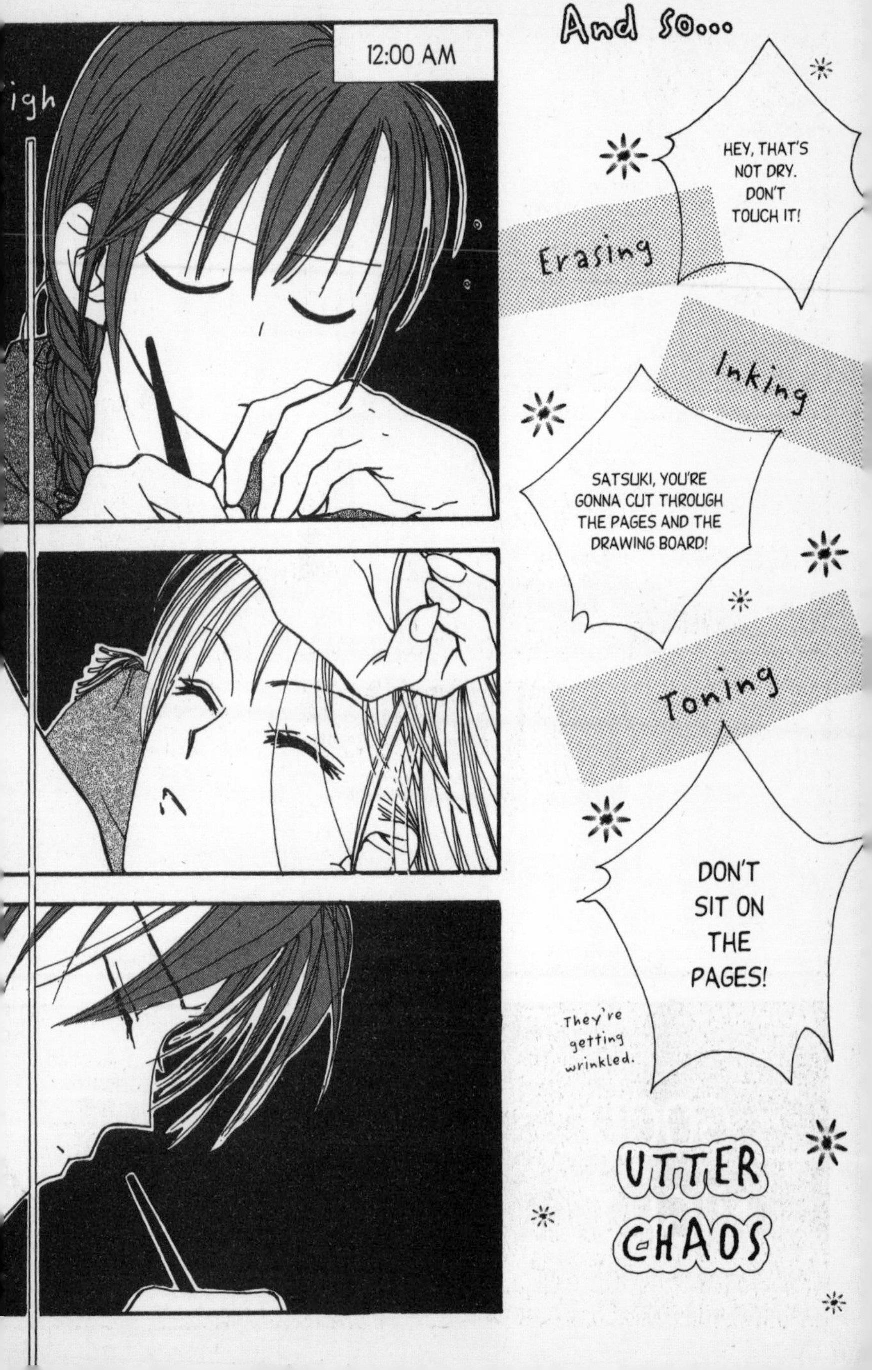
And so...
HEY, THAT'S NOT DRY. DON'T TOUCH IT!
Erasing
Inking
SATSUKI, YOU'RE GONNA CUT THROUGH THE PAGES AND THE DRAWING BOARD!
Toning
DON'T SIT ON THE PAGES!
They're getting wrinkled.
UTTER CHAOS
12:00 AM

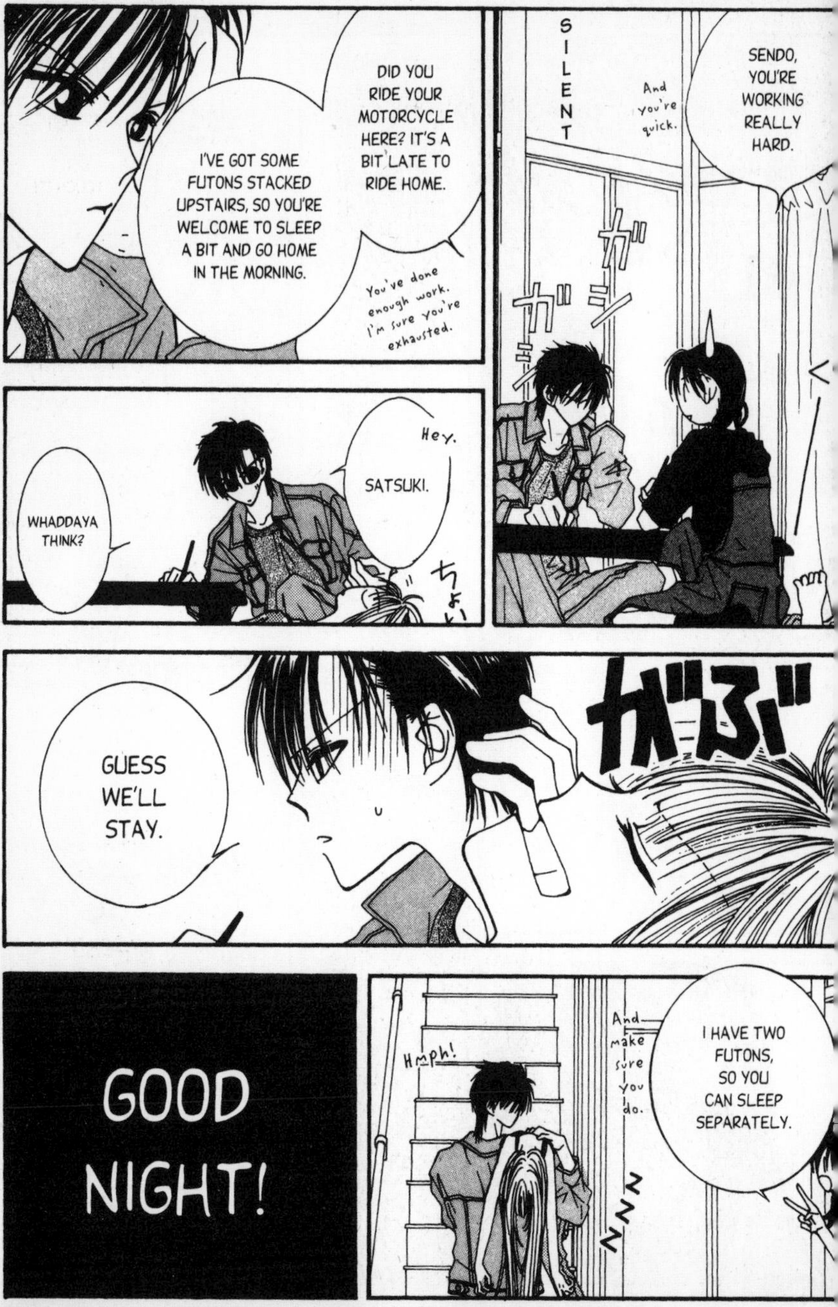
SENDO, YOU'RE WORKING REALLY HARD.
And you're quick.
SILENT
DID YOU RIDE YOUR MOTORCYCLE HERE? IT'S A BIT LATE TO RIDE HOME.
I'VE GOT SOME FUTONS STACKED UPSTAIRS, SO YOU'RE WELCOME TO SLEEP A BIT AND GO HOME IN THE MORNING.
You've done enough work. I'm sure you're exhausted.
Hey.
SATSUKI.
ちょい
WHADDAYA THINK?
がぶ
GUESS WE'LL STAY.
I HAVE TWO FUTONS, SO YOU CAN SLEEP SEPARATELY.
And make sure you do.
Hmph!
GOOD NIGHT!

Yeah right.

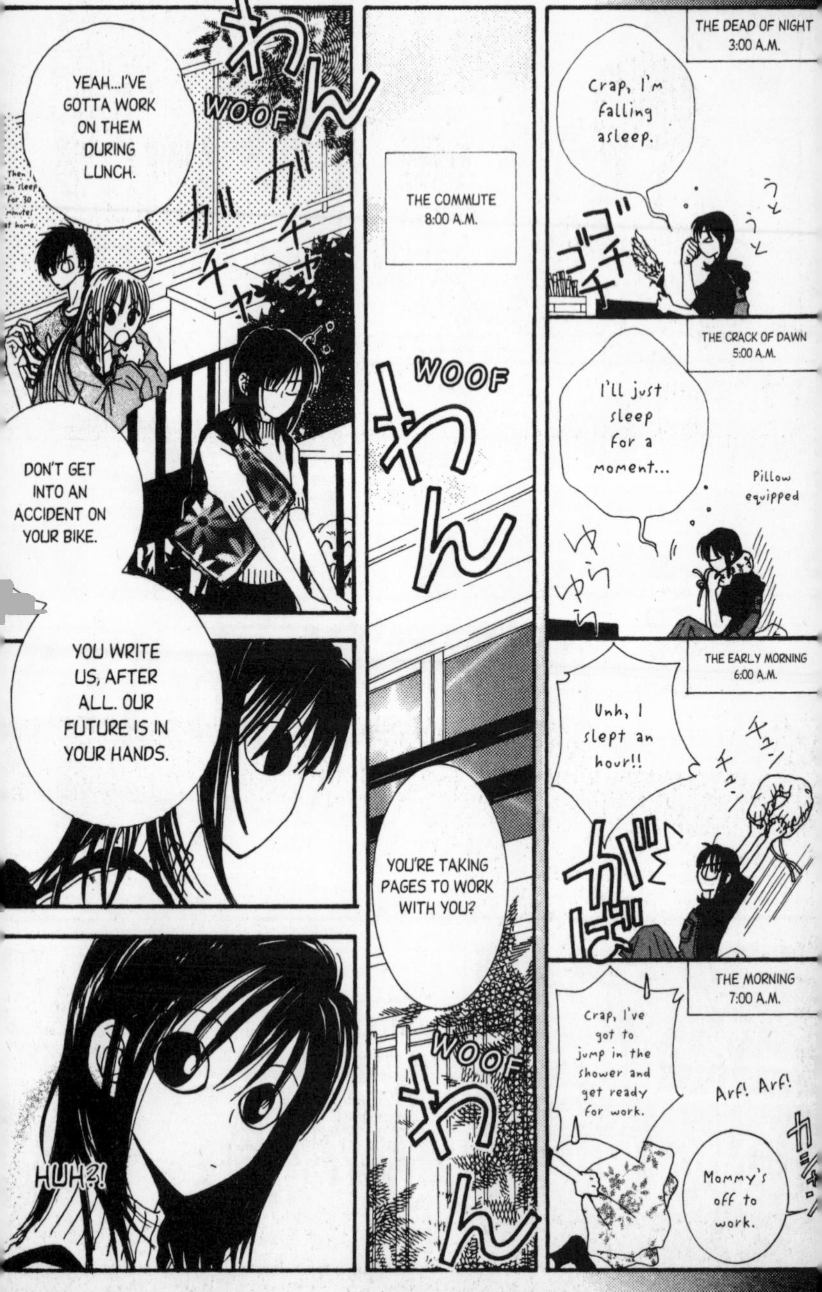

THE DEAD OF NIGHT 3:00 A.M.
Crap, I'm falling asleep.
うと うと
THE CRACK OF DAWN 5:00 A.M.
I'll just sleep for a moment...
Pillow equipped
ゆら ゆら
THE EARLY MORNING 6:00 A.M.
Unh, I slept an hour!!
チュン チュン
THE MORNING 7:00 A.M.
Crap, I've got to jump in the shower and get ready for work.
Arf! Arf!
Mommy's off to work.
THE COMMUTE 8:00 A.M.
WOOF
わん
YOU'RE TAKING PAGES TO WORK WITH YOU?
WOOF
わん
WOOF
わん
YEAH...I'VE GOTTA WORK ON THEM DURING LUNCH.
DON'T GET INTO AN ACCIDENT ON YOUR BIKE.
YOU WRITE US, AFTER ALL. OUR FUTURE IS IN YOUR HANDS.
HUH?!

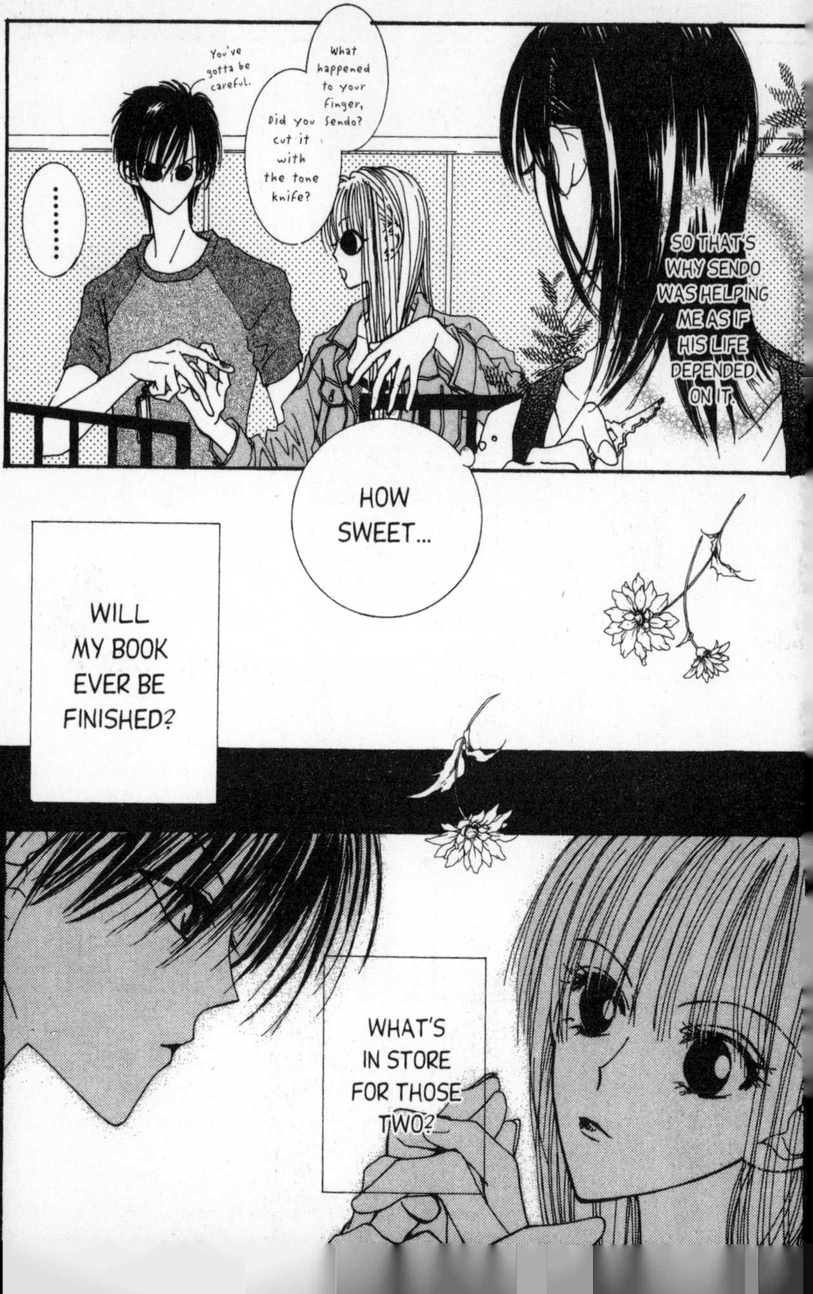
What happened to your finger, Sendo?
Did you cut it with the tone knife?
You've gotta be careful.
....
SO THAT'S WHY SENDO WAS HELPING ME AS IF HIS LIFE DEPENDED ON IT.
HOW SWEET...
WILL MY BOOK EVER BE FINISHED?
WHAT'S IN STORE FOR THOSE TWO?

Many Thanks

I'm writing this in the last possible place. As always, I'm struggling. No matter what I do, I'm a dunce. Oh yeah, I haven't expressed my appreciation yet... let's start this over.

Thank you for coming on this journey with me.

To all of you reading this right now, to those of you who always support me, to those of you who came to help me with my book, to everyone at work who overlooked my horrible attendance record and to my friends, family and editors who, no matter how much I inconvenienced them, remained extremely patient with me. I am really really reaaaaaally full of remorse and gratitude. More than I can express in writing here...

Well, a few things have changed in the many days I spent drawing this manga. I'm now working from home. And my older sister finally came to take her doggie home with her after a period of several years. But I have no time to complain about being lonely. As usual, I'm struggling. No matter what I do, I'm a dunce at it. (I have a feeling I'll be saying that all my life.)

I hope you'll be patient with me. As always, I'm in your hands. *bow*

If you have any complaints--I mean feedback--after reading this book (that includes the paper doll clothes) send them to the Hana to Yume Editorial Department, care of Susugi Sakurai.

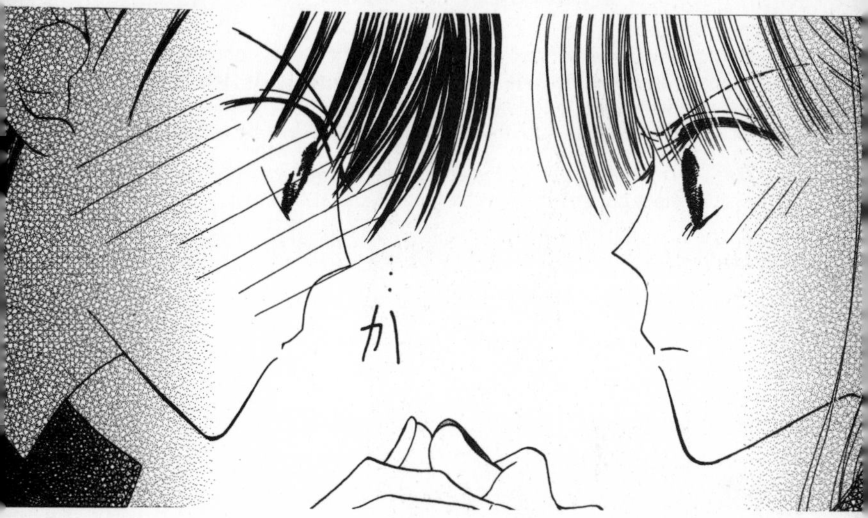
……カ

GLOSSARY

WELCOME TO OSAKA

Osaka, where Satsuki Kurokawa and Aya Sendo live, is a very special place in Japan, known for its unique food and customs. Here's a guide to make you feel more at home in the Kansai region of Japan, although lots of it applies to anywhere in Japan, and some is global.

HONORIFICS

In respect for the Japanese setting, the convention of name honorifics has been retained. In Japan, which suffix one uses when addressing another person, and whether or not one uses their first name indicates the level of respect between two people. When someone chooses not to use honorifics, that can be telling, too.

-san. Equivalent to Mr. or Mrs., but also used between coworkers, acquaintances and friends. This is the most common suffix and the default level of respect.

-kun. Indicates friendly familiarity. Also used by older students to address younger students.

-chan. Indicates friendly familiarity, and is often used for smaller, cuter things than oneself.

-senpai. Used by younger students when speaking to or about older students.

-sensei. Teacher.

-sama. Indicates a great level of respect and is used towards someone much older or of much higher standing.

No suffix: either said out of disrespect or because the speaker and subject are very close.

Page 5	**Okonomiyaki:** Said to have originated in Osaka, okonomiyaki is often described as a "Japanese pizza." Batter is spread on a griddle and the "toppings" include things from fish flakes to cheese noodles.
Page 44	**Iscandar:** The name of a planet at the end of the cosmos in the anime Space Battleship Yamato (aka Star Blazers). Very far away indeed.
Page 57	**Yan:** A honorific suffix used in Kansai.
Page 59	**Paper dolls:** The author uses the word "kisekae." Although it means "paper doll" the same word is used to refer to real doll clothes. Kisekae computer programs also exist where you can change the clothes on a virtual doll.
Page 70	**Bullet trains:** There are two bullet trains. The faster of the two is named Hikari (Light) while the slower is named Kodama (Echo).
Page 75	**Gakuran:** A gakuran is a type of boys' school uniform. The coats vary in length, and a choran is a gakuran with a long coat.
Page 79	**Nosey neighbors:** Often teachers, ex-police officers, and the like take turns patrolling neighborhoods after school. Wearing your school uniform around while goofing off and making your school look bad (like Satsuki and Aya) is a sure way to get in trouble.
Page 80	**Kamaboko:** A molded fish cake. They come in a variety of shapes and are often served in soups.
Page 86	**Male Cheerleaders:** The lanterns in the club room read "Ouendan," which is the Japanese word for a male cheerleading squad. The character Satsuki mentions is from a 1976 movie "Ah!! Hana no Ouendan." There's also a cult-classic Ouendan game released in Japan for the Nintendo DS called "Osu! Tatakae! Ouendan!"
Page 99	**Sarashi:** A sarashi is a sash traditionally worn by samurai around their abdomens as extra protection in a fight. Today, tough guys wear them to show off their toughness. Sarashi also come in handy for binding breasts, as Satsuki did.
Page 113	**Chef's choice:** Ordering chef's choice, or "omakase," is often a way to save money. At sushi restaurants, ordering omakase means you'll get a variety of rolls, but there's no guarantee you'll like any of them.
Page 121	**Short shorts:** In Japan, most manga is released by chapter in weekly, bi-weekly, or monthly manga serial anthologies. The size of these anthologies are about the size of phone books, meaning the pages in the monthlies are larger than in the complied volumes...meaning Satsuki's shorts are very small indeed.
Page 122	**Zelda and Lolita No. 18:** Zelda is an all-girl Japanese rock-band from the 80's and 90's. Lolita No.18 is a current all-girl Japanese punk/hard pop band that started up around 1989.
Page 135	**Negiyaki:** A thinner, more oniony version of okonomiyaki.
Page 138	**Tsutenkaku:** Satsuki actually says "Your standards must be taller than the Tsutenkaku," which is a tall tower located in Osaka.
Page 140	**Kotatsu:** A kotasu is a blanketed table with a heater underneath. See Tramps Like Us vol 8, page 77 for another author's kotatsu fun.
Page 142	**Double eights:** The Japanese character for "eight" resembles the character for "fortune." So double eights is lucky indeed! Abe is 6' and Komugi is 5'9."
Page 158	**Comedy routine:** On this page, the students enact a comedy routine that's typical of Osaka humor. This double bubble is in the form of a comedic duo routine. The first is the "boke" half and the second the "tsukkomi". The boke is the stupid guy, whereas the tsukkomi is the "straight man" who delivers his reprimand with a blow of some form. This is sometimes with a paper fan called "harisen."
Page 159	**Marubiru:** Marubiru is a well known building in Osaka. As the name suggests, it is a rounded (maru) skyscraper (biru).
Page 181	**Shouka:** Traditional educational songs sung in schools originating from the Meiji Era (1868-1912).
	Maki Shinji: A comedic singer/ukulele player.
	The Drifters: Although The Drifters are a well-known soul group in America, it's likely this album could refer to the Japanese comedy group of the same name. The Drifters began their popular TV show in 1964 and were known for their slapstick humor.
	Guitar Wolf: A Japanese garage punk band, founded in the late 80s.
	MAD 3: Another Japanese garage band.
	"Yannachatta Bushi": "Yannachatta Bushi" is a Maki Shinji song that can be loosely translated as the "I've Lost My Motivation To Do Anything" Melody.
	Buritora: Another Japanese band.
	Licensed Characters: Although most of these are well-known in the west, some aren't. Dick Bruna, for instance, is the creator of the super-cute Miffy bunny character. Ping is a female penguin character. Moomin are a set of troll characters that look like hippos.
	Guess How Much I Love You: This is a children's book by Sam McBratney.
	Tenohira Douwa: This is a children's book by Yuuko Ohnari that's title translates to "Palm of the Hand Nursery Tales."
	Hiragana & Katakana: These are the two Japanese syllabaries. All the sounds of Japanese are represented in the hiragana "alphabet" and katakana is a second set of symbols to represent those sounds when they are of foreign origin.
	Peyton Place: A brand of stationary apparently, but might also refer to an old black and white TV series that aired in America in the 1960s. It's possible with Sakurai's tastes that she might have stationary themed from it.
	Anko: Anko is a sweet red bean dessert and/or filling.

In the Next Volume of

SHORT SUNZEN!

IT'S SATSUKI'S BIRTHDAY, AND AYA HAS BRIGHT AND SPARKLY PLANS TO MAKE IT A SMASH AT A FIREWORKS SHOW. WILL AYA GET A CHANCE TO CONFESS HOW HE FEELS OR WILL THE UNLUCKY GUY'S BEST EFFORTS FIZZLE ONCE AGAIN?

STOP!

This is the back of the book.
You wouldn't want to spoil a great ending!

This book is printed "manga-style," in the authentic Japanese right-to-left format. Since none of the artwork has been flipped or altered, readers get to experience the story just as the creator intended. You've been asking for it, so TOKYOPOP® delivered: authentic, hot-off-the-press, and far more fun!

DIRECTIONS

If this is your first time reading manga-style, here's a quick guide to help you understand how it works.

It's easy... just start in the top right panel and follow the numbers. Have fun, and look for more 100% authentic manga from TOKYOPOP®!

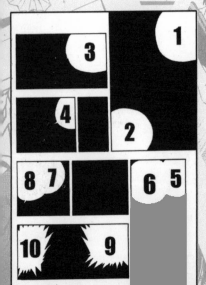